Rethinking the Theatre of the Absurd

Methuen Drama Engage offers original reflections about key practitioners, movements and genres in the fields of modern theatre and performance. Each volume in the series seeks to challenge mainstream critical thought through original and interdisciplinary perspectives on the body of work under examination. By questioning existing critical paradigms, it is hoped that each volume will open up fresh approaches and suggest avenues for further exploration.

Series Editors

Mark Taylor-Batty
Senior Lecturer in Theatre Studies, Workshop Theatre,
University of Leeds, UK

Enoch Brater
Kenneth T. Rowe Collegiate Professor of Dramatic Literature &
Professor of English and Theater, University of Michigan, USA

Titles

Rethinking the Theatre of the Absurd

Ecology, the Environment and the Greening of the Modern Stage

Edited by Carl Lavery
and Clare Finburgh

Series Editors
Enoch Brater and Mark Taylor-Batty

Bloomsbury Methuen Drama
An imprint of Bloomsbury Publishing Plc

B L O O M S B U R Y
LONDON · OXFORD · NEW YORK · NEW DELHI · SYDNEY

Bloomsbury Methuen Drama

An imprint of Bloomsbury Publishing Plc

Imprint previously known as Methuen Drama

50 Bedford Square	1385 Broadway
London	New York
WC1B 3DP	NY 10018
UK	USA

www.bloomsbury.com

**BLOOMSBURY, METHUEN DRAMA and the Diana logo
are trademarks of Bloomsbury Publishing Plc**

First published 2015

© Carl Lavery and Clare Finburgh, 2015

British Library Cataloguing-in-Publication Data
A catalogue record for this book is available from the British Library.

ISBN: HB: 978-1-4725-0667-2
ePDF: 978-1-4725-0576-7
ePub: 978-1-4725-1320-5

Library of Congress Cataloging-in-Publication Data
A catalogue record for this book is available from the Library of Congress.

Typeset by Deanta Global Publishing Services, Chennai, India
Printed and bound in Great Britain

For our Families

CONTENTS

LIST OF
ILLUSTRATIONS

Introduction:
Greening the Absurd

Carl Lavery and Clare Finburgh

Only after the movement of today has been
placed within its historical context can an attempt
be made to assess its significance and to establish its
importance and the part it has to play within the
pattern of contemporary thought.[1]

These Hegelian inflected words from Martin Esslin's *The Theatre of the Absurd*, though descriptive of his own historicization of the work of playwrights such as Samuel Beckett, Arthur Adamov, Eugène Ionesco and Jean Genet (among others), point beyond their immediate historical context. In considering the question of what makes an artwork contemporary, Esslin unconsciously – and perhaps inevitably – undermines the historicity of his study by implying that the significance of absurdist theatre is yet to be grasped, that its meaning lies in the future.[2] Half a century after the publication of the first edition of *The Theatre of the Absurd* in 1961, and speaking back from that future, this collection sets out to respond to the critical challenge implicit in Esslin's remarks by focusing on the relevance of absurdist theatre to twenty-first-century society. For us, this is found in the Theatre of the Absurd's ability to express an emergent sense of ecological and environmental anxiety that today has become so palpable and potentially catastrophic.

It is our contention that the Theatre of the Absurd articulates an important ecological shift in human perception. As the philosopher of science Isabelle Stengers argues, we have been living for the past fifty years or so in a period of 'pharmacological knowledge' in which 'a new kind of memory has come into being'. According to Stengers, this is a return of the 'memory of the unintentional processes that in the past were able to bring about the disappearance of cities, empires, or civilisations, and of the ravages caused by our simplistic industrial, and even "scientific" strategies'.[3] Reflecting the complexity of ecological thought itself, there are numerous reasons why we should see an early appearance of this new, troubling form of remembrance in the absurdist texts of the late 1940s and 1950s. First, the nuclear attacks on Hiroshima and Nagasaki in 1945 produced anxieties about the long-term effects of radiation in the atmosphere; second, the presence of pesticides in the food chain, along with increased levels of carbon monoxide and sulphur dioxide from cars and heavy industry, showed that chemicals and pollutants, and living forms, were inextricably combined; third, the development of ever more powerful hydrogen bombs within the context of the Cold War threw the very existence of life on the planet into question; and fourth the development of consumer capitalism led to an increasing privatization of social life, while intensifying the exploitation of the Earth's natural resources for the purposes of 'growth'.

This list of environmental factors nuances Esslin's reading of the Theatre of the Absurd as a theatrical response to the 'absurdity of the human condition', the cause of which he attributes to 'the decline of religious faith [that] was masked until the end of the Second World War by the substitute religions of faith in progress, nationalism and various totalitarian fictions'.[4] Equally, it explains why, unlike the vast majority of critics who have engaged with the Theatre of the Absurd, we have little enthusiasm for contesting or replacing Esslin's original term with a new appellation such as 'nouveau théâtre', the 'theatre of paradox and protest', 'metatheatre', 'the theatre of discord and revolt', 'dark comedy', 'dissonance' or, more recently, 'parabolic drama'.[5] Our aim in this book is not to discover a more accurate linguistic or conceptual *dispositif* for unlocking the meaning of the Theatre of the Absurd, but rather to provide a series of dramatic, hermeneutic and historical contexts in which its ecological and environmental significance can be recalibrated and its contemporaneity underlined. But what do those contexts consist of, and how do they manifest themselves thematically and formally in absurdist theatre? The remainder of the Introduction sets out to answer these questions and to explain, in some detail, our rationale and methods for 'greening' the Theatre of the Absurd. Realizing that our approach to such canonical texts might appear a little incongruous, perhaps even contentious, we start by providing a historical overview of theatre's somewhat troubled relationship with ecology and environment. After this, we go on to position our green reading within the relatively new field of eco-performance criticism.

Rationale

In the opening pages of *The Natural Contract*, a text that sets itself the urgent task of thinking through what it might mean to live in an utterly new time – the time when 'nature' has entered history as global warming – the philosopher of science Michel Serres provides an illuminating account of Goya's famous painting *Duelo a garrotazos* (*Men Fighting with Sticks*, 1820–3: see Figure 1).[6] In the painting, Goya depicts two cowherds on a deserted marsh, brandishing crude cudgels above their heads, and engaging in what appears to be a grotesque fight to the death. For art historians, Goya's image has been habitually interpreted as an allegory for political discord, a work that throws dark light on the human propensity for violence.[7] None of this Serres would disagree with. However, the originality of his reading is found by following the direction of

FIGURE 1 *Francisco Goya,* Men Fighting with Sticks, *1820–3, oil mural transferred to canvas.*

his gaze. Serres's interest is not in the 'drama' that unfolds between the cowherds; rather, it is with the effect that their actions have on the earth beneath them – how they have reduced the marsh to mud:

> The painter, Goya, has plunged the dualists knee-deep in the mud. With every move they make, a slimy hole swallows them up, so that they are gradually burying themselves together. ... Who will die? we ask. Who will win? they are wondering – and that's the usual question. Let's make a wager. You put your stakes on the right; we've bet on the left. ... But we can identify a third position, outside their squabble: the marsh into which the struggle is sinking.[8]

By wagering on the 'third position' – the marsh – as opposed to the theatricality of the struggle, Serres simultaneously expands and dedramatizes the significance of Goya's painting. In doing so, he interrupts our spectacular fascination with 'spilled blood', which, he suggests, is the motivating force for western art, the depressing meridian that links Homer's *Iliad* to Goya's painting, and beyond:

> Nothing ever interests us but spilled blood, the manhunt, crime stories, the point at which politics turns into murder; we are enthralled only by the corpses of the battlefield, the power and glory of those who hunger for victory and thirst to annihilate the losers; thus entertainment mongers show us only corpses, the vile world of death that founds and traverses history, from the *Iliad* to Goya, and from academic art to prime-time television.[9]

Shortly after this damning passage, Serres makes a point that has radical implications for theatre and performance practitioners and scholars. He claims that theatre, because of its historical obsession with human conflict – in specialist terms, the *agon* or competition that drives so many dramatic plots – is the anthropocentric art form *par excellence*, the medium in which the forgetting of the Earth finds its purest mode of expression. Critiquing theatre for reducing the environment to an abstract backdrop, Serres proceeds to accuse it of 'abhorring the world':

> In the spectacles, which we hope are now a thing of the past, the adversaries most often fight to the death in an abstract space,

where they struggle alone, without marsh or river. Take away the world around the battles, keep only conflicts or debates, thick with humanity and purified of things, and you obtain stage theatre. ... Does anyone ever say *where* the master and slave fight it out?[10]

Numerous examples from theatre history can be marshalled to refute Serres's generalist claim. One thinks, for instance, of the purposefully anti-dramatic 'landscape' performances of Maurice Maeterlinck, Gertrude Stein, Robert Wilson and Goat Island as well as the site-specific happenings and performances of Allan Kaprow, Welfare State International, Brith Gof and Simon Whitehead.[11] Nevertheless, Serres's indictment of the environmental blindness of 'stage theatre' retains its purchase, if applied to the dramaturgical conventions of tragedy, a mode of performance which has dominated the dramatic imagination in the west. Although classical tragedy is not devoid of references to the 'more than human world' – in *Oedipus The King* for instance, the land is blighted, and in *Antigone*, the chorus speaks damningly of the ecological devastation caused by the 'miracle of man' – the focus of the tragic action is always on human protagonists.[12] They dominate our consciousness, and jealously demand our attention. The names of heroes – Oedipus, Antigone, Medea – are what stick in our minds, not the places they inhabit.

According to Peter Szondi, the anthropocentric focus of tragedy became even more pronounced in the seventeenth century as playwrights such as Shakespeare, Pierre Corneille and Jean Racine started to attend, in ever greater detail, to the psychological and social dilemmas of individual characters: 'By deciding to disclose himself to his contemporary world man transformed his internal being into a palpable and dramatic presence'.[13] The effect of this new mode of subjectivity, illustrated in the desire to make the private public, resulted in the radical rejection of everything – nature, animals, the environment – that existed outside the domain of speech. In Szondi's view, modern drama is a drama of and for human subjects alone. In line with Enlightenment thinking, the human world is the only world that counts: 'Most radical of all was the exclusion of that which could not express itself – the world of objects – unless it entered into the realm of interpersonal relationships'.[14] Szondi's anthropocentric reading of western drama is underlined by the theatre historian Erika Fischer-Lichte, who in her *History of European Drama and Theatre* goes as far as to suggest that 'the fundamental theatrical situation ... always symbolizes the *conditio humana*, regardless of its different culturally-historically determined forms'.[15]

In keeping with Serres's point, the comments of Szondi and Fischer-Lichte underline the extent to which, in its dominant forms, the history of theatre has been coterminous with the history of human subjectivity. Even the naturalist plays and performances of Émile Zola, Henrik Ibsen and André Antoine, while purporting to represent human beings as products of their environment, have no interest in the agency of the 'natural world'. Their primary concern is with tracing the impact of the environment on human beings, and in using location as a foil for dramatic action. To that degree, naturalism, as Una Chaudhuri has shown, is simply another form of humanism; in it, 'nature' is a text to be read and deciphered by human agents.[16]

Whether defined in terms of tragedy, naturalist performance and/or melodrama, there is nothing surprising about the environmental limitations of modern stage. Theatre's function as a *theatron* (or site of looking) for the analysis of heightened and destructive human passions and emotions necessarily turns the spectatorial gaze away from the materiality of the external world. For if one wants to examine what is essentially human, as much western theatre purports to do, all that is deemed superfluous to that investigation – here, the environment – needs to be bracketed off. This anthropocentric distillation is mirrored, moreover, by theatre's fundamentally abstract and transcendent geography. One of the great strengths of theatre as a medium has traditionally been its capacity to adopt an inherently plastic and dynamic attitude towards space; one in which the bare boards of the stage can signify any place whatsoever. The title of Peter Brook's famous text *The Empty Stage* (1968) is revealing in this context: it indicates that theatre is a *topos* which is only accorded importance when a human actor enters and is viewed by a human spectator:

> I can take any empty space and call it a bare stage. A man walks across this empty space whilst someone else is watching him, and this is all that is needed for an act of theatre to be engaged.[17]

Faced with theatre's long anthropocentric history, it is little wonder that scholars in Theatre and Performance Studies have been slow in developing a robust, critical language for engaging with the presence of the 'more than human world' in key dramatic texts.[18] While this situation is slowly being rectified by critics interested in animals, cyborgs and objects, the fact remains that the majority of publications in the field continue to pay little or no attention to anything beyond the human realm.[19]

Ironically, in the light of its historical contiguity with the growth of the modern environmental movement, the advent of Performance Studies in the United States in the late 1970s and 1980s has only served to exacerbate this anthropocentric tendency. Despite Richard Schechner's early work on ethology and animal ritual in his 1977 publication *Performance Theory*, most performance scholars, albeit with some major exceptions, have been concerned with cultural performance,[20] with how human beings experiment with, and construct, different forms of sexual, racial and gender identity.[21] In making this claim, we are not suggesting that ecology and environment are exclusive areas of study, sealed off from the cultural domain of identity politics. Rather, we simply want to point out that scholars working in theatre and performance, unlike researchers in, say, literature or philosophy, have been reluctant to engage in what Félix Guattari, among others, terms 'transversal' or 'ecosophical' thinking.[22] For Guattari, this is thinking that seeks to explain how human and 'more than human' worlds intersect and interpenetrate in a dynamic nexus.

A good indication of the belatedness of Theatre and Performance Studies in this important area is found in the opening pages of two recent publications: Downing Cless's *Ecology and Environment in European Drama* (2010) and Wendy Arons and Theresa J. May's *Readings in Performance and Ecology* (2012).[23] In these texts, there is a lament for the failure of theatre scholars to heed Erika Munk's calls in the special edition on ecology published back in 1994 by the US journal *Theater*. In that urgent plea, the first of its kind in Theatre Studies, Munk demands a new form of eco-theatrical analysis that would 'stand at the edge of a vast, open field of histories to be rewritten, styles to rediscuss, contexts to reprieve'.[24] For Munk, theatre's own brand of ecocriticism should situate itself in a generative space, 'somewhere between staged activism and aesthetic analysis, between the ecology of the outside world and the internal ecology of dramatic form'.[25] To convey the political importance of her project, Munk draws an excited analogy. 'Now', she avers enthusiastically, 'it's like the early days of feminism, everything is calling for reinterpretation'.[26]

Munk's comments are nuanced and inclusive. She is not simply urging scholars to write about engaged work *per se* – the type of self-consciously activist stage that we might call, after Kurt Heinlein, 'Green theatre' –[27] and nor does she insist that critical energies should only be directed at performances and practices that deal with ecology and the environment in a direct sense, as witnessed in many of the excellent essays included in three recent special editions of *Canadian Theatre Review*, *Research in Drama and Education: The Journal of Applied Theatre and Performance* and *Performance Research*.[28] Rather, she encourages us to widen the scope of our enquiry and to look back to extant texts, reading them with and against their environmental and ecological grain. The aim, for Munk, is nothing less than the creation of a new form of theatre history that would no longer be limited to 'a history of [human] identity', but, on the contrary, would seek to locate dramatic themes and forms within a larger network of organic and inorganic structures.[29]

This collection joins with the relatively small group of scholars – Wendy Arons, Una Chaudhuri, Downing Cless, Bonnie Marranca, Theresa May, Sheila Rabillard – who have attempted to answer Munk's appeal for a green history by reassessing the ecological potential of canonical classic and modernist dramatic texts.[30] Chaudhuri's *Staging Place: The Geography of Modern Drama*, for instance, looks at the ecological tensions of homecoming in modern and postmodern theatre from the 1870s to the 1990s, while Cless's *Ecology and Environment in European Drama* adopts an even wider remit, focusing on the representation of nature from Aristophanes to Beckett. However, while our collection situates itself, broadly, within this revisionist logic, it distinguishes itself in two specific ways. In contrast with the long *durée* approach of Chaudhuri and Cless, *Rethinking the Theatre of the Absurd: Ecology, Environment and the Greening of the Modern Stage* seeks to explore a relatively specific and delimited period of theatre history that runs from roughly 1948 to the early 1960s. In addition, it aims to reassess the significance of a key critical text, namely, Martin Esslin's *The Theatre of the Absurd*, whose canonical status within theatre scholarship is proved by the fact that it has been published in three different editions, and reissued on numerous occasions.

It is important to understand from the outset that we have little interest in castigating Esslin for paying scant attention to the nascent stages of an ecological crisis that he might only have been dimly aware of (see pp. 12–16). Rather, it is our contention that the sheer influence of his book, caused by its compelling focus on existential and aesthetic issues, has inadvertently dissuaded theatre scholars from grasping the environmental and ecological significance inherent in the Theatre of the Absurd. In the early decades of the twenty-first century, in the age of the Anthropocene, to which we turn presently (see pp. 33–4), this absence needs to be addressed. For the (anti)theatrical sensibility that exploded in Europe and the United States in the late 1940s and 1950s reflects, we believe, a decisive moment in humanity's ability to live on the Earth – the moment when, as a consequence of the nuclear violence inflicted upon Japan in 1945, there was a collective realization that life on the planet could no longer be taken for granted. As the contemporary artist Simon Starling mentions:

> The events that occurred in that unimaginably brief moment caused a fundamental rupture in our relationship with time, but perhaps most significantly in our understanding of the future, which became something to be anticipated precisely and feared.[31]

Contra Esslin who largely limits the discussion to existentialist matters alone (see pp. 12–6), the profound sense of anxiety that emerged in the 1950s is part of a larger, more complex sense of ecological uncertainty that is bound up with the explosion of the atom bomb as well as new knowledge about the disastrous effects of chemical insecticides on the food cycle. In the theatres of Beckett, Adamov, Ionesco and Genet (referred to by Ruby Cohn as 'Esslin's Big Four'[32]), the fundamental principle of ecology – 'the idea that everything and everyone is connected' or, as Guattari would put it, the transversal interplay between environmental, social and mental ecologies[33] – no longer functions in a healthy sense.[34] Instead, we are presented with what the ecocritic Timothy Morton terms a 'dark ecology', a world of toxins and poisons where human characters exist as lonely, alienated monads.[35] In the Theatre of the Absurd, the environmental background is fore-grounded; and 'nature', the phenomenon that since pre-history was regarded 'as an infinite resource', is now seen as both *threatened* and *threatening*.

In Samuel Beckett's second play *Endgame* (1957) for example, the blind Hamm intuits, with some accuracy, the 'dark' ecological mood of the early 1950s when he ruminates, melancholically, that 'no one who ever lived thought as crooked as we'.[36] In the sterile emptiness of *Endgame*, on this 'bitch' of an earth where 'no seeds sprout',[37] Beckett creates a bleak, futural world, in which, as ecocritic Greg Garrard notes, survival is worse than death.[38] In doing so, Beckett demands a confrontation with what the green thinker and anti-nuclear campaigner Joanna Macy might call the 'ecological repressed', the refusal of human beings to accept that their actions have environmental effects, and, consequently, that their fate is bound up with that of the Earth.[39]

Apart from a handful of essays on Beckett, little or no attention to date has been paid to the ecological dimension of the Theatre of the Absurd. In the two most important revisionist accounts to have emerged in recent decades, Enoch Brater and Ruby Cohn's collection *Around the Absurd: Essays on Modern and Postmodern Drama* (1991) and Michael Y. Bennett's *Reassessing the Theatre of the Absurd: Camus, Beckett, Ionesco, Genet, and Pinter* (2011), the focus is resolutely anthropocentric.[40] In the first example, the aim is to trace the influence of absurdist theatre on postmodernist practitioners; and, in the second, Bennett sets out to clarify some longstanding misconceptions about the Theatre of the Absurd's purported lack of a political agenda. Though excellent in their different ways, both of these texts overlook completely the green potential of absurdist theatre that was first hinted at by Theodor Adorno in his seminal essay of 1958, 'Trying to Understand *Endgame*'. In that extraordinary reflection, Adorno offers a sophisticated, if oblique, exposure of the environmental violence that Beckett attributes to the human species. Through his deliberate refusal to represent history according to the coherent and consequential standards of Aristotelian poetics, Beckett allows the spectator, Adorno contends, to feel or intuit the full horror of what it means to live in a time where 'the end of the world is discounted, as if it were a matter of course'.[41] In a passage that historicizes catastrophe in *Endgame* as nuclear catastrophe,

Adorno is the first to point to the ecological significance of Beckett's theatre:

> Every supposed drama of the atomic age would mock itself, if only because its fable would hopelessly falsify the horror of historical anonymity by shoving it into the characters and actions of humans, and possibly by gaping at the 'prominents' who decide whether the button will be pushed. The violence of the unspeakable is mimicked by the timidity to mention it. Beckett keeps it nebulous. One can only speak euphemistically about what is incommensurate with experience.[42]

For Adorno, the accusatory power of Beckett's theatre is found in its negativity. By keeping it nebulous, Beckett conjures an unspoken sense of dread. In this way, he provokes a mood of unease, a kind of haunting that communicates a socio-historical atmosphere that the audience might otherwise prefer to repress or ignore.

Irrespective of formal and thematic differences between individual playwrights, Adorno's reading of Beckett's work is applicable to the ecological sensibility of the Theatre of the Absurd as a whole. One has only to think of the 'unspeakable' terror that so panics the characters of Pinter, Adamov, Ionesco and early Genet to see that the Beckettian scenario in *Endgame* is a widespread feature in absurdist theatre, a kind of environmental primal scene. The nebulousness that so dominates the representational axis in the Theatre of the Absurd has important methodological consequences. It indicates that there is little to be gained in pursuing a form of hermeneutics that would expect to uncover an ideologically coherent position expressed by the practitioners of the Absurd, a set of instructions that audiences could identify and act on. Rather, as Joe Kelleher and Elaine Aston show in their respective essays in this volume on Beckett and Caryl Churchill, it is incumbent upon us to follow Adorno's lead and to concentrate on moments of slippage, negativity and absence. We need to be attentive, in other words, to how absurdist theatre expresses, implicitly, that things ought to be otherwise, even when no direct green message is forthcoming. In this respect, the book situates itself squarely within what Ken Hiltner in a recent anthology terms 'the second wave of ecocriticism'.

In contrast with the first wave that was dominated by celebratory studies of the role of 'nature' in British romantic and American transcendental poetry,[43] second-wave ecocriticism is more concerned with 'sites of environmental devastation' and with subjecting the very idea of 'nature' to scrutiny.[44] Issues of politics, economics and representation come to the fore, and the human body is posited as a fragile site, vulnerable to infection and disease. Rather than making a fetish out of wilderness or place, as the first wave of ecocritics often did, second-wave ecocriticism highlights the extent to which a more progressive ecology might necessitate a new form of human subjectivity, one that is characterized, moreover, by weakness, vulnerability and uncertainty, and which consciously sets out to place the so-called exceptionalism of the human subject in crisis. Timothy Morton provides a typically pithy expression of the stakes involved when he argues that today, 'ecology is the latest in a series of humiliations of the human'.[45]

Martin Esslin, *The Theatre of the Absurd* (1961, 1968, 1980, 2001)

To utter the words 'the Theatre of the Absurd', surely one of the most canonical terms in the theatre lexicon, is to point towards a period and style of theatre that most students, scholars and theatre critics would purport to recognize in an almost *de facto* sense. By way of a definition of the Theatre of the Absurd, Esslin cites Eugène Ionesco, the playwright to whom he devotes the most analysis in his book: 'Absurd is that which is devoid of purpose. ... Cut off from his religious, metaphysical, and transcendental roots, man is lost; all his actions become senseless, absurd, useless'.[46]

To understand this 'world of shattered beliefs', Esslin turned to Albert Camus's 1942 publication *The Myth of Sisyphus*. For Camus, when the Gods 'no longer' provide explanations, human speech and behaviour 'no longer' bear comprehensible meaning: 'In a universe suddenly divested of illusions and lights, man feels an alien, a stranger. His exile is without remedy since it is deprived of a memory of a lost home or the hope of a promised land. This divorce between man and his life, the actor and his setting, is properly the feeling of absurdity'.[47]

Building on Camus's philosophical foundations, Esslin explains that the 'absurd' situation in which humans find themselves in the early 1960s is grounded in historical development. He describes the age in which he wrote the book as 'bewilderingly stratified', since it combines medieval belief systems with Enlightenment rationalism, Marxist progressive politics and twentieth-century fanaticism.[48] The Theatre of the Absurd, for Esslin, has its origins in the specific social, political and economic evolutions that shaped Europe over the twentieth century: the decline in religious belief and the secularization of society; 'the falseness and evil nature of some of the cheap and vulgar substitutes that have been set up to take [God's] place', notably fanaticisms like fascism; the devastating world wars; the impact of the rise of mass media and advertising, and their devaluation of language.[49] Most pertinently for the ecocritical purposes of this book, Esslin makes reference, albeit only on one occasion, to the consequences to humanity of industrialization. Citing the Italian playwright Ezio d'Errico's *The Forest* (1959), whose title refers to a grotesque landscape of derelict telegraph poles, electricity pylons and petrol pumps growing from a soil of concrete, Esslin writes:

> The forest of concrete is an apt poetic image of an industrial civilization, and the characters who inhabit it are all sufferers from its scourges – war, intellectual pride, the suppression of the poetic impulse by commercial pressures, religious doubt, and all the horrors of the concentration camp. ... The play is the passionate outcry of a romantic against the deadening of sensibilities, the loss of contact with organic nature, that the spread of a civilization of concrete and iron has brought about.[50]

Esslin's remark on the destructive impact of industrialization is noteworthy in view of the ecocritical approach that this collection takes. It is all the more striking for the fact that it was written several decades before ecocriticism became an established mode of enquiry. But it remains, for all that, a very minor observation, so minor, in fact, that no commentator has ever mentioned it.

While social, political, economic contexts serve as a backdrop to Esslin's theorization of the Absurd, his overwhelming focus, like Camus's, is on the individual, and that individual's attendant unconscious inner conflicts, needs, desires and neuroses. Perhaps inevitably, given the fact that it predates the emergence of 'green politics', Esslin's philosophical approach is quintessentially anthropocentric. Expressions such as the 'human condition', the 'human situation', 'human endeavour', 'human isolation' and 'man's search for truth' recur repeatedly in *The Theatre of the Absurd*. Esslin perpetuates a deep-seated attachment to a metaphysics of the sovereign human subject, owing to the fact that he nostalgically laments the loss of this subject. Moreover, Esslin speaks frequently of the 'universe', as if the human perspective, notably the European white male perspective, determined the workings of the entire planet and its surrounding solar systems. The intention of this collection is thus to address and to redress this problem, by broadening perspectives in order to locate humans in the works of the playwrights discussed, within wider environmental and ecological contexts.

Esslin describes the aim of his publication to be the presentation of some of the major exponents and works of the Theatre of the Absurd, for instance Beckett's *Waiting for Godot* (1953), which has been seen by millions and has entered vernacular vocabulary. Understandably, Esslin's study focuses on Paris because in the 1950s this capital was, in his words, a 'powerhouse of the modern movement', which attracted highly intellectual artists and audience members. 'There [was] no other place in the world where so many first-rate men of the theatre [could] be found', he declares.[51] One of the many strengths of Esslin's study lies in his inclusion not only of big names like Beckett and Ionesco, but also of Parisian artists who received less attention, for example, Jean Tardieu and Boris Vian, and of a wealth of lesser-known authors hailing from other parts of Europe, like Italy's Ezio d'Errico, already mentioned, or the Catalan author Manuel de Pedrolo. Esslin's book also ends with a highly original *a posteriori* genealogy of the Theatre of the Absurd, the origins of which he traces, for example, back to Shakespeare's clowns, *commedia dell'arte*, Alfred Jarry's *Ubu* plays, and the silent cinema of Charlie Chaplin and Buster Keaton. This small sample of the wealth of influences that Esslin ascribes to the Theatre of the Absurd testifies to his constant reminder to the reader that, in spite of the sense of loss, futility and incomprehension that this theatre evokes, it resiliently clings to comedy, humour and knockabout fun. However, for all of its exhaustive comprehensiveness, in nearly 500 pages, Esslin analyses not a single female theatre-maker.[52] As the quotations from *The Theatre of the Absurd* included in this account of the work illustrate, Esslin's interest focuses on the theatre of 'first-rate men', written on the subject of 'the present situation of Western Man', and 'his' preoccupations, predicaments and struggles.[53] One could argue that when *The Theatre of the Absurd* was re-edited in 2001, these gendered terms for referring to humanity might have been eliminated. Moreover, Esslin adds to this edition authors who, for him, became proselytes of the Theatre of the Absurd towards the end of the twentieth century, for instance the United Kingdom's Tom Stoppard, or Austria's Thomas Bernhard. But he omits crucially important female playwrights from the same countries, like Caryl Churchill and Elfriede Jelinek.

We have already mentioned that Esslin himself gestures, fleetingly, to the ravages visited on the environment of modernity. However, there is a potentially generative way in which Esslin's book might engage with ecocriticism. In *Ecologies of Theatre* (1996), Bonnie Marranca understands ecology both as a regard for the environment, exemplified by the representation of nature, space and landscape in the works of performance-makers like John Cage or Heiner Müller, and as a means 'to contemplate the world of a work as an environment linked to a cultural (aesthetic) system'.[54] She explains how theatrical texts or productions can be like ecosystems – collectives of interrelating, interacting and interdependent scenic elements on stage. *The Theatre of the Absurd* is a significant publication not least because Esslin was highly attentive not only to text and dialogue, but also to all aspects of stagecraft – whether scenography, costumes or acting style – an aspect of theatre that was little discussed by critics before the 1960s, until which point theatre was evaluated according to its literary, rather than its performative qualities. It is telling that, before describing the Absurd as an absence of logic, reason and propriety, Esslin refers to the way in which it can describe music that is 'out of harmony'.[55] He goes on to explain that 'the stage is a multidimensional medium: it allows the simultaneous use of visual elements, movement, light, and language', and he speaks of the 'contrapuntal interaction of all these elements'.[56] These interrelations between a profusion of scenic details on stage can forge an ethics of interconnectedness, exchange, dialogue, reciprocity and democracy – an ecology – where established order between living and nonliving, animate and inanimate forms, is levelled. Whereas Esslin's book predated the availability of critical tools with which to precipitate this ecological dehierarchization, a number of contributors to this collection embrace this ecological schema in order to interrogate human supremacy, thereby opening up the possibility for a greater respect for, and accountability towards, the environment that sustains us.

Greening the absurd

In his Introduction to *The Green Reader*, the political scientist Andrew Dobson offers a useful description of green politics:

> Green politics is more than nature conservation. It begins with environmental problems, but it does not end with them. It seeks the reasons for environmental degradation and finds them in the politics and economics of growth – precisely the politics and economics pursued by virtually every society on the planet.[57]

Dobson's comments illuminate the project of this book. To green the Absurd is not simply to highlight matters of environmental concern (although that, of course, is very much part of our agenda); an equally important task is to question, actively, the supposed exceptionalism of the human subject and to interrogate the politics implicit in its narrowly conceived anthropocentric value system.[58] However, it is crucial that the word 'active' in this collection is not confused with 'activism'. As opposed to contemporary playwrights such as Caridad Svich, Steve Waters, Andrew Bovell and Richard Bean, the writers associated with the Theatre of the Absurd are not green artists in any self-conscious sense.[59] Indeed, if we trace the birth of the modern green movement, as many do, to the 1962 publication of Rachel Carson's influential text *Silent Spring*[60] (swiftly followed by the formation of Friends of the Earth in 1969 and Greenpeace in 1970), it is evident that many of the plays discussed in this collection pre-date the advent of green politics altogether.[61] Confronted with this historical *décalage*, to green the Absurd can only be to engage in an act of historical reclamation, to unfold an ecological significance that was always there but that remained latent and indirect.

But what type of green past are we trying to reclaim? And how might we gain access to it? The history that we are interested in studying in this collection is perhaps most accurately described as an affective history grounded in what Raymond Williams has termed 'structures of feeling'. For Williams, structures of feeling are overarching moods and shared emotions that are fluid, 'in solution', not yet precipitated as crystalline objects or empirical facts to analyse from a distance. 'We are defining', Williams continues, 'a social experience which is still in process, often indeed not yet recognized'.[62] But if a structure of feeling cannot be quantified or understood, this does not mean, Williams reminds us, that it fails to generate social and historical effects: 'Although [structures of feeling] are emergent or pre-emergent, they do not have to await definition, classification, or rationalization before they exert palpable pressures and set effective limits on experience and on action'.[63]

The attempt to chart something as elusive and emergent as an ecological structure of feeling is particularly relevant to the Theatre of the Absurd, for significance in the absurdist text, as all the contributions to this volume demonstrate in one form or another, is affective and allegorical: it expresses itself in rhythms, atmospheres and intensities, and in images of disease, contamination and infection.

For our purposes, the Theatre of the Absurd is best approached as a lived archive of ecological experience, a dramatic articulation of a nascent structure of feeling provoked by the panicked atmosphere of the time – a period where, in the aftermath of Hiroshima and Nagasaki, governments and populations were stumbling towards an understanding of what it meant to live in an epoch where human beings could now destroy the totality of life on the planet and intervene in the geological formation of the Earth itself.[64] As such, and in light of the inarticulate and often opaque quality of historical experience, it is vital, if we are to green the Absurd, that we renounce, in advance, any expectation that we will discover a direct illustration of ecological discourse or environmental critique. The critical challenge lies elsewhere: in unpacking the ecological meanings that are embedded, obliquely, within diverse forms of linguistic, corporeal and emotional alienation that the Theatre of the Absurd was so concerned to evoke.[65]

An equally important objective is to rethink what we conventionally understand by 'nature'. Reflecting the deconstructionist ethos of second-wave ecocriticism, 'nature', in *Rethinking the Theatre of the*

Absurd: Ecology, Environment and the Greening of the Modern Stage, is posed as a problematic concept, an over-determined word with divergent and contested meanings. As Stephen Bottoms, Ralph Yarrow and Clare Finburgh all argue in this collection 'nature' is a loaded signifier, an idea fraught with contradictions, engaged in a persistent to- and fro-ing between physiology and psychology, representation and matter. Any attempt to eradicate these braidings is to mistake the problem for the solution, to perpetuate the Enlightenment desire for neat orderings and boundaries that, for a thinker such as Bruno Latour, has done so much to destroy 'nature' in the first place.[66]

Within such a deconstructionist purview, Clov's reply to Hamm in Beckett's *Endgame*, 'that there is no more nature', is revealing.[67] For what it suggests, perhaps axiomatically given the play's setting, is not simply that 'nature' has been destroyed in some apocalyptic *mise-en-scène*; rather, it confirms a new, deconstructionist awareness that nature was always already an idea, a trope or cultural construct produced by humans for their own purposes.[68] *Endgame*, then, is an ecological play in a double sense. As well as implicitly critiquing human destructiveness, it forecloses any attempt to return to

FIGURE 2 *Yann Collette (Willie) and Natalie Royer (Winnie) in Blandine Savetier's production of Samuel Beckett's* Oh les beaux jours (Happy Days) *at the Comédie de Béthune, 2011.*

'nature' as a place of shelter or redemption, something that humans can exploit again, but this time as a panacea. Clov's words show that to continue to posit 'nature' as a site of authenticity in the wake of nuclear fallout, the acceleration of fossil fuel consumption, and the production of a sinister toxicology of pesticides, polymers and pollutants, is akin to burying one's head in the sand.[69] This point is underlined by the striking scenography in Blandine Savetier's production of another of Beckett's plays, *Oh les beaux jours* (*Happy Days*, 1961) at the Comédie de Béthune in 2011 (see Figure 2). In this performance, a peroxided Winnie, played by Natalie Royer, is entombed up to her neck in a mound of black polythene bin liners that at once highlight the artificiality of 'nature' – the sandy, scorched earth of Beckett's original text is now plastic – while critiquing, through the immediacy of a theatrical image, humanity's despoliation of the planet.[70]

Ecology and environment

To understand further what greening means in this book, we need to distinguish between two terms that we have, until now, used fairly interchangeably: ecology and environment. This is not a simple heuristic exercise, for these idioms give rise to and express very different political agendas. The word environment, for example, is often understood in ecocritical circles to designate the landscape or habitat in which the human beings find themselves. Inherent to the notion of environment, then, is an implicit sense of distance, the designation of a place or milieu that human beings might occupy or construct but are not necessarily part of or affected by. The limitations of the concept are such that Michel Serres urges us to do away with it altogether:

> Forget the word environment. ... It assumes that we humans are at the center of a system of nature. The idea recalls a bygone era, when the Earth (how can one imagine that it used to represent us?) placed in the center of the world, reflected our narcissism, the humanism that makes of us the exact midpoint or excellent culmination of all things. No. The Earth existed without our imaginable ancestors, could well exist today without us, will exist tomorrow ... whereas we can't exist without it.[71]

From Serres's 'deep green perspective' – and we find this reiterated in the work of ecological thinkers as diverse as Arne Naess and Félix Guattari – to think in environmental terms alone ('environmentalism') is to perpetuate, unwittingly, the ideology of the Enlightenment subject who gazes at the environment from the outside, as if it were some aestheticized or intellectual object.[72] In his reflections on technology, Martin Heidegger reiterates the dangers of this predominately visual way of relating to the environment. For Heidegger, transforming the world into a picture (*Gestell*) erases the alterity and agency of 'nature', and results in the resources of the planet being conceived as mere stuff, a 'standing reserve' to be exploited by human beings: 'The world now appears as an object open to the attacks of calculative thought. … Nature becomes a gigantic gas station, an energy resource for modern technology and industry'.[73]

Although important for the attention it places on 'nature', environmentalism does not do enough to challenge, at least not in any fundamental sense, the other-directed violence that lurks at the heart of normative notions of human identity. Rather, as feminist and social ecologists such as Val Plumwood and Murray Bookchin point out, environmentalism can often foster a conservative, patriarchal logic that uses 'nature' as an alibi for a whole series of imaginary 'naturalisations'.[74] In political terms, the difficulties associated with environmentalism are seen in the anxieties that first-wave ecocriticism has sometimes had to confront with respect to the supposedly 'progressive' environmental policies of National Socialism in Germany in the 1930s or the Earth First! movement in the United States in the 1980s and 1990s. In both, 'nature' is accorded a higher value than some human beings, who are now reduced to the condition of 'bare life', which, as Giorgio Agamben shows, is life that can be eradicated with impunity.[75] Despite its avowed biocentrism (extending inalienable rights to nature), this mode of thinking, far from breaking with the anti-ecological logic of the Enlightenment, merely affirms its value system in inverted form. Only now, it is 'nature' that is supposedly deemed authentically transcendent, not culture.

In order to challenge the reactionary elements that haunt the environmental imagination, second-wave ecocritics resist championing a simplistic notion of biocentrism as an alternative value system in and by itself.[76] Instead, they tend to interrogate the very concept of human identity itself and to posit a kind of entanglement or overlap between human and non-human domains. In an essay on Beckett, Paul Davies explains how the ecopolitical dimension of Beckett's writing is found in its capacity for 'defining and contesting subjectivity', in such a way that 'the boundaries of subjectivity, figured as the difference between the outer and inner, echo and resonate with the subject's perception and definition of itself, whether that be in opposition, apposition, or dialogue with the environment'.[77]

Davies's comments underscore the extent to which environmentalism, by itself, is not sufficient to transform our attitudes towards the 'more than human' world. As he argues in his essay, the imperative is to not so much to save 'nature', but rather to interrogate the dangers inherent in binary notions of identity that have done so much to determine our disastrous attitudes towards 'nature' in the first instance. For Davies – and Clare Finburgh is attentive to this in her essay on Genet in this volume – it is impossible to imagine an effective ecology that would not, by extension, critically interrogate the role that orthodox ideas of 'race', gender and sexuality have played in defining our perceptions of 'nature' and vice versa. Progressive ecological thinking, unlike environmentalism, sets out to interrogate unhelpful oppositions and borders, not simply to invert them – hence, the reason why for Timothy Morton, ecology is not about nature *per se*, but about how human beings 'think' 'nature':

> Ecology shows us that all beings are connected. The *ecological thought* is the thinking of interconnectedness. The ecological thought is a thought about ecology, but it's also thinking that is ecological. Thinking the ecological thought is part of an ecological project. The ecological thought doesn't just occur 'in the mind'. It is a practice and a process of becoming fully aware of how human beings are connected with other beings – animal, vegetable, or mineral. Ultimately, this includes thinking about democracy. What would a truly democratic encounter between truly equal beings look like, what would it be … ?[78]

The ideas of Davies and Morton here have much in common with those of Verena Andermatt Conley as articulated in her groundbreaking poststructuralist reading of ecology, *Ecopolitics: The Environment in Poststructuralist Thought* (1997). Citing

Jean-François Lyotard's essay 'Oikos', a text which, along with Guattari's *The Three Ecologies* (1989) and Morton's own *Ecology without Nature: Rethinking Environmental Aesthetics* (2007), figures prominently in this collection, Andermatt Conley insists on aligning ecology with the deconstruction of normative notions of identity. For if, as she proposes, 'being born in the world … inevitably touches on quandaries of dispossession, of severance, and of exile from the idea of a maternal paradise', then 'subjectivity is forcibly … ecological'.[79]

Ecological thinking of the sort advocated by Davies, Morton and Andermatt Conley throws alternative light on Albert Camus's *The Myth of Sisyphus* (1942), a text which, as we have shown (see pp. 12–4), provided Martin Esslin with his philosophical framework for *The Theatre of the Absurd*. However, whereas Esslin's reading of Camus remains resolutely humanist, concerned as it is with the human condition alone, an ecological interpretation of *The Myth of Sisyphus* allows for a very different reading of the Theatre of the Absurd to emerge. To read Camus through a green lens is to grasp how the sense of exile provoked by the Absurd ultimately problematizes the narcissism of the anthropocentric self and, as a consequence, holds out the possibility for a more ecologically viable form of subjectivity. As Camus stresses again and again, and as we explain in more detail presently, ontological exile is always immanent exile; it posits human being as earthly being, existence without hope of transcendence or redemption.

Absurdist ecology and *The Myth of Sisyphus*

The ecological significance of *The Myth of Sisyphus* resides in the fact that, for Camus, the Absurd articulates a radical *décalage* between what human beings want, and what their environment(s) can provide. It is significant that Camus should explain this disjunction by drawing on dramatic metaphors. In the following passage, he insists that the 'essential impulse of the human drama' is to place the human agent at the very centre of the world, so that he or she is the only protagonist worthy of interest. The Absurd shatters this centrality, Camus cautions, by producing an overwhelming sense of strangeness:

> The mind's deepest desire, even in its most elaborate operations, parallels man's unconscious feeling in the face of his universe: it is an

insistence upon familiarity, an appetite for clarity. Understanding the world for a man is reducing it to the human, stamping it with his seal. The cat's universe is not the universe of the anthill. The truism 'All thought is anthropomorphic' has no other meaning. ... That nostalgia for unity, that appetite for the absolute illustrates the essential impulse of the human drama. ... But we must despair of ever reconstructing the familiar, calm surface which would give us peace of heart. ... Forever I shall be a stranger to myself.[80]

This understanding of the Camusian Absurd as a blast of strangeness, a moment of intense existential alienation, is not new.[81] What has been less remarked upon – and Esslin, perhaps understandably, ignores it entirely – is the way in which the Camusian Absurd hints at an implicit relationship between theatre and ecology.[82] For if, as Camus explains here, the logic of human drama is to make the world familiar by draping it in representation, then one way of understanding what an ecological theatre might be, is to approach it as a signifying system that places anthropocentrism in crisis by defamiliarizing our habitual ways of seeing and behaving. Indeed, without ever being conscious of it, Camus appears to suggest as much when discussing the Absurd as a moment when the stage set dissolves:

A step lower and strangeness creeps in: perceiving that the world is 'dense', sensing to what degree a stone is foreign and irreducible to us, with what intensity nature or a landscape can negate us. At the heart of all beauty lies something inhuman, and these hills, the softness of the sky, the outline of these trees, at this very minute lose the illusory meaning with which we have clothed them, henceforth more remote than a lost paradise. The primitive hostility of the world rises up to face us across millennia. For a second we cease to understand it because for centuries we have understood in it solely the images and designs that we had attributed to it beforehand, because henceforth we lack the power to make use of that artifice. The world evades us because it becomes itself again. That stage scenery masked by habit becomes again what it is. It withdraws at a distance from us.[83]

Although he is speaking metaphorically, Camus's description goes some way to explaining the rationale for the ecological potential that we attribute to the Theatre of the Absurd in this collection. For what Camus outlines here is the extent to which theatre, by disorientating and dislocating its spectators, can allow the 'world to evade us' and 'become itself again'. By drawing attention to the falsity of the 'stage scenery' that we ordinarily ignore, and by contesting habitual 'images and designs', theatre permits 'the primitive hostility of the world [to] rise up to face us'. The 'primitive hostility' that Camus draws attention to here carves out a space – an absurdist stage, we might say – where ontology and ecology bleed into each other. In this bleeding, this overlap, a different kind of ecological ethics and politics emerge. For in their confrontation with the absurdity of existence, human beings, Camus implies, are compelled to realize their place in the 'natural world' as human animals, earthly creatures for whom transcendence is replaced with immanence, and whose disappearance is no longer coterminous with the destruction of the world itself. Just as 'landscape negates us', so what Camus refers to as the 'irreducible density of stone' highlights, by contrast, the fleeting and contingent nature of human existence.

Ecologically, this is an extraordinary passage. It suggests that when the narcissistic illusions of theatre are shattered, when, that is, spectators turn their attention away from their obsessions with human passions, they suddenly perceive that to live on the Earth is to live in the midst of what Timothy Morton terms 'strange strangers', uncanny things that trouble the subject/object divide and deconstruct the gap between inside and outside.[84] The paradox of the Camusian Absurd is that the subject is immersed in, and distanced from, the world, in the same impossible moment. In the ontological double-bind that the Absurd brings into being, strangeness does not simply imply separation: on the contrary, it establishes an impossible connection, a relation of non-relation. To borrow the thinking behind Gabriella Giannachi and Nigel Stewart's important collection on environmental performance, the Absurd subject is positioned 'between nature', situated on a restless and permeable borderline, aware of its implication in a world of base materiality that it can never coincide with or lose itself in.[85] Our exile, then, is never absolute, for we are always tethered to the world.

Confronted with the abyssal presence of 'nature', Sisyphus, Camus's hero of the Absurd, acts differently from Roquentin, the protagonist of Jean-Paul Sartre's existentialist novel *Nausea* (1938), who turned away in horror when he chanced upon the muddy roots of an upturned tree. Rather, Sisyphus looks to establish a new relationship with 'nature', a kind of impossible intimacy, in which the foreignness of the world, its 'strange strangeness' is affirmed. In the final essay of the book, after describing Sisyphus's punishment for disobeying the gods in terms of a 'ceaseless rolling of a rock to the top of a mountain, whence the stone would fall back of its own weight', Camus famously decrees that 'one must imagine Sisyphus happy'.[86] A major component of Sisyphus's happiness, Camus proposes, arises from his sudden awareness of immanence, his acceptance that he is part of, and tied to, a complex world of matter from which he can neither escape nor transcend. In this dark illumination, a truce is made with the Absurd in which Sisyphus affirms his impossible exile:

> I leave Sisyphus at the foot of the mountain! One always finds one's burden again. But Sisyphus teaches the higher fidelity that negates gods and raises rocks. He too concludes that all is well. This universe henceforth without a master seems to him neither sterile nor futile. Each atom of the stone, each mineral flake of that night-filled mountain, in itself forms a world.[87]

The lyricism of Camus's conclusion to *The Myth of Sisyphus* resists any temptation one might feel to interpret the Absurd as a form of nihilism. After all, 'The universe without a master', Camus highlights, 'is neither sterile nor futile,' 'each atom forms a world'. Scandalously, and against all common sense, Camus proposes that Sisyphus's awareness of the indifference of the world is the very thing that allows him to respond to its alterity, to respect its strangeness. Ecological ethics and politics, in other words, are found in the human being's ability to affirm the silence of the Earth, to expect no response or help from it in return.[88]

Importantly, in *The Myth of Sisyphus* death is no longer imagined as an exceptional event reserved for human beings alone; rather, the recognition of death – and it is useful to remind ourselves that the starting point for Camus's enquiry was to question the validity of suicide in a universe without God – takes on a planetary dimension as Sisyphus comprehends that the world (and by extension his own body) is made of atoms, matter that transforms and mutates. In this materialist ontology, death is not an end as such; it is a moment of transformation, a different form of becoming, in which humans lose their exceptional status as mortal creatures that think.[89]

Camus's notion of the Absurd reconfigures conventional theories and practices of ecology, a word whose modern-day meaning derives from the amalgamation of the Greek prefix *oikos* ('home' or 'hearth') with the suffix *logos* ('science', 'study', 'law'). In its etymological sense, to be ecological is to be at home in the world, a definition that implies, perhaps dangerously, that to care for the environment is tantamount to caring for one's house. This etymological understanding of ecology has led US bioregionalist thinkers such as Wendell Berry to theorize ecology as a form of home economics, a domestic science rooted in the subject's ability to familiarize itself with its surroundings, to transform the abstractions of space into the lived actualities of place.[90] The difficulty, here, is that the unseizable alterity of the world is erased in favour of an economic worldview, predicated upon ideas of ownership, management and competition. Against this economist and domesticated reading of ecology, Jean François Lyotard proposes an alternative theory of the *oikos*.[91] For Lyotard, ecology and economics, irrespective of their etymological similarities, are fundamentally opposed: 'When *oikos* gives rise to *oikonomikos* or *oikonomikon*', he says, 'a complex transformation of the word *oikos* occurs. ... It implies that the *oikos* has slipped away'.[92] In order to protect the *oikos*, and, by extension, the meaning of ecology as an ethical and political discourse, Lyotard associates it with 'an otherness, an ignored guest who causes some trouble',[93] and whose fate is to remain 'secluded', 'hidden', resistant to communicative language.[94]

Camus's understanding of the Absurd posits a similarly transvalued concept of ecology. Here, ecological ethics are not found in the drive to be at home, but in our capacity to remain *unheimlich*, a stranger suspended between inside and outside, nature and culture, self and other. In a passage that repeats the intimate but impossible relationship that Camus established between ontology and ecology, Morton notes:

> To reintroduce the uncanny into the poetics of the home ... is a political act. Cozy ecological thinking tries to smooth over the uncanny, which is produced by a gap between being human and being a person – by the very culture which is necessitated

ironically because humans emerge from the womb premature, that is, as beings of flesh without a working sense of self.[95]

The 'uncanniness' that Camus, Lyotard and Morton all point to, attests to the ecological significance of the Theatre of the Absurd. In absurdist theatre, homecoming, as in Harold Pinter's 1965 play of the same name, is contested, impossible. At all times, we are presented with geopathological characters, who suffer from what Una Chaudhuri terms, 'homesickness while at home'.[96] In Ionesco's *The Bald Soprano* (1949) and *The Chairs* (1951), as Carl Lavery argues, lonely, disaffected couples drive themselves mad in bell-jars of stifling oppression; similarly, as Franc Chamberlain shows with regard to Adamov's *The Invasion* (1950), the lead character Pierre retreats from the family and appears to commit suicide in his bedroom; and in Pinter's early work, as Mark Taylor-Batty and Carl Lavery highlight, the home is a place of violence and conformity. Crucially, though, we must not see this critique of the *oikos* as a desire to restore a lost value system, an attempt to correct some historically contingent wrong – for it is precisely the desire to return home that is so disabling. Rather, in keeping with the ecology of the Absurd, the more important undertaking is to contest the onto-theological thinking that in monotheistic cultures has posited the world as some originary possession or 'household' gifted to human beings to manage as they see fit. By embracing his homelessness, Sisyphus points to an alternative way of living on the Earth; he accepts himself as a creature of the rock, a stranger divorced from being, happy in his immanence and aware of the impossibility of transcendence.

This ecological reading of Camus's *The Myth of Sisyphus* highlights the important sense in which the Absurd – and thus by extension the Theatre of the Absurd – offers more than a simple critique of what Gregory Bateson calls ecological 'insanity'.[97] Its subversion of the onto-theological structures of the western self holds out the possibility for a more radical intervention, one in which the alterity of the world is both acknowledged and affirmed and where the supremacy of the human subject is undone. It is pertinent to note that Camus's text was published in 1942, one year before the Manhattan Project relocated to Los Alamos in New Mexico, the laboratory where the atom bomb was finally developed in 1945. It is almost as if Camus anticipates how best to respond to a world in which the very presence of life itself is now imagined as 'provisional', as Beckett describes it in his essay 'The Capital of the Ruins' (1946).[98] Within this context of precarity and vulnerability, Camus offers a philosophy for living that avoids both nihilism and repression, each of which tends only to deny the full extent of the ecological crisis that the creation of the atom bomb brought into being.

Environmental history

Within the substantial body of commentary that it has generated, the Theatre of the Absurd has often been described as a theatre created in the shadow of the nuclear attacks on Hiroshima and Nagasaki in August 1945.[99] Strangely, however, there has been no attempt to unpack, in any depth, what such a disturbed theatre might consist of in terms of its representational logic or dramaturgical composition. Similarly – and this absence is perhaps even more glaring – no one has thought to situate the Theatre of the Absurd within the context of the new environmentalist paradigm that emerged in the 1950s.

According to environmental historians, the 1950s marks a crucial moment in the development of ecological awareness. William Cronon notes:

> For a generation growing up in the shadow of the mushroom cloud, the idea that one's own body might harbour the poisonous seeds of future cancers and birth defects became a potent source of both nightmares and political activism. In the history of human fear, the post-Hiroshima age was haunted by new forms of hidden terror that were all the more frightening for lurking so invisibly beneath the bright sunlit surfaces of everyday life. ... What was new, though, was less the poisons themselves than the public awareness of their presence.[100]

What is new about the 1950s, Cronon suggests, is not so much that the atomic age marked the beginning of our current ecological anxiety, but that it brought extant knowledge of that anxiety into public consciousness for the first time. Initially, this was focused on the vulnerability of the human body and its susceptibility to the invisible presence of radioactive particles in the atmosphere. By the mid-1950s rumours and first-hand accounts of cancers, skin diseases and mutations caused by radiation sickness in Hiroshima and Nagasaki began to circulate in the world media as the US censorship of scientific and medical research in Japan was lifted in 1952. This produced a number of papers, journal articles and popular memoirs such as Michihiko Hachiya's influential *Hiroshima Diary: The Journal of a Japanese Physician, August 6 – September 30, 1945*, which was translated into English in 1955.[101] Any doubt that these findings and accounts were politically motivated, an attempt by the Japanese to solicit sympathy for the lifting of economic sanctions, were quashed by the incident of the Lucky Dragon, a Japanese fishing boat whose crew were contaminated by fallout from the detonation of the US hydrogen bomb off Bikini Atoll, and which became a worldwide news story in 1954. On a larger scale, the nuclear standoff between the United States and the USSR over the Cuban Missile Crisis in 1961, as well as the war that threatened to break out between India and China in 1964, proved to many 'that the atomic disaster was not a one-time and locally contained event, but a lasting danger that threatened everyone, even future generations'.[102]

An accurate barometer for gauging the depth of anxiety associated with nuclear fallout is found in the BBC's decision to censor Peter Watkins's *The War Game*, a 1965 documentary drama fictionalizing the destructive chaos unleashed by a nuclear attack on the UK. Unlike earlier representations such as Nevil Shute's novel *A Town Like Alice* (1950) and Stanley Kubrick's film *Dr Strangelove or How I Learned to Stop Worrying and Love the Bomb* (1964), Watkins's docudrama was considered so demoralizing that it was not screened until 1985.

Extant anxieties were further intensified by the construction of nuclear reactors for the production of domestic energy in the United Kingdom, United States and France. The fire at the nuclear generating plant at Windscale in Cumbria in 1957 – still the United Kingdom most serious 'nuclear accident' – emphasized the hazards of nuclear power and created a rupture in how people related to their everyday surroundings. The almost unimaginable longevity of radioactive waste caused by the production of the isotope plutonium 239 in atomic fusion, along with the invisible, boundless threat of radiation sickness, showed that nothing – foetuses, animals, the soil – was immune from death and disease. Integral parts of the ecosystem or *Umwelt* (water, air, the food chain) that had been historically taken for granted by humans were now rendered problematic and suspicious. The world had turned hostile.

As well as provoking a crisis in how bodies related to space, the new and largely unwanted environmental knowledge that came into being in the 1950s transformed how human beings existed in time. Through the advent of what Michel Serres has termed 'world-objects' – objects that are capable of the total annihilation of human and non-human life forms – individuals and the general public in the 1950s were now forced to imagine a world without a future, a world in which the very idea of history as a continuous line joining past, present and future generations, was severed.[103] The historian Dipesh Chakrabarty highlights the existential shock produced by such a violent break, arguing that it throws 'our usual practices for visualising times, past and future … into deep contradiction and confusion. … Our historical sense of the present … has thus become deeply destructive of our general sense of history'.[104]

The experience of historical dislocation that Chakrabarty draws attention to here is ontologically disturbing: it shatters the existential consolations offered by our awareness of belonging to an intergenerational species, a gene pool or form of life that is larger than ourselves and that will continue to exist beyond our death.[105] For many, human existence now seemed devoid of any purpose whatsoever. Indeed, according to Michel Serres, with the invention of the atom bomb death triumphed over life:

> For the first time, reason, science and technology went beyond the deadly laws of life. War for the sake of war prevailed over the struggle for life. The Bomb beat Darwin. … The Second World War marks the moment of reversal: in terms of thanatocracy, we now do better than nature! What an atrocious model for domination! Yes, at that moment humans become more dangerous for humans than the world.[106]

The ontological despair that affected humanity in the 1950s was doubled, moreover, by a profound sense of epistemological uncertainty. As the ecocritic Gabriel Egan shows, the decision to build the first atom bomb created an era of radical doubt. The complexities of nuclear fusion made it impossible for scientists to predict the outcome of their experiments, and no one could say with any certainty what the scale or long-term effects of the atomic reaction would be. Risk and unpredictability replaced the comforting scenario of cause and effect thinking. Ironically, humans were decentred and undone by their own knowledge:

> In the summer of 1942, Edward Teller, one of J. Robert Oppenheimer's team building the first atomic bomb, calculated what would happen in the first millionths of a second after detonations. ... Teller's new calculations started to convince Oppenheimer's team that ... it carried a small, but quite real, chance ... of instantly igniting the world, and they decided to risk it.[107]

What environmentalists criticize as Prometheanism (technological hubris) did not emancipate human beings from 'nature'; ironically, from the 1950s onwards, it tied them even closer to it. After almost two centuries of intensive industrialization, it was becoming apparent that progress in terms of increased life expectancy, better living conditions and more efficient modes of energy and food production had come at a cost. Population numbers were rising; rivers and seas were polluted; species depletion pointed to a new mass extinction event; and even the air itself could no longer be trusted. In the late 1950s, concerns over air pollution in the United States had reached hysterical proportions, as citizens in major cities and industrialized hubs such as Los Angeles and Pittsburgh found it difficult to breathe. Western Europe was gripped by a similar paranoia:

> Medical sociologists Claudine Herzlich and Janine Pierret have pinpointed a secular turning point in France right around 1960: the fear of epidemics and other infectious diseases which had dominated medical anxieties for at least six centuries, now receded into the background rather quickly. ... Instead, fears about illnesses induced by civilisation moved to the top. The findings for France can be generalised to other countries.[108]

Trepidations about the increasing toxicity of the environment were given a powerful, unifying voice by Rachel Carson's 1962 text *Silent Spring*, a worldwide bestseller that provided the impetus for many home-grown environmentalist movements in the United States, Europe and South America. One of the great strengths of Carson's text is the way in which it challenges the misguided idea that human beings are somehow able to stand apart from their environments. As well as describing the decimation of bird life and bee populations in the United States owing to industrial agriculture's use of 'super chemicals' such as aldrin, dieldrin and, most notoriously, DTT (dichloro-diphenyl-trichloroethane), Carson highlighted the dangers that industrial chemical pathogens posed to human life. To communicate this, she tapped into fears about the effects of nuclear radiation on the human body[109]:

> The new environmental health problems are multiple – created by radiation in all its forms, born of the never-ending stream of chemicals of which pesticides are a part, chemicals now pervading the world in which we live, acting upon us directly and indirectly, separately and collectively. Their presence casts a shadow that is no less ominous because it is formless and obscure, no less frightening because it is simply impossible to predict the effects of lifetime exposure to chemical and physical agents that are not part of the biological experience of man.[110]

The anxious futural shadow evoked by Carson's words provides a compelling historical context for reinterpreting a series of striking images and locations found in the work of many absurdist playwrights. When read in conjunction with Carson's text, the mysterious, depopulated landscapes of Beckett's early plays, and Ionesco's obsession with stagnant water, airborne infection and genetic mutation are no longer simple metaphors for the human condition. Rather, they communicate a decidedly literalist vision of the world that is haunted by the spectre of imminent ecological catastrophe, a biosphere that has been rendered toxic.

The troubling uncertainty evoked by Carson's text sheds additional light on the anxious spatiality found in the Theatre of the Absurd. Thrown into a world that could potentially be destroyed by a nuclear attack or ravaged by chemical pollutants, it is not surprising that so many absurdist plays are located in hermetically sealed spaces, offering what the theatre phenomenologist Bert O. States describes as 'great reckonings in small rooms'.[111] Importantly, and differently from what critics such as Kenneth Tynan have argued in their attacks on the supposedly self-obsessed, petit-bourgeois mindset of the Theatre of Absurd, this attempted but doomed retreat from public space to a series of domestic, private *milieu*s is not a denial of history.[112] On the contrary, when considered in terms of an emergent structure of environmental feeling, the move indoors discloses an acute and early sensitivity to a fundamental rift between human beings and 'nature' that sociologists and philosophers only started to pay serious attention to in the late 1960s and 1970s. One of the reasons why so many characters in the Theatre of the Absurd fail to return home is because the support structures that sustain human and non-human life have been destroyed. Beckett's trees are devoid of leaves; Pinter's pond empty of fish; Ionesco's air deadly; Albee's cities hostile; Shepard's America an 'ocean of bones' and buffalo carcasses; and Churchill's landscapes poisoned and polluted, a 'dustbin'.[113]

To place the Theatre of the Absurd alongside the impassioned prose of Carson's *Silent Spring* is to see it performing a forensic role, expressing and foreshadowing, but without ever explaining, a deep-rooted sense of perplexity and despair in the face of an impending ecological crisis. In its images and moods, everyone and everything is shown to be in crisis, fragile, prone to breakdown and malfunction. Like the corpse that grows, magically, in Ionesco's play *Amédée or How to Get Rid of It* (1953), humanity is suffocated by a proliferating, deformed 'nature' whose poisonous growth is now beyond its capacity to manage.[114]

There is an additional, perhaps less obvious, reason for considering why the Theatre of the Absurd expresses a key moment in environmental history. In 2000, the Dutch atmospheric scientist Paul J. Crutzen published an influential paper in which he argued for the existence of the Anthropocene, a term first introduced by the ecologist Eugene F. Stoermer in the 1980s. For Crutzen, the Anthropocene designates nothing less than a new geological epoch, the moment when, as a result of anthropogenic behaviour patterns, no part of the Earth, not even inorganic life, is free from human influence:

> The term Anthropocene ... suggests that the Earth has now left its natural geological epoch, the present interglacial state called the Holocene. Human activities have become so pervasive and profound that they rival the great forces of Nature and are pushing the Earth into planetary *terra incognita*.[115]

At first glance, Crutzen's research would appear to have little in common with the dramatic experiments of the Theatre of the

Absurd – the historical distance between them seems simply too great to warrant meaningful comparison. Such apparent drawbacks, however, become superfluous when two issues are pointed out: first, that the Anthropocene is a name given in retrospect, a signifier that designates a longstanding biochemical process that Crutzen dates to the beginnings of the Industrial Revolution before it accelerated from 1945 onwards; and second, that in addition to its geological meaning, it also describes the coming into being of a new ambivalent and troubling mode of knowledge. For if the Anthropocene is a term that invariably attests to humanity's ability to impact on, and intervene into, 'natural processes', it simultaneously highlights humanity's failure to harness or control such interventions. To live in the Anthropocene is to realize that cause and effect refuse to coincide and that the complexity of an action escapes the intentionality of its agent. Etymologically and ontologically, then, it is tempting to say that the Theatre of the Absurd captures the conceptual meaning of the Anthropocene in nascent form, marking, as it does, the historical moment when the heroic figure of Prometheus is superseded by the tarnished, imprisoned figure of Sisyphus – a shift in consciousness that places limits on human mastery as well as foreclosing any possibility of transcending the Earth.

Anti-humanist aesthetics

By drawing attention to the limits of human understanding, ecological thinking in the age of the Anthropocene is necessarily opposed to the central tenets of humanism, a worldview forged in the Renaissance, which, according to the posthumanist thinker Rosi Braidotti, 'combines the biological, discursive and moral expansion of human capabilities into an idea of teleologically ordained, rational progress'.[116] As Braidotti explains, humanism's commitment to progress as destiny has been environmentally and ecologically disastrous. In her view – and it is difficult to disagree with her – owing to the humanist project, humans have plundered the planet's human and non-human resources, robbing the world of its diversity:

Central to this universalistic posture and its binary logic is the notion of difference as pejoration. Subjectivity is equated with consciousness, universal rationality, and self-regulating ethical behaviour, whereas Otherness is defined as its negative, specular counterpart. In so far as difference spells inferiority, it acquires both essentialist and lethal connotations for people who get branded as 'others'. These are the sexualised, racialised, and naturalised others, who are reduced to the less than human status of disposable bodies.[117]

In line with our thinking, Braidotti's *exposé* of the *imperium* ('the power to command') which resides at the very heart of humanist thinking suggests that the ecocritical potential of a theatre text is not to be found in its content, but, perhaps more pertinently, in its formal dimensions – in the way that it represents the subject and structures the spectator's experience.

As we have already mentioned, Esslin's analysis of the Theatre of the Absurd focuses not only on anthropocentric theatrical elements such as character and dialogue, but also on theatre's status as a 'multidimensional medium' comprising interrelating, interdependent scenic features (see pp. 12–16). Moreover, the experiments conducted by the Theatre of the Absurd with these scenic elements, or formal and linguistic features, often serve to dissolve character and dialogue, or in other words, the ontological foundations of humanist subjectivity – the positing of identity as a unitary substance, uncontaminated by difference. In the opening scenes of Jean Genet's *The Balcony* (1955), for instance, the clients playing the roles of Bishop, Judge and General do not discover the origin or essence of their identities in Irma's brothel (which is a metaphor for theatre in general); rather, they discover that such an essence is impossible to attain. With typical irony, the Envoy points out that the only 'true' things on Earth for human subjects are static images and rigid postures – theatrical phenomena that prevent self-communion:

> **Envoy** Alas, our living eyes will never succeed in seeing ourselves in real death, nor our dead eyes in seeing ourselves in future consciousness, so we have therefore invented and perfected the elegant feat of fixing ourselves in life according to eternal attitudes.[118]

As Clare Finburgh explains (see pp. 191–217), there is no such thing as a fixed character or 'natural' self in Genet's theatre. Human subjectivity is pure artifice, a futile play on the surface of things, a series of empty gestures devoid of a centre.

A similar process of deconstruction is apparent in the work of Pinter, Adamov, Beckett, Albee, Ionesco and Rózewicz. Only, on these occasions, the self is undone by language which, on the one hand, is denuded of all capacity to signify a world beyond itself and, on the other, is posited as a system that produces miscommunication and violence. The tragicomic paradox here is that language, the mechanism that supposedly confirms the human being's transcendence as well its exceptionalism, is now figured as a type of virus, an affliction or addiction that imprisons the subject in a toxic identity. Plays like Beckett's *Krapp's Last Tape* (1958), Adamov's *The Invasion* and Ionesco's *The Bald Soprano* show human beings caught in a double-bind, victims of 'positive feedback', in which empty language produces empty subjects.[119] In these works, where sound and sense, and voice and language are often prised apart and radically juxtaposed, the humanist subject is worn out and exhausted, caught in cycles of endless repetition.

In the absurdist texts of Beckett, Kantor, Rózewicz and Ionesco, characters are no longer believable individuals with whom the audience identifies. More often than not, they are reduced to the status of automatons, strange, uncanny figures who are subjected to stimuli and flows that they have no control over. In Beckett's *Waiting for Godot*, *Endgame* and *Happy Days*, for instance, the protagonists have lost all sense of direction, compelled, as they are, to repeat the same old scenarios, the same tired words and gestures night after night. There is no great drama in these plays, no concern with portraying 'real' people or with representing heroic acts of violence. What we are presented with instead are grotesque representatives – sad, disabled clowns – whose names (Hamm, Clov, Lucky, Pozzo, Winne and Willie) only serve to heighten their distance from the standard – but false – image of humanity conventionally represented on the modern stage.

Like Beckett's, Ionesco's early work sets out to puncture, with manic deliberation, the pretensions of the humanist subject by producing what he defined as 'anti-theatre' – theatre without plot, story and meaningful dialogue. In *The Chairs*, the old man and woman are deprived even of proper names, and are dominated by a proliferation of inhuman objects – the chairs of the title – which they must arrange for their imaginary guests in a rhythm which dominates and dehumanizes them. No longer endowed with free will and intense inner lives, Ionesco's characters are mere parodies, ludic shadows. In this way, Ionesco punctures the humanism of playwrights such as Ibsen, and the early August Strindberg and Anton Chekhov who, for all their professed naturalism, nevertheless continued to present their audiences with subjects whose passions could be read, deciphered and understood according to the spectacular logic of Aristotelian tragedy. By contrast, for Ionesco and Beckett, as indeed for all the Absurdists, the stage is not a space for knowledge but for non-knowledge, a site where characters and spectators alike are subsumed by a world that they are unable to grasp or interpret, a world, that is, which decentres and dethrones the human subject as the superior animal that speaks and reasons. As James Knowlson remarks: 'Beyond mere parody, Ionesco aims to mock, challenge, fragment and ultimately perhaps, explode a cozy, conformist, Cartesian view of reality'.[120]

The Theatre of the Absurd's attack on humanism's 'cozy, conformist' world results, necessarily, in a radically different dramaturgy. As opposed to the organicist unfolding of naturalist and Aristotelian theatre in which the actions and behaviours of characters are determined according to a teleological narrative that starts with an exposition scene and ends in a *dénouement*, absurdist theatre depicts a provisional and equivocal stage. That is to say, a stage that is at once open to chaotic, uncontrollable events (people turn into rhinoceroses, matter endlessly proliferates, objects take on a life of their own) while, at the same time, it is mired in a kind of endless stasis, in which theatre attains a kind of 'zero degree' from which all events, action or drama are virtually expunged. If 'nothing seems to happen' in absurdist theatre, it is because in a world of nuclear fallout and environmental toxins, humanist thought, with its commitment to sameness and will to power, has placed the very possibility of the future in doubt. Where is there to go when the teleological horizon of 'progress' has resulted in ecological catastrophe? What is one to do when any attempt to effect a change in circumstance might make things worse through the production of dangerous, uncontrollable feedback? As Joe Kelleher implies in his reading of Beckett in this volume, the only sensible solution might be to keep still, to do nothing.

Nevertheless, for all its negativity and reticence, things *do* happen in the Theatre of the Absurd. In a manner that pre-empts, by a decade or so, the anti-humanist thinking of poststructuralist philosophers such as Michel Foucault, Jacques Derrida and Félix Guattari, the work of Genet, Ionesco and Beckett opens the audience to a world of contingency, relationality and incompleteness – a world where the human subject is no longer splendidly isolated, but rather implicated in networks and systems that delimit its agency and restrict its room for manoeuvre. Like the actors in Genet's *The Blacks* (1957) who dismantle the edifice of the theatrical spectacle from within, the Theatre of the Absurd, to paraphrase Derrida's definition of deconstruction, 'uses the bricks of the (theatre) house against the (theatre) house'.[121]

Through this explosive *désoeuvrement*, theatre is undomesticated, de-naturalized, left in ruins. Spectators no longer identify with characters like them, but are affected, bodily, by the materiality of what we might call 'theatre things' – bodies, objects, lights and fabrics that insist on their own heterogeneity and which refuse to be drawn into a humanist orbit. To use a phrase from Elinor Fuchs, the Theatre of the Absurd conceives of theatre as an 'elsewhere without an elsewhere', a physical site that does not represent the world but is a world in itself.[122] In this uncanny space, immanent experience (experience of the here and now) triumphs over transcendent experience (experience that is always directed beyond the world). As Ralph Yarrow's essay in this collection explains so well (see pp. 105–25), this shift from the imaginary to the real does not represent ecological experience; it actively produces it. By refusing to be anything other than what is – a decidedly theatrical event – absurdist theatre engages spectators in a world of chaotic systems and unexpected transformations. Matter appears to have a life of its own, to exist beyond human intentionality and desire. On the absurdist stage, the humanist subject is humiliated, compelled, like Sisyphus, to acknowledge that it cannot transcend the Earth. The ruse of the dialectic is at work in this operation. For, as Joe Kelleher proposes in his reading of Winnie's prayer in *Happy Days* (see pp. 127–46), this negation of meaning ultimately holds out the possibility for a new ethics to emerge, one in which human subjects are willing to affirm a world that they are unable to command.[123]

Divergences

The green reading that we are proposing in this collection diverges significantly from William Desmastes's *Theatre of Chaos: Beyond Absurdism into Orderly Disorder* (1998), the one critical monograph to date that has gestured towards the ecological significance of the Theatre of the Absurd (albeit fleetingly).[124] Desmastes's argument is based on a somewhat crude distinction between the ecological potential of absurdist theatre and neo-absurdist theatre.[125] Whereas the 'total randomness' of absurdist theatre results in what Desmastes sees as a kind of nihilistic stasis, neo-absurdist theatre offers, in his view, an optimistic philosophy of the future.[126] This is because in the universes of neo-absurdist playwrights such as Tom Stoppard, Sam Shepard, David Rabe and Marsha Norman, nature is neither 'rational', nor 'vulnerable to human mastery'; rather, it is self-organizing and emergent, an example of 'orderly disorder'.[127] Referring to Ilya Prigogine and Isabelle Stengers, two thinkers whose ideas on chaos theory have influenced a certain strand of second-wave ecocriticism, Desmastes concludes his study by implying that neo-absurdist theatre's acceptance of the limitations of human understanding has the potential to produce a politically progressive model of ecological subjectivity:

> Understanding the possibilities of the individual functioning within natural bounds extends to understanding how society and its political arm can likewise function. Limitations are perhaps difficult to accept for a proud and vain race, but we simply have reached a critical juncture in our existence where denying our limitations could prove catastrophic.[128]

While Desmastes is certainly correct to point out that neo-absurdist theatre questions the agency of the humanist subject, his attempt to dismiss the ecological significance of the Theatre of the Absurd is a little perfunctory.[129] Not only does his reading ignore the sensitivity of absurdist theatre to the new environmental reality that came into being after 1945, a sensitivity that we have carefully contextualized in this Introduction, but it also fails to grasp the dialectical significance of its form. For the playwrights of the Absurd, the negation of the dramatic frame is far from nihilistic; rather, as we have argued throughout this Introduction, it is performative, an attempt to produce an alternative ontology that acknowledges the troubling presence of heterogeneity and difference, and the urgent need to question human supremacy. The ecological significance of this move is underlined by Rosi Braidotti who, in her celebration of 'not-Oneness', draws close to the ecological reading of Camus that we have proposed (see pp. 22–8):

> This humbling experience of not-Oneness, which is constitutive of the non-unitary subject, anchors the subject in an ethical bond to alterity, to the multiple and external others that are constitutive of that entity which, out of laziness and habit, we call 'self'.[130]

Braidotti's comments support our argument that the ecological potential of the Theatre of the Absurd is disclosed by reading it as a critique of the anthropocentric arrogance of humanism. In this way, and in response to Timothy Morton's calls for an alternative, darker form of ecocriticism, the Theatre of the Absurd offers a theory and practice of ecology where chaos is not simply equated with the unpredictable, stochastic processes of quantum physics. Rather, chaos in absurdist work is always double-edged. On the one hand, it is figured as a type of violence inflicted on the planet by human agents; on the other, it is equated with everything that escapes human appropriation, as we have already explained with regard to the Anthropocene. In this respect, the Theatre of the Absurd reflects the profound ambivalence that characterizes existence in the age of Anthropocene. Although the Anthropocene acknowledges the role played by humans in transforming the Earth, it also highlights the limits of their powers. To that extent, and in ways which differ from what Desmastes argues, the Theatre of the Absurd engages in both environmental *and* ecological critique. It draws attention to the despoliation of 'nature', while at the same time stressing the need for an alternative ontology in which human agency is undermined by the radically heterogeneous play of matter.

To read absurdist theatre ecologically *and* environmentally is to contest the erroneous view that playwrights such as Genet and Ionesco are nihilists, and their work devoid of meaning. Conversely, for the contributors to this volume – and here we situate ourselves in a critical lineage that runs from Theodor Adorno to Alain Badiou – the Theatre of the Absurd is radically democratic, a theatre that, through its deconstruction of human exceptionalism, is attentive to the 'more than human' life forms that have been historically denied representation by theatre and performance theory.[131] However, as Adorno explicates in his essay on Beckett's *Endgame*, we should not expect the ecopolitics of the Absurd to be found in green sloganeering or in celebrations of some restored, pastoralist version of 'nature'; rather, they are located in the ability of absurdist work to express the inexpressible through concrete stage images and fragmented dramaturgies which communicate complex and inarticulate emotions. In absurdist performance, spectators are asked to find meaning in the decidedly non-conceptual domain of moods and atmospheres. That we are only starting to make ecological sense of this nascent structure of feeling, some fifty or so years after Martin Esslin published his landmark text, is testament to the contemporary relevance of the Theatre of the Absurd, a theatre that continues to haunt our future in ways that we are perhaps only now beginning to comprehend.

Structure of the book

This collection seeks to expand on Esslin's seminal work in several ways, while recognizing its colossal debt to his *The Theatre of the Absurd*. One aim is to begin to extend the scope of his book in a manner that we hope other scholars will continue to engage with. We therefore open our collection with an essay on a demographic that Esslin all but overlooks, the female author. Subsequent chapters attempt to redress geographical, rather than gender imbalances, by shifting the focus away from western Europe, where the majority of the playwrights in Esslin's corpus lived and wrote, to eastern Europe, and also to the United States. After this attempt to account for the significance of an ecocriticism of the Absurd beyond the authors foregrounded by Esslin, we return to the five major playwrights to whom he devotes extensive analysis. The contributors to this book adopt a variety of strategies in order to engage with playwrights of the Absurd, in keeping with the diversity of meanings inherent in the concept and practice of ecocriticism (animal studies, air pollution, posthumanism, social justice). In addition, where some contributors focus on the totality of a writer's oeuvre, others prefer to concentrate on a select number of texts. Similarly, where some deal in detail with Esslin's work, others engage in a more immediate fashion with environmental and ecological themes. The one constant, however, is found in the way in which all the authors trouble the so-called naturalness of 'nature', which explains why this word is always either placed in inverted commas, or capitalized.

Elaine Aston opens our collection with her essay 'Caryl Churchill's "Dark Ecology"', in which she focuses the reader's attention on arguably the United Kingdom's most important living playwright. For Esslin, Aston recounts, we are anguished by the 'absurdity of the human condition'. For Churchill, however, rather than to any human condition, absurdity must be attributed more specifically to human behaviour, notably, to the human tendency to devalue, damage and 'dehumanise' different life forms. In a world dominated by the inhuman(e) values of global capitalism, warring populations, mobilized only by greed and self-preservation, are pitted against each other, and against the planet. Aston evokes Jacques Rancière who, in his 1995 publication *Disagreement: Politics and Philosophy*, cites Aristotle, for whom, 'man alone among the animals' has been endowed 'with the power of speech'. Rancière develops the notion of being 'animal', where animals represent those who are unable to speak on their own behalf. Aston thus accords Churchill the epithet, 'political-theatre animal', since she champions those without a voice, those who do not count. Despite her pessimistic perspective on a humanity driven to absurd limits by self-interest, Churchill remains resolutely committed to equality and justice not only among humans, but between human and non-human life forms. This egalitarianism is inevitably ecological, since it prioritizes both the human and the non-human. Aston, like a number of other authors in this volume, is inspired by Timothy Morton's concept of 'dark ecology', which chimes with the ethical commitment displayed in Rancière's notion of the 'animal', in the extent to which it calls for everything that is habitually excluded, to be embraced. For humans to engage fully with the ecology around them, they must accept the messy, abject, undesirable, 'dark' aspects of 'nature'. Aston also draws from 'animal compassion' as theorized by feminist philosopher Luce Irigaray, for whom relations with non-human species can teach us more humane ways of treating both other life forms, and each other. In order to demonstrate Churchill's mutual commitment to equality and ecology, Aston analyses three works that account for much of Churchill's expansive career: *The Ants* (1962), *The Skriker* (1994) and *Far Away* (2000). Her detailed analysis both of the play texts and of the plays in production, describes Churchill's 'progressively dark political and ecological critiques'. But for Aston, through the gloom, this 'dark medicine' that Churchill prescribes perhaps offers some hope of a cure. By highlighting so starkly the gross social and ecological inequalities that pervade the planet as we enter the twenty-first century, Churchill warns in salutary tones that the dehumanizing capacities of humans to damage the non-human world will ultimately have repercussions on all life forms, not least on humans.

Like Aston, Stephen Bottoms, in his essay 'The Garden in the Machine: Edward Albee, Sam Shepard and the American Absurd', selects dramatic works that range from the 1960s when Esslin's *The Theatre of the Absurd* was first written, through to the twenty-first century: Edward Albee's *Zoo Story* (1959) and *The Goat or, Who is Sylvia?* (2002); and Sam Shepard's *Rock Garden* (1964), *Fourteen Hundred Thousand* (1966) and *Kicking a Dead Horse* (2007). Aston and Bottoms thus demonstrate how ecological understandings of the Absurd are as relevant today, as fifty years ago, if not more relevant. Whereas Aston draws on Morton's 'dark ecology', Bottoms employs Morton's 'queer ecology'. As Bottoms remarks, and as we have already analysed in this Introduction, Esslin's reading of Camus's *The Myth of Sisyphus* is inflected by his own humanist concerns. Esslin perceives humans and their anguish as the focal point of Camus's Sisyphus story, whereas Camus himself deconstructs human supremacy by embedding humans in the materiality of the planet in ways that anticipate more recent works on ecological thinking, for instance, Jane Bennett's notion of 'vital materialism'. Indeed, Camus even describes Sisyphus as 'happy' in his relationship with earthly matter. The real absurdity, according to Bottoms, derives from the very fact, upheld by Esslin, that humans might perceive themselves as exceptional, as separate, as 'out of harmony' (the Latin etymology of *Absurd*) with 'nature'. Notions of human exceptionalism are particularly pertinent to a US context, Bottoms argues. His essay draws on Leo Marx's *The Machine in the Garden* (1964), the title of which Bottoms reverses in the title of his own essay, and on William Cronon's *Uncommon Ground* (1996). Both of these texts expose the United States's complex relationship with rurality and the wilderness, which often become artifices of a Judeo-Christian Eden that provide false promises that a true, authentic self might be recovered. Accordingly, any pastoralism evoked by Albee and Shepard becomes an absurd delusion, set against a backdrop of industrialization that possesses, domesticates, controls and shrinks the natural world into a 'garden in the machine'. Nature in the plays can only be perceived through the lens of culture and of human desire. Bottoms subsequently theorizes this ambiguity between 'nature' and culture via 'queer ecology': just as queer theory blurs gender and sexuality categories, queer ecology renders porous the boundaries between 'nature' and culture, rural and urban, human and non-human, beings and things. Bottoms also remarks that Morton's queer ecology is apposite to theatre, where any evocation of 'nature' is inevitably conjured through the artifice of performance, and he adds that the playwrights he studies often highlight this equivocation by self-consciously drawing attention to the theatricality of their plays. While, for Bottoms, it is absurd for humans to want to renounce their humanity and become at one with the world, he states that absurdity and anguish are felt by humans precisely *because* they are an inseparable part of the cosmos that surrounds them, even though their culture and self-consciousness result in their feeling so separate from it. Queer ecology, then, leaves us in a hovering, suspensive state, caught between 'nature' and culture. The ethical moment, Bottoms implies, is found in our ability to assent to this in-betweenness, in recognizing the absurdity that ensues when we realize that we are part of, and apart from, the world. Such discomfiting awareness allows for a more ecologically democratic mode of being.

Ralph Yarrow's 'Mutant Bodies: The Absurd in Eastern European Experience', like Aston's essay, roots the Absurd in the specifics of society, politics and history. The precise landscapes described in Yarrow's essay relate to Poland although, as in the theatres of Albee and Shepard, they in no way present naïve pastoral scenes. Rather than an eternal, 'natural' landscape, the twentieth century in Poland, as Yarrow demonstrates, exists as a kind of precariousness precipitated by war and partition, Nazi and Communist occupation, and Jewish pogroms. Yarrow adds to the definition of the Absurd provided by Bottoms, who describes it as 'disharmony', to reveal that *surd* refers to something that adds up, whereas *ab* alludes to the idea of being 'to one side'. The Absurd therefore denotes something that does not add up, that does not fit in. On the stages of the Polish authors that Yarrow discusses, human and non-human forms that do not conform, that refuse to be tidied away – also prevalent among the unpredictable, chaotic, 'dark' figures that populate Churchill's stages – constitute an affirmative force of resistance. According to his readings of Witold Gombrowicz, Tadeusz Kantor, Tadeusz Rózewicz and Stanisław Ignacy Witkiewicz (Witkacy), as well as of Theatre de Complicite's *The Street of Crocodiles* (1992) – an adaptation of a story by Bruno Schulz – their respective theatres resist 'the confinement, mutilation, restriction, amputation and truncation of bodies, lives, organic forms, spaces and modes of relationship', imposed by systematizing definitions and doctrines. For this reason, according to Yarrow, each of these theatre-makers materializes and embodies on stage mutated bodies (explaining the title of his essay): twisted and distorted shapes, disarticulated rhythms, all of which become dramaturgical manifestations of a resistance to hegemonic models that seek to normalize or to neutralize 'nature'. Therefore, theatrical form gives shape to the inchoate, but only momentarily, before it merges back into the liberational chaos from which it emerged. As opposed to the theory of the Anthropocene, where chaos represents the human failure to master the ecological chaos that humans themselves have wrought, here, chaos becomes a form of resistance to hegemonic discourses dictated by those same humans.

Yarrow's essay contains a number of neologisms, such as 'difficultation'. So, too, does Joe Kelleher's, which features terms such as 'endingness', 'world-unendingness' and 'remainingness'. It is as if conventional vocabulary needs somehow to be twisted and contorted in order to accommodate the dark ecologies of unpredictable ideas and concepts that these contributors elaborate in their ecological meditations on the Absurd. In 'Recycling Beckett', Kelleher accounts for the ways in which certain elements of Beckett's oeuvre – stage directions, titles – have been 'recycled' by contemporary visual artists. Gerard Byrne's series of photographs (2006–) of solitary, bare-branched trees alongside country roads inevitably evokes the same scenography in *Waiting for Godot*; and Mirosław Bałka's installation *How It Is* (2009–10) takes its title from Beckett's novel of the same name. Kelleher recounts how, in these visual pieces, the central protagonists of Beckett's drama are removed, leaving empty, depopulated stages. Resonating with Bottoms's account of US theatre, Kelleher describes any evocation of 'nature' in these works as theatrical, as artifice. Concurrently, echoing Yarrow's gloss of the Absurd as something that sits awkwardly, Kelleher suggests that humans do not 'fit in' to these landscapes, that their role is somehow secondary. Humans in Kelleher's essay therefore occupy the ambiguous status of both determining the contours of 'nature', and being eclipsed by them. His account of the works by these two visual artists enables him to look retrospectively at Beckett's texts, and to offer original insights into a range of his works, most notably, *Happy Days*. In relation to the latter, Kelleher cites Morton's scepticism about 'the optimistic aesthetics of a certain strand of ecocriticism' that would posit 'embeddedness' as a value that 'might make us less likely to destroy the world we find ourselves embedded in'. The fact that Winnie is very literally buried up to her neck in her mound is not the thing, for Kelleher, that designates her as a viable ecological subject. On the contrary, it is found in her ridiculous capacity to persist in spite of it all, in her decidedly non-heroic capacity to affirm the relentless coming into being of 'another heavenly day', when everything about her situation suggests the very opposite and should leave her hopeless.

For Franc Chamberlain in 'Rare Butterflies, Persecution, and Pinball Machines: Environment, Subjectivity, and Society in the Theatre of Arthur Adamov', the absurdist playwright presents 'nature' in much the same way as the authors included so far in the collection: it is either contained within human confines, depleted and exhausted, or omitted altogether. Chamberlain mentions Rachel Carson's *Silent Spring* to conjure the barren, desolate 'natural' world represented in Adamov's works, which is populated only by the odd stuffed bird; a river, access to which is prohibited; or butterflies that are collected and commodified into merchandise. As Aston explains, in Churchill's plays the late-capitalist mentality that has eroded collectivity and society has also displayed disrespect, indeed contempt, for the environment. Chamberlain, with reference to Félix Guattari's *Three Ecologies*, also indicates the interrelations between individual, social and environmental systems. For Guattari, the individual's mental subjectivity, her or his existence within society, and the individual's and society's relationship with the environment, are all interpenetrating ecologies. Just as Bottoms remarks that Esslin overlooked Camus's accentuation of the (impossible) human connection with 'nature', so Chamberlain notes that Esslin missed the ecological dimensions to Adamov's short text, *The Confession* (1946). For Esslin, this text centres around the individual's insuperable alienation, whereas Chamblerain highlights Adamov's intense desire for a fusion between humans and the non-human environment, which would enable humans to overcome their sense of solitude and separation. The four plays discussed in Chamberlain's chapter were written during Adamov's early period, before his writing became overtly Marxist: *The Invasion, Professor Taranne* (1951), *Ping Pong* (1955) and *Paolo Paoli* (1957). Chamberlain locates these works carefully within a post-war period of economic liberalism, the rise in the manufacture of commodities, and the rampant consumption of natural resources. Landscapes, as in the US theatre described by Bottoms, are overrun by western modernization, to the point where pinball machines are even installed outdoors. Characters attempt to control the 'natural' world – the 'mud, flesh, and blood', in Adamov's terms – but this ordering, as Aston indicates with respect to Churchill's plays, and Yarrow to Polish theatre, culminates in the oppressive containment and regularization of the 'dark ecologies' of living and non-living entities, that are considered by humans to be insignificant or inferior. It is thus clear that reactionary mentalities impact inevitably upon societal and environmental ecologies. Conversely, argues Chamberlain, modifications to human mentalities can enable 'radical heterotopic possibility', creative spaces for connectivity and reciprocity between the three ecologies.

Like Chamberlain's analysis of Adamov, Carl Lavery's study of Ionesco is located within the post-war context of massive industrialization. In his essay 'Ionesco's Green Lesson: Toxic environments, Ecologies of Air', Lavery focuses on one specific undesirable consequence of rapid modernization: air pollution. Even though Lavery includes the term 'lesson' in his title, he is careful not to counter Ionesco's own contempt for pedagogical, didactic theatre, as he extracts his hermeneutic message obliquely from the playwright's oeuvre. Lavery's analysis of air is influenced by the notion of 'atmoterrorism' set out in *Terror from the Air* (2002), in which Peter Sloterdijk maintains that the toxicological effects of modern industrialization are destroying the very air we breathe. Sloterdijk references in particular the nuclear attacks of Second World War which, for Lavery, haunt Ionesco's theatre more than that of any other author included in Esslin's study. Air, for Sloterdijk, and, by extension for Lavery, is both a biological and political entity, both material and sign. It is the 'natural' matter that sustains life, and also a matter of biopolitical concern, since its state is affected by human actions. Lavery's essay analyses a great range of works from Ionesco's extensive oeuvre, including *The Bald Soprano, The Chairs, Amédée or How to Get Rid of It, Rhinoceros* (1959), *Exit the King* (1962), *A Stroll in the Air* (1963), *Frenzy for Two ... and the same to you* (1963), *Hunger and Thirst* (1968), *The Man with the Suitcases* (1975) and *Journeys to the Underworld* (1980). Lavery exposes the ways in which many of Ionesco's plays critique the atmoterrorism conspiring to destroy our planet: characters are often stifled, or asphyxiated by poisoned atmospheres; and when they succeed in exiting the Earth's atmosphere, it is only to view a devastated planet below. Lavery proceeds to highlight the potential shortcomings of Ionesco's dramaturgy, where characters tend to blockade themselves in, so as not to inhale dangerous toxins. Unlike the necessary connectivity between the individual, society and the environment described by Chamberlain, Ionesco appears to uphold a transcendent, self-sufficient individual. The consequences of this confinement are twofold. First, characters lament the contamination of an Edenic environment that they will never retrieve. Second, they are trapped within an anthropocentric paradigm which is ultimately responsible for the sense of separateness and superiority that leads humans to consider the planet as their property, to be used as they please. Lavery concludes by recuperating Ionesco from this problematic human exceptionalism. Employing Julia Kristeva's notion of 'abject laughter', he suggests that the humour that pervades Ionesco's tragi-comedies re-roots spectators within the messiness and matter of the environmental world, since laughter involves the bodily, animal functions of contracting one's diaphragm and respiratory system to expel air. Laughter thus replaces human transcendence with the kind of immanence already described in this Introduction with regard to Camus, and results in the affirmation of the very thing that Ionesco seeks to escape: mixity.

From the dark ecology of excluded, unwanted, cursed elements evoked in essays by Aston and Kelleher, Clare Finburgh's 'Nettles in the Rose Garden: Ecocentrism in Jean Genet's Theatre', recuperates and champions stinging nettles. Including commentary on each of Genet's plays – *Deathwatch* (1949), *The Maids* (1947), *Splendid's* (1953, published 1993), *The Balcony, The Blacks* (1958),

The Screens (1961), *Elle* (1989) and *The Penal Colony* (1958, published 1994) – Finburgh begins by tracing a movement in his theatre from the claustrophobic interiors of bedrooms and prison cells, to the wide, expansive environments of jungles and deserts. Like Bottoms, Yarrow and Chamberlain, Finburgh notes, however, that these landscapes are always, and inevitably, determined by the social, political and economic factors of a given historical period. Furthermore, as in Bottoms's essay, Finburgh discusses the complex and contradictory relationships that absurdist theatre can have with the pastoral tradition, which tends to depict 'nature' as an eternal, unspoilt wilderness beyond human agency. Finburgh takes the example of flowers that recur across Genet's theatre, novels and poetry, and relates in detail how these elements from 'nature' are self-consciously and artificially reconfigured by Genet in order to bear a profusion of often contradictory significations. The example from Genet's herbarium that spreads like a weed across Finburgh's essay, is nettles. Since nettles show no respect for enclosure, they have entitlement to the whole Earth. At the same time, they are considered to be weeds, and excluded from many gardens – another example of culture determining the contours of 'nature'. Nettles thus come to symbolize the manner in which Genet sanctifies those who are forgotten and marginalized. In addition, nettles can sting, and often represent in Genet's theatre the defiant resistance of the oppressed. Quoting Esslin, Finburgh is aware that this postmodern *mise en abyme*, where the meaning of all elements in Genet's works, not least flowers, is always provisional and shifting, could be incompatible with ecocriticism's concrete commitment to political change. However, she realigns Genet as an ecocritical figure by examining his deconstruction of any definitive meaning and certitude in terms of an active disassembling of the illusion of human separation from, and superiority to, the rest of the animate and inanimate world. Finburgh demonstrates, with reference to a wide range of non-theatrical texts from across Genet's oeuvre, that in his cosmos, humans bear no greater value or significance than non-human animals or, for that matter, the inanimate world. She illustrates how Genet's radical ethics of egalitarianism is materialized in dramaturgical form in his theatre, where meaning is distributed across networks of scenic elements including scenography, costumes, stage properties, lighting, music, acoustics, rhythms and movement. The view that all organisms and inanimate phenomena are part of an interconnected and interdependent network, argues Finburgh, goes some significant way towards demonstrating how Genet engages with a notion of 'deep ecology'.

Our collection ends by returning to the notion of home, or *oikos*, already discussed in this Introduction. Central to the chapter entitled 'The Secluded Voice: The Impossible Call Home in Early Pinter', written by Mark Taylor-Batty with Carl Lavery, are concepts of the home or hearth – the *oikos* – the *domus*, and *habitus*. Whereas in Esslin's analysis the small bedsits and flats that feature across Pinter's early theatre represent a haven, for the authors of this essay they are shifting, unsettling sites of displacement. However, as well as instilling a sense of discomfort, this instability becomes an affirmative force for Taylor-Batty and Lavery, since it can disrupt the normalizing powers of what Lyotard terms the *domus*, and Pierre Bourdieu terms the *habitus*, both of which seek to domesticate, ground or to own the uncanny, the *unheimlich*, or, Morton's 'dark ecology', to which so many contributors to this collection refer. As we have already seen in this Introduction, Lyotard envisages in his essay 'Oikos' a home that, rather than being exclusive and exclusionary, would represent a site that would include and accommodate otherness. These notions of domesticity, ownership, hosting and homecoming, read according to Lyotard's ecological paradigms, are applied by Taylor-Batty and Lavery to Pinter's early theatre: *The Room* (1957), *The Birthday Party* (1958), *The Caretaker* (1960) and *The Homecoming* (1965). In these plays, as read by the two authors, the forcible ejection from the home of undesirable individuals poses a threat to our social ecology and, by extension, to the environment. For them, Pinter creates alternative spaces and modes of dwelling that, while unsettling and disrupted, avoid the stasis of reactionary discourses, and potentially embrace the complexities of entities that are otherwise excluded, or that refuse to belong to official systems and doctrines. When Taylor-Batty and Lavery, along with Aston, Yarrow and Chamberlain, describe the reactionary mentalities that attempt to contain and control the 'dark ecologies' of living and non-living entities that are considered to be undesirable, they perhaps indirectly call for an *oikos*, an open-ended system of reciprocity that might accommodate the alterity of the world without taming it or reducing it to utilitarian functionality.

Our volume ends with an Epilogue by David Williams entitled 'The ruins of time (I've forgotten this before)'. Williams highlights some of the ecocritics that have featured prominently across essays in this collection, notably Bateson, Guattari, Morton and Jane Bennett. According to the theories of so many of these second-wave ecocritics, the subjective, the affective, the sensible and the personal must be enlisted in just the same way as the social, political and environmental, when addressing ecological issues. Williams himself describes the 'inextricable intertwining of thinking and sensibility, social and political structures and material environment'. For this very reason, we feel that Williams's particularly personal perspectives on the Theatre of the Absurd constitute such an appropriate conclusion to our volume. Williams begins by admitting that, as a teenager, he perhaps subscribed to some of the clichés associated with the Theatre of the Absurd, ones that the contributors to this collection have been careful to avoid: *rive gauche* angst chic, hipster cool existential crisis, fashionable nihilism, eternal 'waiting' in bleak no-man's lands. ... Quickly, Williams recuperates the Theatre of the Absurd from these stereotypes of despair and inertia, by highlighting parallels between Beckettian 'not-meaning', and the refusal of conformity represented by counter-cultural moments like the post-punk music scene. However, we have chosen to end our collection with Williams's piece not so much because of the ways in which he indicates the significant part played by the Theatre of the Absurd in past culture. Rather, his piece provides an apt end to the book thanks to its perspectives on the future. He asks, 'What/how one might live in relation to others. What/how one might be. What/how one might do'. Citing theatre director Herbert Blau, who laments humanity's 'suicidal and genocidal' tendencies, Williams draws attention to 'capitalism's pathological stoking of the infinite desire and drive to possess and consume yet more "stuff" in the face of diminishing, finite resources'. At the same time, Williams shares with many contributors to this collection the affirmative hope that, should we let go of our anxious desire for control, permanence and stasis, and should we embrace transience, impermanence and the 'ecological becomings of things and of *the others that are us* – for our fictions', then we might just be able to 'turn a death story into a life story'. Indeed, we might be better placed to 'inherit the Earth'.

The body of absurdist authors analysed through the lens of ecocriticism in these chapters is neither exhaustive nor exclusive. Like the Lyotardian *oikos*, we hope that the project begun in this book will destabilize notions of exclusivity and certainty, in order to host the possibility for other thinkers and practitioners to continue our dialogue, by reflecting more widely on the ecocritical potential of the Absurd in theatre and performance.

Works cited

Abel, Lionel, *Metatheatre: A New View of Dramatic Form*. New York: Hill and Wang, 1963.

Abrams, David, *The Spell of the Sensuous: Perception and Language in a More Than Human World*. New York: Vintage, 1996.

Adorno, Theodor, 'Trying to Understand Endgame', trans. M. T. Jones, *New German Critique*, vol. 26 (1982) [1958], pp. 119–50.

Agamben, Giorgio, *State of Exception*, trans. K. Attell. Chicago, IL: University of Chicago Press, 2005 [2003].

Andermatt Conley, Verena, *Ecopolitics: The Environment in Poststructuralist Thought*. London and New York: Routledge, 1997.

Arons, Wendy and Theresa J. May (eds), *Readings in Performance and Ecology*. Basingstoke: Palgrave Macmillan, 2012.

Badiou, Alain, *On Beckett*, trans. N. Power and A. Toscano. London: Clinamen, 2002.

Bate, Jonathan, *The Song of the Earth*. Cambridge, MA: Harvard University Press, 2000.

Bateson, Gregory, *Steps to an Ecology of Mind*. Chicago: University of Chicago Press, 2000 [1972].

Beckett, Samuel, *Endgame* in *Samuel Beckett: The Complete Dramatic Works*. London: Faber and Faber, 1986.

Beckett, Samuel, 'Faux Départs', in S. E Gontarski (ed.), *Samuel Beckett: The Complete Short Prose 1929-1989*. New York: The Grove Press, 1995, pp. 271–4.

Beckett, Samuel, 'The Capital of the Ruins', in S. E. Gontarski (ed.), *Samuel Beckett: The Complete Short Prose 1929-1989*. New York: The Grove Press, 1995, pp. 275–8.

Bennett, Michael Y., *Reassessing the Theatre of the Absurd: Camus, Beckett, Ionesco, Genet and Pinter*. Basingstoke: Palgrave Macmillan, 2011.

Berry, Wendell, *Home Economics: Fourteen Essays by Wendell Berry*. New York: North Point Press, 1987.

Bookchin, Murray, *Philosophy of Social Ecology: Essays on Dialectical Naturalism*, 2nd revised edn. Montreal: Black Rose Books, 1995.

Bottoms, Stephen and Matthew Goulish, *Small Acts of Repair: Performance, Ecology and Goat Island*. London and New York: Routledge, 2008.

Bottoms, Stephen, Aron Franks and Paula Kramer (eds), 'On Ecology', *Performance Research*, vol. 17, no. 4, (2012).

Bowker, Matthew H., *Rethinking the Politics of Absurdity: Albert Camus, Postmodernity, and the Survival of Innocence*. London and New York: Routledge, 2013.

Braidotti, Rosi, *The Posthuman*. Cambridge, MA: Polity Press, 2013.

Brater, Enoch and Ruby Cohn (eds), *Around the Absurd: Essays on Modern and Postmodern Drama*. Ann Arbor, MI: University of Michigan Press, 1990.

Brook, Peter, *The Empty Space*. London: Penguin, 1990 [1968].

Brustein, Robert, *The Theatre of Revolt: Studies in Modern Drama from Ibsen to Genet*. Boston, MA: Little and Brown, 1964.

Buell, Laurence, *The Environmental Imagination: Thoreau, Nature Writing and the Formation of American Culture*. Cambridge, MA: Harvard University Press, 1995.

Camus, Albert, *The Myth of Sisyphus and Other Essays*, trans. J. O'Brien. New York: Alfred A. Knopf, 1955 [1942].

Carson, Rachel, *Silent Spring*. New York: Houghton Mifflin, 2002 [1962].

Chakrabarty, Dipesh, 'The Climate of History: Four Theses', *Critical Enquiry*, vol. 35, no. 2 (2009), pp. 197–222.

Chamberlain, Franc, Carl Lavery and Ralph Yarrow, 'Steps Towards an Ecology of Performance', *University of Bucharest Review*, vol. XIX, no. 1 (2012), pp. 1–37.

Chaudhuri, Una, '"There Must be a Lot of Fish in that Lake": Toward an Ecological Theater', *Theater*, vol. 25, no. 1 (1994), pp. 23–31.

Chaudhuri, Una, *Staging Place: The Geography of Modern Drama*. Ann Arbor, MI: University of Michigan Press, 1996.

Clark, Nigel, *Inhuman Nature: Sociable Life on a Dynamic Planet*. London: Sage, 2012.

Cless, Downing, *Ecology and Environment in European Drama*. London: Routledge, 2010.

Cohn, Ruby, 'Introduction: Around the Absurd', in Enoch Brater and Ruby Cohn (eds), *Around the Absurd: Essays on Modern and Postmodern Drama*. Ann Arbor, MI: University of Michigan Press, 1990, pp. 1–9.

Collingwood, R. G., *The Idea of Nature*. Oxford: Oxford University Press, 1960.

Cronon, William, 'Foreword: The Pain of a Poisoned World', in Brett L. Walker (ed.), *Toxic Archipelago: A History of Industrial Disease in Japan*. Seattle, WA: University of Washington Press, 2010, pp. ix–xvi.

Davies, Paul, 'Strange Weather: Beckett from the Perspective of Ecocriticism', in S. E. Gontarski and Anthony Uhlmann (eds), *Beckett After Beckett*. Gainesville, FL: University of Florida Press, 2006, pp. 66–78.

Derrida, Jacques, *Margins of Philosophy*, trans. A. Bass. Chicago, IL: University of Chicago Press, 1982.

Desmastes, William, *Theatre of Chaos: Beyond Absurdism into Orderly Disorder*. Cambridge: Cambridge University Press, 1998.

Dobson, Andrew, *The Green Reader*. London: Andre Deutsch, 1998.

Donald, Minty, 'The Urban River and Site-Specific Performance', *Contemporary Theatre Review*, vol. 22, no. 2 (2012), pp. 213–23.

Egan, Gabriel, 'Ecopolitics/Ecocriticism', in Ken Hiltner (ed.), *Ecocriticism: The Essential Reader*. London: Routledge, 2015, pp. 278–300.

Esslin, Martin, *The Theatre of the Absurd*, 3rd revised and enlarged edn. Harmondsworth: Penguin, 1980.

Fishcher-Lichte, Erica., *History of European Drama and Theatre*, trans. J. Riley, London and New York: Routledge, 2002 [1990].

Fuchs, Elinor, 'Another Version of Pastoral', in *The Death of Character: Perspectives on Theater After Modernism*. Bloomington, IN: Indiana University Press, 1996, pp. 92–107.

Gardner, Lynn, http://www.theguardian.com/stage/theatreblog/2011/may/23/beckett-happy-days-father-ted.

Garrard, Greg, '*Endgame*: Beckett's Ecological Thought', in Yann Mével, Dominique Rabaté and Sjef Houppermans (eds), *Samuel Beckett Today/Aujourd' hui 23*. Amsterdam: Rodopoi, 2011, pp. 383–97.

Garrard, Greg, *Ecocriticism*, 2nd edn. London: Routledge, 2012 [2004].

Genet, Jean, *The Balcony*, trans. B. Wright and T. Hands. London: Faber and Faber, 1991.

Giannachi, Gabriella and Nigel Stewart (eds), *Performing Nature: Explorations in Ecology and the Arts*. Bern: Peter Lang, 2005.

Glotfelty, Cheryll, 'Introduction: Literary Studies in an Age of Environmental Crisis', in Cheryll Glotflety and Harold Fromm (eds), *The Ecocriticism Reader: Landmarks in Literary Ecology*. Athens, GA: University of Georgia Press, 1966, pp. xv–xxxvii.

Goodall, Jane, *Performance and Evolution in the Age of Darwin: Out of the Natural Order*. London and New York: Routledge, 2002.

Gray, Nelson and Sheila Rabillard (eds), 'Theatre in an Age of Eco-Crisis', *Canadian Theatre Review*, vol. 144 (2010).

Groys, Boris, 'Comrades of Time', *E-Flux Journal* 11, December 2009.

Guattari, Félix, *The Three Ecologies*, trans. I. Pindar and P. Sutton. London: Continuum, 2008 [1989].

Hachiya, Michihiko, *Hiroshima Diary: The Journal of a Japanese Physician, August 6 – September 30, 1945*, ed. and trans. W. Ellis. Charlotte, NC: North Carolina Press, 1955.

Hagood, Amanda, 'Wonders with the Sea: Rachel Carson's Ecological Aesthetic and the Mid-Century Reader', *Environmental Humanities*, vol. 2 (2013), pp. 57–77.

Heddon, Dee and Sally Mackey (eds), 'Environmentalism', *Research in Drama and Education: The Journal of Applied Theatre and Performance*, vol. 17, no. 2 (2012).

Heidegger, Martin, *Discourse on Thinking*, trans. J. Anderson and E. Freund. New York: Harper and Row, 1966.

Heim, Wallace, Bron Szerzynski and Clare Waterton (eds), *Nature Performed: Environment, Culture and Performance*. Oxford: Blackwell, 2003.

Heinlein, Kurt, *Green Theatre: Promoting Ecological Preservation and Advancing the Sustainability of Human and Nature*. Saarbrücken: VDM Verlag, 2007.

Hiltner, Ken (ed.), *Ecocriticism: The Essential Reader*. London and New York: Routledge, 2015, pp. 131–3.

Hughes, Edward J. (ed.), *The Cambridge Companion to Camus*. Cambridge: Cambridge University Press, 2007.

Hughes, Robert, *Goya*. London: Vintage, 2004.

Ionesco, Eugène, *Notes and Counter Notes: Writings on Theatre*, trans. Donald Watson. New York: Grove Press, 1964.

Junquera, Juan José, *The Black Paintings of Goya*. London and New York: Scala, 1999.

Kershaw, Baz, *Theatre Ecology: Environments and Performance Events*. Cambridge: Cambridge University Press, 2007.

Knowlson, James, 'Tradition and Innovation in Ionesco's *La Cantatrice chauve*', in Enoch Brater and Ruby Cohn (eds), *Around the Absurd: Essays on Modern and Postmodern Drama*. Ann Arbor, MI: University of Michigan Press, 1990, pp. 57–72.

Latour, Bruno, *We Have Never Been Modern*, trans. C. Porter. Cambridge, MA: Harvard University Press, 1993 [1991].

Lavery, Carl, 'The Ecology of the Image: The Environmental Politics of Philippe Quesne and Vivarium Studio', *French Cultural Studies*, vol. 24, no. 3 (2013), pp. 264–78.

Lavery, Carl and Simon Whitehead, 'Bringing it all Back Home: Towards an Ecology of Place', *Performance Research*, vol. 17, no. 4 (2012), pp. 111–19.

Lehmann, Hans-Thies, *Postdramatic Theatre*, trans. K. Jürs-Munby. London and New York: Routledge, 2006 [1999].

Lyotard, Jean François, 'Oikos', in *Political Writings*, trans. B. Readings with K. Geiman. London: UCL Press, 1991, pp. 96–107.

Macy, Joanna and Molly Young Brown, *Coming Back to Life: Practices to Reconnect Our Lives, Our World*. Gabriola Island: British Columbia, 1998.

Marranca, Bonnie, *Ecologies of Theatre*. Baltimore, MD: John Hopkins University, 1996.

Mayberry, Robert, *Theatre of Discord: Dissonance in Beckett, Albee and Pinter*. Rutherford, PA: Fairleigh Dickinson University Press, 1989.

Morton, Timothy, *Ecology without Nature: Rethinking Environmental Aesthetics*. Cambridge, MA: Harvard University Press, 2007.

Morton, Timothy, *The Ecological Thought*. Cambridge, MA: Harvard University Press, 2010.

Morton, Timothy, 'Queer Ecology', *PMLA*, vol. 125 (2010), pp. 273–82.

Munk, Erika, 'Introduction', *Theater*, vol. 25, no. 1 (1994), pp. 5–6.

Naess, Arne, 'The Deep Ecological Movement: Some Philosophical Aspects', *Philosophical Enquiry*, vol. 8, no. 1 (1986), pp. 10–31.

Orozco, Lourdes, *Theatre and Animals*. Basingstoke: Palgrave Macmillan, 2013.

Parker-Starbuck, Jennifer, *Cyborg Theatre: Corporeal/Technological Intersections in Multi-Media Performance*. Basingstoke: Palgrave Macmillan, 2011.

Plumwood, Val, *Feminism and the Mastery of Nature*. London: Routledge, 1993.

Rabillard, Sheila, '*Fen* and the Production of a Feminist Ecotheater', *Theater*, vol. 25, no. 1 (1994), pp. 62–71.

Radkau, Joachim, *Nature and Power: A Global History of the Environment*, trans. T. Dunlap. Cambridge: Cambridge University Press, 2008 [2002].

Read, Alan, *Theatre, Intimacy and Engagement: The Last Human Venue*. Basingstoke: Palgrave Macmillan, 2008.

Schechner, Richard, 'The End of Humanism', *Performing Arts Journal*, vol. 4, no. 1/2 (1979), pp. 9–22.

Schechner, Richard, *Performance Theory*, 2nd revised and enlarged edn. London and New York: Routledge, 2004 [1977].

Schweitzer, Marlis and Joanne Zerdy (eds), *Performing Objects and Theatrical Things*. Basingstoke: Palgrave Macmillan, 2014.

Serreau, Geneviève, *Histoire du nouveau theater*. Paris: Gallimard, 1966.

Serres, Michel, *The Natural Contract*, trans. E. MacArthur and W. Paulson. Ann Arbor, MI: University of Michigan, 1995 [1990].

Serres, Michel, *Times of Crisis: What the Financial Crisis Revealed and How to Reinvent Our Lives and Future*, trans. A. Feenberg-Dibbon. London: Bloomsbury, 2014 [2009].

Starling, Simon, 'Never the Same River (Possible Futures, Probable Pasts)', in Amelia Groom (ed.), *Time: Documents of Contemporary Art*. Cambridge, MA and London: MIT Press, 2013, pp. 30–4.

States, Bert O., *Great Reckonings in Little Rooms: On the Phenomenology of Theatre*. Berkeley, CA: University of California Press, 1985.

Steffen, Will, Paul J. Crutzen and John R. McNeill, 'The Anthropocene: Are Humans Now Overwhelming the Great Forces of Nature?', *Ambio*, vol. 38 (2007), pp. 614–21.

Stengers, Isabelle, *Cosmopolitics I*, trans. R. Bononno, Minneapolis, MN: University of Minnesota Press, 2010.

Styan, J. L., *Dark Comedy: The Development of Modern Comic Tragedy*, 2nd edn. Cambridge: Cambridge University Press, 1968.

Szondi, Peter, *Theory of the Modern Drama*, trans. M. Hays. Cambridge: Polity Press, 1987 [1965].

Walker, Kenny, '"Without Evidence, there is No Answer": Uncertainty and Scientific Ethos in Silent Springs of Rachel Carson', *Environmental Humanities*, vol. 2 (2013), pp. 101–16.

Wellwarth, George, *The Theatre of Protest and Paradox: Developments in the Avant-garde Drama*. New York: New York University, 1971.

Williams, David, in Alan Read (ed.), 'The Right Horse, The Animal Eye: Bartabas and Théâtre Zingaro', 'On Animals': *Performance Research*, vol 5, no. 2 (2000), pp. 29–40.

Williams, Raymond, *Marxism and Literature*. Oxford: Oxford University Press, 1977.

1

Caryl Churchill's 'Dark Ecology'[1]

Elaine Aston

Caryl Churchill is a rare breed of playwright: a dramatist endowed with a trenchant political voice and a capacity for formal invention that is unsurpassed on the mid- to late-twentieth and twenty-first century British stage. A majority of her plays have been performed at London's premier new playwriting venue, The Royal Court Theatre, where, as former Artistic Director Max Stafford-Clark, Churchill's long-term collaborator, observes, she figures among those writers whose propensity for the 'unconventional' has opened up and challenged the theatre's dominant strains of social realism.[2] As a political playwright, she understandably found inspiration in Brechtian dramaturgy, but also, as Stafford-Clark attests, was 'influenced considerably by Ionesco and by the Theatre of the Absurd'.[3]

However, in the interests of this essay collection with its focus on the Absurd and the ecological, to understand the absurdist strains within the constantly mutating DNA of Churchillian theatre is to see how these differ from the Theatre of the Absurd as Martin Esslin categorizes and defines it through his all-male cast of mid-twentieth-century playwrights – principally Samuel Beckett, Arthur Adamov, Eugène Ionesco, Jean Genet and Harold Pinter. Within Esslin's critical framework, it is the 'metaphysical anguish at the absurdity of the human condition'[4] that is posited as what, in form and content, these 'masters of the Absurd' sought to express.[5] That understanding has since been reconsidered, most notably by Michael Y. Bennett who contends that Esslin misreads the Absurd, making a counterargument for the Theatre of the Absurd as 'not about absurdity, but about making life meaningful given our absurd situation'.[6] Equally, I would argue that Churchill's theatre anguishes not over the 'absurdity of the human condition', but the absurdity of a world enmeshed in values that threaten to devalue all kinds of life forms. Hence, including this essay on Churchill in *Rethinking the Theatre of the Absurd* affords an opportunity to examine how the absurdist strains threaded through the fabric of her theatre evince a political commitment to critiquing and opposing the dehumanizing values that govern the human *and non-human* condition, thereby complementing other contributions to this volume whose primary concern is to 'green' Esslin's treatment of the dramatic exponents of the Absurd.

As she embarked on her professional writing career in the 1960s, Churchill's departure from the Esslin-derived notion of 'the absurdity of the human condition' was in part born out of her understanding that in keeping with shifting social, cultural and political landscapes, theatre needed to change or renew its direction with respect to both form and content. Enquiring after a direction for drama in her essay 'Not Ordinary, Not Safe' published in 1960, for instance, she acknowledges the significance of plays by the likes of Beckett, Pinter and Ionesco, at the same time as expressing her frustration with the failure to move beyond the trope of the endless wait: 'I can't go on like this, says Estragon. He does, but do we have to?'[7] As a riposte to the 'everlasting flat depression' Churchill perceived as shaping the dramatic landscape formed by either the Absurdists or the realists,[8] she called on playwrights to broaden their 'range, and without ignoring our problems get them into a different perspective'.[9] 'To tell us to care isn't enough,' she elaborated, 'we have to be shown what we're to care about in a way that makes us care'.[10]

Churchill's commitment to socialism and feminism constantly informs her views on 'what we're to care about'. She once described her ideal society as 'decentralized, nonauthoritarian, communist, non-sexist – a society in which people can be in touch with their feelings, and in control of their lives'. Thereafter, she observed, 'But it always sounds both ridiculous and unattainable when you put it into words'.[11] Over time, Churchill's vision has appeared less and less realizable, rendering it absurdly 'unattainable' given the various erosions of socialist and feminist ideologies.[12] This erosion of an egalitarian landscape, in turn, accounts for the progressively dark political and ecological critiques in Churchill's theatre: her critical sensing of the damage done to human and non-human life forms when all that remains are the inhuman(e) values of an increasingly aggressive capitalist system.

A political-theatre animal

In short, Churchill's relentless commitment to questions of equality and social justice marks her out as a political-theatre animal. In everyday terms, to describe a person as a political animal is to signal her or his active interests in politics. But I want to propose a conceptualization of this term in the interests of more fully introducing, understanding and explaining how Churchill's valuing of the egalitarian comes to map with the ecological.

In his seminal 1995 text *Disagreement: Politics and Philosophy*, Jacque Rancière begins by returning to Aristotle's *Politics* to recapitulate on 'the eminently political nature of the human animal',[13] quoting the passage in which Aristotle states that 'nature, as we say, does nothing without some purpose; and she has endowed man alone among the animals with the power of speech'.[14] Further, within the Aristotelian frame, 'speech' is contrasted with 'voice'. Animals can voice their 'pain or pleasure', but 'speech', logos, is reserved exclusively for humankind, the only species who 'have perception of good and evil, the just and the unjust', thereby enabling 'a common view in these matters that makes a household and a state'.[15] Rancière's subsequent intervention is not to undo this binary between human/speech and animal/voice, but rather to point out the social inequalities in human terms of the visible and the invisible, those endowed with speech and those without logos. In terms of politics, Rancière elaborates:

> Politics does not exist because men, through the privilege of speech, place their interests in common. Politics exists because those who have no right to be counted as speaking beings make themselves of some account, setting up a community by the fact of placing in common a wrong that is nothing more than this

very confrontation, the contradiction of two worlds in a single world.[16]

Following Rancière, to be among the unaccountable, to be without speech is, as it were, to be animal. Therefore, to insist on the 'right to be counted' is to become a political animal: the one who is not-quite-human righting the 'wrong' by dissenting from the inequalities of the social order, disavowing, for instance, the 'common view' that kept in place the Athenian 'household' and 'state'.

Similarly, Churchill populates her contemporary theatre with questions of inequality and social justice by giving us characters deprived of logos, who 'speak' out of environmentally unfriendly terrains such as the family, home or nation. However, taking the part of the speech-less, or taking the part of 'those who have no part',[17] also brings Churchill into an ecological alignment with all life forms 'who have no part'. In other words, a capacity to right the 'wrong' may not be a matter of coming into the logos of the human but to become animal – to decentre human interests in favour of the coexistence of the human and non-human. This, therefore, makes the political animal the one who also looks in a different direction: away from the entry into logos and towards the non-human/animal world. As a political-theatre animal, then, Churchill's mode of looking is, of necessity, Janus-faced: looking both to questions of inequalities within the human ordering of the world and towards a horizontal (rather than hierarchical) realignment between the human and the non-human.

To trace the doubling of Churchill's political concern for the egalitarian and the ecological, I turn to three of her works: the early radio drama *The Ants* (1962) and two of her later plays *The Skriker* (1994) and *Far Away* (2000). Ultimately, all three plays demonstrate that to discount the non-human world is to risk a damaged ecology of all forms of life. In order to show this in a way 'that makes us care', Churchill deploys absurdist sensibilities that shapeshift through this trio of dramas to create affectively nauseous theatrical environments. This is not the nausea of existential despair, but the sickening feeling that ensues when we are caught up in, and affected by, Churchill's critical sensing of both the enduring inequalities of the human-to-not-quite-human and the abject failure to acknowledge the co-existence of the human with the worlds of the non-human.

The Ants – 'Animal Compassion'

Interviewed at the time of her first professionally produced play *Owners* (1972) at The Royal Court Theatre, Churchill explained her interest not in the Absurd but in the absurdity of people's value- and judgement-making: 'The absurd things people take for granted, and the whole different systems people have for judging whether things are important or not'.[18] 'If I cut my finger now,' she continued, 'it would be an awful thing, but obviously much worse things are happening far away and one can't relate to them'.[19] As a playwright, therefore, she perceived the necessity of defamiliarizing the 'absurdities of positions' people perceive to be 'normal', by taking them 'out of the context which makes them seem all right'. For to 'take the context away', she argued, could make it more difficult for people to be accepting of the 'horrible things' they do that are 'made to seem perfectly all right by their context'.[20] In brief, her reflections gesture towards decontextualizing or defamiliarizing strategies as an aesthetic means to reveal the absurd reckonings of the human species, a preoccupation of hers that she acknowledges can be traced back to her first professionally produced radio play, *The Ants*.

As a title, *The Ants* foregrounds a non-human species as its putative subject. It is, however, the dehumanizing capacities of the human that come fully into focus. A divorcing couple, Jane and Stewart, are in dispute over who is to have custody of their son, Tim. Alienated by parental squabbling, Tim finds solace in the company of his grandfather and a colony of ants. Perversely, however, Grandfather gradually infects Tim with a sense of his own disillusionment about the loveless nature of the adult world: his endorsement of the solitary life, which he purports to be preferable to the disappointments and estrangements that come from losing the love of others. Hence, while the ants are at first a source of pleasure for the boy, at the close of the play Tim is infected by his grandfather's logic and joins the older man in dousing them in petrol to exterminate the colony.

A question the play poses regards what hope there is for humans as a species when they value only those matters that are of immediate, personal concern. It does so by revealing the absurdity of a horizon of looking that is determined by and confined to internecine, familial hostilities. A report of the 'outside' world comes via a newspaper brought by Stewart, occasioning Grandfather to comment, 'Yes, you forget there's a world outside and a war on. You can't imagine a war down here, but there's always one somewhere'.[21] 'Down here' in Grandfather's house by the shores of the sea, a place where 'nothing happens', the momentous, militaristic happenings in the world at large are deemed unremarkable. The failure of the characters to allow the 'outside' into their lives registers as Jane reads in the paper that 'somewhere' far away from 'here' a bomb has been dropped[22]:

Jane	They've dropped a big bomb.
Grandfather	Which side?
Jane	Us.
Grandfather	Dropped it on us?
Jane	No, we dropped it.
Grandfather	I suppose that's just as well.[23]

These elliptical lines speak volumes about the human capacity to dehumanize: to annihilate a faceless, nameless, human other in the interests of self-preservation – 'just as well' it's not 'us'.

The faraway bombing of those who are not 'us' appears close up, is brought home (in both senses) in the petrol bombing of the ants. Killing the ants is a metaphorical expression of the 'natural' enmity towards distant, not-quite-human others; it is also a literal act of aggression against the non-human world of insects. From an adult's perspective, insects are enemy invaders. They crawl through Grandfather's house. It is 'disgusting, earwigs in the kitchen, there's something moving wherever you look', complains Jane.[24] As creatures that disgust, they must be destroyed. Exceptionally, the child is on the side of the ants insisting they should not be harmed, should not be killed. These creatures initially delight rather than disgust him; they provide comfort from the persistent parental squabbles over custody. Writing on 'animal compassion', feminist philosopher Luce Irigaray observes of her own childhood experiences how 'unhoped for support' came from animals in stressful, 'critical' times.[25] Recollections of her sensory, experiential contact with animals invite her to reflect philosophically on how relations with other species might be instructive for humanity, a humanity that, thus far, is ill-prepared for, if not failing in, its compassionless encounters with others.[26] It is possible, Irigaray argues, to redress this, to find a way back to the 'sense capabilities' of other species that 'we, as humans, have lost', but only and crucially 'on condition that we do not use their assistance to pursue our project of arrogant world domination'.[27] In Churchill's play, the child loses his compassion for the ants because he learns from the adults the 'value' of killing in the interests of 'world domination'. Compassion turns to enmity as one particular reddish ant, whom he has befriended and named Bill, is no longer identifiable among the crawling masses, and the human-indoctrinated instinct to dominate takes hold. The initial joy of observing and touching the insects turns to horror as they swarm up his arm, and finally to hysterical delight as he '*shrieks with laughter*' at their burning.[28] Hence, the unlooked-for succour of the insect world is irretrievably lost as the child is lost to a humanity that knows only aggression practised as a means of self-preservation. In brief, extinguished along with the ants is the possibility of worlding pacific relations between humans and between human and other life forms.

Churchill originally conceived *The Ants* as a play for television, but her agent, Peggy Ramsay, envisaged difficulties with how the drama would work for this medium: 'On television, my dear, if a play is set during the war, it's a *war play!!* The filming of the ants sequence, too, isn't easy, as it would have to be specially done in order to "match up" with the "live" scenes. Honestly I think this is a subject for SOUND'.[29] On Ramsay's advice, Churchill's play was submitted for radio broadcast (BBC Radio 3, 27 November 1962), and was presented to listeners rather than viewers. As Elin Diamond insightfully observes in her discussion of *The Ants*, radio has 'a distinguished history in producing terror, for what imagination "sees" is far more terrifying than any embodiment'; it allows Churchill, for instance, to verbalize the terror of the faraway bombing that is 'out there' as 'instantly "here"', thus affording the listener an affective sensing of the war the characters refuse to see.[30] In another way, how, in the visual medium of theatre, to embody non-human life forms in order to posit the ecological necessity of achieving pacific relations between the human and the non-human remains a challenge. To address this difficulty, in her stage play *The Skriker*, Churchill gives us the coexisting worlds of humans and spirits.

The Skriker – the absurdity of cosmic capitalism

The Skriker's aesthetic is akin to Salvador Dali's 'lobster telephone': a surreal doubling of the human world with the spirit world of the Skriker, '*a shape shifter and death portent, ancient and damaged*'.[31] 'Look and look again', Churchill admonishes as she schizophrenically splits and troubles the spectatorial gaze between damaged humans and poisoned spirits.[32] In her script, the mainly mute, non-human world of the spirits is set out in the form of a series of stage directions which direct the reader's attention to the composition of the stage: to the non-verbal, physical layering of the spirits' stories woven into the dramatic text. Choreographing the dark underworld for the play's premiere in 1994 at the Cottesloe, The Royal National Theatre, London, Ian Spink engaged performers in a movement-based language to populate the stage with these other-worldly creatures, divisible and distinguishable from, and yet penetrating, the human world/space with their strange, haunting presence.[33] These are creatures who are, to borrow from Jacques Derrida, 'beyond the edge of the *so-called* human'; their presence calls into question the binarized abjection of all those marked out and named as non-human.[34] This is not least because the spirits do not conform to one uniform, other-than-human kind. Rather, in appearance, shape or movement, the spirits are representative of multiple species from the Kelpie (part man and part horse) to Thrumpins who ride on the backs of unwitting businessmen.

The human world of *The Skriker* is reduced to just two young women: Josie who has killed her baby, and Lily who is pregnant and all alone but for Josie and the shape-shifting Skriker. The two teenage mothers are genealogically related to the disadvantaged, working-class girl, Angie, in *Top Girls* (1982), Churchill's socialist-feminist critique of a society divided by 'us' and 'them', of a masculinist economy of the feminine rooted in material gain, capitalist greed. The future Angie foresees at the close of the play is 'frightening', a nightmare world of compassionless inequality.[35] Throughout the 1980s, Brechtian refrains dominated the Churchillian landscape as she persisted in warning of the human desire to have and to own, from the corporate ownership of land that controls and determines the lives of the agrarian women labourers in *Fen* (1983) to the money-making classes in *Serious Money* (1987).[36] However, the collapse of Communism at the close of the decade and the relentless advances of late-twentieth-century capitalism occasioned a shapeshifting in Churchill's aesthetic as she sought to give form to the absurdity of a humanity increasingly lost to the inhumanity of a capitalist system gone global. Where Esslin conceived of the Theatre of the Absurd as giving expression to the 'absence' of a 'generally accepted cosmic system of values',[37] Churchill, by contrast, takes issue with capitalism now felt as a global, cosmic system governing the value of all human and non-human life. Redoubling her efforts in *The Skriker* to take the part of 'those who have no part' (Josie and Lily), she gives us the uncanny coupling of the human and non-human to make us feel the toxicity of a globe poisoned by the creed of human greed. This involves her in a return to the ecological dystopia that haunts *The Ants,* but in increasingly darker hues and absurdist tones.

'Dark ecology' is how Timothy Morton nuances deep ecology, the body of thought that attempts to think beyond the green credentials of human-centred relations with the environment and towards a horizontal, transversal acknowledgement of all life forms.[38] For Morton, 'dark ecology' is necessary for 'ecological thought': 'The only way out is down. It is the ultimate detox. But like homoeopathy, it uses poison as medicine'.[39] The aesthetics of a 'dark ecology' he posits as embracing 'negativity and irony, ugliness and horror'.[40] All the way down to the poisoned underworld of Skriker is where Churchill's play takes us in the hope that we might recover a sense of egalitarian and ecological well-being. For the hoped-for recovery resides not in the poetic vision that gives us the wonder of 'Nature' as an antidote to the social and planetary ills that ail us, but in the formation of 'ugliness and horror', the medicinal poison we must swallow if we are ever to gain a perspective on cosmic capitalism as that which radically disagrees with us.

In *The Ants,* Grandfather explains to Tim that while the insects might 'know' things like 'sugar' or a 'twig' when these are placed before them, what 'they don't know' is 'you', the human.[41] However, Skriker, '*ancient and damaged*', has long known the human race as a damaging species; as R. Darren Gobert insightfully observes, 'The creature's damage originates in environmental devastation'.[42] Dimly, she can recollect a time when humans were kinder to

spirits, but 'now they hate us and hurt hurtle faster and master'.[43]
Nourished by cruelty rather than kindness, her species has survived
by feeding off the toxicity of the 'master' race and yet perversely
she remains needy of their withheld affection. In the role of Skriker
in the National's production, Kathryn Hunter depicted the spirit
as the kind of insect-like creature that provokes human disgust:
a winged insect, moth rather than butterfly, black and grey, not
brightly coloured. A 'spidery tangle of arms legs and black wings',
she delivered the Skriker's opening monologue as a crawling,
creeping and creepy creature.[44] Towards the close of the monologue,
her diminutive body cast a gigantic, portentous shadow across the
stage: her insect-like form, now with wings unfurled, twisted away
from the audience as, poised for flight up into the human world, she
bellowed her wrath-fuelled claims on the species that had damaged
her spirit world.

Equally, Skriker's animalistic howl of the wrong done to her own
species pierces the speech she has learned from human tongues.
Being on the side of the animal/non-human, of those who do not

FIGURE 3 *Kathryn Hunter playing the Skriker in Caryl Churchill's* The
Skriker *directed by Les Waters at the Cottesloe Royal National Theatre,
1994.* © *Hugh Glendinning.*

count, she cannot command language. Hers is a damaged logos which refuses to obey the orderly, ordering of speech as a meaning-making system of human communication. Instead, her language 'rhymes and associates' so that it 'goes off on other trains of thought within a sentence'.[45] That said, her language is far from nonsense: her excessive speech conjures up tales of fairy folklore. As her monologue begins, the tales she spins spin out from Rumplestiltskin, the story that tells of a miller's daughter whose father boasts to the king that his 'daughter could spin span spick and spun the lowest form of wheat straw into gold'.[46] The price of spinning straw into gold set by the fairy trickster who comes to the woman's magical aid is the life of her first-born child, but she out-tricks the trickster by correctly guessing the riddle of his name. Skriker embodies the fairy's fury at being out-tricked and would sooner forego and forget the human world. But its 'poison' runs through her 'rivers of blood', pulling her back to wreck her 'revengeance' by trading in the currency on which the human world turns – 'gold mine, sweet'.[47]

In her human disguises, many of them figuring beings in need of care and compassion, she preys on those who are in desperate need, those who, within a capitalist ecology, figure as the socially unworthy and undeserving poor – damaged young women like Josie the child-killer and the single mother Lily. These girls become dependent on Skriker's magical powers as their only means of economic survival.[48] Lily, the good, who comforts Skriker dissembling as an impoverished, old woman, is rewarded for her altruism in 'gold speaking pound coins'[49]: when she speaks, her speech produces money (unlike compassionless Josie who is made to speak toads). While Lily may look kindly on Skriker, her goodness cannot, however, prevail in an economy of capitalism. Indebted to the 'bloodmoney'[50]-sucking Skriker who is riddled with curiosity about the human world, Lily, like her fairy-tale counterpart, must quench the spirit's thirst to know how things work (and ultimately to repay her debt with the life of her child). In a hotel bar in London, encountering Skriker in her guise as a US woman tourist, Lily is at a loss for words as she is unable to give an adequate explanation for how a television set works – to explain the inner workings of satellite communications, 'up in space'.[51] Lily's failure to grasp the flow of technological power is symptomatic of her inability to see the invisible current of capitalism whose workings determine her state-less position as an impoverished, lone mother.[52] Coming to her rescue as the 'good fairy' capitalist, Skriker sets her straight:

Skriker	Where do you think your money comes from?
Lily	I'm not ungrateful.
Skriker	You're the one I've chosen out of everyone in the world.
Lily	Why?
Skriker	Because you're beautiful and good. Don't you think you are? Yes everyone sometimes thinks they're beautiful and good and deserve better than this and so they do. Are you telling me I made a mistake? I'd be sorry to think I'd made a mistake.[53]

Singled out to 'deserve better', Lily, along with Josie, is weighed down by the spirit's parasitic attachments to her host body. But, equally, neither of the girls feels capable of giving up the powers and pleasures of consumption she grants them. Lily will not wish her away, the Skriker challenges, 'because I might give [her] nice things. And Josie wants nice things. That's why she wants me. Not to help Lily. So you both want me/That's nice'.[54]

Lured by greed to Skriker's underworld and failing to heed the warnings not to consume its deceptive 'glamour',[55] Josie is forced to live out her years in the spirit world, while, so the Skriker relates, the human world is a 'wide open wide world hurled hurtling hurting hurt very badly' and her vampiric feeding off humans increasingly fails to satisfy, given their 'toxic' rather than 'sweet flesh'.[56] In the time–space continuum of the spirit world, Josie's wait is not the Beckettian wait that marks the futility and absurdity of the looked-for purpose or meaning to life. Rather, her waiting elicits a recovered feeling for the world she has lost – 'a little bit of stony ground', 'the stones' she remembers as a child pulling her back to Earth as she out-tricks the Skriker by disobeying her command not 'to touch the water in the fountain'.[57] In accordance with fairy logic, however, time in the human world has not moved on: Josie returns to the moment of her leaving. Thereafter, the irony is that Josie's only means of saving Lily/the world from Skriker's harm is to go 'further and murther in the dark', doing 'terrible things' to keep the spirit 'sated seated besotted'.[58] An even deeper, darker, ironic twist to Churchill's tale follows: in a final attempt at global salvation, Lily agrees to repeat Josie's journey to the underworld, believing she will also be reunited with her child and rejoin the world in the moment of her leaving it. But Lily is 'tricked tracked wracked' as she lands in the apocalyptic future of the human to face the '*wordless rage*' of her daughter's offspring.[59]

This 'horror storybook ending' which eschews the happy-ever-after convention of the fairy tale is the dark medicine of 'ecological thought' and consolidates the play's overall composition as surreal, slippery and tricksterish.[60] Uncertainties abound in the drama's changeling-like aesthetic, rendering what is dream, nightmare or reality tenuous; the slipperiness of its fairy logic wormholes space and time to permit the uncanny crossings between the parallel worlds of the human and non-human. The epicentre of trickery, the forked-tongued Skriker dissembles and deceives, twisting words and worlds into the dark-light, messianic seeing of the truth of the human/non-human condition as Churchill intuits it.[61] What she tellingly reveals is that in a world conditioned by human greed, nothing is more certain than the damaged future the play portends: a world in which 'Spring will return and nothing will grow'[62] and everything is 'dustbin'.[63]

Far Away – the undoing of democracy

As Churchill gives us Skriker's dark imagining of a cosmos reduced to 'dustbin', so she demolishes the mythical conceit of Nature that 'has been a comfort to people as long as they've existed'.[64] For as Morton advises, the 'comfort' derived from thinking of Nature 'as a reified thing in the distance, under the sidewalk, on the other side where the grass is always greener', impedes ecological thought.[65] For ecological thinking must discomfort rather than comfort, go deeper and darker if it is to think in terms of the coexistence of all life forms. However, Morton also observes that this is hard to achieve because 'one of the things that modern society has damaged, along with ecosystems and species and the global climate, is *thinking*'.[66] What Churchill, in turn, reveals is that the capacity to think of ourselves in relation to human and non-human others is so damaged, the idea of coexistence so unthinkable in a world shaped by the inequalities of a capitalist ecology, that we risk the apocalyptic extinction of all forms of life. At the turn of the millennium, Churchill returns to this darkest of thoughts in *Far Away* (2000).

When the play premiered in the Theatre Upstairs at the Royal Court, the feeling of a world edging still further into darkness was visually encoded in its staging. Where, in the National's production of *The Skriker*, the space of the human world was mapped by Annie Smart's design of a white, clinical box set inside a larger structure, whose architecture was disturbed by the haunting presence of the non-human world of the spirits, in *Far Away* remnants of the human were evoked by a sparsely furnished domestic environment enveloped in darkness. Nature with a capital 'N' was stripped away before the opening scene: a painted front cloth, depicting a brightly coloured, country idyll and accompanied by a sound-scape of bird song and running water, was removed to reveal the dark reality of the domestic interior.[67]

Reduced to just three characters – Harper, Joan and Todd – *Far Away* consists of three elliptically formed parts. The first introduces Joan as a child staying in her Aunt Harper's house and struggling to make sense of the violence she perceives around her. Part Two depicts Joan as a young woman in the workplace, making designer hats with her co-worker Todd, hats that are to be worn by condemned prisoners paraded on their way to execution. The final, third part returns to Harper's house several years later to reveal all three characters caught up in global warfare.

Joan, the child, like Angie in *Top Girls*, senses that she is surrounded by a 'frightening' world, but the violence she witnesses outside Harper's house – her uncle beating up people, including children – is made 'safe' by her aunt's account of these bloody events as acts of succour and hospitality: 'Your uncle is helping these people. He's helping them escape. He's giving them shelter'.[68] Each time the child relates the disturbing things she has seen or heard (events which the audience do not see), the adult twists them into an understanding of how they serve 'to make things better'.[69] For instance, the unnatural sounds of a 'person screaming' are attributed by Harper to nature – to an owl, one of many types of bird she claims to inhabit the 'beautiful place' where her home is located.[70] Nature is not only the scapegoat for human-to-human violence but is itself contaminated by the violent behaviour; there is blood on the ground seeping into the Earth. The child who steps into the blood is sworn to keeping the darkest of secrets and initiated into thinking she is doing 'good': 'You can look at the stars and think here we are in our little bit of space, and I'm on the side of the people who are putting things right, and your soul will expand right into the sky'.[71] Hence, virtuous humanity mutates into its inhuman opposite: the child is unwittingly damaged by and lost to a belief system devoid of an ethical care for others, an order of thinking which, in Irigaray's terms, works absolutely and resolutely against 'the accomplishment of our humanity'.[72]

When, in Part Three, Joan as an adult and married to Todd, returns to Harper's house, she is the one who comes seeking refuge and an escape from the violence which has escalated from the local hostilities she witnessed as a child into epic, global warfare. This part is a powerful, poetic expression of a Hobbesian war of all against all, which Churchill presents as the 'logical' outcome of late-twentieth-century, globally occurring capitalism: the warring of peoples mobilized by self(ish)-interests and preservation. Except that in forming her warring landscape, Churchill imagines this not just as the hostilities of all humans against all humans, but of all species against all species. Cats have 'been killing babies',[73] relates Harper to Todd; deer 'storm down from mountains and terrorise shopping malls',[74] while mallards 'commit rape, and they're on the side of the elephants and the Koreans'.[75] With the exception of crocodiles who are, according to Harper, 'always in the wrong', it is impossible to know which species are on which side. [76]

Akin to the grotesque comedy of the rhinoceros-invaded town in Ionesco's *Rhinoceros*, these reports of species on the rampage are laced with absurdist humour. But ultimately, *Far Away* arguably strikes a comparatively deeper and darker note of discord than Ionesco's play whose leading protagonist, Berenger, at least survives as a lone but emancipatory figure resistant to the mass metamorphosis of humans into rhinos. For as the conversational tones of Todd and Harper collide with their absurd reckonings about which nations, peoples or animal species are the enemy, so Churchill elicits a critical sensing of a humanity entirely devoid of the capacity to conceive of caring for any kind of life form. The killing on the part of Todd and Joan is indiscriminate: Todd relates how he has 'shot cattle and children in Ethiopia' and 'gassed mixed troops of Spanish, computer programmers and dogs'[77]; Joan, en route to Todd, 'killed two cats and a child under five', not so very different from when she is licensed to kill on a 'mission'.[78] Where Joan and Todd come to appear 'thing-like' as desensitized killing machines, the fact that 'everything's been recruited' means that all 'things', organic or inorganic, are, in an opposite way, animated by the power to kill[79]: 'There were piles of bodies and if you stopped to find out there was one killed by coffee or one killed by pins, they were killed by heroin, petrol, chainsaws, hairspray, bleach, foxgloves'.[80] Steeped in war, nature turns a hostile gaze on the human. Birds, which Irigaray claims as the species who might support us the most and help us 'furthest along the way' towards achieving 'our humanity',[81] are now to be feared, although more fearful still is 'the weather' that's 'on the side of the Japanese'.[82] Thus Churchill's absurdist strains form the nightmare reality of nations competing for the control and domination of natural resources: 'Bolivians are working with gravity,' relates Joan, 'but we're getting further with noise and there's thousands dead of light in Madagascar'. So 'who', she wonders, 'is going to mobilise darkness and silence?'[83]

The play's second part provides a telling link between the child as a witness to violence and the adult as a desensitized killing machine. Its workplace setting sets the scene for labour relations tied to the production of extravagant, ridiculously over-sized, designer hats to be worn by condemned prisoners. Under sentence of death, the women, children and men parade as a silent speech-less body. Evocative of the holocaust in its staging,[84] the condemned appear like 'the walking corpses' which Bruno Bettelheim witnessed in the concentration camps: those prisoners who, utterly defeated by the extreme deprivation of their prison environment, surrender any chance of leaving the camp other than as a corpse.[85]

Complicit in a fascist regime by dint of their labour, Joan and Todd are also on their way to becoming 'walking corpses'. Todd, the more experienced worker compared to the novice, Joan, regards himself as the only principled person in the workplace, which he knows to be corrupt. In turn, he encourages Joan to 'think in different ways'. 'I'd never have thought about how this place is run and now I see how important it is', she admits to Todd.[86] But such thinking is incapacitated and curtailed by an inability to grasp the totality of the corrupt system in which their lives are enmeshed. They might reflect on and speak out about the wrongs of the hat parade at the risk of losing their jobs; they might get as far as thinking that 'all the parades are corrupt', but what remains unthinkable, unimaginable, is an alternative, democratic, social order in which all people are valued, counted rather than discounted.[87] As Todd and Joan relinquish any feeling for 'those who have no part' (the prisoners), politics is glimpsed at the point of vanishing.[88] In short, Churchill's strategy of presenting the word-less parading of human degradation is an invitation to her audience to see that which the young couple fail to see: the spectacular defeat of politics, of democracy.[89]

To recognize the absurdity of the inhuman condition under capitalism is, however, what Churchill, the political-theatre animal, reveals as that which is vital to our recovery, to feeling our way back to a democratic pulse. A democratic pulse is also an ecological pulse, pulsating with the egalitarian and ethical rhythms of human-to-human and human-to-non-human existence. That pulse may be weak at times and increasingly harder to find going into the twenty-first century, as the world marches on to the beat of capitalism. Yet, without it, Churchill warns, we risk a damaged ecology and the deepest and darkest irony of all – to be human is to join the ranks of 'walking corpses'.

Works cited

Amich, Candice, 'Bringing the Global Home: The Commitment of Caryl Churchill's *The Skriker*', *Modern Drama*, vol. 50, no. 3 (Fall 2007), pp. 394–413.

Aragay, Mireia, Hildegard Klein, Enric Monforte and Pilar Zozaya (eds), *British Theatre of the 1990s: Interviews with Directors, Playwrights, Critics and Academics*. Basingstoke: Palgrave Macmillan, 2007.

Aston, Elaine, *Caryl Churchill*, 3rd edn. Tavistock: Northcote House, 2010.

Aston, Elaine, 'Feeling the Loss of Feminism: Sarah Kane's *Blasted* and an Experiential Genealogy of Contemporary Women's Playwriting', *Theatre Journal*, vol. 62 (2010), pp. 575–91.

Bennett, Michael Y., *Reassessing The Theatre of the Absurd: Camus, Beckett, Ionesco, Genet, and Pinter*. Basingstoke: Palgrave Macmillan, 2011.

Bettelheim, Bruno, *The Informed Heart: Autonomy in a Mass Age*. New York: The Free Press, 1960.

Churchill, Caryl, 'Not Ordinary, Not Safe: A Direction for Drama?', *The Twentieth Century* (November 1960), pp. 443–51.

Churchill, Caryl, *The Ants*, in *New English Dramatists*, vol. 12, Harmondsworth: Penguin, 1969.

Churchill, Caryl, 'Introduction', *Caryl Churchill: Plays 3*. London: Nick Hern books, 1998, pp. vii–viii.

Churchill, Caryl, Interview, *Plays and Players* (January 1973), p. 1.

Churchill, Caryl, *Top Girls*. London: Methuen, 1982.

Churchill, Caryl, Interview. *Late Theatre*, BBC2, January 1994.

Churchill, Caryl, *The Skriker*. London: Nick Hern Books, 1994.

Churchill, Caryl, *Far Away*. London: Nick Hern Books, 2000.

Derrida, Jacques, 'The Animal that Therefore I am (More to Follow)', *Critical Enquiry*, vol. 28, no. 2 (Winter 2002), pp. 369–418.

Diamond, Elin, 'On Churchill and Terror', in Elaine Aston and Elin Diamond (eds), *The Cambridge Companion to Caryl Churchill*. Cambridge: Cambridge University Press, 2009, pp. 125–43.

Esslin, Martin, *The Theatre of the Absurd*, 3rd revised and enlarged edn. London: Methuen, 2001.

Gobert, R. Darren, *The Theatre of Caryl Churchill*. London: Bloomsbury Methuen Drama, 2014.

Irigaray, Luce, 'Animal Compassion', in Peter Atterton and Matthew Calarco (eds), *Animal Philosophy: Essential Readings in Continental Thought*. London: Continuum, 2004, pp. 195–201.

Morton, Timothy, *The Ecological Thought*. Cambridge, MA: Harvard University Press, 2010.

Nightingale, Benedict, *The Times*, 29 January, p. 16.

Rabillard, Sheila, '*Fen* and the Production of a Feminist Ecotheater', *Theater*, vol. 25, no. 1 (1994), pp. 62–71.

Rancière, Jacques, *Disagreement: Politics and Philosophy*, trans. J. Rose. Minneapolis, MN: University of Minnesota Press, 1999 [1995].

Roberts, Philip, *About Churchill: The Playwright & The Work*. London: Faber & Faber, 2008.

Thurman, Judith, 'The Playwright Who Makes you Laugh about Orgasm, Racism, Class Struggle, Homophobia, Woman-Hating, the British Empire, and the Irrepressible Strangeness of the Human Heart', *Ms* (May 1982), pp. 51–7.

2

The Garden in the Machine: Edward Albee, Sam Shepard and the American Absurd

Stephen Bottoms

At the heart of Sam Shepard's 1992 western film *Silent Tongue* lies a short scene in which a horse-drawn cart, bearing a rag-tag group of medicine show musicians and comedians, is seen heading back east across the New Mexico prairie wilderness, in search of something resembling civilization. They spy, some distance away, a grizzled, elderly figure on foot. Pushing a wheelbarrow piled high with all his worldly possessions, he is heading in the opposite direction – west. One of the party stands and hollers a question across the void: 'Where to!' The Lone Man (Tim Scott) stops for a moment, stares with haunted eyes into the distance, and calls back a single word: 'Land!'[1]

This moment is as distilled and pointed an encapsulation of the Absurd as anything to be found in Beckett. It also exposes the hollowness of Horace Greeley's mythic injunction to 'Go West, Young Man'.[2] For there is land all around – an ocean of it. The Lone Man, we must presume, has another kind of land in mind, some pastoral ideal of a place where he can set down roots, and reproduce the very domesticity that he has abandoned to pursue his ruggedly individualistic quest. Yet, out here on the lone prairie, there is not even a landscape to possess with the *eye* – no spectacular, red-rock vista of the type beloved of John Ford westerns, and referenced in Shepard's earlier film collaboration with Wim Wenders, *Paris, Texas* (1984). This is just flat, desolate scrubland, neither hostile nor remotely welcoming. Whatever the Lone Man is looking for, he has not found it, and the Sisyphean image of his lonely struggle strongly hints that he never will. 'In a universe suddenly divested of illusions and lights,' Albert Camus writes in *The Myth of Sisyphus*, 'man feels an alien, a stranger. His exile is without remedy because he is deprived of the memory of a lost home or the hope of a promised land'.[3]

This chapter is concerned with the triangle of tropes that connect in the Lone Man's futile quest: the environment, the American and the Absurd. These links are important to establish because Martin Esslin's *The Theatre of the Absurd*, for all its epoch-defining importance in dramatic circles, conspicuously failed to make them. Despite opening his book with an anecdote about Herbert Blau's production of *Waiting for Godot* at California's San Quentin penitentiary in 1957, Esslin displays a dismissive disregard for the American context. In its revised, enlarged second edition of 1968, *The Theatre of the Absurd* dedicates less than six of its 424 pages to American dramatists. Esslin excuses himself from looking any closer by asserting that

> the Absurd springs from a feeling of deep disillusionment, the draining away of the sense of meaning and purpose in life, which has been characteristic of countries like France and Britain in the years after the Second World War. In the United States there has been no corresponding loss of meaning and purpose. The American dream of the good life is still very strong.[4]

If Esslin's Eurocentrism rings hollow, it is because the questioning of that febrile dream had long been central to American drama and literature. Existentially oriented plays were not difficult to find in the United States at this time, but Esslin gives only a brief, slighting account of Edward Albee's early work, and skates over fellow Off-Broadway playwrights Jack Gelber and Arthur Kopit in a few sentences. He also completely overlooks the rich landscape of New York's alternative, Off-Off-Broadway playwriting scene of the 1960s – a scene whose small, makeshift, underfunded venues were not dissimilar to the 'pocket theatres' of Paris in which the

Theatre of the Absurd had flourished to begin with.[5] By 1967 (in time for Esslin's revisions, had he been paying attention), the most celebrated of the underground scene's young writers, Sam Shepard, had published his first collection of *Five Plays* – on which Samuel Beckett was the clearest dramatic influence.

If Esslin's disregard for American playwrights is disappointing, however, his lack of interest in the natural environment seems positively myopic, given its centrality within the book that he takes as the inspiration for his title, terminology and argument – Camus's *The Myth of Sisyphus*. Esslin's précis misleadingly emphasizes rather abstractly 'the metaphysical anguish at the absurdity of the human condition' that he claims is Camus's concern.[6] Yet, Camus himself advocates neither anguish nor human exceptionalism. *The Myth of Sisyphus* is concerned less with a broken, vertical relationship between man and a meaning-giving God (whose absence Camus simply takes as read) than with our horizontal relations with the material realities of Earth: 'The Absurd is not in man (if such a metaphor could have meaning) nor in the world, but in their presence together'.[7] 'If I were a tree among trees, a cat among animals,' he writes, 'I should belong to this world. I should *be* this world to which I am now opposed by my whole consciousness'.[8] Being human, I am, in other words, 'out of harmony' with nature. (The Latin root word *absurdus* is a musical term literally meaning 'out of tune'.) And for Camus, the bleak irony is that this acute sense of disattunement with our surroundings comes into focus at precisely the moment when – in all humility – we stop perceiving the world as a projection or possession of human consciousness, and instead begin

> sensing to what degree a stone is foreign and irreducible to us, with what intensity nature or a landscape can negate us. At the heart of all beauty lies something inhuman, and these hills, the softness of the sky, the outline of these trees at this very minute lose the illusory meaning with which we had clothed them, henceforth more remote than a lost paradise. ... The world evades us because it becomes itself again.[9]

Camus's nuanced perspective here is very much *in* tune with aspects of more recent thinking such as Jane Bennett's work on 'vital materialism': 'To begin to *experience* the relationship between persons and other materialities more horizontally,' she argues, 'is to take a step toward a more ecological sensibility'.[10]

The relevance of all this to the American context is particularly pronounced, because this is a nation founded on the pastoral dream of recovering some kind of prelapsarian harmony with nature. As Leo Marx argues in his seminal work of ecocriticism, *The Machine in the Garden* (1964), 'The pastoral ideal has been used to define the meaning of America ever since the age of discovery, and it has not yet lost its hold upon the native imagination'.[11] Pastoral literature has, since classical times, always already been a product of city living, with country life being viewed idealistically or nostalgically by those who no longer experience its rigours directly. In the nineteenth century, the vogue for romantic pastoralism sparked by poets such as Wordsworth obliquely reflected a period of mass urbanization, which – as Greg Garrard notes – 'made these contrasts relevant to many more people than ever before'.[12] Yet, in America, the notion of a vast, 'virgin land' (its native peoples mysteriously absented) had been foundational since the earliest colonial settlements. 'The European mind was dazzled by the prospect', Marx writes, because 'it seemed that mankind actually might realize what had been thought a poetic fantasy. The dream of a retreat to an oasis of harmony and joy ... was embodied in the various utopian schemes for making America the site of a new beginning for Western society'.[13]

Marx's *Machine in the Garden* analyses the development of this American pastoral tradition in forensic detail, and helpfully distinguishes between a naively sentimental pastoral, still manifest in many a Hollywood film, and what he calls 'complex pastoral'.[14] Traceable in the works of major American writers from Washington Irving to Nathaniel Hawthorne, Herman Melville and Henry David Thoreau, this more complex literary tradition presents meditations on nature's power and beauty that are persistently punctuated by sights and sounds that remind the reader of the disattuning proximity of the man-made, mechanized world of railroads, ships, factories and so forth. In this chapter, however, in reversing the terms of Marx's title, I want to argue that Albee and Shepard – arguably America's pre-eminent playwrights of the Absurd – manifest an awareness that pastoralism of any sort is an absurd delusion. The mechanization of culture and nation has long since been completed, and the natural world is only conceivable from within an alienated, acculturated perspective – the garden in the machine. Such a reversal of perspective is, of course, entirely appropriate to the theatrical medium, in which the mechanics and artifice of staging pre-condition any thoughts that might emerge about other, less man-made environments. From within this aesthetic context, though, the question for Albee and Shepard, as for Camus, is whether a sharpened awareness of our human limits might invite a humbler, more reflective relationship with the other inhabitants of the Earth (animal, vegetable and mineral) from which our very self-consciousness forever separates us.

Given the limits of space, I have elected in what follows to illustrate these arguments by focusing on selected plays from opposite ends of each playwright's career to date. This chapter examines examples both from the 1950s–60s, on which Esslin focuses, and from recent work from the 2000s. Other moments could also have been selected (the mid-1970s of Albee's *Seascape* and Shepard's *Buried Child*, for example), but my 'bookending' approach should be taken as gesturing towards the sustaining and developing of certain ongoing concerns throughout these playwrights' careers. The chapter also charts a path of sorts through different conceptual landscapes – from city, to woodland, to farmland, to wilderness – while journeying from East coast to Midwest to Southwest ('go west, Lone Man'). In each topography, the plays' characters vainly attempt to find harmony, intimacy, connectivity, with the more-than-human environment from which they remain so absurdly separated.

City

In *The Myth of Sisyphus*, Camus presents the unexamined life in terms both urban and theatrical. 'It happens that the stage-sets collapse', he announces of the moment in which the absurd person singular becomes suddenly aware of living an empty, habituated existence: 'Rising, tram, four hours in the office or factory, meal, tram, four hours of work, meal, sleep and Monday, Tuesday, Wednesday, Thursday, Friday and Saturday, according to the same rhythm. ... But one day the "why" arises and everything begins'.[15] Edward Albee's first, landmark play *The Zoo Story* (1959) dramatizes just such a moment of possible beginning for Peter, an archetypal bourgeois family man, who lives in comfort with a wife, two daughters, two parakeets and an unspecified number of cats. His daily moment of pastoral repose on a bench in Central Park is shattered by the arrival of Jerry – a stranger, an outsider (any translation of Camus's 1942 novel *L'Étranger* will do) – who regales him with curious stories of his socially alienated life before manufacturing his own death on a blade held by Peter.

Central Park is a pointed location for these events. Opened in 1857, this man-made garden within the machine of New York was designed (by renowned landscape architect Frederick Law Olmsted) to provide the denizens of a rapidly expanding city with the simple pleasures of grass, trees and ponds. Albee's stage directions nod towards 'foliage, trees, sky' that might be visible behind Peter's bench, but the theatrical reality of the play – which helped make its initial, off-Broadway staging economically viable – is that it requires almost no set at all.[16] Taking inspiration from *Waiting for Godot* (1953), Albee replaced Beckett's tree with a bench, and let the otherwise empty stage contain the action. Thus, despite its ostensible setting, *Zoo Story* is locked within the framed artifice of the theatre just as surely as Central Park itself is a theatrically green artifice locked within the city grid – and just as surely as the animals in the nearby city zoo (itself contained within the park) are contained within cages. As Philip Kolin notes, Albee's text foregrounds 'cages, boxes, frames, bars, encasements, the shrinking territorialities of prison cell or madhouse', and the park is by no means exempt from this heavily policed scheme.[17] Indeed, Jerry notes, Peter won't find any police officers on this east side of the park, because they are all over on the 'wild west' side, 'chasing fairies down from trees or out of the bushes'.[18] This is just one of the play's allusions to the repression of sexuality – in this case a homosexuality still proscribed by law when the play was written. 'Nature' is to be contained and cultivated, but undesirable weeds (and unnatural fairies) are ruthlessly rooted out.

Though it predates his thought by four decades, we might see *Zoo Story* in relation to Timothy Morton's 2010 call for a 'queer ecology'. Developments in evolutionary theory, Morton notes, have decisively 'abolished rigid boundaries between and within species' just as queer theory has blurred traditional boundaries of gender and sexuality: 'Life-forms constitute a mesh, a nontotalizable, open-ended concatenation of interrelations that blur and confound boundaries at practically any level'.[19] In the play, Jerry is the queer disruptor, the unruly force of nature – and while *Zoo Story* has often been read as a coded dramatization of a gay pick-up, Jerry's more obvious role is to confound Peter more than seduce him, to destabilize his ordered worldview with a dazzling barrage of oddly intimate, often confessional language. Jerry satirizes the city's functions as a stratifying machine for regulating and separating people from each other ('what's the line between upper-middle-middle-class and lower-upper-middle class?'[20]), and highlights the marginalized status of those living in 'the sickening rooming houses on the West side of New York City, the greatest city in the world. Amen'.[21] Jerry himself lives in one such building, in a single, tiny room, subdivided by beaverboard from another, in claustrophobic proximity to the 'colored queen' next door, and an entire Puerto Rican family crammed into another single room. This great city, reproducing the squalor and inequity of its European precursors, is a long way from the egalitarian ideals of America's founding fathers.

The realities described by Jerry are so far from Peter's sheltered experience that he proves slightly incredulous: 'I find it hard to believe that people such as that really *are*'.[22] Yet, for Jerry, Peter's very indifference to the lives of others is also, paradoxically, something they hold *in common*: 'We neither love nor hurt because we do not try to reach each other'.[23] His own awareness of such separation, Jerry explains, was brought to him by his discovery of surprising commonality with a 'mere' animal – his landlady's neglected, malnourished dog. This 'black monster of a beast ... bloodshot, infected maybe; and a body you can see the ribs through the skin', embodies the city's brutalizing effects on the non-human as well as the human.[24] (There are echoes here, perhaps conscious on Albee's part, of a similar mangy dog in Meursault's boarding house in *The Outsider*.) Jerry describes the dog as both the proverbial caged animal and a queer kind of sexual predator – coming at him like 'malevolence with an erection' whenever he sets foot in the entrance hall of the rooming house.[25] Jerry regales Peter with a vivid account of his attempts first to bribe the dog into passivity with meat treats, and then (when that fails) to murder it with rat poison. Rather than actually dying, however, the abused dog merely learns to steer clear of Jerry. Now, he explains, 'whenever the dog and I see each other ... we regard each other with a mixture of sadness and suspicion, and then we feign indifference'.[26] Such distance had been Jerry's goal throughout, and yet – he now realizes – this new coldness is a source of pain. The stage set has, so to speak, collapsed, and Jerry has realized both his profound alienation from, and newfound need for contact with, an entire urban ecology of beings and things: 'A person has to have some way of dealing with SOMETHING. If not with people ... if not with people ... SOMETHING. With a bed, with a cockroach ... with a carpet, a roll of toilet paper'.[27]

Jerry's rambling speech, emphasizing his intimate interdependence with non-human others (both animate and inanimate), suggests a tormented variation on Camus's 'sensing to what degree a stone is foreign and irreducible to us'. His desire to overcome indifference has driven him to the city zoo, 'to find out more about the way people exist with animals'. However, he notes, this 'probably wasn't a fair test, what with everyone separated by bars from everyone else'.[28] Consequently, he has opted to force himself on Peter much as the dog forced itself on him, by treating the park bench as a heterotopic space akin to the entrance hall – a site for horizontal encounters between those whose socially policed paths might never otherwise cross.

Following the conclusion of his dog story, Jerry attempts to 'communicate' with Peter – to prevent him from leaving this place unmoved, indifferent – via queerly intimate, physical means. First he attacks him with tickling, rendering the giggling Peter physically incapable of walking away. Then he ups the ante by attempting to force Peter off the bench – a move which has the desired effect of igniting Peter's possessive defiance: 'This is my bench, and you have no right to take it away from me ... I've come here for years'.[29] Peter's determination to protect his territorial rights results in a resort to atavistic violence (the bourgeois family man as snarling dog?), violence whose stakes Jerry purposely heightens by throwing him a knife and daring him to fight. Once Peter takes up the knife, however, Jerry hurls himself into an embrace with his opponent, thereby impaling himself. This climactic, tableau-like image, besides being oddly erotic, begs the critical question of agency. Does Jerry mean to kill himself? Does Peter mean to stab him? Or, indeed, does the presence of the blade itself complete a kind of actantial circuit between flesh and metal? Bruno Latour defines an actant as 'something that acts or to which activity is granted by others'.[30] A weapon possesses precisely this potential, its deadly materiality almost requiring it to perform in human hands, with or without conscious will. It is, of course, another such question of material intent around which Camus's *The Outsider* also revolves: does Meursault mean to kill the unnamed Arab, or is it the sun in the sky and the gun in his hand that impel the pulling of the trigger?[31]

Perhaps Jerry's death is more a matter of animal instinct than conscious agency on his part. Certainly, Albee tells us, his agonized scream '*must be the sound of an infuriated and fatally wounded animal*'.[32] Yet, as Peter hurries away, Jerry calls after him pointedly that 'you're not really a vegetable; it's all right; you're an animal. You're an animal, too'.[33] This parting shot suggests that understanding oneself as an animal is preferable, superior even, to Peter's previously unexamined, sleeping life, while the 'too' implies a final gesture towards a queer commonality. In (literally) closing the gap between them, however, Jerry also brings about his death. It is as if he has given up on attempting to overcome the separation between people and things, in the very act of attempting it.

According to Esslin, Camus's *Myth of Sisyphus* had asked 'why, since life had lost all meaning, man should not seek escape in suicide'.[34] What he neglects to mention is that Camus had also answered this question in no uncertain terms: 'Suicide is a repudiation. The absurd man can only drain everything to the bitter end'; 'Living an experience, a particular fate, is accepting it fully'.[35] In this light, Jerry's apparent death wish might suggest a failure to embrace the full absurdity of his situation, an urge for some kind of divine transcendence: 'Oh ... my ... God' is his and the play's final line, to be played, Albee tells us, with '*a combination of scornful mimicry and supplication*', in a prayer-like appeal to an absent creator.[36] In Jerry's defence, though, we might cite Theodor Adorno's paradoxical observation that 'the transcendent is, and it is not. ... Nothing could be experienced as truly alive if something that transcends life were not promised also'.[37] Albee's playwriting, here and elsewhere, often seems driven by the agitating urge to become more 'truly alive' – to transcend, however impossibly, the deadening forces of circumstance. In this respect, however, his work is a long way from the cool, observational acceptance of Camus, for whom 'transcendency has been eliminated'. The alternative, he proposes, is to embrace 'a sort of fragmentary immanence which restores to the universe its depth'.[38]

Wood

The experience of immanence is central to that greatest work of American pastoral, Henry David Thoreau's *Walden; or, Life in the Woods* (1854). Thoreau's aim, he tells us, in living in solitude in the Massachusetts woods for two years, was 'to anticipate, not the sunrise and the dawn merely, but, if possible, Nature herself. ... It is true, I never assisted the sun materially in his rising, but, doubt not, it was of the last importance only to be present at it'.[39] Such moments of communion are necessarily fragmentary, however, because as Thoreau himself observes, there is no true intimacy to be had: 'Nature puts no question and answers none which we mortals ask'.[40]

Thoreau's retreat to the woods represented a self-conscious escape from the enervating pressures of the city. The inhabitants of Concord 'have appeared to me to be doing penance in a thousand remarkable ways'; 'The mass of men lead lives of quiet desperation'.[41] Paradoxically, however, these famously dissenting remarks place Thoreau within the canonical mainstream of American thought: as Leo Marx notes, 'An inchoate longing for a more "natural" environment enters into the contemptuous attitude that many Americans adopt toward urban life'. The result of such repudiation, he adds, is that 'we neglect our cities and desert them for the suburbs'.[42] Yet, the suburbs still represent an environment under careful control – a blurred border zone between (alienating) civilization and (unnaturally manipulated) nature.

Sam Shepard's work is characteristically set in such liminal territory, rather than in the urban contexts favoured by Albee. His earliest extant play, *Rock Garden* (1964), written when he was only twenty-one years old, takes place in what appears to be a suburban Californian home akin to the one that he had not long since abandoned to shape an adulthood in New York. The play hinges around an unresolved tension between the domestic/ inside and the natural/outside, as a teenage Boy is lectured first by his mother and then by his father. The bed-bound Woman states that she probably 'caught this cold ... from being out in the rain too much', and repeatedly emphasizes the need to properly insulate the house against the elements – a task which, she maintains, her husband is neglecting to accomplish.[43] Yet, the

Woman also seems seduced by the very externalities she seeks protection from:

> I love the rain and whenever I get the chance I walk in it. I like it after the rain stops, too. I mean the way everything smells and looks. Right after a good hard rain. Those are two of my favorite times, when it's raining and right after it rains. I like it before it rains too but that's different. It's not the same.[44]

The Man represents a kind of converse mirror image of the Woman's queer sense of intimacy with the elements. Where she stays inside but desires the outside, he wants to bring the outside inside – to domesticate nature. Where she speaks of rain, he speaks of sprinkler heads for the lawn and irrigation pipes for the orchard. His stereotypically masculine fascination with the great outdoors prompts recurring suggestions that 'maybe we can go to Arizona' – to the vast, wilderness state of Grand Canyon and Painted Desert. Yet, his sole reason for doing so is to collect rocks for his garden. It is almost as if he dreams of domesticating the desert as a kind of ersatz simulacrum of itself:

> **Man** We could start another garden. A bigger one. ... All you need is some rocks. ... We went to Arizona before and we found a lot of rocks. We could really have some nice gardens like the one I have now. Only bigger and more fancy. I saw one with a fountain in it. We could put a fountain in ours. ... You come up the street and there'd be a nice green lawn with a lot of rock gardens and the irrigation running and the new trees all – all sort of green.[45]

Such desirous blurring of inside and outside, nature and culture, feminine and masculine, is, according to Timothy Morton, another reason to align the ecological and the queer: 'All life-forms, along with the environments they compose and inhabit, defy boundaries between inside and outside at every level. When we examine the environment, it shimmers, and figures emerge in a "strange distortion"'.[46]

Shepard further accentuates this 'sort of green' perspective in *Fourteen Hundred Thousand* (1966), the lead text in his *Five Plays* collection. The play begins with Ed telling his friend

Tom about a one-room cabin in the woods that he has just been to, given 'in the spirit of a donation' by an unnamed benefactor – a gift which places the cabin outside the market economy that Thoreau was so intent on escaping.[47] Like Thoreau, Ed will have to fix the cabin up to make it habitable, but he sees it as a potential place of retreat, 'a place for resting and walking and not doing much else'.[48] On hearing of the cabin, Tom's partner Donna and her mother wax ironically lyrical about the potential delights of living out in nature:

Donna	Such peace in the mountains!
Mom	Yes! And birds!
Ed	Singing all the time!
Donna	Such fun!
Mom	Lovely! Lovely![49]

Donna also makes it clear, however, that she does not want Ed to leave for the woods until he has completed the task he and Tom are engaged in – building a vast bookcase to store the 'fourteen hundred thousand' books she has accumulated. This unfinished structure, Shepard's stage directions note, '*stands from floor to ceiling*' against a white, upstage wall.[50] The irregular bursts of hammering, deriving from the men's construction attempts, creates a jarringly theatrical noise-scape that shatters any possibility of 'peace' for these characters. Yet, the dramatic irony is that the shelves are themselves made from wood – the trees outside brought inside. So too are the books that will line the shelves, which begin appearing onstage in teetering piles as Mom and Dad carry them in. The group's labours, Donna stresses, will not be at an end until the towering bookcase is 'waxed, polished, and smells like the great outdoors!'[51]

Ed's retreat to nature involves a converse form of domestication. He wants to live in the great outdoors, but to do so he must construct an indoors: 'I have to finish the cabin before it snows'; 'I haven't even built the chimney yet'.[52] Ed's first mention of snow occasions Donna's arrival with tins of white paint for the shelving, while Tom mocks Ed with talk of 'a raging blizzard' that will completely white out the woodland landscape. This neatly prefigures a later sequence of choreographed chaos in which Tom and Donna become a kind of interior blizzard: at odds over how to complete the shelving, they engage in a full-on paint fight: '*They charge and viciously paint each other with the brushes ... they are both covered with white paint*.[53] Thus, these humans mimic natural forces even as they try to insulate themselves against them.

Descriptions of a woodland landscape entirely submerged in snow dominate the closing, 'winter' chapters of Thoreau's *Walden*: 'When the snow lay deepest no wanderer ventured near my house for a week or fortnight at a time'.[54] That sense of utter isolation is extrapolated in *Fourteen Hundred Thousand* into a picture of human redundancy which is tantamount to death. Donna imagines any occupant of Ed's cabin becoming invisible, whited out, and the cabin itself simply continuing its 'natural' cycles unaided by human hand: 'Somehow I see it lost in the woods and nobody even living there. It turns on its own lights at night and then turns them off again in the morning. It even flushes its own toilet and builds its own fires and makes its little bed'.[55] Towards the end of the play, a further monologue imagines the cabin becoming deluged in a snowdrift of biblical proportions (akin, perhaps, to 'the Great Snow of 1717' alluded to by Thoreau). Speaking in unison, as if themselves absorbed into some greater force of nature that robs them of independent agency, Donna's Mom and Pop describe the snow 'getting thicker and thicker so the people went outside but it didn't get any better. It got thicker and thicker and covered all their trees. ... It got so bad that they had to climb a hill and watch from the top while their houses disappeared'.[56] The monologue keeps snowballing, gradually absorbing the entire cast of five with its relentless, unifying force, as they describe a crowd of people vanishing into the whiteness of the landscape without trace: 'They never got tired and they never got strong and they didn't feel a thing. And nobody knows how they ever got lost, how they ever got away'.[57]

Oneness with nature, as Camus indicates in his reference to trees and cats, also implies an erasure of individual consciousness, a kind of oblivion. Perhaps this is why even Thoreau himself returned to the society he had so forcefully critiqued: 'At present', he acknowledges in *Walden*'s opening paragraph, 'I am a sojourner in civilized life again'.[58] Human culture is, by definition, an attempt to create structural difference from nature, and in *Fourteen Hundred Thousand*, the building of the bookcase operates as a microcosm of civilization itself, by providing a forward purpose and linear chronology rather than the oblivion of immanence: 'It gives you something to project into the future', Donna notes of the men's

industry, 'as a kind of guidepost'.[59] Once complete, the bookcase –
with its books neatly ordered according to colour and size – will
provide a sense of cultural and aesthetic solidity. And yet, she notes,
it too will become redundant, forgotten: 'We just pass through the
room and take the whole shmear for granted'.[60] At that point, new
distractions will be needed to stem the slide into oblivion. 'Libraries
fascinate me to death,' Mom observes: 'Like ancient tapestry or
Chinese urns or butterfly collections'.[61] The detritus of civilization
keeps piling up, and the books appearing on stage, a papery mirror
for the woodland deluge: 'Anyone would think you were flooded
with books'.[62] Yet, the Sisyphean task of construction will never
be done, which is why Ed will never get out to his cabin. 'It's an
impossibility,' Tom observes: 'We'll be here forever'.[63]

Shepard's critique of the absurdity of Americans' simultaneous
attraction to, and repulsion from, nature is brilliantly encapsulated
in the closing section of the play. As the other actors systematically
erase the marks of their own presence – dismantling the set to leave
only a bare stage, while humming the tune of 'White Christmas' –
Mom and Pop read alternately from a book lifted from one of the
many piles. The narrative they recite tells of how humans have
always built cities 'more out of a state of frenzy' than any forward
planning, creating 'radial' structures whose ego-driven intensity
is focused at their urban heart: 'The farther one gets from this
center point the less one is aware of the excitement. As one moves
toward the country and more rural areas the excitement has all
but disappeared'.[64] And yet, Pop recites, the people in the cities still
miss the 'open green space' outside, and (as *Zoo Story* had also
reminded us) 'city parks are nothing more than tiny breathing
spaces or overly synthetic versions of the real thing and they also
make it tremendously difficult to forget the city (if that be their
function) for the simple fact that they were conceived in the midst
of horrendous skyscrapers'.[65]

The narration thus proposes a new, utopian solution. The radial
and vertical city is to be replaced with the *linear* city. This concept,
originally proposed by the nineteenth-century Spanish architect
Arturo Soria y Mata, and championed by Soviet planner Nikolai
Milyutin in the 1920s, is appropriated by Shepard as extravagantly
American: 'As an example the city would stretch in a line from the
tip of Maine to the tip of Florida [that is, down the entire Eastern
seaboard] and be no wider than a mile. ... This would allow any

citizen with the ability to use his or her legs to walk from the midst of the city into the midst of the country'.[66] Mom and Pop expound on the further advantages of this system – simple, rapid transit along the length of the linear city; cultural facilities evenly distributed at regular intervals; 'Employment opportunities would vastly increase'; 'Water shortage would be extinct'.[67] But just as it all begins to sound wonderful, we are reminded that the urge to keep building, keep growing, keep expanding, will never be satiated. Shepard describes 'cross-country linear cities' developing east to west, to complement the north-south axes, 'forming ten mile squares of country in between'.[68] The rural landscape becomes literally the garden in the machine, but it doesn't stop there. Next come 'Ocean cities and sky cities and cities underground', and the gardens keep getting smaller: 'Forming five mile squares in between. ... Forming two-mile squares in between./Cities enclosed in glass to see the sky./Forming one-mile squares./Cities in the sky to see the glass./Forming squares in between'.[69] Thus, the self-contradictory urge both to separate ourselves from nature (for the sake of shelter and 'excitement') and to be close to it (for the sake of 'peace') results in its systematic eradication. Failure to acknowledge our absurd condition (that we are 'out of harmony' with the natural world) results in a second order of apocalyptic absurdity.[70] While for Shepard, in the 1960s, this was still paranoid science fiction, in the globally warming twenty-first century, it is fast becoming our eco-reality.

Farm

Edward Albee's *The Goat; or, Who is Sylvia?*, which premiered early in the twenty-first century (2002), critiques American pastoralism with a ferocious new twist. Like *Fourteen Hundred Thousand*, this play hinges on a gargantuan utopian fantasy: the protagonist, Martin, is a prize-winning architect who has designed 'World City' – a 'twenty-seven billion dollar' Oz that will rise up amidst 'the wheatfields of Kansas, or whatever', and will strike a perfectly designed balance between nature and culture: 'Verdancy: flowers and green leaves against steel and stone'.[71] This urge to blend urban and rural living has prompted Martin himself (in an inversion of Shepard's linear city premise) to scout out a new country home for his family, which is 'no more than an hour or so from [the city]'.[72] Closeness; intimacy; what can possibly go wrong?

The Goat is structured in three scenes, and in the first two Martin is compelled to give similar accounts of a single, life-changing encounter – first to his friend Ross, and then (after Ross has spilled the beans) to his wife Stevie. In dramatic terms, the narrative repetition suggests a kind of traumatic return, but what Martin returns to is a vision of the rural as a bounteous cornucopia: 'The roadside stands, with corn and other stuff piled high, and baskets full of other things – beans and tomatoes and those great white peaches you only get late summer'.[73] This is farm country as Eden – 'the garden of the world'[74] – where human stewardship of nature is abundantly rewarded by divine approval. In Eden, however, there is always temptation. It was harvest time, Martin tells Stevie:

> fall, the leaves turning ... a regular bucolic. I stopped and got us things, vegetables and things ... and it was then that I saw her. And she was looking at me with ... with those eyes. ... And what I felt was ... it was unlike anything I'd ever felt before. It was so ... amazing. There she was.[75]

She is a goat, an ordinary farm animal with whom Martin has become so smitten that he is enjoying regular and – he claims – consensual sexual relations with her. (Queer ecology, indeed.) And note that it was the eyes that drew him in. In The Animal That Therefore I Am (2008), Jacques Derrida reflects at length on his human perception of an animal's gaze – so inherently other and unknowable that it becomes too easily anthropomorphized as either 'a benevolent or pitiless gaze, surprised or cognisant. The gaze of a seer, a visionary or extra-lucid blind one'.[76]Albee takes such romanticization, literalizes it as 'love at first sight', and so pushes the pastoral ideal of man finding 'unity' with nature into territory that is both farcical and terrible. Farcical because the whole scenario seems calculatedly ridiculous; terrible because the play also deftly succeeds in persuading the spectator of its underlying emotional truth. As Stevie notes of the moment Ross told her of Martin's infidelity:

> Some things are so awful you have to laugh – and then I listened to myself laughing, and I began to wonder why I was – laughing. ... I stopped laughing. I realised – probably in the way if you

suddenly fell off a building – 'oh shit, I've fallen off a building and I'm going to die; I'm going to go splat on the sidewalk'; like *that* – that it wasn't a joke at all; it was awful and absurd, but it wasn't a joke.[77]

The Goat collides the comic and tragic to extraordinary effect. As J. Ellen Gainor has pointed out, Albee's specific literary reference point is Shakespeare's *Two Gentlemen of Verona*, which 'Northrop Frye famously singled out ... as exemplifying the "green world" of romantic comedy'.[78] Martin's goat is christened Sylvia after Shakespeare's Silvia, 'both a specific character, representing generosity of spirit and faithful love, and a pastoral ideal, the "nymph" to Valentine's "swain"'.[79] Indeed, Stevie deftly paraphrases Shakespeare in her interrogation of her erring husband:

Stevie   Why do you call her Sylvia, by the way? Did she have a tag, or something? Or, was it more: 'Who is Sylvia,/ What is she/That all our Goats commend her ...'[80]

Martin   (*trying to be rational*) No, it just seemed right. Very good, by the way.

Stevie   Thank you.[81]

The fact that, in the midst of a scene of grinding marital anguish (see Figure 4), this couple can trade literary quips and compliment each other on their word-play (one of *The Goat*'s most insistent features) demonstrates a level of cultural artifice and self-consciousness that, far from being merely indulgent on Albee's part, is key to the play's absurdist critique of pastoralism. Set in Martin and Stevie's tastefully decorated home, filled with valuable ornaments and furniture that Stevie proceeds systematically to trash in her rage with Martin (with hilarious and shattering effect), *The Goat* emphasizes the yawning size of the gulf between rural idyll and sophisticated urbanity. 'God, I wish you were stupid,' Stevie remarks sadly at one point; 'Yes; I wish *you* were stupid too,' Martin responds.[82] Perhaps they imagine that simpler people (or animals?) would respond more directly and spontaneously to happenstance – much as Thoreau romanticizes the 'wild man' he sees in the woods: 'I love to see Nature carried out in him'.[83] But this couple cannot help but speak self-referentially, habitually querying each other's grammar and syntax ('Women in deep woe often mix their metaphors'), in a manner that seems

FIGURE 4 *Jonathan Pryce (Martin) and Kate Fahy (Stevie) in Edward Albee's* The Goat; or, Who is Sylvia? *directed by Anthony Page at the Almeida Theatre, London, 2004.* © *John Haynes.*

constantly to set them at a remove from the primal realities they are trying to confront.[84] When Martin at one point exhorts Stevie to 'be serious!' she responds bitingly: 'No! It's too serious for that'.[85]

Put simply, Albee's characters do not know how to talk about what has happened, because they have no reference points for it. Albee's concern here, articulated in the play's second subtitle, *Notes toward a definition of tragedy,* seems to be to evoke something of the ancient force of Greek tragedy – of cataclysmic fate being visited on the protagonists beyond any real choice or control of their own. (The Greek word *tragedy* literally translates as 'song of the goat'.) 'We prepare for ... things,' Stevie notes, 'and we think we can handle everything, whatever comes along', never realizing that

> something can happen that's outside the rules, that doesn't relate to The Way The Game Is Played. Death before you're ready to even think about it – that's part of the game. A stroke that leaves you sitting looking at an eggplant that the week before had been your husband – that's another. ... The fucking of animals! No, that's one thing you haven't thought about, one thing you've overlooked as a byway on the road of life.[86]

Martin, too, speaks of struggling to comprehend what has happened to him. He has been overtaken, he claims, by 'an ecstasy and a purity, and a ... love of a ... (*dogmatic*) un-i-mag-in-able kind'.[87] In an attempt at rationalizing the situation, he has been to visit an Alcoholics Anonymous-style meeting for bestiality addicts, only to discover that he cannot identify with the assembled pig, dog and goose lovers. They all feel guilt and shame for their peccadilloes, but for Martin, Sylvia represents inexplicable joy. He is off the cultural map entirely, staring rapturously into the abyss.

The *Goat* thus resonates strongly with Derrida's suggestion that 'the gaze called "animal" offers to my sight the abyssal limit of the human ... that is to say, the bordercrossing from which vantage man dares to announce himself to himself'.[88] Crossing that border means breaching cultural taboo, transgressing the boundaries by which we have separated what we deem 'human' (clean, rational, civilized) from what we deem 'animal' (dirty, instinctive, savage). Yet, crucially, as long as a breach of taboo remains unknown or uncomprehended, the sky does not fall. Indeed, Martin's life seems more (pastoral) comedy than tragedy at the play's outset. It takes the (mis)speaking and (mis)knowing of his liaison with Sylvia to bring about tragic consequences – to break what cannot be fixed. This is why, in the third and final scene, Martin bitterly berates Ross for breaking confidence and telling Stevie. 'I could have worked it out!' he insists of his goat-love, 'I could have stopped, and nobody would have known. [But] now nothing can *ever* be put back together. *Ever*!'[89] It is evident, however, that Ross spilled the beans precisely because he is the *most* taboo-bound of the play's characters. Although perfectly happy to admit his own everyday hypocrisies and sexual double standards, Ross is so appalled at Martin's confession that he renders his friend the *scapegoat* for all other breaches of social convention.

The Greek term *tragos apopompaios* means, literally, the goat that departs, or is sent away. The scapegoat is an object of ritualized repudiation: the impure or taboo is expelled from the social body (the inside) into the realm of wild or primitive (outside). When Martin protests to Stevie that 'it isn't about fucking', her retort is telling: 'Yes! It is about fucking! It is about you being an animal!'[90] Where *Zoo Story* had concluded with Jerry's invocation of animal commonality, *The Goat* reminds us sharply that conceptions of what is 'human' are always already predicated on a relegation of animal nature to an external realm beyond. Even so, social taboos are historically constituted and thus mutable: in the play's final scene, through confrontations between Ross, Martin and his son Billy, Albee teasingly juxtaposes bestiality with homosexuality (once taboo, now widely accepted) and paedophilia (demonized today, yet normal to Plato's Greeks). Times change, but taboo remains – as a structural necessity in order for the human being 'to call himself by the name that he believes he gives himself'.[91]

The Goat's central irony, then, is that if one were to take seriously the 'harmony with nature' to which the pastoral imagination has always aspired (or even if one were simply to allow 'human nature' free rein), one might also very quickly find oneself – as Billy puts it – 'beyond all the rules'.[92] But the human animal's absurd condition, as Camus surmised, is that cultural self-consciousness has forever separated us from our surroundings: even as we remain physically dependent on nature's bounty, we imagine ourselves elsewhere, and we need rules in order to police this self-imposed bordercrossing. Equally clear is that non-human nature will pay the price for this absurdity. In the play's closing image, Stevie returns to the decimated living room of the stage, dragging the bloodied corpse of a goat. 'Why are you surprised?' she asks the distraught Martin: 'What did you expect me to do?'[93]

Wilderness

As the scapegoat knows all too well, wilderness has, in western thought, traditionally been figured as the barren outside, east of Eden, into which repudiated things are cast. It is a peculiar quirk of American history, then, that somewhere around the mid-nineteenth century, wilderness became 'frequently likened to Eden itself'.[94] 'In Wildness', Thoreau famously declared, 'is the preservation of the World'.[95] In a nation whose mythically vast, open spaces were fast becoming colonized or privatized, it became necessary to preserve the notion of 'the wild frontier' via an imaginative extension of the pastoral tradition. With farmland becoming too cultivated, too *feminized*, it was only in 'beyondness' that the lone, questing (invariably masculine) individual could find union with nature.

As its title perhaps implies, Shepard's *Kicking a Dead Horse* (2007) engages with this mythos still more directly than his film

FIGURE 5 *Stephen Rea (Hobart Struther) in* Kicking a Dead Horse, *written and directed by Sam Shepard, and premièred at the Abbey Theatre, Dublin, 2007.* © *Ros Kavanagh.*

Silent Tongue (which concentrates its critical attention on the rape and dispossession of Native peoples). The play's lone protagonist is Hobart Struther, who – like Albee's Martin – is a successful, East Coast professional, with an apparently happy marriage. Hobart has cast *himself* out of civilization, however, in the hope of reconnecting with a deeper reality. The play is set on an unspecified patch of ground in the New Mexico wilderness (again – the bleak, flat prairie of *Silent Tongue*): Hobart and his horse have left truck and trailer miles behind, striking out in search of some inarticulable communion with the land. Yet the horse, having inadvertently inhaled a nosebag of oats, has keeled over dead, leaving Hobart in something of a quandary.

Commissioned by Dublin's Abbey Theatre, *Kicking a Dead Horse* is Shepard's most knowingly Beckettian play to date. It is both a confrontation with existential realities in an empty theatrical landscape, and a kind of music hall routine. A role written for Shepard's long-time collaborator, the Irish actor Stephen Rea, Hobart is a kind of sad clown figure, delivering a rambling, bleakly comic monologue as he prepares a grave for his dead horse, recounting 'all the shit that rolls through your numb skull as you shovel, one scoop at a time'.[96] Like Beckett's Hamm and Clov, Hobart is given to occasional meta-commentary on the progress of the play's action

('This is getting dire. This is getting dark and dire'[97]), and to staring out at an audience whose presence he simultaneously acknowledges and denies: 'You've spent a solid day digging; rambling on to imagined faceless souls'.[98]

The play's inherent meta-theatricality performs at least two key dramatic functions. First, Hobart's need to 'imagine' an audience for himself highlights again the binary structuring of consciousness in terms of self and other, identification and repudiation. Indeed, as the play progresses, Hobart resorts to arguing with himself, as if to keep himself awake and alert, through a kind of schizophrenic personality division:

> Snap out of it.
> What? Sorry.
> There's times I don't recognise you at all.
> Like when?[99]

Second, the play's meta-theatricality also serves to prevent any sense of unification in the representational apparatus: we are *both* in the wilderness *and* in the theatre. Indeed, the play's original production, directed by Shepard himself, persistently alerted the audience to the stage artifice through a deft choreography of sudden lighting shifts and abrupt sound effects, intricately paced with the rhythms of Hobart's 'routine'. Whenever he attempts, and fails, to move the dead horse, for example, the corpse falls back into place with the 'boom' of an amplified kettle drum.

Such strategies fracture the spectator's experience of dramatic fiction, and are particularly telling in this context: the wilderness *is* theatre. As Adam Sweeting and Thomas Crochunis have argued, there is an analogical relationship between traditional, realist theatre (with its unfractured representationality) and conventional representations of wilderness, in which landscapes are treated as if they are completely unaffected by the observing human presence. Just as the proscenium arch separates stage and auditorium, they suggest, so 'wilderness zones, by definition, are bureaucratically distinguished from the land from which they have been carved. [Our] experiences of both efface the cultural assumptions and structures that shape our performances, encouraging audiences or wilderness visitors to observe events as though they simply unfold on their own'.[100] Wilderness zones, in short, are the rock garden in the machine.

This line of argument was most controversially advanced by William Cronon in his book *Uncommon Ground* (1996). The modern concept of wilderness, he asserted, is an artifice of Judeo-Christian American culture, 'the natural, unfallen antithesis of an unnatural civilization that has lost its soul. It is a place of freedom in which we can recover our true selves. ... Most of all, it is the ultimate landscape of authenticity'.[101] Shepard's Hobart invokes precisely this idea in his repeated, capitalized claim that 'AUTHENTICITY' is what he has come out here looking for: 'The sense of being inside my own skin. That's what I missed'.[102] Surveying the wreckage of his ruggedly individualistic quest, however, Hobart bitterly recriminates himself for this 'haunted, ghostly idea' of 'weighing the true against the false'.[103] What was he even thinking? 'I'd get out here, miles from nowhere, and somehow feel miraculously at peace? One with the wilderness? ... After a whole lifetime of being fractured, busted up, I'd suddenly become whole? The imagination is a terrible thing'.[104] Hobart feels, acutely, Camus's sense of the foreignness of matter, the intensity with which 'nature or a landscape can negate us'. The stage set has fallen away and he is now experiencing the prairie *as* prairie, rather than as myth: 'Maybe all it ever is is blinded by the dreaming of what it might become'.[105]

Attempting to recall a lost youth in which he felt more at peace with himself, Hobart speaks of 'the days of AUTHENTICITY – when I rode for the brand, as they say: mending fences, doctoring calves, culling cows'.[106] But this invocation of the traditional cowboy lifestyle, whether real or imagined on Hobart's part, tellingly emphasizes the intrusion of market forces into wild places – branding, parcelling land, slaughtering for meat product. Considered in context, the myth of 'The "Wild Wild West"' is, Hobart notes, 'sentimental claptrap', which functions to facilitate another form of marketization ('*nature as commodity*', Cronon calls it).[107] He has come west equipped with top-of-the-range leisure equipment, including a designer cowboy hat: 'Brand new Resistol. Quadruple X Beaver'.[108] But as Shepard's stage directions state at the outset, '*he should look more like an urban businessman who has suddenly decided to rough it*'.[109] 'When the Sierra Club argues for more "'wilderness"', Greg Garrard observes dryly, 'they are in practice representing the interests of wealthy suburbanites rather than rural working people'.[110]

Hobart recalls that his transition from cowboy to businessman was facilitated by an eye for lost art treasures: 'These masterful western murals nobody could recognise any more through the piled-up years of grime, tobacco juice and bar-room brawl blood'.[111] Buying such forgotten works for a song from their owners, and then selling them at enormous profit has turned him into a wealthy art dealer, but his story epitomizes in microcosm the *extraction* of resources from the western landscape – a process indulged in by everyone from museum curators to oil men: 'The history of it. The dinosaur. Bones. Ancient aching bones. The fossil fuels'.[112] So domesticated has the west become that Hobart – as if personifying the nation itself – finally wonders how it is that he is helpless before the elements, facing his own extinction:

> I do not understand why I'm having so much trouble taming the Wild. I've done this already. Haven't I already been through this? We closed the frontier in 1890-something, didn't we? Didn't we already accomplish that? The Iron Horse – coast to coast. Blasted all the buffalo out of there. An ocean of bones from sea to shining sea. Chased the heathen Redman down to Florida. Trails of tears. Paid the Niggers off in mules and rich black dirt. ... Sucked these hills barren of gold. Ripped the top soil as far as the eye can see. Dammed up all the rivers and flooded the valleys for recreational purposes. Run off the small farmers. Destroyed education. Turned our children into criminals. Demolished art. Invaded sovereign nations. What else can we possibly do?[113]

The satiric tone of this speech does not disguise the seriousness of Shepard's concerns. The ever-extending linear city in *Fourteen Hundred Thousand* is here re-figured in more historically apposite terms: the American imperialist quest to possess and control territory, in the name of 'Manifest Destiny', has enslaved non-white peoples, despoiled the environment and even legitimated the conquest of the oil-rich Middle East. None of this means anything, however, in the face of mortality itself – the *ne plus ultra* of that which cannot be 'tamed'. Stranded in the middle of the lone prairie with nothing but a dead horse for company, Hobart finds himself radically humbled, no more vital than inanimate materials. 'What are we going to do?' he asks his dead steed: 'Huh? Just lay out here and get rained on like a couple of rocks?'[114] As if mocked by the theatrical apparatus, he finds himself beset by a storm of thunder and lightning effects – forced to take shelter in the lee of the horse.

In theory, of course, Hobart does have the choice to leave the stage – to strike out on foot across the prairie while he still has some energy and supplies to attempt it. As if restaging *Antigone* in miniature, Hobart debates with himself whether to simply leave the horse unburied, as carrion. 'He deserves better than that,' he decides, and yet the corpse stiffly refuses to be coaxed into the grave Hobart has dug for it, repeatedly slamming back to Earth on the wrong side of the hole: 'Why doesn't this fucking horse want to go down in the hole!'[115] The horse, it is worth adding, is stubbornly, materially real, 'vibrant matter' with kettle-drum resonance. It should, Shepard's stage directions stress, '*be as realistic as possible, with no attempt to stylise or cartoon him in any way. In fact, it should actually be a dead horse*'.[116] Hobart shouts and swears at this massive object; he wrestles with it, drags and (as the title insists) kicks it, but it will not oblige him. Still, Hobart does not desert this Sisyphean task of burial, and gradually – like the absurd hero discussed by Camus – Hobart comes to accept the absurdity of his fate: that in burying the horse he is also burying himself. Together, he concludes, they at least offer each other 'Company – some – warmth'; 'If I was to jump down in there with you, would you be a little more co-operative? ... Would you maybe be less lonely?'[117]

There are echoes, perhaps, in this queer moment of inter-species togetherness, of Albee's Jerry – seeking commonality with anyone or anything who will listen. Unlike Jerry, however, Hobart makes no attempt to cry out to an absent creator: 'I don't think I can think of God'.[118] Instead, at the last, he calls only on the fragmentary immanence of the elements ('a bright – shining – sunny – day') and the intransigent materiality of his companion.[119] An absurd parody of the classic western hero, Hobart and his horse are, finally, bound together like Camus's Sisyphus and his boulder: 'His fate belongs to him. His rock is his thing. ... Each atom of that stone, each mineral flake of that night-filled mountain, in itself forms a world. The struggle itself towards the heights is enough to fill a man's heart. One must imagine Sisyphus happy'.[120]

Finally, also (and notwithstanding Esslin), one must imagine the Absurd and the American in a warmly grave embrace. 'We need', William Cronon writes,

> to embrace the full continuum of a natural landscape that is also cultural, in which the city, the suburb, the pastoral, and the wild each has its proper place, which we permit ourselves to celebrate without needlessly denigrating the others. We need to honor the Other within and the Other next door ... and to discover a common middle ground in which all these things, from the city to the wilderness, can somehow be encompassed in the word 'home'.[121]

Works cited

Adorno, Theodor, *Negative Dialectics*, trans. E. B. Ashton. New York: Continuum, 1973.

Albee, Edward, *The American Dream and The Zoo Story*. New York: Signet, 1961.

Albee, Edward, *The Goat; or, Who is Sylvia?*. London: Methuen, 2004.

Bennett, Jane, *Vibrant Matter: A Political Ecology of Things*. Durham, NC and London: Duke University Press, 2010.

Camus, Albert, *The Myth of Sisyphus*, trans. J. O'Brien. New York: Random House, 1955 [1942].

Camus, Albert, *The Outsider*, trans. S. Smith. London: Penguin, 2013 [1942].

Cohn, Ruby, *From Desire to Godot: Pocket Theater of Postwar Paris*. London: Calder, 1998.

Cronon, William (ed.), *Uncommon Ground: Rethinking The Human Place in Nature*. London: Norton, 1996.

Derrida, Jacques, *The Animal That Therefore I Am*, trans. D. Wills. New York: Fordham University Press, 2008 [2006].

Esslin, Martin, *The Theatre of the Absurd*, 2nd revised and enlarged edn. Harmondsworth: Penguin, 1968.

Gainor, J. Ellen, 'Albee's *The Goat*: Rethinking Tragedy for the 21st Century', in Stephen Bottoms (ed.), *The Cambridge Companion to Edward Albee*. Cambridge: Cambridge University Press, 2005, pp. 199–216.

Garrard, Greg, *Ecocriticism*. London and New York: Routledge, 2004.

Kolin, Philip C., 'Albee's early one-act plays: "A New American Playwright from whom Much is to be Expected"', in Stephen

Bottoms (ed.), *The Cambridge Companion to Edward Albee*. Cambridge: Cambridge University Press, 2005, pp. 16–38.

Marx, Leo, *The Machine in the Garden: Technology and the Pastoral Ideal in America*. New York: Oxford University Press, 1964.

Morton, Timothy, 'Queer Ecology', *PMLA*, vol. 125, no. 2 (2010), pp. 273–82.

Shepard, Sam, *States of Shock, Far North, Silent Tongue: A Play and Two Screenplays*. New York: Vintage, 1993.

Shepard, Sam, *Fifteen One-Act Plays*. New York: Vintage, 2002.

Shepard, Sam, *Kicking a Dead Horse*. London: Faber and Faber, 2007.

Smith, Henry Nash, *Virgin Land: The American West as Symbol and Myth*. Cambridge, MA: Harvard University Press, 1974.

Sweeting, Adam and Thomas C. Crochunis, 'Performing the Wild: Rethinking Wilderness and Theater Spaces', in K. Armbruster and K. R. Wallace (eds), *Beyond Nature Writing: Expanding the Boundaries of Ecocriticism*. London: University Press of Virginia, 2001, pp. 325–40.

Thoreau, Henry David, *Walden; or, Life in the Woods*. Mineola, NY: Dover, 1995.

3

Mutant Bodies: The Absurd in Eastern European Experience

Ralph Yarrow

Introduction

Martin Esslin's *The Theatre of the Absurd* (1961) famously describes the Absurd in terms of 'metaphysical anguish' and despair – in his reading, the world seems pointless, all action futile.[1] However, playwrights frequently use it somewhat differently to signal a protest against the confinement, mutilation, restriction, amputation and truncation of bodies, lives, organic forms, spaces and modes of relationship by closed 'systems' doctrines, definitions. The Absurd is a way of materializing dissonance with logocentricity and systematization, a dissonance which bursts out in speaking shapes. It blows open, explodes, excoriates, exfoliates. It is an energy, a refusal to submit. It foregrounds that which sticks out, is a remainder, can't be tidied away, doesn't add up. Chaplin's and Tati's (later John Cleese's) walks. Too many corpses to be covered up. Too many chairs to fit in. In this respect the Absurd may be seen as ecological; not because it offers a nostalgia for the pastoral, but because it embraces and operates, if slightly less ironically, Thomas Mann's implication in his 1924 novel *The Magic Mountain* that life is a disease of matter,[2] and does so by means of processes which celebrate 'multiplicities, disparate causalities, and unintentional creations of meaning', as Isabelle Stengers puts it in her 2010 text *Cosmopolitics I*.[3]

The Absurd reconfigures the relationship of inside and outside. I become the violence which is being vested on the world (a rhinoceros, a bug, an empty space haunted by the voices of the dead). A being whose crushed sensitivity sprouts as antennae, vulnerable legs and underbelly, beneath the ludicrous umbrella of a carapace; others who carry their atrophied childhood on their backs, signing as monsters the violence enacted upon them. In absurdist theatre, closed or protective structures and systems (including rooms and cities) reveal the deadliness at the heart of bourgeois conformity and comfort. They become places and modes haunted by a sense of menace. The closed system is not so much a place of security as an ineffectual and increasingly desperate attempt to preserve it at all costs – 'an ecology of bad ideas', as Félix Guattari (citing Gregory Bateson) might say.[4]

The situation is such that the Absurd is the only proper way to articulate it, that is to say improperly and disarticulately. Distortion and damage is effected on bodies, language, connectivities and conjunctions; it is inscribed on, in and through them. These bodies speak their awryness, they shriek their wrack, they stagger their uncouth dance of death, speaking for that which is cut off, squeezed out, disallowed. Their gait is awkward, ungainly, staccato, their trajectory tangential, their voices squeaky; they are a kind of luxury imbalance.

Such are the modes of their existence and so the bodies through which it emerges must inhabit this long scream. A theatre in which this occurs must also be a place of contradiction, of refusal, or disarticulation. It is another way of knowing: visceral, fractured, puzzling to the residual habit of logic, open to the affirmative disruptions of chaos.

Surd is that which adds up. Ab, as a Germanic prefix, indicates something which is 'off', 'to one side' ('Abort', the old word for toilet, offers an excruciating euphemism, somewhere that is a sort of unmentionable location). That which is Absurd adds up tangentially, differentially, inexactly. All its component parts contribute to and articulate this disharmony, this not-fitting-together.

But not fitting into a precast mould is also a sign of a different kind of materiality, which recognizes and rejoices in the dysfunctional, the digressive, the 'alienatory', the strangeness of making: Tadeusz Rózewicz's Hero in *The Card Index* (1960) and Witold

Gombrowicz's Ivona in *Princess Ivona* (1938) opt out of action and speech and scandalize others who expect 'proper' behaviour (Elders, court hierarchies); their non-action and not-speaking are, however, actions, in director Max Stafford-Clark's sense, and they disrupt the machine of conformist behaviour.[5] Kantor's bio-object bodies in *Dead Class* (1975), for instance, refuse to discard or suppress the traumas, guilt and losses of their past, displaying them as mutely and grotesquely ineradicable.

These characters, these bodies, signal not just a refusal of inclusion (in the given), but more actively a form of reincorporation, of re-inclusion, of admitting not only that which is elegant and polite but also – or more urgently – that which is neither, not so much the golden mean as the blue mean[y]; what Timothy Morton calls 'dark ecology', perhaps, in recognition of the ambiguity of all environmental process, as opposed to the externalized neatness of more conventional concepts like 'nature'.[6] Evolution may operate also, or more dynamically, through excrescence. And so, writing about this may be not so much the usual academic exegesis of clarification and explication, as a kind of paradoxicalization or difficultation. This has resonances with what Baz Kershaw in *Theatre and Ecology: Environments and Performance Events* (2007) terms 'a paradoxology of performance', the idea that dissonance, chaos or 'negative feedback' is vital to the functioning of any healthy ecosystem, even writing.[7]

In this essay I want to think about how the paradoxical ecology of the Absurd is embodied in Polish Theatre in the twentieth century (though Poland, as Jarry said, is also anywhere), and also to rehistoricize and relocate the Polish experience to claim its generic function as iconic of an essentially ecological mode of operation. Absurdity was part of Polish experience, as I point out below, over a much more extensive period than that in which Esslin's category of the Theatre of the Absurd is located.[8] Thus the plays which I discuss here, by Witold Gombrowicz, Tadeusz Kantor, Tadeusz Rózewicz and Stanisław Ignacy Witkiewicz (Witkacy), overlap this period, but are not contained by it. I will explore them as performing a problematic and dynamic ecology, adding to the mix of plays, Theatre de Complicite's disruptively inventive *The Street of Crocodiles* (1992), a text adapted from the fragmented and explosive narratives of Bruno Schulz (killed by a Gestapo officer in 1942).

I am taking it as axiomatic that the Absurd is a reaction: to the closure and enclosure of closed ecosystems, to the inability to get out of them – including the autonomic system that condemns us all to death – and to the stultification, mental, physical and emotional, which this situation causes. There are, of course, also systems of habit, as Beckett and Ionesco make clear, which work similarly and perhaps even more perniciously.

Thus the Absurd, as I define it here, is also a performance – an ecological response to the oppression exercised by these systems and, particularly in the examples I am going to explore, systems of political and social control which determine the mobility or rather lack of mobility of the oppressed, and deny them the access to, or the right of, thinking, feeling and behaving in ways other than those prescribed. In the case of Eastern Europe and especially Poland in the early part of the twentieth century, this nexus of control is directly experienced in terms of incarceration or construction by an 'external' system, which operates physically through denial or restriction of living space, through prohibition of relational activities (personal or political, as under apartheid in South Africa) and compulsion or control of the forms of motion or position that bodies and persons could adopt. It may be interpreted more generically as a manipulation of identity, role, status – towards the mechanized, the oppressed, the subaltern. But it is felt viscerally, directly, somatically in the body, as a twisting into shapes or a tying into knots, as a hugging of walls and a fear of open spaces, as a sound-track (internalized or external) of orders and instructions in another language, of alien noise, of the marching of feet across an inner and outer landscape (as in *The Street of Crocodiles*).

Feeling is squeezed into these protective or resistant modes, and bodies are the sites where it occurs. So, it is with the expressive articulation of these bodies that I am concerned, for they perform, voluntarily or involuntarily, the configurations into which they have been twisted, in order to allow the screams to be articulated. Yet, in so doing they also speak an investment in the articulateness of forms, in the potential of those energies to be what they are and, in so doing, to reclaim an ecology which is apparently prohibited. They disclose themselves too as the storehouse and activation of the memories of a culture, somewhere between being written off or consigned to dust and becoming an agent of transformation and magic.

Poland

From 1742 until 1989, Poland (never exactly the same geographical space) was partitioned, reconfigured, its territory, status, political systems, even its language, determined by others: most noticeably in the twentieth century by Nazi Germany and Soviet Russia. In this era, it is also not merely the territory of Warsaw, Auschwitz and Treblinka, but also of an intense and enduring ambivalence – as in many occupied countries – about its own complicity. Concepts such as 'The Nation' and 'The People' become mere slogans, and even the attempt to retain or regain a Polish identity is treated as suspicious. All systems of power and forms of discourse appear hollow: mere variations of style. Tadeusz Kantor's 'Theatre of Death' is only one example of the way in which the presence of death and dying is recognized not merely as ubiquitous but also as ambiguous. In Witkacy's *The Water Hen* (1921), the eponymous heroine is shot at her own request several times over, and each time it signals something different: a melodramatic gesture, a statement of boredom or despair, an incitement to her lover to take responsibility for his life, a resurrection, a proclamation. Kantor's *Dead Class* (1975), operating under the shadow of the Charlady Death figure of the Putzfrau, her school-cleaner's broom turned into a scythe, both recalls and laments this long process of dying as a pedagogy, but also thereby suggests, Kafka-like, that this stumbling and painful celebration may also exist as the only impossible way out of the thrall.[9] The Priest in *Wielopole/Wielopole* (1981) is dead (as a mannequin) and dying (as actor), expressing both the dead weight of the past and the horrors of many periods of Polish experience. Death and dying occur in these works as a remarkable diversity of powerful and distorted shapes – the extremes of life pulled into speaking and symbolic form.

Polish twentieth-century theatre emerges, in the plays I discuss and in others like Grotowski's *Apocalypsis cum Figuris* (1969), Rózewicz's *The Trap* (1982), Kantor's *Lovelies and Dowdies* (1974) and the work of companies like Gardzienice and Teatr Osnia Dnia, as an often extraordinarily physically intense and bizarre response to this situation. This is not a theatre which generalizes, but one which materializes the situation as specifics of bodies and processes, always particular, 'peculiar' to the moment, the place, the events, the discourses. Grotowski's 'laboratory' work and the locus and operation of Gardzienice, for instance, have also been fully discussed elsewhere as examples of the 'artistic retreat' to nature, and to that extent they represent the attempt to explore and invest in a kind of seamlessness between performer and environment, a re-immersion in the forces of the natural world, which was largely disrupted by preceding history.[10] Acknowledging this, I am here more concerned with the quality of the ambivalent and bizarre production of 'nature' that emerges in many plays across a fairly large historical period, and to ask if, in spite of immediate appearance to the contrary, some kinds of strange but important ecological activity are in process. This activity, in the Poland of the twentieth century, is primarily directed towards what Carl Lavery calls 'radical immanence': an eccentric and disruptive production, an expressive and difficult articulation of that which has been denied life, and a mnemonics, a rematerialization and immersion in space, time and being.[11]

Experiencing this Absurd is, in the first instance, akin to living in a world where any clear sense of who, where, what and why one can be is regularly problematized or dismantled. George Hyde notes the Polish capacity to negotiate this continual revision of orientation, acquired from long experience and thus an indication of the way in which living with unpredictability generates the capacity to operate within and with it: even the Communist slogans in the street (in 1976) 'become entirely metaphorical, a succession of "as if" propositions about the deceptiveness of reality'.[12]

The Absurd here materializes dissonance with the logos, the logocentric, the logic of systematization. Bodies grow, swell, shrink, change; lose bits (Beckett) or add bits (Kantor); become animal (Ionesco); go floppy (Gombrowicz); get cooked (Różewicz). The dignity of known contours, including those of 'the theatre' in a variety of senses, erodes, explodes, implodes. 'Self' is extruded, no longer contained by previously assumed boundaries.

There are other kinds of bodies in operation, too: those of the audience and the performers, and that of the space in which performance is (perhaps) enclosed, all of which may both protect contours and also disclose their vulnerability, providing a kind of porosity which redraws boundaries between inside and outside, between what can be contained and what spills over or invades. Schulz explains: 'There is no such thing as a dead object, a hard-edged object, an object with strict limits. Everything flows beyond its boundaries, as if trying to break free of them at the earliest opportunity'.[13] Kantor notes: 'I keep coming back to the problem of the imperative need to destroy this artistic space, to exit from the reservation labelled "art"'.[14] This liminality – or what Stengers calls 'symbiosis' – signals a two-way relationship of self/the human and 'nature', in which 'bodies' start to break out of the corrals, to invade each other.[15]

What, too, is the 'landscape' of the Polish twentieth-century plays I want to explore? There isn't much countryside in Polish absurdist work, any more than in, say, Ionesco, Pinter or Beckett. Where there is, it either takes the form of an uncritical – and thus ironized – nostalgia for youth, for a kind of mental and emotional 'greenness' (explored especially by Gombrowicz in his novels *Ferdydurke* (1937) and *Pornografia* (1960)) which keeps the populace in a state of infantilism; or it is implied as a form of authenticity only by its absence. Landscape has become aestheticized and distanced; it is an imaginary, assimilated to the 'good form' and self-consciously arty elitist discourse of superior intellectuals (Gombrowicz in *Princess Ivona* as well as the aforementioned novels, Witkacy in *The Water Hen*). In Poland, as Timothy Morton puts it, 'the aesthetic has become commodified, and the commodity has become aestheticized'.[16] It is another country, seemingly lost (like Clov's report in *Endgame* (1956), 'there's no more nature'), or simply a kind of pastoral decorative art, its placidity and irrelevance only occasionally disrupted by excessively material or functional objects.[17] Frederick in *Pornografia* is outraged to find the scene of rural idyllic life he is trying to compose rudely disrupted by the messy and inelegant physicality of 'the barrel!'[18] The tools of actual work are a rude reminder that other, less elegant and comfortable kinds of process might be involved in any direct encounter with the natural world.

Everywhere you look in the Polish Theatre of the Absurd, 'nature' is edited out as irrelevant or outdated or a naïve concept or perhaps an unwanted violence. That is to say, the potentials it represents (and in saying 'nature' I don't construct it as separate from but as contiguous to or indivisible from the human and social) are recorded in this work as somehow relegated to elsewhere in time and space. 'Greenness', in this context, identifies and satirizes a dangerous ecology, an infantilization which acts as an oppression, like Nazi versions of the 'natural'. Thus the job of the Absurd here may precisely be to present the 'natural' as strange, *un*natural bodies, growths, energies. The unnaturalness is materialized, embodied. Because to do so is to question the hegemonic violence that maintains a certain model – in the case of Poland, one in which any potentially disruptive elements are distanced or neutralized. So the Absurd brings them nearer and activates them. In so being they speak for a 'nature' which has not been naturalized, a 'nature' which is also eccentric, unpredictable, which moves not in gently successive narrative sequence but may bubble out in bursts and boils, in quantum leaps of non-linear bypass/trespass, as an alternative to the prescribed flow of the 'fittest evolutionary mechanism', where 'fittest' equals that which fits into the model. There is another 'nature' within us and without. There may be a key to this in Mickiewicz's nineteenth-century play *Forefathers' Eve* (1823–32), which includes a Strindbergian solsticial feast, evoking an anarchic, dangerous energy via 'a kind of vibrant silence inhabited by the dead', and reflecting the inability of a 'partitioned, oppressed and divided nation' to speak out differently.[19] The ways in which this is made available to audiences are through 'difficultation', making things uncomfortable, redrawing the contours and unsettling the expectations of sound and silence, of spaces and the relationships they posit and compose. It is a case, then, as Timothy Morton proposes, of 'finding ways to stick around with the sticky mess that we are in and that we are, making thinking dirtier, identifying with ugliness, practicing [sic] "hauntology" (Derrida's phrase) rather than ontology'.[20] This is a rather different and darker kind of 'greenness' than the essentially conservationist logic satirized by Gombrowicz.

Kantor

Kantor's *Wielopole/Wielopole* (1981), in spite of recomposing the memories of a rural village, takes place in a 'room', a framework for the emergence of part-real and part-imagined versions of people from the past. The retracing of that past does not overtly draw on much in the way of embeddedness of their lives in the rural. Kantor's animation and actualization of framed entities, signalled in the title, posits two versions of a remembered/real locus. 'Poland', says George Hyde, is both '"real" and "represented"',[21] and the continuous disruption and unsettling of actions, like the fumbling attempts to get things – doors, windows, instruments – to work, likewise challenges any continuity of feeling, speaking and doing.

Territory here is *meaning*, the imagined space of an act of recollection, signalling both the loss and fragmentation and the capacity to reconstitute it, albeit differently, awkwardly, hesitantly, through gaps. It's an attempt to relocate people, relationships, utterances, things. They are re-imagined in a room, which is the whole time and space of their lives, so now the stages and events of those lives crowd upon each other – they lie next to or on top of each other in the same (rotating, machine-like) bed, they move around each other, through each other in the room and the large wardrobe opening to both back and front, but their interaction is neither coherent nor complete. The room itself is not a single, coherent, comfortable or secure place, but a locus of invasive and disturbing otherness; memory is not something which confirms, but something which interrupts, disrupts and unsettles. The composer (Kantor, the artist) doesn't know if their lives were 'really' like this. The characters '"hired" ... sinister, mediocre and suspect creatures' are evoked by a process which is 'suspect and none too clean'.[22] In the work, the discrete moments reconstruct themselves, stacked upon each other, as they are performed by memory, itself a hazardous and mendacious operation. Bodies and words and moves and objects interfere with each other, across resistances, blanks, implausibilities. The past is another country, but there is no security as to its status. Family life is disrupted by war, invaded by a Platoon, which performs a rape and is represented doubly, like the Priest, by live actors and dummies; each protagonist 'tries to hold on to his vision of a common family room'.[23] But this and the Uncles' attempts at reconstruction are largely unsuccessful. So is the notion of country or countryside, and Wielopole itself is both geographically 'hidden in its depression' and 'forgotten by history'.[24] What there is for sure is the reconstructive process, not the content. So the whole piece emanates not just this impossibility of recapturing any kind of arcadia, of *Heimat*, of secure origin, but also the resolute difficulty of producing a mimetic equivalent of how it is/was. It is a kind of chaos theory in action, proceeding by indirection and interruption to chart a different but tactilely recognizable kind of remembering, as its audience, like that of a Beckettian play, has to experience the nature of pause and fragment and effort.[25] This is a paradoxical and complex mode of representation which functions to deconstruct the sense in which 'nature has become a transcendental principle'.[26]

As Milija Gluhovic points out, the 'mnemotechnics' of the play do not operate a cathartic reordering of fragments into a whole, but a 'repetitive and obsessive' procedure, a 'way of inducing anxiety'.[27] Consequently, 'anamnesic activity does not lead to a presence grasped on stage' or recreate an 'Edenic microcosm'[28]; rather, it takes the form of continual disruption, problematic collage, juxtaposition of frames, styles, genres. Traumatic memory 'can operate in different registers of truth at the same time'.[29] This kind of history cannot be possessed simplistically, but it can perhaps be re-collected by the kind of juxtaposition of register mooted above. For Jean-François Lyotard, this (entropic) process is a characteristic of *oikeion* (belonging): not memory which we could 'describe ... in terms of function', but more precisely dysfunctional.[30] In Lyotard's understanding of *oikos* (and ecology), home is not homely, nor exclusively a place of safety, but, rather, the unknown, the uncanny/*unheimlich*, from which we come and with which, in spite of our attempts to circumscribe and delimit ourselves and our world, we are continually and inescapably contiguous.[31] Thus, memory here is really *anamnesis*, in which the conventional self and its function as a 'filter or ... screen preserving our quietness' are also disturbed.[32] Belonging (as in Lyotard's example of the dog) is actually a kind of substratum of feeling integrated with what we are not. What is being tracked is experience on the edges of consciousness, partly suppressed, partly emerging haphazardly or erratically.[33] A plural, paradoxical or conflictual aesthetic is the appropriate vehicle for its encounter, instigating a kind of ecological 'field awareness' rather than a sequential progress or exegesis. Such a mode registers differently, more 'holistically' perhaps. It edits out less, is more active as a process of immersion, apprehension and relation, makes less distinction between different orders, and allows the uncomfortable and the disruptive a place within the act of composition. This is an eco-aesthetics of open systems, an ecologic that allows for what Stengers terms disparity and dissensus to come into play: 'The "ecological perspective" invites us not to mistake a consensus situation, where the population of our practices finds itself subjected to criteria that transcend their diversity in the name of shared intent, a superior good, for an ideal peace. Ecology doesn't provide any examples of such submission'.[34]

Rózewicz

Rózewicz's *The Witnesses* (1963) consists of two brief texts, which laconically present a mode of uninvolved observation of scenarios where neither life nor death incites any participation or concern, except on a very banal level – characters merely move (go, come) or don't move, usually for no apparent reason. They are bizarre, non-action pieces in which:

i) Outside a kitten is drowned, buried and trampled, in a conventionally pretty postcard landscape (pool, sand) by a nasty little boy, *watched* by a nice little girl (who does nothing), while a married couple also *observe* from their window above, while discussing in an unemotional and tepid kind of way the imminent arrival of Mummy, who has announced that she will be moving in. They will need to divide a room and move the furniture, they say. He must buy a chicken to make broth. She doesn't seem likely to go out.

ii) Two men sit in a kind of inside/outside location, facing opposite ways, and converse desultorily about being there, going away. One of them does go away, for a bit, while the other 'confesses' his not very interesting life, and intermittently describes a dog which progressively drowns in its own shit and decays. He *watches* it, very close to his chair. This seems to suggest a long expanse of time, though there are no other indicators of action or movement.

Not much happens, but there is a clear absence of emotional or physical communication between humans and animals. It seems as though life is so banal (after the war, in comparatively easy but unexciting circumstances) that there is only boredom or death or indifference or inability to react, to feel, to express any particular concern or care. Animals are killed, children are vicious, adults are indifferent. We are in a kind of proto-Sarah Kane country, without even the flicker of disgust. What Rózewicz makes available to the audience, as they are required to experience *themselves* as witnesses, is the recognition, as perhaps with Kane, of the degree to which we have become desensitized, detached, without any sense of our co-substantiality with the world of animals or others.

In Rózewicz's *The Card Index* (1960), the Hero is not a singularity but a kind of succession – he is addressed by a succession of different names by different characters who pass through his space; he is as it were a stack of randomly shuffled cards, a sequence of inadequacies (as good child, student, lover, businessman, etc.) whose life is and has been a series of events in which he has been less than an agent and which do not add up to a coherent or convincing story. In spite of the Elders' remonstrances, warnings, encouragements and laments, he never makes anything of himself. People pass through his room, reconfiguring it for their own purposes (as a café, an office and so on), measuring it, attempting unsuccessfully to fit it and him into their own stories and worlds. 'He' is in one sense Poland, invaded and reconfigured over the ages, its language and laws imposed by others.

Apples, girls, commercial possibilities never quite deliver. A German girl brings an apple, leaves it behind; the possibility of Eden is, however, blotted out by a concentration camp loudspeaker blaring insults.[35] There are few, if any, ecological or environmental references; those that are there suggest unfulfilled promises or worse: forests are where people 'hunted each other'.[36] In this world there is not much 'nature', and natural references point only to its absence. It is a world in which expectations of conformity and disapproval of anything seen as aberrant, devious or rebellious are voiced by Elders, parents and others disappointed that the Hero does not fit the mould; and further exemplification of this mode is manifested by a man who behaves as a dog (crawls, begs). So all forms of self-generated, spontaneous, non-conformist behaviour are seen as shocking:

> **Father** 'He's playing a nasty game under those bedclothes, I'm sure of it. All by himself'.[37]

The shock is not only confirmed but exponentially magnified and relocated by events and admissions from the Hero's position – there are not only suspect hands but also a woman under the bedclothes (though she too is an agent of conformity, encouraging him to prepare himself for a business meeting). He 'admits' to poisoning Granny and 'planning to remove Dad',[38] contradicting the Elders' idealistic vision that he might become a heroic figure from accepted romantic/nationalistic legend 'cutting off Hydra's head' and 'gathering laurels in Heaven'.[39]

What is expected is the suppression of the 'natural', its replacement by ideological stereotype and its relegation to a symbolic nostalgia. Thus the 'natural' or self-generative life of Poland and its people has been turned into a space inhabited by successive strands of manipulation. It is a world in which life is squeezed out or compressed into corners, both with expectations of conformity (your country is just another café) and with the immanence of threat and oppression. In one scene, the Chorus of Elders function as teachers who expect and/or praise the mindless regurgitation of historical facts as the correct way to acquire a school-leaving certificate; in a reinforcement of this deadly banality, they begin towards the end of the play to fire out onomatopeically linked words, rather like the Smiths and Martins in Ionesco's *The Bald Prima Donna* (1948). The same attitude emanates from the Elders' threatening rendering of 'Hushabye baby',[40] and their suspicion of hidden meanings in the Hero's talk of flies in the beer; and the sense of menace is intensified by references to (red and black) stains.[41] The effects on the Hero are evident: 'There were so many different things in me and now there is nothing'.[42]

However, what also occurs is the frequent, but usually unexpected and illogical, eruption in and from this space of occurrences and phenomena, which materialize and thus foreground the repression (or the fear of its absence) – the woman, the dog/man, the girl who orders coffee and cake. Life erupts in the sudden materializations and shifts (of time, genre, register, topic, character, place), that is to say as *acts*. They each reset the frame and reconfigure the world of the play. Each time this recalls a further instance of the Hero's continuing reduction or of the attempt to remould him to conformist status. So the dynamism expresses the weight and accretion of deadliness. At the end he is indifferent, incapable of reaction in the interview scene: 'What are you going to do about the nuclear threat?' 'Nothing'.[43] The manifestation of this 'nothing' (the play) is both a lament and a triumph of the emergence of the odd, the unexpected and unassimilable. The Hero's room, like that of *Wielopole/Wielopole*, is quite explicitly a place of interruption, of otherness. Instead of 'doing something', as the Elders urge, the Hero enacts a kind of entropy. But his inaction is itself a (scandalous) kind of action. It also manifests a deliberate non-engagement with the methodologies of knowing and performing in the world that are paraded before him as desirable.

Gombrowicz

Gombrowicz's *Princess Ivona* (1938) exemplifies the deadly entrapment of the attempt to maintain appearances at all costs. While on one level it is a relatively recognizable ironic fairy tale (deconstructing the Cinderella version of acceding to the aristocracy and exposing the grasp, voracity and murderous retentiveness of those in power), it adds the particularly Gombrowiczian analysis that this behaviour is bolstered and justified by the insistence on adherence to good form. This peculiarly lifeless and pretentious construct – one thinks, for instance, of the absurd uniform worn by Erich von Strohheim in the film *La Grande Illusion* (1937) – turns creativity to ceremony in life and art. Nature here is a backdrop for the display of charitable concern, as the royal family make an evening appearance in the park:

> **Queen** What a wonderful sunset ...
> **King**   My Lord Chamberlain, give him [the Beggar] a crown.
>   Let the people know we have their welfare at heart. ...
>   Right now. Let's go. ... We've still got to make a tour of
>   the Gardens to mingle freely with our loyal subjects.[44]

In addition, Gombrowicz creates an outstandingly articulate and original paradox, an eponymous protagonist who remains almost entirely silent. The centre of his play is thus what Prince Philip, who has rashly decided to propose to the awkward, ungainly and taciturn Ivona in order to exhibit some youthful (but entirely predictable and thus essentially, in the Gombrowiczian sense, 'green') evidence of rebelling against his parents and his status, astutely identifies as a threat: 'You are the universal irritant'.[45] That is to say, that which rubs up everything the wrong way, undercuts any sense of dignity, rightness or comfort, whips up a frenzy. She might also be described, *pace* Lyotard, as an 'ignored guest who produces some trouble'; like Różewicz's Hero, she refuses all stereotypes and definition, not least those of Princess or bride-to-be.[46]

Ivona's silence sucks out all the paranoia of those who are desperate not to be found out, not to have their established status and power revealed as hollow. Philip, his father King Ignatius – abetted by the Chamberlain – and his mother Queen Margaret, all resort to plots to rid themselves of Ivona's threat. The latter notably fears that Ivona's influence will cause her to reveal 'what fumbles inside', while the King and the Chamberlain skate around admissions of depravity.[47] (Lyotard describes the actions of those who want to maintain the status quo as the 'autopoeisis of the great monad'.[48]) So the 'irritant' in effect works like a black hole, which is an extraordinarily energetic phenomenon. The rhythm of the play follows the classic escalation of farce, as the royals lose all dignity in their increasingly ludicrous machinations. The black hole of Ivona seems to exert an increasing velocity of chaos upon the established order. She serves thus as a sign of the power of the Absurd itself in the absurd constellation of events visited upon Poland by a whole succession of powers between the eighteenth and twentieth centuries. The Absurd is apparently misbegotten, ugly, incomprehensible, inarticulate and unapproachable, but resolutely present, the materialization of a subaltern, outsider, discordant and disruptive energy which works not to maintain but to destroy. If this were India, we might call it Kali or Durga, and we might have a metaphysic which had a place for it in the scheme of forces. Quantum physics might also recognize that dynamic, involving paradox, probability and indeterminacy – the forces of chaos. Such is the otherwise entirely unpretentious Ivona, and even when they do come up with a scheme to do away with her – the Chamberlain's dastardly plot to serve pike at a formal dinner and embarrass her while eating, so she chokes on the bones – they succeed only in monumentalizing her power. Ivona puts the skids under the stultifying morbidity of good form and the viciously murderous attempt to maintain it ultimately by her *death*. In a last attempt to preserve formalities, they all (royal family, courtiers, etc.) kneel to her corpse, thinking they are doing the right thing. Yet, in so doing they, in fact, *immortalize* her as 'the universal irritant', the black hole of all their pretence. She is now not just 'universal' but also eternal, a ceremoniously omnipresent vortex, recalling Kantor's definition of his 'Zero Theatre', which occurs 'down below the normal order of things, by way of the slackening of bonds, by way of a loss of energy ... towards the void, to the zero region'.[49]

In these plays, the Absurd operates an *epoché* (or bracketing), a Shklovskian moment of defamiliarization, by foregrounding the uncomfortable, the indigestible, the unnatural, which marks the recognition that nature is what we make of it: it is both an other phenomenon and the discourses and/or channels of perception by which we represent that to ourselves (i.e. a simulacrum, *pace* Jean Baudrillard). To recognize this requires a pulling-up-short, a gap, a hiatus: precisely what is operated by Ivona's silence and ugliness and by Kantor's intrusive and manipulative presence in the environment of his work. It is impossible to receive this then as what we expect a play to be, so its form operates a dislocative act which reconfigures the 'natural', similar to what Maurice Blanchot calls *désoeuvrement*, something which undoes the work at the same time as it creates it.[50] 'Acknowledging the gap is a paradoxical way of having greater fidelity to things'.[51] This strange 'fidelity' uncovers a different, more ambivalent relationship with the ecological. It too, as that which is both within and without, before and after us, is the uncanny home in and as which we never rest. You can't really live these plays without experiencing that uncanniness, which undoes the 'natural' form of knowledge-at-a-distance. It may release a knowing which is more miscegenous, more confused, a kind of 'touch' perhaps, as Lyotard suggests.[52]

Theatre de Complicite

At the end of the Theatre de Complicite production of Bruno Schulz's short story *The Street of Crocodiles*, the characters 'disappear ... into the light'[53]; these oppressed and ultimately annihilated bodies (Jewish, as are those of Schulz himself, Kantor and Rózewicz) – in performance those of actors from many countries, all other to each other – reclaim, in the action and imagination of performance, their power as agents. They have created a performance in which bodies and books become birds, people walk down walls, the matter of earth and zinc and wood becomes malleable and transformable as well as tactile and memorious, materializing places, interactions, the imaginative and emotional life of a whole historical, cultural and family reality. From the initial destruction of the library 'under Gestapo authority',[54] books as entities and the languages of living that they contain are reclaimed and reconfigured in, by and through the bodies of the performers, in an act of transformation that is also an act of resistance and an act of memorialization.

The Street of Crocodiles is not, properly speaking, an absurdist play, but it speaks of the conditions in which much absurd work emerged, and it pinpoints the vectors of energy which drive the Absurd. From the Complicite production, I remember the materiality of bodies and things; the rhythm of marching feet underneath the action; shifts of species and function and place; the stage as a dining room, a farm, a school, as the locus of warmth, of the production and communal consumption of food; and as that which is no longer, which has been swept away and is only memory. Silence also speaks. In Rózewicz's The Card Index, the Hero remembers, 'I clapped. I cheered'. The consequences of this act of acquiescence resonate within him so that 'sometimes there is such a colossal clapping in me. I am empty like a cathedral at night'.[55] In this emptiness the past reverberates, just as Kantor's bodies are freighted with the weight of what they once were. This is a reaching across time in which the hiatus between was and am, between that to which I was reduced and that which I might be, is bridged; though neither in The Street of Crocodiles nor in previous discussions of the Absurd have these things been theorized as an ecology, they nevertheless function ecologically as a crossing of those boundaries that have fenced off the flow of being and the potential of significance.

Here 'there is no dead matter. Lifelessness is only a disguise behind which lie unknown forms of life'.[56] Wood is alive, an example of what Jane Bennett calls 'vibrant matter'.[57] The woodwork class turns into a dance of death. 'How much ancient suffering is there in the varnished grain of an old familiar wardrobe?'[58] Chests and tables are 'quickly nailed together, crucified timbers, silent martyrs'.[59] Bundles of cloth produce music, in a scene which talks about the marvels of the electric bell and the relationship between nature and invention. Here is a world in which anything can become anything else. Something else is always happening in-between, behind, to the side: something is about to become something else (actors, furniture, the space). Here maybe is a dynamic of rhizomic pattern made available to the awareness: it is in production that life occurs, via generation from the apparently dead (compare Kantor's Dead Class where a class is produced from death).

The Kantoresque conductor of this activity of transformation in The Street of Crocodiles is Father, whose 'heresy is to charge inanimate matter with life'.[60] As both traumatic manipulator and demiurge, Father's production is no less ambiguous than Kantor's in *Wielopole/Wielopole*, in part because it is set against the growing menace of those marching feet, underlined by the frequent repetition of Goethe's 1782 poem 'The Erlking' building towards the child's death with increasing urgency and mirrored by Leon's appearance as Death. Then the gale erupts into and across the space, dragging and bending the characters with it, turning action into a Bergmanesque dance of death. The rhythm of the poem's delivery, by individual actors and then as a chorus, seeds this ungraspable menace and the wind sweeps everything up and away. The set too continually fragments and the central memorious figure of Father is constructed and then sawn apart as a wooden puppet, his birds swept out of the attic and the pages of the books strewn and incinerated.

'Es zerfällt', says Rainer Maria Rilke (in the *Eighth Duino Elegy* (1923)): 'wir ordnens wieder und zerfallen selbst' ('It fragments: we put it back in order and fall apart ourselves').[61] Rereading the script of *The Street of Crocodiles* I am amazed at how all this could be done, acted, materialized – sometimes by simple but inventive technology, more often by the actors themselves. But I remember that this continuous reordering and redisintegrating was the dynamic of the production, as it was also the story of the country and civilizations it recalled, and as it is also in a sense the story of all our lives. So in this context the Absurd is presentation, materialization, of that inescapable dance of form and death, each configuration as awful and as marvellous, as chaotic, and as much about rescuing form from that chaos and seeing it merge back into it, as each other. Rather like a Japanese Noh stage or a Beckett short, everything about the performance is slightly oblique, off-centre, constantly surprising in its angles and refractions, right from the initial entry of some characters vertically down the back wall. This seems like a testimony to the fact that Schulz 'writes from within a world where not to be of the centre is the only tenable kind of centrality'.[62] On the back cover of the script, a quote from the *New York Times* review says: 'When you leave the theatre you expect the ground beneath your feet to give way'. Substitute 'sky' for 'ground' and 'fall' for 'give way' and we are in an Artaudian zone. The production seems to have generated this extraordinary sense of living in the precarious, which could be its most potent way of inciting entry to an ecology which constantly shifts across boundaries and juxtaposes opposites. There are hugely destructive political, social and historical forces on the march throughout; the production did not seek to dodge them, but rather to engage and mobilize them, if only in the recognition that the 'ordering' so wrested could only ever be transient. As Goethe puts it in the poem 'Legacy' (1829): 'Das Ewige regt sich fort in allen' ('The Eternal manifests continuously in all things')[63], and he characterizes its action in 'Parabase' (1817) as 'gestaltend umgestaltend' ('forming and reforming'), destruction and creation in one.[64]

For many writers of absurdist theatre, 'the time is out of joint', but instead of trying to 'put it right', they exemplify it in their dramaturgical structures, embody it in their movements and attitudes, disarticulate it in the disjunction of their speech-rhythms and the lacunae between words and meanings. The world exists as our knowing. The knowing here is (by reference to the known) skewed, skewered, screwed up. Seeing, walking, speaking it can only be oblique, staccato. But thus the 'natural' is seen, moved through, spoken as strange, incomprehensible, impossible to accept in its bland and blind violence; and its opposite is allowed to flower, like the growing corpses of Ionesco's *Amédée, Or How to Get Rid of It* (1953). In Gareth White's gloss of Nicolas Bourriaud, 'art has the capacity for thermodynamic effects: melting the frozen relations produced by homogenising culture'.[65] I have written principally about the aesthetics of this process, but this aesthetic is also a politics and a challenge to live on the Earth differently.

Theatre has the capacity to tend towards openness: it is dialogue, it constitutes an offer. Much of this absurdist work identifies the forces that seek to close, but its energies, its images and its methods, operating a continual re-contouring of bodies and a rupturing of boundaries, incite a different relationship with natural and social ecologies, one that is both more troubled and more troubling, but also more intimate and more inclusive. To allow this to occur may move us from resilient monads towards more dynamic and open-ended zones of exchange.

Works cited

Beckett, Samuel, *Endgame*. London: Faber and Faber, 1964.
Bennett, Jane, *Vibrant Matter: A Political Ecology of Things*. Durham, NC: Duke University Press, 2010.

Blanchot, Maurice, *Writing the Disaster*, trans. A Smock. Lincoln, NE: University of Nebraska Press, 1986 [1980].

Bystydzieńska, Grazyna and Emma Harris (eds), *From Norwich to Kantor: Essays on Polish Modernism dedicated to Professor G.M. Hyde*. Warsaw: University of Warsaw Press, 1999.

Esslin, Martin, *The Theatre of the Absurd*, 3rd expanded and enlarged edn. Harmondsworth: Penguin, 1980.

Gluhovic, Milija, 'The mnemonics of Kantor's *Wielopole, Wielopole*', *Toronto Slavic Quarterly*, no. 14 (2005), Online journal: http://www. utoronto.ca/tsq/14/gluhovic14.shtml [accessed 31 January 2014].

Grace, Daphne, *Beyond Bodies: Gender, Literature and the Enigma of Consciousness*. Amsterdam and New York: Rodopi, 2014.

Goethe, J. W., *Gedichte, Erster Band*. Stuttgart: Verlag der J. C. Cottaschen Buchhandlung, 1868.

Gombrowicz, Witold, *Pornografia*, trans. A. Hamilton. London: Penguin, 1966.

Gombrowicz, Witold, *Princess Ivona*, trans. K. Griffith-Jones and C. Robins. London: Calder and Boyars, 1969.

Guattari, Félix, *The Three Ecologies*, trans. I. Pindar and P. Sutton. London: Continuum, 2008.

Hyde, George, 'The word unheard: "Form" in Modern Polish Drama', *Word and Image*, vol. 4, no. 3–4 (1988), pp. 719–31.

Hyde, George, 'Poland', in Ralph Yarrow (ed.), *European Theatre 1960-1990: Cross-Cultural Perspectives*. London: Routledge, 1992, pp. 182–218.

Kantor, Tadeusz, *Wielopole/Wielopole*, trans. M. Tchorek and G. M. Hyde. London and New York: Marion Boyars, 1990.

Kantor, Tadeusz, 'Programme for the performance of *Wielopole/ Wielopole*', Kraków, Crikoteka, n.d.

Kershaw, Baz, *Theatre Ecology: Environments and Performance Events*. Cambridge: Cambridge University Press, 2007.

Kumiega, Jennifer, *The Theatre of Grotowski*. London: Methuen, 1987.

Lyotard, Jean-François, 'Oikos', in *Political Writings*, trans. B. Readings with K. Geiman. London: UCL Press, 1993, pp. 96–107.

Mann, Thomas, *The Magic Mountain*, trans. H. T. Lowe-Porter. London: Vintage, 1999.

Miklaszewski, Krzysztof, *Encounters with Tadeusz Kantor*. London and New York: Routledge, 2002.

Morton, Timothy, *Ecology Without Nature: Rethinking Environmental Aesthetics*. Cambridge, MA: Harvard University Press, 2007.

Rilke, R. M., *Duineser Elegien*, ed. E. L. Stahl. Oxford: Blackwell, 1965.

Rózewicz, Tadeusz, *The Card Index and Other Plays*, trans. A. Czerniawski. London: Calder and Boyars, 1969.

Stafford-Clark, Max *Letters to George: The Account of a Rehearsal*, London: Nick Hern Books, 1997.

Stengers, Elizabeth, *Cosmopolitics I*, trans. R. Bononno. Minneapolis, MN: University of Minnesota Press, 2010.

Theatre de Complicite, *The Street of Crocodiles*. London: Methuen, 1999.

Walker, Janet, 'The Traumatic Paradox: Autobiographical Documentary and the Psychology of Memory', in Susannah Radstone and Katherine Hodgkin (eds), *Regimes of Memory*. London and New York: Routledge, pp. 104–19.

White, Gareth, *Audience Participation in Theatre*. London: Palgrave, 2013.

4

Recycling Beckett

Joe Kelleher

Poisoned ground

The current volume situates Samuel Beckett's work and that of other European writers of the so-called mid-twentieth century Theatre of the Absurd within a history of meaning making, and so a history to be contested, in ethical or political or, specifically here, ecological terms. This means understanding historical works – texts, plays, theatrical productions and the like – not simply 'in the context' of what was going on when they were being written and staged (as if such a context were ever given in full sight, and for however far it extends), but also in dynamic relation to any such context, any such understanding, as it were in the glimmer of an extinguishing illumination, or else – it may be – one coming luridly to full blaze. It calls for sensitivity to events and processes from before the plays were written, along with what was on the horizon of these works' circulation and reception, and their own imagination and articulation of possible futures. It also means making sense and meaning in the face of an impossibility of imagining (Beckett: 'I can't go on, I'll go on'[1]; 'Imagination dead imagine'[2]), in the face of what fades and blazes all at once: 'not only ... the aftermath of World War Two – burnt-out cities, death camps, traumatised landscapes – [but also] the "white heat" of capitalist modernisation', and what falls out of all that, the depletion of 'resources', the dispersal of 'inhabitants', the exhaustion of 'worlds'.[3] Ultimately – which is to say also at the start of the show, as the stage is lit and the actors appear, again, 'to play' – it would be to encounter the works as speaking from the 'poisoned ground', as the editors for this volume have put it, of 'a world gone wrong', and in the strange light of what theorist Timothy Morton has called 'dark ecology'.[4] This latter, in Morton's words, asserts 'the contingent and necessarily queer idea that we want to stay with a dying world', where a sense of being 'suspended in the possibility of acting without being able to act' may give birth to 'the awareness of the intensity and constraint of critical choice'.[5] That latter – or so I understand Morton's formulations – involves not only an immediate and a 'precarious leap' into commitment and action, irrespective of the modes of responsibility we have been trained to observe (in defiance of consumerism, 'critical choice shuts down the possibility of choosing again'[6]). It also has about it a hauntedness that can't help but hang listening, not for what speaks to us, in 'the environment' as it were, echoing our projective sensibilities, but for what is already dead in the ground, ourselves in part already down there with it, and which speaks to us not at all. Haunted, that is to say, not by voices – not even silent voices – but by silence as such, the coming of which chills, or burns, with the realization that we know nothing of what is to come, other than it must be 'here'.[7] An intimacy of relation, then, although it may be the more intimate we find it, the more unfamiliar it is, the more out of sight. Beckett's character Winnie, 'embedded' up to her waist in a mound of earth, sees an 'emmet' (an ant) go by in Act One of *Happy Days*, carrying its egg-sac.[8] It, or its offspring, is likely to be in the earth with her in Act Two, when she is embedded up to her neck.

We won't have any trouble recognizing the landscape that Clov looks out on in Beckett's *Endgame* (1957), or the one that Winnie and Willie inhabit in *Happy Days* (1961) – '*Expanse of scorched grass rising centre to low mound*'[9] – as images of a ground that has been poisoned somehow.[10] Clov anyway, with his telescope at the window, is quite definitive: 'Corpsed. (*Pause.*)' Given such an unequivocal account, there would be nothing at this distance (Clov again at the window: 'Nothing ... nothing ... good ... good ... nothing ... goo-') that requires seeing or saying that isn't already being seen and said, out there and back then, on the stage and in the text.[11] Leave aside that at this particular point in the text, Clov, too, is about to spot something moving out there. Clov had the words for it from the start: 'Finished, it's finished, nearly finished, it must be nearly finished'.[12]

This being so – if indeed it is so – what is it that happens when others come along, when we ourselves come along as if from out of nowhere, with something to add (whatever it is we have in our sacks) to the ecology of meaning making that is already going on here? As, of course, we always do – it goes without saying – every time an audience turns up to a production of one of the plays. But then, how does the theatricality of this historical work – an absurd theatricality, shall we call it? – infect the ecology of our thought? I am curious, for instance, about contemporary practices and processes that return to such works as a resource for thinking and for making anew in other forms than theatre. In the essay that follows, I start out considering works by twenty-first-century artists Gerard Byrne and Mirosław Bałka, which perform their own sort of 'recycling' of small elements of Beckett's oeuvre, in particular some of the words that orientate and set things going, stage directions and titles and suchlike. As I shall try to set out, some peculiar effects are produced, akin to a poisoning – or shall we say curing? – of theatricality as such. One of which is that these contemporary artworks can appear like unpopulated, empty stages – or waiting rooms – where a dramatic protagonist is still to appear. Or if a protagonist were, indeed, to appear, she or he would be unlikely somehow to 'fit in' with the situation, or likely to be out of place, out of time, estranged by the very stage that appears to be constructed for her or his appearing. As if the people – or here the characters – around whom the dramas exist, and without whom the dramas do not happen, cannot be there anymore. Or else, can only be there – we shall come back to this – ridiculously. In coming back to that we will come back to Beckett, specifically *Happy Days*. But for the moment, where are we now?

Recycling Beckett

The photographs have long titles such as *A country road. A tree. Evening. The road to Glencullen between the Glendoo and Tibradden Mountains,*[13] *Dublin Mountains* (2007); or, *A country road. A tree. Evening. Somewhere between Tonygarrow and Cloon Wood, below Prince William's Seat, Glencree, County Wicklow* (2007); or, *Route à la campagne, avec arbre. Soir. À côté du hameau 'Le Sage' au Nord-Est de Roussillon, faisant face au Pie de Boeuf et au Vergilas* (2008). Particular places, spots on the map, visited at a certain moment, although you might have trouble if you were so minded finding those places again ('somewhere between'), or making much of those moments. Come at it another way, it is always more or less the same place and time (a country road, evening), although in its own particular *hic et nunc* and with its own particular tree. The photographs are from a series (ongoing since 2006) by the artist Gerard Byrne, taken in rural locations near Dublin or outside the village of Roussillon in France, places that Samuel Beckett could feasibly have passed by when he lived in the areas, places that might – or so the conceit goes – have inspired the opening stage direction of the writer's 1953 play *Waiting for Godot*.[14] If these are not real-world sources for the literary scene, they are doing the job fine enough now, standing in for the famous setting and as theatrical as you like, as if the landscape itself were auditioning for the part.

True to Beckett's text, Byrne takes the photographs only at dusk, during winter, when there are leafless trees to be found, illuminating the locations with bright, coloured lights that give an odd sort of artificial quality to the final images: as if these environments, for all their pulsing purples and yellows, their bare-branched and bony winter whites, their fire-red foregrounds and deep-set blues, were somehow weather-less, without humidity or determinate temperature, like stage sets can sometimes appear to be, depending upon the action that takes place and the words that will be spoken in the course of a drama to heat things up or cool them down. Nor is there anything momentary about the flash of light in which these scenes are captured, nothing lightning-like about any of them; they remain, as if waiting for whoever might 'come on' from the right or the left of the picture. Except, of course, that nobody does, nor will, and not just because these are photographs. There is something about the distance in these images between now and then, something to do with the way in which one sort of present (call it a present that belongs to a more or less distant past) withdraws itself from another (the present tense of Byrne's displayed images). For one thing – and it is an aspect I have never felt to the same extent in any stage production I have seen of *Waiting for Godot* – those are real roads in the photographs, with decent tarmac these days. They are designed for motor vehicles to pass along at some speed, not for pedestrians to stand around, philosophizing and what have you while they wait for something to happen, such as happens in Beckett's play. Waiting around, philosophizing and so on are activities more likely to be interrupted in places like these by someone stopping in her or his car to offer a lift. Or so the images seem to say.

Byrne's pursuit of a sort of theatricalized criticality, unsettling our sense of what makes up a present through re-working some of the recovered scripts of other presents, in the past, is well-established.[15] He is probably best known for a number of video works based on decades-old magazine conversations between public figures – writers, artists, intellectuals of their day. The videos are often fragmented into parts, installed in galleries on free-standing surfaces you can walk around, sometimes accompanied by seemingly related still photos, like elements of some sort of archaeological find that happen to be still talking: except that they are very conspicuously constructed and acted out. These videos deal with moments when 'modern' thoughts, vanguard ideas as it were from outside the popular sphere, appeared to present themselves to consumerist culture, to enter the swim of mainstream awareness, and become part of the immediacy and the disposability of newsstand media. *A Man and a Woman Make Love* (2012) features 1920s surrealists André Breton, Jacques Prévert and Yves Tanguy conversing – excruciatingly for the large part – on sexual mores, recycled in a mode resembling a television drama of our own time, the surrealists portrayed by contemporary actors. *1984 and Beyond* (2005–7) revisits a 1963 *Playboy* discussion about possible human futures between prominent Cold War era science fiction writers such as Arthur C. Clark and Isaac Asimov, filmed in a modernist gallery and sculpture park, the parts played by Dutch actors: the accents, the architecturally aspirational setting, let alone the substance of the conversation, situating the speakers in an ambience, a world and time of their own, which appears to have been deposited – an odd sort of serious-minded, elegantly dressed and located, thinking-speaking artefact – into our here and now. We, in our world, probably did not turn out as they imagined we might, but then, neither do they. We are 'strange strangers' to each other, indeed.[16]

At least, though, there are people in these videos, even if they are actors pretending to be people from the past. Not even that much can be said for the country road photographs, and that fact strikes you; at least, it struck this viewer when I visited a retrospective of Byrne's work at the Whitechapel Gallery in London in 2012. There

are – simply – no people there in the images, which is not how it
is – ever – in Beckett's theatre. In the plays there is always someone
already there (in *Waiting for Godot* it is Estragon, one of the two
tramps). Beckett's stage settings do not wait for someone to come
along and inhabit them; they are, as the lights come up, always
already environments for some sort of human creature at least.[17]
In Byrne's photographic scenes, we might feel, if someone were
to come on, it would be a peculiar business, awkward somehow.
Which is not to say his environments are unpopulated (if we could
conceive of such a thing as an unpopulated environment): there
are still those auditioning trees, or bushes or shrubs, those bits of
fencing and tarmacadam, on show and – you have to grant it, for
all the actorliness involved – all pretty believable.

There are no people there either – or not yet, not until they choose
to enter of their own accord – in Mirosław Bałka's sculpture *How It
Is*, which occupied the Turbine Hall of London's Tate Modern for
several months over 2009–10. Byrne's country road photographs, as
we saw, recycled a short Beckett text, a stage direction, a landscape
caption, to pick out fragments of the world as candidates for a sort
of 'found' installation that pays homage to a memory, or a kind of
performative echo, of twentieth-century literary or theatrical history
in our 'own' times and places. Bałka does something similar to the
extent that he borrows the English title of Beckett's early 1960s
novel for his own work, although he has said in a public discussion
that the phrase only came to him after the sculpture was planned,
when he saw the cover of the original Grove Press edition in the
Strand Bookstore in New York.[18] What Bałka's work presents is a
volume of pitch darkness, led up to by a steel ramp, inside a 30 metre
long (and 13 metre high) rusted steel box, perched on its 2 metre
high stilts, the whole structure echoing the steel framework of the
converted power station in which it stands, and resembling perhaps
some sort of oversize transport container. The inside is lined with a
velvet-like cloth, absorbing sound and light, making it hard to tell
how deep it goes. I say resembling: resembling or reminding of this
or that. It is hard not to start speaking of the work in these sorts of
allusive ways. That borrowed title is itself an allusion, of course, to
Beckett's tale of aloneness and dependence, of a voice heard in the
dark, of movement that stops and starts, a journey through mud
that continues as long as there are others there, to crawl from or
towards. What the title might seem to do here at Tate Modern is

bracket out everything else and point towards the presentness of the heavyweight sculpture and the darkness it harbours. Approach it; take a walk around; step inside if you will: this is how it is. The allusions, then, belong to the ambience of the work. They are part of the air. They are in the overtones.[19]

They 'go in' with you as you go. Even the pun in Beckett's original 1961 French title *Comment c'est* is drawn into the matter. So it is that the image of disorientating blackness confronting us at the opening of Bałka's sculpture is cut with an impulse to *commencer*, to move and to think and to feel: 'to start to touch the darkness'.[20] A sort of anti-image perhaps, like the blackness that anticipates, surrounds and eventually swallows the orientating image of the actor in later Beckett plays such as *Not I* or *Footfalls* or *Rockaby*.[21] Except that here the actor, the protagonist, will not appear.

Just how much goes into that ambience is set out in a long catalogue essay by art critic Paolo Herkenhoff, ground that is covered again in a public discussion between Herkenhoff and Bałka that took place at Tate Modern during the exhibition.[22] But we can also make up our own; we do not need to be told. We may, for example, notice in our approach to the sculpture the already-mentioned resemblance to a transport container and register, as it were on behalf of our own world and times, the machinery of a dark commerce, the movement of commodities – the movement of people as commodities – across a world of global economic and political inequality. Or we may recall at the ramp – that word still carries a resonance into our own century – the transports and the mass murders in Europe of the mid-twentieth century, only a lifetime or so ago. To start listing the topics in this way is, perhaps, to betray with the implication of equivalence any one of them, as if to hurry on the reflection that would pause amongst the layers. Except that there is no delaying all of the everything and anything else that might come to mind also in face of the work, not least if we attend to the supplementary materials accompanying the exhibition. There is so much of it, and all of it pulling back into one sort of darkness or another: from Plato's cave and Jonah's whale to fox holes in twentieth-century battlefields and black holes in outer space, the myth of Hades, the sight of an open grave, an open mouth, a submarine, the memory of a cellar entrance in your parents' home, let alone the family resemblance of art historical allusions ranging from Kasmir Malevic's *Black Square* (1915) back to Gustave Courbet's *L'Origine du monde* (1866), and beyond. And Beckett – we are probably supposed to know something about Beckett too, aren't we? But then are we, at all?

I recall a line from a feature by Gerard Byrne in *Frieze* magazine, where he talks about seeing 'European art house cinema' for the first time as a teenager on Channel 4 in 1980s Dublin. 'A slow realisation dawned: there were other societies who couldn't care less about the social mores we agonized over, and didn't feel obliged to narrate everything through hackneyed idioms. We didn't really understand anything much, except that everything interesting was coming from elsewhere.'[23] Even, perhaps, by that point the writings of the Dubliner Samuel Beckett. Then again, close to home can also be a world away, and vice versa. The sculptor Bałka, in a short documentary film about his life and locale that appears on the Tate website, speaks of knowing nothing when he was young, until he found out for himself, about the transport in the 1940s of three-quarters of the population of his home town of Otwock to the death camp of Treblinka.[24] Nor is it a matter just of what we know, but how we know it. Someone of another generation than Byrne or Bałka, the French philosopher Alain Badiou, who began reading Beckett, he tells us, in the mid-1950s, writes forty years later that he was a 'young cretin' when he did so.[25] It is easy enough in one's youth, says Badiou, to want to change the world, but it is more difficult to take on the labour of 'subtract[ing]' one's thinking from the conventional formulations of the day. And so, 'I could only see in Beckett what everybody else did. A writer of the absurd, of despair, of empty skies, of incommunicability and of eternal solitude.' In other words, 'A Beckett convinced that beyond the obstinacy of words there is nothing but darkness and void.'[26] As opposed, Badiou writes, to what he has come to recognize and value in Beckett since: 'a lesson in measure, exactitude and courage'.[27] To return to Bałka's *How It Is*, we might argue that none of the 'overtones' are explicitly given in a work whose own measure and exactitude is a weighted muteness, itself a subtraction from what might be thought and said, taciturn enough anyway to make us feel that we will have to do the work ourselves, of imagining an ambience that may be there if we want to listen for it, but does not demand that we do that.[28] So it is, perhaps, that Herkenhoff writes of the Polish visual artist borrowing from the earlier Irish writer an impulse 'to extinguish the images by which we define ourselves'.[29] We come back to the fact that the 'mouth' of the sculpture at Tate

Modern is dark and – of its own accord at least – speechless. Is this the sculpture's way of soliciting our attention 'even so'? Shall we speak on that mouth's behalf and say that if Bałka's darkness is an extinguishing darkness, then it is also an echoing one, whether we hear it or not? Shall we insist, in spite of the cloth-lined, muffled interior, that something sounds at this distance?

Or put it this way. The sculpture has been conceived and installed in a world where there are now some matters it should be impossible not to know, and to take account of. This is how it is. And this is not about the availability of facts and data – or not merely that – nor is it about ourselves, with the superiority of hindsight, knowing more or understanding better than what authors of an earlier period, or even an author's fictional characters, let alone their readers, spectators and critics, knew and understood in theirs. It has to do, rather, with a certain melancholy of knowing, or a sort of *ecological* memory. I'm thinking, for instance, of historian of science Isabelle Stengers's proposal that ecological practices have brought 'a new kind of memory ... into being', a memory of 'unintentional processes that in the past were able to bring about the disappearance of cities, empires, or civilisations', a memory that records 'the ravages caused by our simplistic industrial, and even "scientific," strategies (the "DDT strategy")'.[30] This new kind of memory, Stengers says, is now 'part of the present', and is the basis for the cultivation in the present of 'pharmacological knowledge' (derived from the concept of the *pharmakon*, the drug that can both cure and poison),[31] which is to say a knowledge of how even the best-intentioned actions can have disastrous consequences, and how there is no 'actor' (human or otherwise) that is independent of the world that both grounds that actor's appearing and can cause it to change its meaning.[32] And the 'actors' are here, just as they are in Byrne's photographs, and maybe, after all, they fit just fine.

I implied that Bałka's sculpture *How It Is* is dark, empty, silent and unpopulated. In fact, it is nothing of the sort; at least, any time I visited the work during the period of its installation at Tate Modern, there were many people going in and out of the sculpture, running and laughing and screaming, and managing to see their way around with light from their mobile phones. This behaviour of the public has been commented upon. To take just one example, Herkenhoff, in his public discussion with Bałka mentioned above, at one point mutters something about an 'impairing' of the artist's work.[33] I'm reminded again of Clov with his telescope at the window, looking out with mordant satisfaction and seeing 'nothing ... good ... good ... nothing ...' until a small boy appears, or what looks like a small boy. Clov is dismayed, and ready to 'take the gaff' to the creature, until Hamm stops him. What's the point after all? 'If he exists he'll die there or he'll come here'.[34] Well, at Tate Modern he exists for sure; he is legion, and he has all his fellows and family with him. There have been other views on the matter. Helen Sainsbury, the editor of the exhibition catalogue, writes – rather 'politically', perhaps – of how artists who make work for the Turbine Hall are unable to control how the public behave, something that Bałka was well aware of, and she takes satisfaction in the way that responses to the work combine thoughtfulness with playful sociality.[35] Making a related point, political in an inflected sense, Zygmunt Bauman in his catalogue essay writes of 'the presence of strangers, miraculously transformed into fellow human beings: a presence emanating confidence, not anxiety'.[36] It is the sort of observation made more recently by Jen Harvie in her discussion of how other commissions for the Turbine Hall by Carsten Höller, Olafur Eliasson, Tino Sehgal and others 'cultivate social interaction rather than private contemplation', and how the 'content' of these works might be not so much objects 'as social interactions and relations'.[37] This seems fair to me, although I would have to admit to 'missing' the promised darkness in *How It Is*, the way one can feel sometimes that 'getting the point' is somewhere on the horizon of one's experience, if not necessarily in the immediacy of one's environment. What we seem to have here – with all the running and the standing still, the feeling one's way, amidst the chatter and squeal of acquaintances and strangers and the flickering of phone lights – is something like an over-riding, or an unplugging of that 'ambience of allusion' I was referring to earlier. Which may be to suggest some other sort of 'reciprocal capture' is going on – to borrow another phrase from Stengers – a sort of social ecology of foreign bodies (we might think along the lines of parasitism or predation, which is not to say we won't also think along the lines of fascination, or even love), encounters that take place between the light and the dark, between the on and the off, and which may not be the same thing from the one side as from the other. It may be that none of that meaning making – 'usual drivel', 'usual tosh' – matters really now; or, it doesn't matter *like that*.[38]

The ridiculous subject

To recap, Gerard Byrne and Mirosław Bałka propose extensions of the Beckettian environment as it were beyond the plays and novels and into a world of phenomenal and temporal actualities – a country road, a tree, evening; a massive steel container placed in the main hall of a free-to-enter public gallery. In so doing, they each re-theatricalize that environment as a sort of stage set on which an actor – or any human inhabitant – has yet to appear. In Byrne's photographs, the actors won't or don't or can't enter, although the trees and other landscape elements put on a good enough show in the meantime. In Bałka's sculpture, the place of the actors has been taken by members of the public, but they aren't saying their lines or even listening for their cues; they are playing with their mobile phones and enjoying themselves. Of course, Byrne and Bałka are not the only ones to work with Beckett's texts and images in these sorts of ways. As Steven Connor has remarked, 'In his time and ours, Beckett's work has been subject to huge amplification and enlargement – across genres, media, languages and cultures.'[39] For Connor this is something of a problem, to the extent that these amplifications have tended to betray what he takes to be a commitment in Beckett's work to an aesthetics of the finite, making the Irish author into 'the centrepiece of what might be called a contemporary aesthetics of the inexhaustible, which assumes the sovereign value of endless propagation and maintains a horror of any kind of limit. Beckett found himself', Connor continues, 'as part of his own historical finitude, having to invent, always anew, even in the middle way, the means of his abstention from this infinitising'.[40] Connor concludes with a warning against seeing the work as 'a source for henceforth unconstrained performative reappropriations', although perhaps the very problem that Connor identifies begins to account for why it is that the contemporary works we have been looking at are not as infinitizing as Connor fears, or at least why their stages are as vacated as they are, or why it might be so difficult for someone to come along and be the person who is supposed to be in that place.[41]

It was difficult enough in Beckett's own dramas and stories where, as is the case with Winnie in *Happy Days*, although the character *sticks out* so from the poisoned ground (Winnie fantasizes at one point that if it weren't for the pull of gravity she might 'simply float up into the blue'), there appears little chance of her being 'sucked up' out of a pictured world that she herself, in large part, constitutes, and narrates into being.[42] She is there for life, as it were. This is how it is in Beckett's theatrical installations, these pictorial and architectural situations – in the case of *Happy Days* a geological-domestic situation maybe – that are illuminated for a certain duration, looked at and listened to by people who do not get to come and go at will and who have bought tickets for the privilege, and which are always – as remarked already – occupied, or inhabited by a someone who is stuck in it from the start, and who will still be stuck in it (even more so, most likely) at the end.[43] Works such as these tend to be reflexive about their theatricality, often ironically so (Clov with his telescope again, but looking into the auditorium this time: 'I see ... a multitude ... in transports of joy'[44]). This sort of modernist irony plays, these days (it was probably ever thus), as a rather old-fashioned fourth-wall-teasing gag, although it also touches on what Morton, in the context of the ecological discourse we've been shadowing, refers to as 'the refreshing and consistent noncoincidence of what is in our heads with what is the case'.[45] In the sense, that is to say, that this non-coincidence with where – and when – one is, *is* where one is and nowhere else. The effect, then, for figures such as these – for a character such as Winnie – is that 'nature' is experienced as akin to theatre (or whatever representational medium the work happens to belong to); at the very least it brings to bear theatre-like conditions. Those conditions, as set out below, will appear as a series of ironies, through which nature and theatricality, the how it is and the how it happens to appear, entangle with each other, in singular strangeness and at the same time seemingly inexhaustible repeatability.

There is, of course, the to-be-expected condition of being watched, a sense of being on show ('Strange feeling that someone is looking at me'), which is only an iota of subtraction away from an intimation, a fear maybe, of being abandoned, to indifference, or worse, neither looked at nor listened to nor thought about at all. 'I am clear, then dim, then gone, then dim again, then clear again, and so on, back and forth, in and out of someone's eye. ... Strange? ... No, here all is strange'.[46] There is also – to return to Connor's general topic, although this one again is something of a theatrical speciality – a peculiar relation to the finitude of things: their endingness, their everyday deficiency, and also the remarkable

FIGURE 6 *Yann Collette (Willie) and Natalie Royer (Winnie) in Blandine Savetier's production of Samuel Beckett's* Oh les beaux jours (Happy Days) *at the Comédie de Béthune, 2011.*

capacity of things – especially under theatrical conditions – to stand in for other things, as like themselves as damn it. So, in *Happy Days* – at least in the first act of the play when she still has the use of her arms – Winnie occupies herself by withdrawing bizarre objects from her capacious handbag. I say bizarre. The objects are ordinary enough – toothbrush, toothpaste, spectacles and so on (there is also a not-so-ordinary revolver at one point, there are always strange strangers amongst the familiar) – but Winnie finds inexhaustible bemusement in them, as have Beckett's audiences, for aeons. The toothpaste, the cream, is always almost run out – but never quite – each time the scene is played. And Winnie perceives that 'each time' aspect no less than we do. She breaks the looking glass, she throws away the tonic bottle; she knows they will be back in the bag on the next occasion. Meanwhile, she does all this under a 'blazing light' that is both the light of the sun where, we might say, her character is really, and also – or almost also – a very bright theatre lantern shining down from a few metres away on where she is now, no less really, recycling her phrases, chivvying and consoling Willie, telling her story, singing her song, all in front

of a *trompe-l'oeil* backcloth representing the unbroken plain and
sky where – for real this time, and next time too – she is just about
the only thing, just about the only sort of someone, sticking out of
the pictorial ground, the place, the situation, the historical moment
that will suck her down into it a little more every succeeding day.
She is, as Beckett's stage direction has it, 'embedded' in it all, up to
her neck in it by the end, which – embeddedness – is another figure
that Connor offers for thinking about finitude, 'the impossibility of
ever being otherwise than at a specific place and time, "*en situation*",
in a specific set of circumstances that cannot be discounted or set
aside as merely incidental',[47] and which is also, as it happens, a
figure that Morton deploys to characterize the optimistic aesthetics
of a certain strain of ecocriticism: the experience of connectedness
that supposedly might make us less likely to destroy the world we
find ourselves embedded in, and less inclined to persevere with out-
moded subject–object dualities.[48] As it is, the world that Winnie
is embedded in is pretty much fucked already, and the Cartesian
dualities are just about the only things that keep her going (she is
all subject and hanging on to every ounce; everything else is object
enough: '(*gazing at zenith*). Another heavenly day'[49]). And so she
carries on as best she can, 'persevering without project', or so we
might take it (her actions after all are so ordinary, so making-do)
although she claims something else, asserts something more in the
teeth of it all: that if she can carry on, and if the world – things,
Willie, and whatever else remains – can carry on for her (or perhaps
just 'carry on' will do), this will have been 'another happy day'.[50]

And so, in a sense, it proves. World, things, Willie, whatever
else, the here and now itself, is all, indeed, there again the next
time, miraculously, hideously enough. It is, as we've been saying, a
simple theatrical fact: finitude returned, or soon returning. It is also
absurd, although perhaps not so much in the mid-twentieth century
existentialist sense evoked by Martin Esslin in *The Theatre of the
Absurd* (Esslin cites Camus: 'This divorce between man and his life, the
actor and his setting, truly constitutes the feeling of Absurdity'[51]), but
something akin to what Kierkegaard sets out in his 1843 book *Fear and
Trembling*, where resignation to loss is overturned in the miraculous
return of everything that was to be lost, 'by virtue of the absurd'.[52]
That is to say without any cause or guarantee (God's guarantee
excepted) that links a subjective commitment – or a 'movement',
to use the Kierkegaardian vocabulary – and its consequence or

FIGURE 7 *Yann Collette (Willie) and Natalie Royer (Winnie) in Blandine Savetier's production of Samuel Beckett's* Oh les beaux jours *(Happy Days) at the Comédie de Béthune, 2011.*

outcome (or not even an outcome, but what comes out in spite). Or so it goes for the faithful, for those who perform the terrible mystery of faith, such as Abraham in the episode of the prevented sacrifice of his son Isaac. That said, things have come down somewhat by Winnie's day. Winnie is faithful-*sounding* enough (the first phrases of her monologue rehearse a little prayer: 'For Jesus Christ Amen ... World without end Amen'), but what is returned to her in Beckett's play, for all the dreadful world-unendingness that comes with it, is so finite, her reduced companion Willie not least, but all the rest of it too, a few small necessaries, stage props, some words to say. Compared to the knight of faith, who is imaged, from outside as it were, according to the rather theatrical ironies of Kierkegaard's text both as an indefatigably complaisant petit-bourgeois ('He lounges at an open window and looks out on the square on which he lives; he is interested in everything that goes on'[53]) and as a virtuoso performance artist ('But to be able to fall down in such a way that the same second it looks as if one were standing and walking, to transform the leap of life into a walk'), Winnie's situation (she has no window, she makes no leaps) is not so much absurd as ridiculous.[54]

Esslin doesn't have much to say about the ridiculous. As he remarks in the Introduction to his book, "absurd" may simply mean "ridiculous", but this is not the sense in which Camus uses the word, and in which it is used when we speak of the Theatre of the Absurd'.[55] The word does, though, come up a couple more times in Esslin's volume, once in reference to a clumsy screen adaptation of Genet's 1947 play *The Maids* that turned out 'faintly ridiculous, almost a self-parody',[56] and once more in a brief reference to Raymond Radiguet's play *The Pelicans* (1921), about the Pelican family who are 'anxious to do great deeds to make their name so famous that it will no longer sound ridiculous'.[57] The ridiculous, then, as a state of exposure, of being on show, specifically the putting on show of the one who acts, who makes a movement (however minimal the movement, however small the deeds), for the sake of a future, or a redemption of the present (however meagre the redemption) for which there is no guarantee, no discernible likelihood, no reasonable hope. We get a glimpse of how it goes in the Shower or Cooker episode. Winnie tells a story. She remembers a couple who came by, male and female, hand in hand, carrying bags. She can't remember the name, Shower or Cooker, one who shows or one who looks, cold or hot, who is to say. They gaze upon the spectacle of her suffering, as if this really were a theatrical installation, nature made theatre and she an actor in it, for good or ill. 'What's she doing?' says Mr Shower, or Cooker. 'What's the idea?' 'What does it mean?' And then 'Why doesn't he dig her out?' referring to Willie. And, later, 'I'd dig her out with my bare hands'. Except that he doesn't, or won't, or can't, and after a squabble with Mrs Cooker, or Shower – 'And you, she says, what's the idea of you, she says, what are you meant to mean?' – they depart, ridiculed themselves now in their facile demand for meaning and their incapacity to act, by Winnie herself – ridiculous subject *extraordinaire*, burning subject *ne plus ultra* – and, given the allegorical temper of the episode, by her author, Beckett.[58]

It is hard to say if the happy day that Winnie invokes is the most selfless of projections (a happiness not even her own, a curing of the poisoned ground for a future that won't even have her in it) or something more *self*-sustaining: something for her soul, let's say, here and now also ('Oh this *is* a happy day'[59]). Maybe they come down to the same, or nearly the same, the difference between a smile put on for others and for oneself, an *effort* such as that which switches itself on and off. Maybe it does not matter; maybe what matters, the thing to be valued, or the relation to be established, at this distance is with certain qualities that go with the ridiculous: qualities of persistence, of remainingness, resistance to any sort of conspicuous heroism, and the refusal of adaptability, not least the sorts of inexhaustible adaptability – although exhaustion can come about soon enough – that are demanded of us, and that we commit ourselves to, in our own times and places.[60] For instance, where a capacity to adapt to precarious and invidious economic and societal situations is experienced as a complicity and perpetuation of such situations, as much as a necessary survival 'instinct'. No wonder, then, that various returns to the Beckettian example seek to perform – however appropriative the gesture – not an adaptation of that example so much as a sort of transliteration, as if picking up what Stanley Cavell some time ago identified as Beckett's own 'strategy of literalisation'.[61] This anyway is what both Byrne and Bałka do: taking up in the end a writer's words – stage directions, a title – and nothing but the words, just as Winnie does in her way with her repertoire of immortal lines and 'homely sayings', not even demanding, or pretending, that they are worth much too anymore.[62] What such contemporary works also do – as it were in the light of a 'pharmacological knowledge' that takes in its ecological stride the ridiculous pretension to link action and process with consequences worth believing in – is that they present a vacated stage: a stage, as in Byrne's photographs, for the non-human actors to show what they can do; or else, at the site of Bałka's sculpture, for social actors to come on without instructions, without scripts, and do whatever they will invent to do; or else, as in any production of Beckett's dramas – and they still go on – for a theatre actor to be there, in the place of Winnie or whoever, and to do exactly what it says in the script, or as near as damn it.

Works cited

Adorno, Theodor, 'Trying to Understand *Endgame*', trans. M. T. Jones, *New German Critique*, vol. 26 (Spring–Summer 1982 [1958]), pp. 119–50.

Badiou, Alain, *On Beckett*, ed. and trans. Nina Power and Alberto Toscano. Manchester: Clinamen Press, 2003.

Badiou, Alain and Elie During, 'A Theatre of Operations: A Discussion between Alain Badiou and Elie During', in Manuel J. Borja-Villel, Bernard Blistène and Yann Chateigné (eds), *A Theater Without Theater*. Barcelona: MACBA, 2008, pp. 22–7.

Bałka, Mirosław, 'Mirosław Bałka in Conversation' (2009), http://www. tate.org.uk/context-comment/video/Mirosław-Bałka-conversation.

Bauman, Zygmunt, 'Strangers Are Dangers ... Are They?', in Helen Sainsbury (ed.), *Mirosław Bałka: How It Is*. London: Tate Publishing, 2009, pp. 14–25.

Beckett, Samuel, *Three Novels*, trans P. Bowles and S. Beckett. New York: Grove Press, 1965.

Beckett, Samuel, *Endgame*. London: Faber, 1968.

Beckett, Samuel, *Happy Days*. London: Faber, 1970.

Beckett, Samuel, *Collected Shorter Plays*. London: Faber, 1984.

Beckett, Samuel, *Six Residua*. London: Jonathan Cape, 1999.

Byrne, Gerard, 'Life in Film', *Frieze Magazine*, Issue 123 (May 2009), https://www.frieze.com/issue/article/gerard_byrne_film/.

Cavell, Stanley, *Must We Mean What We Say?*. Cambridge: Cambridge University Press, 2002 [1969], pp. 115–62.

Connor, Steven, 'On Such and Such a Day ... In Such a World: Beckett's Radical Finitude', in Minako Okamuro, Naoya Mori, Bruno Clément, Sjef Houppermans, Angela Moorjani and Anthony Uhlmann (eds), *Borderless Beckett/Beckett sans frontières*, *Samuel Beckett Today/Aujourd'hui*. Amsterdam and New York: Rodopi, 2008, pp. 35–50.

Egoyan, Atom, *Steenbeckett*, http://www.artangel.org.uk/projects/2002/ steenbeckett.

Esslin, Martin, *The Theatre of the Absurd*, 3rd revised and enlarged edn. Harmondsworth: Penguin, 1983.

Funcke, Bettina, 'You See? Gerard Byrne's Reconstructions', *Afterall*, vol. 17 (Spring 2008), www.afterall.org.

Godfrey, Mark, Catherine Wood and Lytle Shaw, *The Present Tense Through the Ages: On the Recent Work of Gerard Byrne*. London: Koenig Books, 2007.

Hallward, Peter, *Badiou: A Subject to Truth*. Minneapolis, MN: University of Minnesota Press, 2003.

Harmon, Maurice (ed.), *No Author Better Served: The Correspondence of Samuel Beckett and Alan Schneider*. Cambridge, MA: Harvard University Press, 1998.

Harvie, Jen, *Fair Play: Art, Performance and Neoliberalism*. London and New York: Palgrave Macmillan, 2013.

Herkenhoff, Paolo, 'The Illuminating Darkness of "How It Is"', in Helen Sainsbury (ed.), *How It Is*, London: Tate Publishing, 2009, pp. 50–105.

'How It Is App'. *The Unilever Series: Mirosław Bałka How It Is* (2009), http://www2.tate.org.uk/MirosławBałka/website.

Kierkegaard, Søren, *Fear and Trembling and The Sickness Unto Death*, trans. W. Lowrie. Princeton, NJ: Princeton University Press, 2013 [1843].

Loock, Ulrich, 'Some Notes on Mirosław Bałka's Work', *Cura Magazine*, no. 4 (April–June 2010), p. 84.

Morton, Timothy, *Ecology Without Nature: Rethinking Environmental Aesthetics*. Cambridge, MA: Harvard University Press, 2007.

Morton, Timothy, *The Ecological Thought*. Cambridge, MA: Harvard University Press, 2010.

Morton, Timothy, 'Thinking Ecology: The Mesh, the Strange Stranger, and the Beautiful Soul', *Collapse*, vol. 6 (2010), pp. 195–223.

Price, James, *Mirosław Bałka: How It Is* (2009), http://vimeo.com/11669764.

Sainsbury, Helen (ed.), *Mirosław Bałka: How It Is*. London: Tate Publishing, 2009.

Stengers, Isabelle, *Cosmopolitics I*, trans. R. Bononno. Minneapolis, MN: University of Minnesota Press, 2010.

Worth, Katharine, *Samuel Beckett's Theatre: Life Journeys*. Oxford: Clarendon Press, 1999.

5

Rare Butterflies, Persecution and Pinball Machines: Environment, Subjectivity and Society in the Theatre of Arthur Adamov

Franc Chamberlain

Introduction

A striking absence of the living, non-human world haunts the dramatic works of Arthur Adamov. The plays exist in a 'silent spring' where not only birds, but also all non-human voices are rendered mute. The sound of horses' hooves under the crack of a whip in *Dead Souls* (1959), Adamov's dramatic adaptation of Nikolai Gogol's novel, is an exception to this silence and there are, in the same play, references to living trees and the appearance of (domesticated) horses on a projection screen.[1] While Adamov's version does carry over some of the details of the natural world that appear in the source text, the playwright drastically reduces the rich vitality of the Earth that features in Gogol's novel. The varietal abundance of bird life detailed in Gogol, for example, is replaced in Adamov's script by a single stuffed bird of an unspecified kind.[2] The descriptions of forests, ploughed fields and brooks that populate Gogol's novel become images of 'vast desolate landscapes' in Adamov's play.[3] This sense of desolation echoes the post-apocalyptic scenarios in Beckett's *Endgame* (1957) and Ionesco's *The Chairs* (1952), written after the bombing of Hiroshima and Nagasaki in August 1945, when the world was freshly aware of the threat of nuclear devastation and soon to become conscious of the destruction caused by dichlorodiphenyltrichloroethane (DDT), as a result of Rachel Carson's best-selling text *Silent Spring* (1962).[4]

The absence of nature in Adamov's theatre is symptomatic of our inability to maintain a healthy relationship with our environment, as we continue to engage in behaviours that unbalance our ecosystem in ways that not only lead to the extinction of other life forms, but also disturb our social behaviour and individual psyches. Adamov's primary focus is on the individual psyche and social relationships, but the disturbed connection to the wider environment is visible through fragments that are present in his dramatic texts like dead birds in a coal mine.

The disturbed interdependency of complex individual, social and environmental systems, mainly implicit in Adamov's texts, was made explicit in the writings of Gregory Bateson,[5] and later developed in the work of Félix Guattari.[6] The bleak and forceful opening paragraph of Guattari's *The Three Ecologies* articulates the problem in words that echo themes and concerns not only of Adamov's theatre in particular, but of the Theatre of the Absurd in general:

> The Earth is undergoing a period of intense techno-scientific transformations. If no remedy is found, the ecological disequilibrium this has generated will ultimately threaten life on the planet's surface. Alongside these upheavals, human modes of life, both individual and collective, are progressively deteriorating. Kinship networks tend to be reduced to a bare minimum; domestic life is being poisoned by the gangrene of mass-media consumption; family and married life are frequently 'ossified' by a sort of standardization of behaviour; and neighbourhood relations are generally reduced to their meanest expression … .
> It is the movement between subjectivity and its exteriority – be it social, animal, vegetable or Cosmic – that is compromised in this way, in a sort of general movement of implosion and regressive infantalization.[7]

All of the major themes in this passage concerned Adamov, and particularly visible in the plays are the deterioration of individual and collective modes of life brought about by technological change, mass media propaganda and the standardization of behaviour. Guattari, with a nod to Bateson, emphasizes three levels or 'ecological registers': human subjectivity, social relations and environment.[8] This tripartite formulation of ecology offers a way of investigating Adamov's drama from an ecological perspective that takes into account environmental issues, while at the same time considering social and mental dimensions. A transformation of subjectivities and social circumstances is, for both Adamov and Guattari, the key to producing a meaningful relationship between the three registers. As Guattari puts it:

> How do we change mentalities, how do we reinvent social practices that would give back to humanity – if it ever had it – a sense of responsibility, not only for its own survival, but equally for the future of all life on the planet, for animal and vegetable species, likewise for incorporeal species such as music, the arts, cinema, the relation with time, love and compassion for others, the feeling of fusion at the heart of the cosmos?[9]

The 'feeling of fusion' that Guattari mentions, as well as its opposite – a sense of separation from the heart of the cosmos – is present in a short text that Adamov published in 1946, *The Confession* (described by Esslin as 'among the most terrifying and ruthless documents of self-revelation in world literature').[10] An early section of this text, written in 1939, was translated into English as a stand-alone piece entitled 'The Endless Humiliation' and, in it, Adamov writes of a sense of intense alienation, which he calls 'Separation'.[11] But 'Separation from what?', he asks, before continuing:

> I do not know. All that I know is that I am suffering, and that if I am suffering it is because at the source of myself there is mutilation, separation. I do not know what name to give what I am separated from, but I am separated from it. Once it was called God. Now there is no longer any name.[12]

This sense of separation, intensely felt by the individual, is described by Adamov elsewhere in the text as a 'neurosis' and identified as a cultural symptom. It is a disturbance in our collective mental ecology, which 'exhibits all the horror of our history, in which the unconscious can no longer find a common mode of expression that will liberate it'.[13] At the same time, neurosis has a positive aspect because it produces 'consciousness of separation', and, as such, has the potential to provoke the subject into experimenting with alternative ways of accepting or engaging with alienation, rather than undergoing it, for example, in silence and despair.[14]

The bulk of 'The Endless Humiliation' concerns Adamov's obsessive desire to be sexually humiliated by women, and his pursuit of that obsession, as a process of liberation through debasement, is akin to that of Genet. This route through humiliation is complemented, however, by a process of reconnection with a felt sense of a living cosmos:

> On an evening in spring the air is transparent, offered to the silent penetration of the mind. Rain has fallen upon the leaves, all green and growing things are exalted. It is a resurrection of colours, the promise of the world redeemed.[15]

Adamov follows this intense lyricism with a description of a personal ritual, or magical process, which involves the touching of wood and earth and the avoidance of iron; a match is struck to provide a flame, for instance. Initially, Adamov is in a 'flux of anxiety'; however, this gradually subsides as he stabilizes himself through these ritual interactions with his environment.[16] Notably, the tree holds a particular significance for him[17]:

> Man seeks to enter into relation with an effective symbol of perpetuity, of that unanimous becoming which acts in terms of metamorphosis rather than of death. And wood is par excellence the great life-bearer, the reservoir of profound energies. Wood is the life that springs out of the earth. It is the subterranean summons from the sucking octopus of the roots, from the sap, purest of all life's juices, cold fire and white blood issuing from the abyss and rising towards the moving leaves by innumerable delicate ways, bundles of liquid jets which, thickening at the contact of the air, become the living flesh of trunk and branches and, once dead, their toughest armour.

> Wood of the tree of life, in touching you I touch the solidified
> witness of the great vertical flow of desire, the stratified sign of
> the clear blood's ascension from the abyss toward the light.
> Wood patient as life itself, the slow petrifying agent of forms,
> you grow so gently that your flesh assuages even human pain.[18]

This poetic and intensely emotional engagement with the tree
is, for Adamov, a means of re-establishing the previously severed
connection between human and non-human worlds; it bridges the
gap between the 'human mind and the structure of the universe'.[19]
It also has something of the intensity that Antonin Artaud imagined
for his 'theatre of cruelty'.[20] Nevertheless, when Adamov touches the
tree, the more accurate resonances are with the work of C. G. Jung[21]:

> Whenever we touch nature we get clean. ... People who have got
> dirty through too much civilisation take a walk in the woods, or
> a bath in the sea. They may rationalise it in this way or that way,
> but they shake off the fetters and allow nature to touch them.[22]

According to Jung, touching and being touched by nature, as a
means of restoring a more balanced relationship to the wider
environment, carries the possibility of feeling fusion at the heart
of the cosmos. Esslin suggests that one of the aims of the Theatre
of the Absurd was to restore a 'lost sense of cosmic wonder and
primeval anguish'[23] and to 'return to the original, religious function
of the theatre',[24] in a world where there is no longer any 'generally
accepted cosmic system of values'.[25] Esslin, Adamov, Guattari,
Artaud and Jung are all in agreement that pre-industrial societies
were better at integrating the three ecologies of mind, society and
environment than our own.

This lack of integration so omnipresent in modern industrial
society is evident in Adamov's theatre. However, nowhere in his
dramatic texts are there elements of such intense affect in relation
to the environment to compare with the passage from 'The Endless
Humiliation'. In contrast to his own vital connection with non-
human biosphere, Adamov's dramatic characters seem deracinated.
While Pierre in *The Invasion* (1950) is aware of a missing dimension
to his existence, he does nothing to overcome it, merely expressing
his lack of connection in terms of a flattening of experience:

'I can only say this much: everything that I have brought to life seems desperately lifeless. Flat. ... Do you know what that means? Flattened? Suddenly removed from space'.[26] This flatness indicates a disruption in Pierre's relationship to himself, to his social circle and to the environment.

Although the problem of ecological disruption is not addressed directly in terms of the environment in Adamov's work, it is implicitly approached through the treatment of mental and social ecologies and the barren and lifeless fragments of the wider biosphere that are scattered throughout the plays. To an extent, this is mirrored, too, in Guattari's *The Three Ecologies* (1989), and also in *Chaosmosis: An Ethico-Aesthetic Paradigm* (1992), where there can be no doubt as to the importance of environmental ecology, but where these environmental problems are seen primarily in terms of human attitudes and social organization.

Adamov takes a number of different approaches to these problems in his drama and indicates the need for the reconfiguration of mentalities and social practices, without coming up with ready-made solutions. The four plays discussed here – *The Invasion*, *Professor Taranne*, *Ping Pong* and *Paolo Paoli* – are all from the 1950s, a decade in which the major works of the Theatre of the Absurd were created, and before Adamov switched to a more explicitly Marxist approach in his work.[27]

Neither Adamov nor Guattari emphasize healing or repairing the environment, as both are aware that a purely technical solution is neither possible, nor desirable. From that point of view, Adamov's plays serve the 'two-fold function' of the Theatre of the Absurd as identified by Esslin. Not only do they expose the 'absurdity of inauthentic ways of life' that holds out the possibility of being rectified for the better, but they also engage with a more profound sense of Absurdity which refuses any form of social solution: namely the question of value in a world that is bereft of certainties, and where 'life must be faced in its ultimate, stark, reality'.[28] The reality, as both Adamov and Guattari realize all too well, is that there will be no divine intervention to restore our lives, societies and environment to some prelapsarian Edenic state where everything is in ideal harmony. Confronted with the irreconcilable presence of the Absurd, the most – the best – we can do, perhaps, is to follow the example of Camus's Sisyphus and to find a way of living with meaninglessness without succumbing to nihilism. In what follows,

I will investigate Adamov's theatrical response to what we might call 'an absurdist ecology'. In an attempt to remain consistent with the focus of this collection, the discussion of each play will begin with an environmental fragment as a springboard to considering a selection of Adamov's plays in relation to all three of Guattari's ecologies.

The Invasion (1950)

In *The Invasion*, there is a single reference to the landscape at the end of Act III. Pierre's wife, Agnès, is leaving him for her new lover and she remarks that they will 'be going near the Nive', a river in the Basque region, which rises in the Pyrenees and joins the Adour at Bayonne/Baiona.[29] Agnès mentions that she has been there once before with Pierre and that 'it was raining and we got soaked', a specific reference to the heavy rains typical of the area. Here the desire to return suggests the possibility of a reconnection with environmental flows, but Agnès also comments that, on her previous visit, 'The whole length of it was fenced off' and 'I wonder why they are always working around there'.[30] The river is subject to enclosure, no longer accessible to the general public, and the fence blocks Agnès's contact with the river and, potentially, to an ecstatic re-connection that echoes Adamov's own experience with the tree. The fencing off of the river also points to the break in the flow of affection between Agnès and Pierre, as well as her (forlorn) hope that things will improve in her new relationship with the First Caller.

The fencing-off is not simply a barrier that prevents Agnès and Pierre from accessing the river; it is a reminder that streams of water, libido, money, information and so on are captured and subjected to a regime of management which seeks to control and dominate them, rather than open up possibilities for transformation. This regime is expressed through Pierre's mother (The Mother) and her allies, First Caller and The Woman Friend. The absence of proper names, in this context, indicates that they are standardized, one-dimensional figures in contrast to the more complex characters of Pierre, Agnès and Tradel. Dividing the cast in this way shifts the focus away from Pierre as the protagonist of the text and pits the forces of singularization against the forces of conservatism and standardization. Pierre, Agnès and Tradel, their friend and collaborator, are in disagreement among themselves and unable to achieve a collective resingularization that would enable them to effectively resist the invasion of The Mother and her accomplices. Guattari distinguished between processes of desingularization, where there is a reduction to a standardized, 'unidimensional subjectivity' and those of resingularization, which allow for a multidimensional subjectivity.[31] While Pierre, Agnès and Tradel all try to escape from the process of desingularization, they are unable to form a group to assist each other.

Esslin and Carlos Lynes each view the disorder of the stage, with papers scattered on every surface throughout the first three acts of The Invasion, as a metaphor for the disorder of the characters' minds. Significantly, they consider the restoration of order as a solution to the chaos of matter out of place.[32] Neither critic notices, however, that this is the imposition (or re-imposition) of an oppressive order. In terms of the broader picture, Esslin amplifies the view of the reactionary Mother figure claiming that the disorder of the room is 'matched by the disorder of the whole country: immigrants are streaming across the frontiers, the social structure is disintegrating'.[33] In addition, both Esslin and John H. Reilly suggest that Agnès is the source of the chaos in the home: 'It almost seems that Agnès stands for disorder'[34] and '[Pierre's] household is a series of disorders, seemingly caused by his wife'.[35] Reilly does, nevertheless, note that the Mother's order brings a 'sense of sterility and hopelessness' as well as causing the expulsion of Agnès and the immigrants.[36]

The Mother's perspective would be familiar to the supporters of right-wing parties in contemporary Europe. Her ever-present newspaper provides stories to develop and maintain her views: 'It's unbelievable!' she exclaims. 'This business about immigration has been going on for months'.[37] In The Three Ecologies, Guattari, thinking about this resurgence of reactionary right-wing politics in the 1980s, commented, 'We are witnessing a reinforcement of segregationist attitudes vis-à-vis immigrants, women, the young and the elderly'.[38] The Mother is an invader. She takes up residence in her son's apartment and gradually imposes her own standards of order upon it. At the beginning of Act IV, the stage directions indicate that The Mother is seated centre stage and that 'one must get the idea, as soon as the curtain goes up, that she is now mistress *of the house*'.[39] The room is neatly ordered and immigration has been stopped. As the scene progresses, Pierre disappears to his room and dies alone. Whether he commits suicide or not is unclear, but by encouraging Agnès's exit and then blocking her return, The Mother certainly contributes to his death.

The imposition of order on a potentially creative chaos creates a toxic environment in the home and in the *socius* that supports a conservative subjectivity inhibiting creative transformations and progressive resingularizations. By the end of the play, everything is effectively fenced off, and the situation is, to use Guattari's words, 'dominated by reactionary nationalist enterprises hostile to any innovation, oppressing women, children, and the marginalised'.[40] For Guattari, such a suffocating and stagnant state of affairs is always the case in any social ecology, 'unless a politically coherent stance is taken by collective praxes'.[41] In *The Invasion*, Pierre, Agnès and Tradel are unable to connect and devise a strategy to resist the conservative forces because they do not appear to realize their shared interests. The audience can see the power grab of The Mother, but it is not visible to those who will suffer most from it.

Professor Taranne (1951)

The only references to the environmental landscape in *Professor Taranne* are those to the beach where the eponymous Professor has been accused of exposing himself to young girls. The reasons he gives for undressing on the beach are twofold: first, he has forgotten his money and is unable to hire a cabin, and second, 'You tell me you can always go behind the cabins, but there the sand's never changed and it's so dirty,' Taranne says.[42] A significant part of the Professor's defence against the accusation of the young girls is that local environmental degradation prevents him from getting changed more discreetly. But it is more than the beach that has been soiled and degraded; the episode with the girls and Taranne's act of removing his clothes at the end of the play signal difficulties with sexuality and the naked body. Furthermore, Taranne is accused of plagiarizing the work of another academic in another instance of degrading exposure.

Professor Taranne is a transcribed dream and Adamov claimed to have made only a single change: replacing a reference to himself with the name of Taranne.[43] The disgrace of Taranne's exposure to the girls directly echoes that of Adamov in 'The Endless Humiliation', where he remembers a rainy afternoon in his childhood: 'I remember ... lying down on the sidewalk of a deserted suburb having taken off all my clothes, trembling in both terror and desire to be discovered in this degrading attitude'.[44] The desire to be seen naked and accepted is an acknowledgement of the continuity of human and non-human in the biosphere, but, as Adamov states in 'The Endless Humiliation', 'modern man cannot bear to have near him even one of the great defining images which permit a glimpse of the creature of mud, flesh, and blood'.[45] The conflict between the desire to be observed naked in public and societal norms is part of the disturbance in Adamov/Taranne's psychic ecology that is connected to the process of separating the social from the environmental, the human from the animal. To move beyond this binary is to engage in what Deleuze and Guattari refer to as 'becoming-animal', a form of ecstatic and collective emancipation that the authorities always move quickly to prevent on account of how 'packs' or 'swarms' are more difficult to contain than solitary individuals.[46]

Without effecting a significant change in the social ecology, what might be an appropriate mode of expression for Adamov/Taranne's desire to be naked? At the end of the play, Taranne hangs up a large map on the wall: '*The map is a large expanse, grey, uniform, absolutely empty,*' then he '*looks at it for a long moment [and] very slowly begins to take off his clothes*'.[47] The blankness of the map indicates a no-place, a utopia, where it is possible for Taranne's desire for exposure to be expressed without resulting in legal action or feeding the fear that its expression will cause harm to others. Guattari recognizes the need to provide opportunities and spaces for the expression of unconventional desire and fantasies – in fact, for him, it is a marker of social ecological health:

> It is, of course, legitimate to repress the 'acting out' of certain fantasies. But initially it is necessary for even negative and destructive phantasmagorias to acquire modes of expression – as in the treatment of psychosis – that allow them to be 'abreacted' in order to re-anchor existential Territories that are drifting away.[48]

Rather than being a blank place on the map where such fantasies could find a mode of expression, La Borde, the clinic where Guattari worked, provided a place of radical heterotopic possibility for the exploration of mental and social ecology as well as the potential for exploring these in relation to the wider environment. In 1987, Guattari invited the Japanese Butoh artist Tanaka Min to La Borde and one event involved the performer dancing naked with the elements in the grounds of the clinic.[49]

In *Professor Taranne* and 'The Endless Humiliation', Adamov reminds us of the way in which our culture involves the cloaking of the intimate relationship between the human body and the environment, a cloaking that blocks our thinking about the effects that humans have on the biosphere. The illusion that human beings are separate from nature and, so, free to exploit it, has led to a growing alienation from the environment where human technological mastery over the biosphere hides our interdependence with non-human life. The relationship between humans and the wider environment is also presented via fragments in *Ping Pong*, a play in which Adamov moves to a more direct exploration of social ecology and analyses the impact of mechanization and commodification on the mentalities and social interactions of the players who are obsessed with the famous, coin-operated arcade game.

Ping Pong (1955)

In *Ping Pong*, one character, Roger, has a flower in his buttonhole; another, Sutter, claims to have ridden a horse across a desert, to have had a son who drowned in a lake, and he has a dream of cornfields in India; later, a garden is mentioned. The only one of these fragments that is present on stage is Roger's flower, yet this marks a difference from *The Invasion* and *Professor Taranne*, where fragments of the natural environment are merely referenced rather than being present as material objects. Roger is the only character in the first part of the play who has no interest in the general obsession with pinball, either as a means of generating money, or as a mode of entertainment. His flower indicates that he still has some romantic idealism but, at the same time, a cut flower is an ambivalent marker of separation, a trace of a connection with the earth that once was vital. He is in amorous pursuit of a young woman, Annette, who becomes caught up in the world of pinball and looks for opportunities to make money by proposing improvements in the mechanism. The flower remains in Roger's buttonhole throughout the play except on two occasions: first, when Annette removes it in her concern that he will be 'a laughing stock' among the punters in the newly emerging arcades, and, second, when it is replaced by a mourning ribbon after the Old Man dies.[50]

Throughout *Ping Pong*, the characters' lives are changed by the appearance and development of the pinball machines. Electronic machines were developed in Chicago during the 1930s, and later spread to Europe. In Adamov's play, they stand for the economic liberalism sponsored by the post-war Marshall Plan. Like the commodities that flooded Europe in the late 1940s and 1950s, once electronic machines appear in *Ping Pong*, they seduce customers in the cafés. At first, only a few machines are present, but, as their numbers grow and they are given various enhancements, more and more people join with them. Eventually the machines are moved out of the cafés and into specialist arcades. The lives of the individual characters become centred around the game, and they put themselves in service to the machine and its producers, The Organization. The changes in the café environment and culture and the interactions between pinball machine and human create a new model of subjectivity. Here, creativity loses its diversity and is channelled, instead, into improving the machine and maximizing income for The Organization. The (misplaced) hope is that some money will trickle down. Tragically and absurdly, the immense creative energy of the characters in *Ping Pong* is not turned towards solving the problems of mental, social or environmental ecology. Rather, their desires are distorted through their involvement with the pinball machine.

One of the characters, Arthur, for example, comes up with a solution to the regular jamming of the pinball machine. The implication is that the players, not the design or manufacture of the machine, are at fault because they 'shake the table too much'.[51] Arthur's idea is for the machine to be redesigned in such a way that the player can then drop in another coin and the machine will reset. But Arthur does not demonstrate any technical knowledge. He has an idea that he proposes to take to The Old Man, the head of The Organization, and imagines that he will be paid, like one of the inventors. This promises to shift his relationship to the machine. There is the possibility, for instance, that he might exist as an active collaborator rather than a passive consumer. Victor, a medical student, refuses to believe that The Organization will support the proposal, but goes along with Arthur to see the corporate head, The Old Man, who, as it turns out, thinks it a 'terrific' idea. The difficulty here, though, is that they are not the only ones to have proposed it, and the idea is already accompanied by a name, 'Tilt'.[52] 'Tilt' is a way of indicating that the player, not the machine, is at fault, and leads to the player putting in more money rather than abandoning the machine because it is malfunctioning.

On numerous occasions in the play, which covers several decades, Arthur suggests a number of possible improvements, sometimes on his own, sometimes with Annette. One idea that Annette and Arthur come up with, and which is rejected by The Old Man, is to have a graphic image of the stage at which a player is in the game. They propose that as soon as a player progresses in the game, a rocket flashes and appears to move towards a moon. When the rocket reaches its destination, the moon lights up, and the player gets an extra ball.

The inventions are designed to capture and bind the players more strongly to the pinball machine. The intention of the additional graphic design is to seduce spectators so that, instead of sitting at a distance complaining about the presence of the machine in their social space, they are drawn to observe and, finally, to play. The situation in *Ping Pong* is paralleled by analogous processes in the gaming world today. As we move from mechanical and electronic pinball to the virtual apps of smart phones and tablets, we find that we no longer need to place actual money into a machine's slot, but that we can buy the game online and can play it any time we like. The other scenario is that we get the game for free and are bombarded by adverts or given opportunities to move the game along faster with in-app purchases. It is not the playing of a game as such that is a problem, but, rather, that it dissuades people from participating in other leisure and social activities. As a consequence, they tend to become sedated and their psychic, social and environmental ecologies degrade. Arthur, Annette and Roger, for example, all see their relationships become impoverished, as their lives revolve, increasingly, around pinball. Despite the fact that Adamov doesn't explicitly discuss environmental ecology, it is telling that machines are 'even installed ... in the gardens'.[53] There is, in other words, no environment that is free from the invasion of the techno-capitalist profit machine.

Paolo Paoli (1957)

In *Paolo Paoli*, there are a greater number of fragments from the natural world than in any of Adamov's plays discussed so far; indeed, there are more references to and appearances of 'nature' than in all of the other plays put together. But while butterflies and beetles, flowers and feathers are present, they have all been extracted, and are either dead (butterflies and beetles), soon-to-be dead (cut flowers) or exist as signs of a possible death to come (feathers). The situation with butterflies, flowers, beetles and feathers is the same throughout the play. They are mere commodities for trade. Flowers and birds are not seen as having an intrinsic value and one commodity can easily replace another. One character, Cécile, says: 'The flower will oust the feather', not for any particular reason, except for fashion.[54] The disconnection from the natural world is a theme that subtly runs through Adamov's plays, but in *Paolo Paoli* it is much bolder.

The action of the play is set in Paris in the years leading up to First World War and Paolo Paoli, a dealer in rare butterflies, purchases his stock from places around the world where the French have a colonial interest. Paoli's main customer is Hulot-Vasseur, a dealer in feathers for fashion, and a slide at the beginning of the play informs the audience that, in 1900, products from the feather industry were France's fourth largest export.

During the play, ten species of butterfly are named: *Morpho Eugenia*, *Morpho Rethenor*, *Zalmoxis*, *Copiopteryx Semiramis*, *Thecla Coronata*, *Charaxes Acroides*, *Macrodontia Cervicornis*, *Titanus Giganteus*, *Dynastes Hercules* and *Hecubia*. There is no celebration of these butterflies as living creatures in motion; they are admired as examples of fixed and frozen beauty, objects for sale. Paolo draws attention to features of a butterfly when selling one to Hulot-Vasseur, for example: 'Have a look at those blue streaks – there, under the belly. Don't you agree that those warm tones ... ?'[55] The list and the descriptions are, however, an implicit invitation for the audience to learn more about the various species of butterfly and become aware of their specificity, their natural habitat and their scarcity. Paoli claims that he makes his money 'without harming a single creature – except these short-lived insects', and shows no concern about potential species extinction.[56] Indeed, the fewer butterflies of a particular kind there are, the greater their economic value. Demand outstrips supply. Paoli claims a Rothschild as one of his friends and patrons and Adamov is almost certainly referring to Walter Rothschild (1868–1937), a remarkable collector of dead creatures and who, at the time of his death, had a collection of over two million butterflies.[57]

Birds receive a treatment similar to that of butterflies, although Adamov mentions fewer species. The fashion for including a part of or even a whole bird on women's hats had become big business in the late nineteenth century and there was a growing opposition to the practice, led by the Audubon Societies in the United States. In 1886, one American opponent of the fashion, Frank Chapman, set out on a fact-finding expedition across Manhattan to Fourteenth Street – into the heart of the fashion district – where he counted every bird species he could identify on women's hats. In two afternoon trips, he saw 'the stuffed wings, heads, tails and bodies of three bluebirds, two red-headed woodpeckers, nine Baltimore orioles, five blue jays, twenty-one common terns, a prairie hen, a saw-whet owl ... and 132 other birds'.[58]

Towards the end of the play, Hulot-Vasseur's business is affected by the imposition of an import tariff on feathers for the fashion industry from the United States. There is a brief reference to the Audubon Society and its role in the new import restrictions, and the Abbé Saulnier makes reference to 'all those dead birds doomed to reappear on ladies' hats'.[59] In 1911 the Audubon Plumage Bill was passed, which banned the trade in all native bird feathers, and the 1913 Tariff Bill, which is referred to in *Paolo Paoli*, 'banned the import of wild-bird plumes from other countries'.[60] In *Paolo Paoli*, Adamov points towards some of the complexities involved in the relationship between environmental awareness, conservation, industry, ethics and people's livelihoods. The emphasis of the play is still on social rather than environmental ecology, but now Adamov explicitly demonstrates how the two are inextricably linked. While Marxism was to provide Adamov with a possible solution to the problems of social ecology articulated in *Paolo Paoli*, the contemporary examples of Communist states in the 1950s would not have offered hope for solutions to environmental ecology. The reduction of Gogol's rich countryside with its variety of species to a stuffed bird and desolate landscapes, mentioned at the beginning of this essay, can be taken as a reference to Stalin's Soviet Union. Stalin, like a contemporary climate-change denier, rejected the ecological objections to giant grain factories and supported the subordination of ecology, and natural science in general, to Marxist 'science'.[61]

Conclusion

Throughout Adamov's plays discussed here, 'nature' is either commodified or exhausted. While, for the most part, the natural world is pushed into the margins, its absence from Adamov's work amplifies the workings of an absurd culture that cuts itself off from its environment and, in the process, creates a system of exploitation that threatens to destroy not only environmental ecology but also mental and social ecologies. In *Paolo Paoli*, Adamov's aim is not to provide a direct critique of a society whose destruction of 'nature' was eventually to lead directly to the carnage of First World War. Rather, by focusing on the actions and motivations of characters engaged in the trade of feathers and butterflies, Adamov defamiliarizes expectations and, at the same time, highlights the need to think of ecology in a holistic and multiple sense. For what Adamov's apparently whimsical and absurdist allegory shows is that the same social and mental ecology that was willing to slaughter birds and butterflies by the millions for decoration, and present it as the most 'natural' thing in the world, would treat its young men in the same way. Paradoxically and ironically, Adamov's silence amplifies the tragedy – the absurd tragedy – of twentieth-century history, a century where, for the first time, humankind waged an all-out war on itself and the environment that supported it, offering white feathers to those who refused the invitation to the *danse macabre*.

There are figures in Adamov's plays who resist the exploitation: Robert Marpeaux in *Paolo Paoli* and Sutter in *Ping Pong* both become politicized as a result of their experiences, but neither is able to envision the full extent of the problem. Ultimately, though, throughout the plays there is a sense of exhaustion and defeat; the future appears bleak, dystopian, resigned to its absurd fate. Read with the help of Guattari's *Three Ecologies*, however, the environmental fragments in Adamov's plays serve to render clear the disruptions in the relationships between the ecological levels and invite us to come up with creative possibilities for change.

Works cited

Adamov, Arthur, 'The Endless Humiliation', *The Evergreen Review*, vol. 2, no. 8 (1959), pp. 64–95.

Adamov, Arthur, *Paolo Paoli: The Years of the Butterfly, A Play in Twelve Scenes*, trans. G. Brereton. London: John Calder, 1959.

Adamov, Arthur, *Two Plays: Professor Taranne and Ping Pong*, trans. P. Meyer and D. Prouse. London: John Calder, 1962.

Adamov, Arthur, *The Invasion*, in Bert Cardullo and Robert Knopf (eds), *Theater of the Avant-Garde 1890-1950: A Critical Anthology*. New Haven, CT: Yale University Press, 2001.

Adamov, Arthur, *Dead Souls & Spring 71*, trans. P. Meyer. London: Oberon Books, 2006.

Bateson, Gregory, *Steps To an Ecology of Mind: Collected Essays in Anthropology, Psychiatry, Evolution and Epistemology*. St. Albans: Granada Publishing, 1973 [1972].

Carson, Rachel, *Silent Spring*. Harmondsworth: Penguin Classics, 2000 [1962].

Conley, Verena Andermatt, *Ecopolitics: The Environment in Poststructuralist Thought*. London: Routledge, 1997.

Deleuze, Gilles and Félix Guattari, *A Thousand Plateaus: Capitalism and Schizophrenia*, trans. Brian Massumi. London: The Athlone Press, 1988.

Esslin, Martin, *The Theatre of the Absurd*, 3rd revised and enlarged edn. Harmondsworth: Penguin, 1983.

Genosko, Gary, *Félix Guattari: An Aberrant Introduction*. London: Continuum, 2002.

Guattari, Félix, *Chaosmosis: An Ethico-Aesthetic Paradigm*, trans. P. Bains and J. Pefanis. Bloomington, IN: Indiana University Press, 1995.

Guattari, Félix, *The Three Ecologies*, trans. I. Pindar and P. Sutton. London: Continuum, 2008.

Guattari, Joséphine and François Pain, (dir.) *Tanaka Min à La Borde*. Paris: L'INA & le CPA, 1987, https://www.youtube.com/watch?v=IrHGwSRTjKQ.

Jung, C. G., *Two Essays on Analytical Psychology: The Collected Works of C.G. Jung*, vol. 7, trans. R. F. C. Hull. Princeton, NJ: Princeton University Press, 1966.

Lynes, Carlos Jr., 'Adamov or "le sens littéral" in the Theatre', *Yale French Studies*, vol. 14 (1954), pp. 48–56.

Price, Jennifer, *Flight Maps: Adventures with Nature in Modern America*. New York: Basic Books, 1999.

Price, Jennifer, 'Hats Off to Audubon', *The Audubon Magazine*
(December 2004), http://archive.audubonmagazine.org/features0412/
hats.html.
Reilly, John H., 'Deciphering the Indecipherable', in Bert Cardullo
and Robert Knopf (eds), *Theater of the Avant-garde 1890-1950:
A Critical Anthology*. New Haven CT: Yale University Press, 2001,
pp. 468–71.
Sabini, Meredith (ed.), *The Earth has a Soul: C.G.Jung on Nature,
Technology, and Modern Life*. Berkeley, CA: North Atlantic Books,
2002.
Taylor-Batty, Mark, *Roger Blin: Collaborations and Methodologies*.
Berne: Peter Lang, 2007.
Weiner, Douglas R., 'Community Ecology in Stalin's Russia: "Socialist" and
"Bourgeois" Science', *Isis*, vol. 75, no. 4 (December 1984), pp. 684–96.

6

Ionesco's Green Lesson: Toxic Environments, Ecologies of Air

Carl Lavery

*Having become aware of the primary and secondary
greenhouse effects, living and breathing under open skies
can no longer hold the same meaning as before.
From the open-air homeland that mortals have had
since time eternity, something uncanny, uninhabitable,
unbreathable was withdrawn.*[1]

Introduction

Anyone familiar with the work of the Franco-Romanian playwright
Eugène Ionesco might find it perverse that this essay, as its title
suggests, seeks to distil a 'green lesson' from his work. Throughout
his career, Ionesco was unremitting in his condemnation of
pedagogical theatre, and in texts such as *The Alma Impromptu*
(1955) and *Hunger and Thirst* (1968), went out of his way to satirize
Brechtian-inspired critics such as Roland Barthes and Bernard Dort,
who, in France in the 1950s, were associated with the left-wing

journal *Théâtre populaire*.[2] In the Anglophone world, by contrast, Ionesco's anti-didacticism is perhaps better known as a consequence of the dispute he waged with the critic Kenneth Tynan in the pages of the UK newspaper *The Observer* in the summer of 1958. Against Tynan's calls for a socially engaged theatre that would inform audiences about the current state of the world, Ionesco retorted that, for him, 'a work of art has nothing to do with doctrine … an ideological play can be no more than the vulgarisation of an ideology. In my own view, a work of art has its own unique system of expression, its own means of directly apprehending the real'.[3]

As Ionesco has it – and he makes this clear in a second letter to Tynan – plays that seek to deny the autonomous logic of the artwork and provide a hopeful message in clear, precise terms are not only aesthetically vacuous; they are also politically dangerous, since their *raison d'être* is to impose a homogenous model of truth that eradicates difference. This line of reasoning is well dramatized in Ionesco's allegory *The Lesson* (1954), which traces the destructive rationality that leads a Professor to kill his student when she both resists his ideas and is unable to follow his methods. In a tragic-comic take on J. L. Austin's performative theory of language, words in *The Lesson* have the force of things, and it is telling that the Professor should murder the girl as she struggles to pronounce the word *couteau* (knife) – a development which underlines the murderous semiotics of pedagogy, the sense in which abstract ideas exert material effects.[4] The final image of the play, which specifies that the girl dies 'in an immodest position' with 'her legs apart' in a chair, suggests that the pupil has been 'raped' by knowledge, forced to submit to the phallocentric desire of the master.[5]

Given Ionesco's hostility towards pedagogy, is my attempt to draw a 'green lesson' from his work – a lesson that is both environmental and ecological, terms that I define presently – a betrayal, then, of its very meaning, a dangerous and reductive simplification? Not necessarily, I would suggest, for Ionesco is not castigating teaching *per se* in his diatribes and texts; rather, he is opposed to instrumentalized teaching that seeks to impart a message, to render spectators passive. Somewhat paradoxically – and this is what Tynan was reluctant to admit in his debate with Ionesco – the artwork that insists on its own autonomy might have greater pedagogical value than the didactic work, in the extent to which it encourages spectators to produce their own interpretations, to 'emancipate' the text from the intentions of the author.[6] In what follows, I intend to test this hypothesis by reading Ionesco's theatre with and against its 'environmental grain' to see what, if anything, can be learnt from it.

Such an approach is vital not only for showing how we might 'green' a theatre text, but also because Ionesco tends to be read in the same way by critics, most of whom, like Martin Esslin in the longest chapter of the third edition of *The Theatre of the Absurd* (1980), feel duty-bound to refer to his copious commentaries on his own plays.[7] Ironically, given Ionesco's distaste for pedagogy, his critical writing has resulted in at least two generations of critics being stultified. Too often, commentators have responded to his plays as the authentic expression of the metaphysical dilemmas of Ionesco the subject, rather than the more open-ended inventions of Ionesco the playwright. This tendency has been a constant feature in Ionesco criticism from the 1950s onwards, and arguably goes some way to explaining why Ionesco's work has fallen out of critical favour in recent years. In order to reinvent Ionesco for contemporary ecological purposes, it is necessary to put his autobiographical reflections to one side and to concentrate instead on the work itself, which is precisely the methodology I have adopted for this essay.[8]

My argument for 'greening' Ionesco is based on a nuanced and sometimes complex distinction between environmentalism (a measure of the quality and health of a given habitat, in which humans are affected, but nevertheless retain their unique status) and ecology (a form of thinking/mode of being that questions human exceptionalism by stressing the value of interconnectedness and interdependence). For reasons that will soon become clear, Ionesco's work defies a straightforward ecocritical reading in the extent to which its environmentalism is at odds with its ecology. This, in turn, necessitates a dialectical structure in which the green credentials of Ionesco's theatre are first affirmed, then questioned, then reaffirmed. The first part of the essay shows how Ionesco articulates a profound sense of environmental disquiet about the future of the planet in a century haunted by what the German philosopher Peter Sloterdijk has called 'atmoterrorism' – a type of terrorism that is not content to destroy the enemy but which seeks to render the totality of its life-world suspect, by 'using violence against the very air that groups breathe'.[9] According to Sloterdijk, atmoterrorism is a consequence of western modernity. In his 2002 publication *Terror from the Air*, he traces its genealogy to the release of mustard gas in the trenches at Ypres in April 1915, before proceeding to demonstrate how it has proliferated throughout the twentieth century, reaching its most spectacular apogee in the atomic attics launched against Hiroshima and Nagasaki in August 1956. Sloterdijk's ideas are particularly useful for reading Ionesco's theatre since they explain how 'air' in his work is simultaneously literal and metaphorical, a trope that highlights the entanglement of 'nature' and 'culture'.

The remainder of the essay unfolds somewhat differently. Whereas part one celebrates the sophisticated and expanded environmentalism implicit in Ionesco's critique of atmoterrorism, part two discloses the ecological limits of his thinking. Here I explain how Ionesco's quest to (re)locate an essentialized sense of self – his metaphysical drive for transcendence – results in an unhelpful anthropocentric paradigm that contradicts one of the fundamental principles of ecology: namely, that everything is part of everything else. As such, if we are to draw a positive ecological lesson from Ionesco's theatre, his attachment to what I call 'a proper view of self' needs to be contested and its ecological limitations acknowledged. In my attempt to do this in part three, I adopt a more critical strategy than Una Chaudhuri who, in a recent revisionist essay of his 1959 play *Rhinoceros* (Ionesco's most popular play in Anglophone theatre circles), disclosed a vitalist desire in Ionesco's work to 'become animal'.[10] Instead, I contrast Ionesco's primarily metaphysical or humanist model of subjectivity with the more biocentric ideas of Gregory Bateson, Donna Haraway and Timothy Morton, before concluding with an exploration of how Julia Kristeva's notion of 'abject laughter' might allow for a more progressive 'green' reading of his texts, one that celebrates the immanence of bodily existence. In this way, I aim to arrive at a dialectical interpretation of Ionesco's theatre that, while always aware of its tensions and ambiguities, manages to affirm its ecological potential.

A final point: I am not the first scholar to research Ionesco's obsession with air. In the 1960s and 1970s, critics such as Rosette C. Lamont, Jacques Guicharnaud and Mircea Eliade interpreted the elemental dimensions of air and Earth in Ionesco's theatre through the lenses of structuralism and comparative religion.[11] However, whereas their reliance on the theories of Carl G. Jung and the material phenomenology of Gaston Bachelard tended to underscore the timelessness of Ionesco's work, I prefer to concentrate on the contingencies and specificities of history. By doing so, I seek to show

how the air in Ionesco's dramas is a matter of biopolitical concern, an element that, as a result of the dangers posed by nuclear and chemical pollutants in the twentieth century, makes any attempt to separate the social from the environmental impossible, not to mention foolhardy.

Part one

Terror from the sky

Perhaps more than any other playwright associated by Martin Esslin with the Theatre of the Absurd, Ionesco's work is haunted, explicitly, by images of nuclear catastrophe.[12] While Beckett, as Theodor Adorno points out in 'Trying to Understand *Endgame*' (1982), makes indirect reference to the nuclear bomb, Ionesco's plays, time and again, show cities, worlds and planets being exploded in all-consuming acts of violence.[13] In *The Chairs* (1951), a play whose watery setting has resonances with J. G. Ballard's novel *The Drowned World* (1962),[14] the audience is told that Paris, 'the city of light', has 'fallen into ruins', and 'faded right away four hundred thousand years ago': 'There's nothing of it now, except a song'.[15] In keeping with the aesthetic incongruity that characterizes absurdist drama – the willingness of characters to accept, at face value, the strangeness of the quotidian world they inhabit – no information is forthcoming about the reason for Paris's destruction in *The Chairs*. It has simply taken place, a source for dark comedy.

A clue for the withdrawn but violent event that dominates *The Chairs* is given in *Exit the King* (1962), the final installment in the series of plays featuring the character of Bérenger as Ionesco's absurdist Everyman.[16] In *Exit the King*, the French title of which, *Le Roi se meurt*, conveys a sense of death as process, the whole society is threatened with atmoterrorism, total atomic devastation.[17] In his account of the country's defeat by a neighbouring power, the Doctor, a bacteriologist, no less, evokes the nuclear winter scenario that haunted military and civilian thinking during the Cold War:

> **Doctor** Three days ago, your empire was flourishing. In those three days, you've lost all the wars you've ever won. ... Our

continent has become a desert. ... Yesterday evening it was spring. It left us two hours and thirty minutes ago. Now it's November. All the cows are calving twice a day. ... The brittle leaves are peeling off. The trees are sighing and dying. The earth is quaking rather more than usual. ...[18]

Reflecting twentieth-century concerns, while at the same time anticipating twenty-first-century ones, *Exit the King* shows a society reeling from ecological catastrophe – the climate has changed, plant life is dying, birth cycles are disrupted. In a phrase that resonates, uncannily, with testimonial reports about the infernos of Dresden, Hiroshima and Nagasaki, the Doctor talks of how the bodies of twenty-five civilians, caught under a strange lightning cloud, were vaporized, reduced to nothing but ash. 'The lightning's struck in the sky, the clouds are raining frogs, the thunder's rumbling. Twenty-five of our countrymen have been liquefied'.[19]

A similar anxiety about atmoterrorism is seen in *A Stroll in the Air* (1963). Here, Bérenger, depicted now as a famous writer living, somewhat incongruously, in Gloucestershire, has his cottage flattened by a bomb dropped from a German plane, a bizarre, surreal remnant from Second World War. Although he emerges from the ruins of the building, safe but soot-stained, Bérenger seems hardly to notice the destruction of his cottage, overwhelmed as he is with hope and optimism. His enthusiasm is caused by the appearance of the fantastical messenger from the 'anti-world' who periodically walks in the skies above him and holds out the hope – at least initially – for a sense of transcendence, a meaning to life, an elevation beyond the mundane. Nevertheless, as the play progresses, the violence of the earlier bombing, too quickly ignored, develops ominous portents.

On learning how to fly, Bérenger is initially overjoyed. Everything is light, translucent, clean. Gravity, the force that roots human beings to the Earth, is overcome. A new life, a different type of breathing, beckons:

Bérenger I've never been so relaxed; I've never been so happy. I've never felt so light, so weightless. ... It's all very concrete. This happiness is something physical. I can feel it here. The air that fills my lungs is more rarified than air. It gives off vapours that are going to my head. A sort of divine intoxication.[20]

The mood shifts, however, the higher Bérenger soars. On exiting the Earth, in exchanging atmosphere for ether, Bérenger sees into the future, and what he discovers there leaves him broken and defeated. Like the Bérenger figure in all of the plays in Ionesco's middle period, the character in *A Stroll in the Air* undergoes a kind of tragic *Bildung*. For what Bérenger brings back from his voyage into the cosmos – and it is tempting to see the play as a sobering, gloomy response to the first orbiting of the Earth made by the Soviet astronaut Yuri Gagarin in 1961 – is knowledge of the planet's destruction. When asked by a journalist to communicate his experience, Bérenger can only provide a litany of catastrophe. In a manner reminiscent of Walter Benjamin's 'angel of history' (but in reverse), he speaks of seeing 'bottomless pits', populated by 'columns of guillotined men, marching along without their heads', and of gazing at 'tremendous curtains of fire'.[21] In Bérenger's account, this human-made apocalypse is followed by a natural disaster that melts first the Earth's crust ('the earth was cracking, the mountains were caving in') and then the universe itself ('I saw millions of exploding stars … infinite wastes of ice, then the fire and ice again … all coming slowly towards us … nearer and nearer and nearer').[22]

In keeping with Sloterdijk's idea about atmoterrorism, the air in Ionesco's play has lost its innocence, and can no longer be trusted. To take to the skies in *A Stroll in the Air*, is not to affirm the cosmic energy of *rêverie* as Gaston Bachelard famously argued in his elemental reading of Shelley and Nietzsche in *Air and Dreams: An Essay on the Imagination of Movement* (1943).[23] And nor is it to partake in a deterritorializing line of flight that French philosopher Luce Irigaray, in her critique of Heidegger's obsession with Earth in *The Forgetting of Air in Martin Heidegger* (1983), posits, optimistically, as a jump into infinite (feminine) possibility, an escape from patriarchal attempts to police and patrol gender identity.[24] Conversely, Bérenger's apocalyptic orbit documents a Promethean vision gone awry. In *A Stroll in the Air*, technology, represented by the messenger from the *anti-monde*, has rendered the atmosphere finite, restricted, catastrophic.[25] Splitting the atom and space exploration are sure signs, for Ionesco, of an apocalypse to come.

Within the Cold War context in which they were written, *Exit the King* and *A Stroll in the Air* are best seen as traumatized texts, plays haunted by the premonition of some environmental cataclysm.

Here, absurdism is no longer simply a philosophical concept, something that stems from a loss of faith in previous metaphysical certainties, as Esslin explains it in *The Theatre of Absurd*, and which Michael Y. Bennett continues to reiterate, albeit in different terms, in his recent book *Reassessing The Absurd: Camus, Beckett, Ionesco, Genet and Pinter* (2010).[26] Rather, the Absurd here is historically determined, a mode of anxious dwelling that marks a major transformation in what might be called, after Steven Connor, 'the materialist imagination' – the type of imagination that is produced in and through our interaction with 'the material world of substances and processes'.[27]

Read through the materialist imagination, the Absurd still is, as it always was, a type of sensate experience, produced through a corporeal engagement with 'nature' (see the section on Camus on pp. 22–8 of the 'Introduction'). Except that now this experience is historicized through and through, and addressed to the mechanisms by which technology in the twentieth century has transformed air and sky into sites of nebulous terror. What could be more absurd, indeed, than an intelligent creature whose intelligence only serves to destroy it? In this respect, it does not appear too far-fetched to compare Bérenger's disabused trajectory in *A Stroll in the Air* with that of the US scientist Robert Oppenheimer, the leader of the Manhattan Project, who was so horrified at the utilization of the atom bomb he had helped create in the laboratories of Los Alamos in 1945, that he compared himself to 'death the destroyer of worlds'.[28] Bérenger's loss of faith has parallels, too, with the members of the science and security board of the Bulletin of Atomic Scientists who, at the University of Chicago in 1947, set the Doomsday Clock to 11.53 pm. In this calendar, midnight is the hour when the world will be annihilated.

Although certainly more emphatic than Beckett, Ionesco does not address nuclear anxieties through a conventional issue-based aesthetic. *The Chairs, A Stroll in the Air* and *Exit the King* are dream visions, plays that mine the *insolite*, the magical and fantastical. In these texts, realist notions of character, history, setting and speech are abandoned. Meaning is communicated elliptically through the unspoken significance inherent in compact scenic images – a stage of empty chairs, a character flying through air, a broken king in a fissured castle – and audiences are confronted with the affective unfolding of incongruous and chaotic dramaturgies where objects proliferate, autonomously, in unexpected sizes and intensities. Ionesco has little interest, then, in explaining our fear of nuclear terrorism by producing a sense of critical distance, as Brecht did in his revised version of *The Life of Galileo* (1955); or in critiquing it satirically, like the Theatre Workshop, in their agit-prop production *Uranium 235* (1946). For him, there is no way to think ourselves out of the environmental anxiety that the advent of the atom bomb has occasioned. Rather, rationality might well be, as his contemporaries Theodor Adorno and Max Horkheimer also suggested, part of the problem rather than the solution, an insanity built into reason itself.[29] As such, the only alternative is an oblique one. Ionesco wants us to experience the shock, to register the loss, to feel the absurdity of the situation as a stimulus to change. In this respect, Ionesco, like Beckett and Pinter, gives us what Michel Serres in his text *Genesis* (1997) calls an 'ichnography' as opposed to an 'iconography' of disaster, the background atmosphere rather than the crystalline object, the evocation rather than the articulation, the poison rather than the cure.[30]

The failure of immunization

Ionesco's characters are not only terrorized *from* the air; they are also terrorized *by* it. A glance at contemporary history explains why. In the two decades following the atomic attacks on Hiroshima and Nagasaki on 6 and 9 August 1945, respectively, radiation sickness caused by nuclear fallout became a new high-profile issue in the world media once news censorship in Japan ended in 1952. For the first time in medical and military history, weaponry did not simply cause death at the moment of impact, but rather continued long after the initial event, working invisibly in the bodies of survivors who had been contaminated by breathing in radioactive dust. Short- and long-term consequences included the increased risk of carcinogenesis, cataract formation, chronic radiodermatitis, decreased fertility and genetic mutations. Fears about 'nucleated' air were compounded when the United States and the United Kingdom tested new types of hydrogen bombs in Bikini Atoll and Maralinga in Australia in the 1950s, as well as by their decisions to use the by-products of plutonium research for the production of domestic energy. Calder Hall in the village of Windscale, Cumbria, the United Kingdom's first nuclear processing plant, was opened in 1956.

France, the country where Ionesco spent the majority of his adult life, was equally implicated in nuclear activity. Between 1960 and 1998, France carried out 210 nuclear tests, most of which were performed in its former colonies in North Africa and *départements et territoires d'outre-mer* (DOM-TOM) in the Pacific Ocean. While other countries were increasingly minded to conduct their nuclear experiments underground for fear of contaminating locals and destroying indigenous ecosystems, France, along with China, persisted with open-air testing until 1968. After the detonation of France's first thermo-nuclear bomb in the Pacific, this technique of explosion was abandoned due to public protests and pressure from the newly established Green Party – Les Verts. The decision was heavily influenced by the reporting of the 'Beryl incident' in 1962 when French soldiers were exposed to nuclear radiation, and also by concerns over the fate of Algerian and Polynesian civilians who were in the vicinity of many of the detonations without being given adequate warning or provided with protective clothing.

The atmospheric anxieties induced among the public by what the US poet Gary Snyder has termed a 'plutonium based economy' were intensified by additional environmental threats such as smog and lead pollution and by the invention of new super insecticides such as DDT (dichloro-diphenyl-trichloroethane) and chlorfenapyr, which were used by farmers to increase their crop yield.[31] These synthetic, chlorinated hydrocarbons were the same ones that the marine biologist and conservationist Rachel Carson famously drew attention to in her bestseller *Silent Spring* (1962), when she compared their effects to those of nuclear fallout.[32] Although first published in English, *Silent Spring* was a notable success in France. Translated into French in 1963 as *Le Printemps silencieux*, it helped galvanize the French environmental movement under the leadership of René Dumont in the 1960s.

The sense of panic generated by the toxicological effects of nuclear radiation and synthetic chemicals manifests itself in Ionesco's theatre, allegorically, through a mistrust of the molecular, the bacterial and the atmospheric. In *Rhinoceros* (1959), for instance, it is significant that each time a rhinoceros appears, a subsequent decrease in air quality ensues. As the animals stampede throughout the town, they stir up particles, spread germs. In his stage directions,

Ionesco specifies that the stage should be awash with clouds of dust: '*A great noise of rhinoceroses traveling very fast is heard outside. ... The sound of a wall crumbling is heard. Dust covers part of the stage, enveloping if possible, the characters. They are heard speaking through it*'.[33] Remembering how Jean was infected with 'rhinoceritis' through a pulmonary infection,[34] Bérenger and Daisy seek immunity from the pandemic by barricading themselves inside Bérenger's flat: 'Shut the window, darling. They're making such a noise. And the dust is rising even up to here. Everything will get filthy'.[35] As with nuclear and chemical pollution, however, the human body can do little to protect itself against the pathogens in the atmosphere. The disease functions microbiologically by attacking the very air that we breathe. There is no escape; nowhere to go. Significantly, at the end of the play, after Daisy has transformed into a rhinoceros, an increasingly hysterical Bérenger is left locked in his tiny room, choking on dust clouds, 'the last man left'.[36]

The dark climatology that permeates social life in *Rhinoceros* is evident, too, in *The Killing Game* (1970), a play in which, over eighteen episodic scenes, a nameless but typically French town is all but eradicated as an epidemic sweeps through it, causing people to drop dead on the spot, 'victims of an absurd illness'.[37] The plague knows no frontiers; it penetrates walls, and seeps through skin. To open a window is to succumb; to breathe is to die. Like radioactive particles in the atmosphere, the virus in *The Killing Game* is invisible: it is nebulous, everywhere and nowhere.

We should not be surprised by the failure of immunization in *The Killing Game* and *Rhinoceros*. In most, if not all, of Ionesco's plays, the desire to protect oneself by retreating from the world is impossible. Intimate or domestic sites are just as troubled and contaminated as public spaces.[38] In keeping with Sloterdijk's ideas, discussed in greater detail presently (see pp 175–80), the air in Ionesco's theatre is double; biological and political at the same time, it is an element that reveals how 'nature' and 'culture' are involved in interdependent exchanges that undo all attempts to differentiate between them. The promiscuous, double-edged meaning that Ionesco attaches to both air and breathing is well illustrated in his earliest play *The Bald Soprano* (1949). Throughout the play, the interchangeable couples, the Smiths and the Martins, talk in order not to speak. It is as though they are terrified by knowledge, panicked by the possibility of discovering the horror that awaits them in the outside world. In her extraordinary 'Fire' poem that takes place towards the middle of the play, Mary, the maid, discloses the possible source of this terror when, as if from nowhere, she evokes the spectre of total nuclear annihilation:

Men on fire
Women on fire
Eyes on fires
The blood caught fire
The sand caught fire
The birds caught fire
The fish caught fire
The moon caught fire. ...[39]

Mary's poem is semantically and structurally integral to the ecological meaning of the piece. Not only do her words, with their associations of smoke and billowing heat, exist as an environmental analogue to the suffocating social atmosphere of the Smiths's living room, but also her poem evokes the repressed event – the reality or possibility of nuclear catastrophe – that produces the social madness in the first place and which, in turn, must be forgotten. It is surely no coincidence, in this context, that the mood between the couples quickly deteriorates in the wake of her impromptu performance. By revealing the trauma, Mary's poem allows something to shift. However, instead of helping the couples to show solidarity with each other, the lifting of repression in *The Bald Soprano* only produces violence. Trapped in their will to ignorance, the Smiths and Martins prefer to turn on each other than to confront the terrible reality of what it means to live under the shadow of the atom bomb. Infected by the toxicity of the atmosphere, language dissolves into a series of nonsense phrases and non sequiturs:

Mrs Smith	A motor car travels very fast, but I'd rather have a cook to cook the dinner.
Mr Smith	Don't be a silly goose, kiss the conspirator instead.
Mr Martin	*Honi soit qui mal y pense.*
Mrs Smith	I'm waiting for mahomet to come to my mountain.
Mr Martin	Social progress is much better coated with sugar.
Mr Smith	Down with polishing (*He throws up the cards, upsets the table and removes it*).

(The others are silent for a moment, stupefied, while the clock chimes intensely. They all rise to their feet and move frenziedly about the stage until at the end of the scene the four characters are standing up, face to face, close together, shouting at each other, raising their fists, ready to hurl themselves at each other's throats).[40]

In *The Bald Soprano*, social, linguistic and environmental ecologies are shown to be inherently relational and interdependent. To pollute the air is to pollute minds, to manufacture an overwhelming sense of insanity that threatens all life forms.

The ecological feedback loop of *The Bald Soprano* is replayed in *Amédée or How to Get Rid of It* (1953). Here, the dead corpse of an adolescent body magically swells in a bedroom before inflating to take up the whole space of the flat itself. Tellingly, the married couple who live in the apartment, Amédée and Madeleine, experience the invasion of the corpse as a form of claustrophobia, a crisis of air. They are stifled by its pneumatic growth:

Madeleine	It's so hot in here. I'm stifling. ... Open the door, and let's have a little air. ... I'm too hot. I want a breath of air. ... Give me a moment to breathe.
Amédée	No I shall never be able to. ... We shan't even be able to breathe in this atmosphere.[41]

In *Amédée or How to Get Rid of It,* asphyxiation is a psychosomatic condition. Psychological fears – Amédée's writing block, Madeleine's depression, their mutual unhappiness – manifest themselves in physical symptoms, and vice versa. As with *The Bald Soprano*, poisoned environments produce toxic interpersonal relationships.

Ionesco's literal and allegorical depiction of breathing difficulties in his early plays has much in common with Elias Canetti's reading of Hermann Broch's notion of atmospheric warfare. In a speech given on the occasion of Broch's fiftieth birthday in Vienna in 1936 – and cited extensively by Sloterdijk in *Terror from the Air* – Canetti discloses how, for Broch, the physiological and psychological effects generated by the release of poison gas in the trenches at Ypres far exceeded their immediate historical context: 'Hermann Broch's work stands between war and war, gas war and gas war. It could be that he still somewhere feels the poisonous particles of the last war. ... What is certain, however, is that he, who knows how to breathe better than we do, is already choking on the gas that shall claim our breath'.[42]

In Canetti's interpretation, the 'poisonous particles' that Broch still feels in his lungs are a metaphor for social and environmental catastrophe. According to Canetti, this is because the future ecological war anticipated by Broch in 1936 (and evidenced by the development of nuclear weapons during the 1940s) will be a total war waged in such a way that old distinctions between nature and culture are dissolved. In addition to destroying the adversary's physical environment with chemical weapons, the aim is to target the enemy's mental health through the diffusion of propaganda.[43] In Canetti's 'metabolism of breathing', the invention of the wireless is an analogue to the gas canister; the insubstantial words, images and voices broadcast by the radio or wireless are as noxious and contagious as chemical pathogens. They produce 'bell jars' of oppression, in which everything and everyone is mistrusted.[44] Tragically, as Sloterdijk explains in *Terror from the Air*, when this double-bind occurs, people become their own contaminants: 'What then proves particularly dangerous are the climatic toxins emitted from people themselves, since desperately agitated, they stand sealed together under a communication bell jar: in the pathogenic air conditions of agitated and subjugated publics, inhabitants are constantly re-inhaling their own exhalate'.[45]

What makes Sloterdijk's and Canetti's 'black environmentalism' so relevant to Ionesco's theatre is the way in which pollution – 'bad air' – is figured as both psychological *and* physiological at the same time. Because of the diffuse nature of mediatized broadcasting, the spectre of absolute communication, the retreat into domestic space, be that private or national, does not allow for better respiration; it simply intensifies toxicity, 'worsens' the atmosphere, and creates poisonous ideologies. As in *Rhinoceros*, fears of contagion turn individuals and collectives against each other in the same way that allergens provoke an abnormally intense response when the immune system feels itself under threat.

In *Frenzy for Two ... and the same to you* (1963), a one-act play whose depiction of domesticity has much in common with *The Chairs* and *Amédée or How to Get Rid of It*, the anonymous protagonists, He and She, attempt to protect themselves from the atmosphere of violence that is escalating in the streets outside by sealing the air vents of their flat with a mattress and a wardrobe. The retreat from aggression, however, does not inoculate against it. Rather, in this noxious environment, where they have resigned themselves 'to being asphyxiated', the couple find themselves locked into a relationship of mutual self-loathing[46]:

She What are you going to do? You've got me into a fine fix!
He Who cares! We'd better hide.
She Give me a hand. Lazy devil! Seducer! [*They block the window with the mattress and stop up the doors, while through the ruined walls of the room you can see figures and brass bands passing*]
He Tortoise!
She Slug! [*They slap each other's faces and without pausing set to work again*].[47]

Frenzy for Two highlights the environmental complexity of Ionesco's theatre. In it, pollution functions according to a terrible feedback loop, in which fears of contamination produce a sense of social asphyxiation. This, in turn, creates a kind of collective pathology, in which people are so terrified of the outside world that they retreat to enclosed spaces and inhale the ideas and concepts that led to the production of dangerous toxins in the first instance – human exceptionalism, the survival of the fittest, the value of competition, the naturalness of war, self-sufficient individualism, etc.

Ionesco's sensitivity to the toxic atmosphere of mid-to-late-twentieth-century modernity has important diagnostic value: it discloses how environmentalism has little to do with the protection or conservation of nature alone; rather, it is always bound up with social factors, with how human beings coexist with each other. But for all its implied critique, it is noticeable that Ionesco appears to offer no alternative to the dark climatology that so oppresses and infects his characters; rather, he seems content, simply, to register the carnage. With this in mind, is the environmental knowledge that his theatre imparts sufficient to warrant a 'green lesson'? Or is something more affirmative needed? In what follows, I shift direction and investigate whether Ionesco's plays might offer a sense of hope, no matter how miniscule, for living differently on the planet.

Part two

Against transcendence

The finitized, toxic air that Ionesco's theatre gives expression to transforms, radically, the capacity of human beings to dwell on the Earth. Anticipating Sloterdijk's recent study of the relationship between morphology and ontology in the trilogy *Spheres* (1998, 1999, 2004), Ionesco, like Pinter and Beckett, documents the moment when sphereological existence, the space of enclosure, is replaced with immensity, the space of exposure.[48] In this shift from house to sky, Ionesco's characters exist as unprotected beings, infected by atmospheric systems that domestic shelters are powerless to withstand.

Strangely, however, at this moment when everything is calling out for a fundamental re-evaluation of how human beings might relate to and inhabit the Earth, Ionesco's environmentalism reveals its limitations. In a world where 'all that is solid' has, quite literally, 'vanished into air', the only solution that Ionesco offers to the toxic atmospheres of the twentieth century is found in a regressive desire for transcendence.[49] In *The Killer*, for instance, Bérenger initially sees the 'City of Light', designed by the architect, as a form of consolation. With its good air-conditioning, clean streets and rational geometry, Bérenger, like his namesake in *A Stroll in the Air*, is reminded of a mystical moment when he was emancipated from the base materiality of the world:

> Bérenger   I was deeply aware of the unique joy of being alive.
> I'd forgotten everything, all I could think of was those
> houses, that deep sky and sun, which seemed to be
> coming nearer, within my grasp, a world that was
> made for me. ... Suddenly the joy became more intense,
> breaking all bounds! And then, oh what indescribable
> bliss took hold of me! The light grew more and more
> brilliant, and still lost none of its softness, it was so
> dense you could almost breathe it, it had become the
> air itself, you could drink it like clear water.[50]

In Bérenger's experience of transcendence, the atmosphere, tellingly, is no longer dense with bacterial perturbations and toxic turbulence; it is purified, transparent, shining. Bérenger can breathe again. He has become one with the light, desubstantiated.

In plays such as *Hunger and Thirst* (1968), *The Man with the Suitcases* (1975) and *Journeys to the Underworld* (1980), this desire for transcendence takes on a more explicitly theological significance, as Ionesco's characters set out on what is perhaps best termed as a Strindbergian 'soul journey', a redemptive quest for wholeness and totality.[51] In *Hunger and Thirst*, Jean is determined to leave the family home, a swampy prison where he imagines his lungs filling with water and mud:

> Jean It's an absolute nightmare. My nightmare. I've always known it, since I was a child. I often woke up in the morning choking with fear. Because I've been dreaming of some ghastly house half sunk in the ground, half under water, oozing with mud.[52]

Like Bérenger in *The Killer*, Jean seeks to abscond from the mephitic fumes of the 'ghastly house' and to breathe instead the pure crystalline atmosphere of his childhood, 'way above the wintry valleys ... on the highest spur ... there stands the princess's palace ... in the middle of a sunlit park'.[53] By transforming 'nature' into an abstract ideal, Jean's objective is to triumph over the body's inevitable putrefaction and death, to become wholly spiritual substance: 'Where can I find earth that's not hard, water that won't scald me, a dressing that heals, a bush without thorns?'[54] Although Jean succeeds in experiencing flashes of salvation in which it 'was as if I was the centre of the universe', and 'out of this world', his rediscovery of the lost paradise is momentary and ultimately unsustainable.[55] At the end of the play, Jean is trapped in finitude, imprisoned by the bodily desires of 'thirst and hunger'.

The failure of transcendence in *Hunger and Thirst* is nothing new in Ionesco's work. In all his later plays, the desire to locate a place of immunity – a comforting centre – beyond the toxicity of the world is shown to be impossible. The only consolation that remains – and it is a false consolation – is the faint memory (or fantasy) of a brilliantly transfigured world, a world of breathable, unperturbed air. This memory, rightly critiqued by Jean's wife Marie in *Hunger and Thirst* as 'a hopeless case of nostalgia', does not liberate Ionesco's characters; it simply condemns them to a life where all that one can do is to rail, uselessly, against the contaminated atmosphere of the world and to bemoan the irrecoverable presence of a paradise that has gone.[56]

For all the acuity of its environmental critique then, Ionesco's theatre only gets us so far in attempting to rethink our relationship to the planet and to each other.[57] If we want to draw a more progressive 'green lesson' from his work, we need to set out on a different path, reading his plays against their environmental grain, in such a way that the transcendent model of subjectivity that he invests in is problematized and ultimately abandoned.

Part three

For immanence

A good place to start this work of ecological revisionism is by contrasting Ionesco's notion of subjectivity with those of key ecological thinkers such as Gregory Bateson and Donna Haraway. Irrespective of his interest in the Absurd, Ionesco, as I have pointed out, is attached to a normative, ontotheological model of identity. In the Bérenger cycle as well as in his later, more explicitly religious plays, the goal is always to overcome alienation, to eradicate difference. In the language of the neo-Lacanian psychoanalyst Julia Kristeva, Ionesco is engaged in an impossible quest for *propriété*, a complex word that in French poststructuralist thought fuses metaphysical notions of subjectivity with ideas of cleanliness and property owning. The 'clean and proper subject', as Jacques Derrida points out, is a subject who attempts to eradicate all difference, to exist as inviolable ego.[58] Such a desire to transcend the world is not only destined to fail in an age of atmoterrorism (how can one escape the everywhere and nowhere quality of air?); it is ecologically disastrous. As Rosi Braidotti has argued in her 2013 publication *The Posthuman*, transcendent notions of selfhood, be they theological or philosophical, produce destructive behaviour patterns. In her reading, the quest to exist as a unitary subject eradicates the autonomy of the 'non-human' world by positing it as 'dumb material' for human agents to exploit as they see fit.[59] Faced with such narcissistic fantasies, it is no longer enough to want to protect the environment as a thing in itself; rather, the more urgent task is to rethink our current notions of subjectivity so that the quest for clean air is not confused, as it is in Ionesco, with the desire for *propriété*.

Gregory Bateson's famous definition of ecology in *Steps To an Ecology of Mind: Collected Essays in Anthropology, Psychiatry, Evolution, and Epistemology* (1972) as the relationship of 'organism + environment' offers a useful corrective to Ionesco's view of self.[60] In Bateson's expansive ecology, the human being is an ecological subject, precisely because its existence is bound up with and dependent upon the health of a larger ecosystem. We cannot act on the environment without affecting ourselves. There is simply no way out of this relationship. This mutual situation is, for Bateson, what being in the world is: namely, a network of connected and interdependent things. In Bateson's view – and this is why Ionesco's transcendent concept of self is so dangerously regressive – to deny this interdependence is to invest in a disastrous ecology, where the human subject finishes by driving itself and the world insane:

> When you narrow down your epistemology and act on the premise 'What interests me is me, or my organisation, or my species', you chop off consideration of other loops of the loop structure. You decide that you want to get rid of the by-products of human life and that Lake Erie will be a good place to put them. You forget that the eco-mental system called Lake Erie is part of *your* wider eco-mental system – and that if Lake Erie is driven insane, its insanity is incorporated in the larger system of *your* thought and experience.[61]

The feminist philosopher of science Donna Haraway underscores the relational logic behind Bateson's notion of ecology by insisting on the generative powers of 'mixity'. In the opening pages of *When Species Meet* (2008), Haraway indirectly counters the compulsion that Ionesco's characters have to exit the world by insisting that 'she is a creature of the mud, not the sky'.[62] From Haraway's post-humanist perspective, immunization is not a good in itself, a metaphysical value to be sought after. As she points out in a chapter on the work of biologist Lynn Margulis, evolution is driven by a process of virology in which different organisms and cells mingle with each other at a bacterial level, and so give birth to new life forms. In Margulis's symbiotic theory of biology, there is no such thing as a clean and proper subject; human beings are born infected. Without this prior contamination, there would be no human being – indeed, no life – at all. Haraway notes: 'Reading Margulis over the years, I get the idea that she believes everything interesting on earth happened among the bacteria ... some of which is the vehicle for new sorts of complex patternings of ones and manys in entangled association'.[63]

Between them Haraway and Bateson offer a very different perspective on toxicity from the one advanced by Ionesco. For them, the composite, the contingent and the infected are constituent elements of being itself. To breathe is to accept that we are always immersed in the world, entwined in matter that refuses to remain enclosed and separate.

This celebration of connectedness and virology does not mean, of course, that one should simply ignore the pollution that human activity has wreaked on the planet. That simply repeats the classic anthropocentric desire to leave the Earth behind, to abdicate all responsibility for human actions. What is required, instead, is an alternative ontology, a commitment to the world as it is, an acceptance of its abject state, its immanence. Timothy Morton puts this well in the final sentence of his provocative text *Ecology without Nature: Rethinking Environmental Aesthetics* (2007), when he urges the reader to 'choose this poisoned ground ... to be equal to this senseless actuality'.[64]

Morton's comments allow us to reconfigure Ionesco's metaphysical version of the Absurd for ecological purposes. For if one of the consequences of Morton's affirmation of 'senseless actuality' is that 'we choose and accept our own death, and the fact of mortality among species and ecosystems', then death, the event that, for Ionesco, makes existence so alienating and melancholic, is no longer a concern for individual beings alone; it is now figured as a collective issue, a planetary affair.[65] In ecological thinking, 'life forms', as Morton reminds us, 'are made of other life forms', the death of one organism is an opportunity for another, a necessary part of an evolutionary process that humans themselves have benefited from.[66] From this perspective, ecological ethics and politics are always, in a sense, absurdist, for they entail a willingness to embrace a world that, as Camus points out in *The Myth of Sisyphus* (see Introduction, pp 63), is destined to remain indifferent to us, even though it is perhaps the most intimate thing that we will ever know.[67]

That Ionesco is not oblivious to the relationship between the Absurd and ecology is seen in *Exit the King*. In the play's long and profound meditation on death, Bérenger's refusal to die results in a sequence of egotistical fantasies in which he is willing to sacrifice the world for immortality:

King   It's not natural to die, because no one ever wants to. I want to exist.[68]

King   Sun, sun, will you miss me? Good little sun, protect me! And if you're in need of some small sacrifice, then parch and wither up the world. Let every human creature die provided *I* can live for ever, even alone in a limitless desert. I'll come to terms with solitude. ... Light of our days come and save me![69]

King   I die, so let everything die.[70]

Tragically *and* comically, Bérenger's narcissistic compulsion to transcend death in *Exit the King* produces environmental destruction. This point is underlined in the anguished dialogue that ensues between Marguerite, the Doctor and the servant Juliette towards the end of the play:

Marguerite   There's nothing but the crust left. We'll soon be adrift in space.

Doctor   And it's all his fault! He never cared what came after him. He never thought about his successors. After him the deluge. Worse than the deluge, after him there's nothing! Selfish bungler!

Juliette   The earth collapses with him. Suns are growing dim. Water, fire, air, ours and every universe, the whole lot disappears.[71]

Ionesco's awareness of the dangers of transcendence reveals a conflict at the very heart of this thinking. For while he knows that the rejection of finitude is environmentally damaging – hence the need, in allegorical terms, to 'exit the king' (the self) – he is unable to posit an alternative mode of subjectivity that might make death less agonistic and singular. Differently from Haraway and Morton, and despite his pointed critique of human hubris in *Exit the King*, Ionesco continues then to conceive of death as the anthropocentric moment par excellence, the event that distinguishes our exceptionality as a species. In doing so, he persists, like Bérenger, in severing death from its generative role in the continued production of life by imagining it as something 'unnatural'– an affliction or punishment that somehow transgresses the human desire for a logos (a God, a meaning, a word). Ultimately, then, behind Ionesco's critique of Bérenger's ridiculous and unsustainable refusal to die, there lies, yet again, the spectre of transcendence, the belief that life has to have a purpose or *telos* if it is to be deemed worthwhile. Unlike Camus's Sisyphus, immanence for Ionesco is never enough. He remains bound to a transcendent horizon.

Given the existential factors that determine Bérenger's disastrous ontotheology in *Exit the King*, perhaps the most effective ecological lesson that we can take from Ionesco's theatre is to expand the ethical remit of the Absurd, to widen its focus of concern. Ecologically, the properly absurdist task would be to confront our mortality (which Bérenger does) while affirming our debt to a planet that we are undone by and responsible to (which Bérenger does not do). But how to make this 'more than human' move with respect to Ionesco's theatre? Where to start? Perhaps by returning to the laughter that pervades his tragicomedies.[72]

In the final chapter of her 1982 publication *The Powers of Horror: An Essay on Abjection*, Julia Kristeva argues that laughter allows the subject to confront death in a manner that forecloses the possibility of transcendence. In her writing on the novelist Louis Ferdinand Céline, Kristeva points out how laughter produces a 'kind of infinite catharsis' by, on the one hand, tapping the horror of extinction, and, on the other, by allowing readers to expel their dread in a physical exhalation:

> With Céline we are elsewhere. As in apocalyptic or prophetic utterances, he speaks out on horror. But while the former can be withstood because of a distance that allows for judging, lamenting, condemning, Céline – who speaks from within – has no threats to utter, no morality to defend. In the name of what would he do it? So his laughter bursts out, facing abjection, and always originating at the same source. ... A laughing apocalypse is an apocalypse without God. Black mysticism of transcendental collapse. The resulting scription is perhaps the ultimate form of a secular attitude without morality, without judgment, without hope.[73]

Kristeva's reading of Célinian abjection has much in common with Ionesco's understanding of the Absurd. In both instances, the world is devoid of sense, deprived of redemption and radically immanent. However, although Ionesco is intellectually aware of this, he seems unable to abandon his nostalgic attachment to a transcendent self, desiring, as he does, to escape the abject materiality – the dirt – of the world. Kristeva highlights the futility of such a venture. 'A laughing apocalypse', she reminds us in her analysis of Céline, 'is an apocalypse without God'. By stressing the disenchanted reality of this decidedly non-theistic apocalypse, Kristeva helps us to see anew the ecological significance of Ionesco's theatre, in ways that circumvent the unhelpful intentions of the author. In spite of his reactionary desire to exist as 'a clean and proper self', the great contradiction – and thus the great potential – in Ionesco's work, if viewed through a Kristevan lens, is that its production of laughter replaces transcendence with immanence. For when we laugh we are rooted, bodily, in the world. In laughter, the abdomen, intestines, thorax all come to the fore, and words vanish.

There is, then, in Ionesco's work a radical but generative *décalage* between what his plays say and what they do in performance. In *Exit the King*, Bérenger's predicament, his horror of disappearing into the void, compels the audience to encounter the anguish of death. However, Ionesco's ability to balance this tragic confrontation with elements of comedy – think of the ridiculous moment when Bérenger's 'dying' causes him to acclaim the sublime beauty of the carrot – creates a form of dark laughter that allows the audience to expel, with an outpouring of exhalate, the fear of its own dissolution.[74] In these moments, the audience is returned to the immanent reality of the body, and through that return, offered a kind of corporeal sublimation, in which the act of laughing simultaneously confronts and displaces death. In the emptying provoked by the absurdist laughter of *Exit the King*, there is no possibility of escaping the world, for the catharsis of abjection never comes to an end. Rather, like theatre itself, it is an act that needs to be performed again and again, in full knowledge of the futility of the venture. However, through this always physicalized emptying of death, this expulsion of breath, it becomes possible to affirm our attachment to the Earth, to come to terms with the mud that Ionesco's elevated obsession with the sky seems so often to avoid on the semantic level of his plays.[75]

I would like to bring this essay to a tentative close by emphasizing the environmental and ecological dissonance of Ionesco's theatre and by arguing for an active method of interpretation that is sensitive to both its 'green' strengths and weaknesses. As I have demonstrated, it is not enough to celebrate Ionesco's environmentalist critique of the poisoned atmosphere of the twentieth century. Rather, if we are to grasp the full ecological import of Ionesco's plays for contemporary audiences, it is incumbent upon us to pay attention to their ambivalences and tensions. In doing so, it is possible to show that the ecological potential of Ionesco's work is paradoxically located in the very thing he strives, but fails, to transcend: the seething immanence of the world. For by producing plays that simultaneously confront and laugh at death, Ionesco allows us to release our pathogenic breath in the public space of the theatre, and in that shared experience to discover a way of existing together in a corporeal confederacy with both human and non-human others.

To return to the premise of this essay, my conclusion is that Ionesco's theatre *does* offer a positive 'green lesson'. Importantly, though, this lesson exceeds its environmentalism and ends by affirming a form of embodied subjectivity that neither Ionesco nor his characters seem able to embrace. Notwithstanding the author's distrust of didactics, Ionesco's production of laughter produces what I see as a pedagogy of humility, which, as the Latin and Greek roots of that word acknowledge, owes more to materiality than to religion. To be humble (*humilis*) in Latin and Greek is to be born low, to be of the soil (*humus*). In this way, Ionesco's theatre, when read against its quest for transcendence, reminds us that as human beings, we are composed of humus, bodily creatures whose nostalgia for an impossible and dangerous oneness is thwarted by the fact that we live and die in mixity, in an immanent relationship to the Earth.

Works cited

Adorno, Theodor, 'Trying to Understand *Endgame*', trans. M. T. Jones, *New German Critique*, vol. 26 (1982) [1958], pp. 119–50.

Adorno, Theodor and Max Horkheimer, *Dialectic of Enlightenment*, trans. J. Cumming. London: Verso, 1997 [1944].

Bachelard, Gaston, *Air and Dreams: An Essay on the Imagination of Movement*, trans. E. and F. Farrell. Dallas, TX: Dallas Institute of Humanities and Culture, 2002 [1943].

Bateson, Gregory, *Steps to an Ecology of Mind: Collected Essays in Anthropology, Psychiatry, Evolution, and Epistemology*. Chicago, IL: University of Chicago Press, 1990 [1972].

Benjamin, Walter, 'Theses on the Philosophy of History', in *Illuminations: Essays and Reflections*, trans. H. Zorn. New York: Harcourt Brace, 1968 [1955], pp. 245–58.

Bennett, Michael Y., *Reassessing the Theatre of The Absurd, Camus, Beckett, Ionesco, Genet and Pinter*. Basingstoke: Palgrave Macmillan, 2011.

Braidotti, Rosi, *The Posthuman*. Cambridge, MA: Polity Press, 2013.

Camus, Albert, *The Myth of Sisyphus and Other Essays*, trans. J. O'Brien. New York: Alfred A. Knopf, 1955.

Carson, Rachel, *Silent Spring*. Boston, MA: Houghton Miffin, 1962.

Chaudhuri, Una, 'Becoming Rhinoceros: Therio-Theatricality as Problem and Promise in Western Drama', in Garry Marvin and Susan McHugh (eds), *Routledge Handbook on Animals*. London and New York: Routledge, 2014, pp. 194–207.

Connor, Steven, *The Matter of Air: Science and the Art of the Ethereal*. London: Reaktion, 2010.

Critchley Simon, 'Interview with Simon Critchley', http://www.necronauts.org/interviews_simon.htm.

Derrida, Jacques, *Spurs: Nietzsche's Style*, trans. B. Harlow. Chicago, IL: University of Chicago Press, 1979 [1978].

Eliade, Mircea, 'Lumière et transcendance dans l'oeuvre d' Eugène Ionesco', in Marie-France Ionesco and Paul Vernois (eds), *Ionesco: Situations et Perspectives*. Paris: Pierre Belfond, 1980, pp. 117–28.

Esslin, Martin, *The Theatre of the Absurd*, 3rd revised and enlarged edn. Harmondsworth: Penguin, 1980.

Guicharnaud, Jacques (with June Guicharnaud), *Modern French Theatre from Giraudox to Genet*. Yale, CT: Yale University Press, 1967.

Haraway, Donna, *When Species Meet*. Minneapolis, MN: University of Minnesota Press, 2008.

Hubert, Marie-Claude, *Eugène Ionesco*. Paris: Seuil, 1990.

Ionesco, Eugène, *Amédée or How to Get Rid of it: A Comedy*, in *Plays*, vol. 2, trans. D. Watson. London: Calder and Boyars, 1954.

Ionesco, Eugène, *The Bald Prima Donna: A Pseudo-Play in One Act*, trans. Donald Watson. London: Samuel French, 1958.

Ionesco, Eugène, *The Chairs: A Tragic Farce*, in *Plays*, vol. I, trans. D. Watson. London: Calder and Boyars, 1958.

Ionesco, Eugène, *The Killer*, in *Plays*, vol. 3, trans. D. Watson. London: John Calder, 1960.

Ionesco, Eugène, *The Lesson* in *Rhinoceros and Other Plays*, trans. D. Watson. Harmondsworth: Penguin, 1962.

Ionesco, Eugène, *Rhinoceros* in *Rhinoceros and Other Plays*, trans. D. Prouse. Harmondsworth: Penguin, 1962.

Ionesco, Eugène, *Exit the King*, in *Plays*, vol. 5, trans. D. Watson. London: Calder and Boyars, 1963.

Ionesco, Eugène, *Notes and Counter Notes: Writings on Theatre*, trans.
D. Watson. New York: Grove Press, 1964.

Ionesco, Eugène, *Frenzy For Two … and the same to you*, in *Plays*, vol. 6,
trans. Donald Watson. London: John Calder, 1965.

Ionesco, Eugène, *A Stroll in the Air*, in *Plays*, vol. 6, trans. D. Watson.
London: Calder and Boyars, 1965.

Ionesco, Eugène, *Hunger and Thirst*, in *Plays*, vol. 7, trans. D. Watson.
London: John Calder, 1968.

Ionesco, Eugène, *Present Past Past Present: A Personal Memoir*, trans.
H. Lane. New York: Grove Press, 1971.

Ionesco, Eugène, *Eugène Ionesco: Théâtre Complet*, ed. Emmanuel
Jacquart. Paris: Gallimard, 1990.

Ionesco, Eugène, in Emmanuel Jacquart (ed.), *Eugène Ionesco: Théâtre
Complet*. Paris: Gallimard, 1991.

Irigaray, Luce, *The Forgetting of Air in Martin Heidegger*, trans.
M. Mader. Austin, TX: University of Texas Press, 1999 [1983].

Jacquart, Emmanuel, 'Introduction', in Emmanuel Jacquart (ed.), *Eugène
Ionesco: Théâtre Complet*. . Paris: Gallimard, 1991, pp. i–ix.

Kristeva, Julia, *The Powers of Horror: An Essay on Abjection*, trans. Leon
S. Roudiez. New York: University of Columbia Press, 1983.

Lamont, Rosette C, 'Air and Matter', *French Review*, vol. 38 (1965),
pp. 349–61.

Marx, Karl and Friedrich Engels, *The Communist Manifesto*. London:
Verso, 2012 [1848].

Morton, Timothy, *Ecology without Nature: Rethinking Environmental
Aesthetics*. New Haven: Harvard University Press, 2007.

Morton, Timothy, 'Queer Ecology', *PMLA*, vol. 125, no. 2 (2010),
pp. 273–82.

Onimus, Jean, 'Quand le terrible éclate de rire', in Marie-France Ionesco
and Paul Vernois (eds), *Ionesco: Situations et Perspectives*. Paris: Pierre
Belfond, 1980, pp. 143–57.

Rancière, Jacques, *The Ignorant Schoolmaster: Five Lessons in Intellectual
Emancipation*, trans. K. Ross. Stanford, CA: Stanford University Press,
1991 [1987].

Serres, Michel, *Genesis*, trans. G. James and J. Nielson. Ann Arbor, MN:
University of Michigan Press, 1997 [1982].

Sloterdijk, Peter, *Terror from the Air*, trans. A. Patton and S. Corcoran.
Los Angeles: Semiotext(e), 2009 [2002].

Sloterdijk, Peter, *Spheres. Volume 1: Bubbles – Microspherology*, trans. W.
Hoban. Los Angeles, CA: Semiotext (e), 2010 [1998].

Smith, Steve (ed.), *Nottingham French Studies*, vol. 35, no. 1 (1996).

Snyder, Gary, 'Four Changes', in *Turtle Island*. New York: New
Directions, 1974.

7

Nettles in the Rose Garden: Ecocentrism in Jean Genet's Theatre[1]

Clare Finburgh

Jasmine, mimosa, dog rose, peonies, pansies, anemones, lilies, tulips, irises, lilacs, gladioli, broom – Genet's (1910–86) namesake – nettles, and above all, roses. Flora, and, indeed, fauna and the inanimate world, occupy a position in Genet's oeuvre that is at times no less important than that of the animal species known as human.

Not only do Genet's works contain a veritable herbarium, but they are produced according to a 'herbaceous' aesthetic. Rather than growing from a central trunk or stem like a tree, herbaceous plants – nettles for example – spread from underground networks of rhizomes or tubers.[2] Entwined narratives, motifs that recur with garland-like circularity, luxuriant and sinuous syntax, symbols grafted onto other symbols, metaphors that shoot from other metaphors like buds, branches or roots, signs gathered into bouquets, figures that cross-pollinate with others to create hybrid variations – all these devices serve in Genet's theatre to supplant the conventional theatrical components of linear plot, clearly defined character and readily comprehensible dialogue. In words with which Genet could have describe his own dramatic works, the Moon declares to the Sun in his play *The Penal Colony* (1958, published 1994), 'To the vertical ease of cypresses, I oppose the confusion of creepers'.[3] Two decades before this play was posthumously published, philosopher Jacques Derrida appropriately wrote in *Glas*, a study which offers the most remarkable analysis of the role played by flowers in Genet's works, '[Genet's] text is composed in creepers and ivy ... rolled up, woven, and braided like creepers'.[4] To account for the ecological ethics of Genet's theatre, it is necessary for me, too, to write 'herbaceously'. I interlace my analysis of his theatre with references to his poetry, novels, and essays on art and politics. This enables me first to trace a movement from the enclosed spaces of rooms and cells, into the wide, expansive environments that pervade his later plays. I remark, however, that, rather than placing landscapes centre-stage in some splendid, self-determined, romantic isolation, Genet highlights how they are always and inevitably perceived via constructed ideological discourses. I then take the example of flowers, detailing how Genet attributes all manner of unpredictable and contradictory meanings to them. Evoking Martin Esslin, I suggest that this postmodern *mise en abyme*, where meaning is constantly destabilized, could precipitate a sense of the meaningless 'absurdity' of existence, which might be incompatible with an ecological concern for safeguarding the environment in meaningful, concrete ways. Writing of the 'feeling of helplessness when confronted with the vast intricacy of the modern world, and the individual's impotence in making his own influence felt on that intricate and mysterious machinery', Esslin seems to suggest that an 'absurd' world presents individuals or groups with few, or no, possibilities for affirmative action: 'Nothing the individual can do can have meaning in a world on the brink of annihilation'.[5] However, I propose that the elements in Genet's work which make it so hospitable to a poststructuralist reading, notably the ways in which he radically deconstructs human superiority, could promote an ecological project. The author who tends in his literary garden to nettles as much as to roses, accords equal importance, as I demonstrate, to human and non-human animals, to flowers and plants, and to animate and inanimate entities.

Since the 1990s, environmentalism has moved beyond natural sciences like geography and population biology, into the arts and humanities. This is explained partly because everybody, without exception, has a stake in the survival of the planet. In addition, the arts are no longer considered by ecologists simply as leisure pursuits, but can be evaluated in terms of their responses to the most significant emergency in the history of our planet, the environmental crisis. For Richard Kerridge, co-editor of *Writing the Environment*, the environmental crisis also constitutes a cultural crisis, a crisis of how to represent the environment in narrative, discursive terms.[6] Consideration of the form that texts take is, of course, the very *raison d'être* of literature and theatre. With reference to performance, Wendy Arons and Theresa May describe 'ecodramaturgy' as 'theater and performance making that puts ecological reciprocity and community at the center of its theatrical and thematic intent'; drama in which the non-human world is taken as seriously as the human dimensions of society and culture, and which makes us aware of the 'inescapable interdependencies and shared contingencies between our species and the millions of micro- and macro-organisms with which we share both a gene pool and a planetary ecosystem'.[7] It might be far-fetched to consider Genet an eco-activist. At no point in his extensive oeuvre does he consciously defend animal rights, or promote respect for the environment. Yet, he constantly poses himself the intellectual and theatrical dilemma of how to represent non-human agency, to speak on behalf of, and to stage, non-human entities. By abolishing perceived hierarchies between human and non-human, animate and inanimate, Genet's theatre foregrounds their mutualities and reciprocities. If ecocriticism is understood as a methodology for evaluating the ethical and aesthetic representation of our planet and the usefulness that these representations might bear as a response to our environmental crisis, I suggest, then, that Genet's theatre provides an essential object of analysis.

From the boudoir to the bush

As Genet's playwriting developed over time, his settings broke from the claustrophobic interiors and airless atmospheres of prison cells and bedrooms characteristic of his early theatre – *Deathwatch* (1949), *The Maids* (1947) and *Splendid's* (1953, published 1993) – to survey expansive panoramic vistas incorporating forests, jungles, deserts and oceans. *The Balcony* (1956) was written in the mid-1950s, in the course of a prolific period during which Genet also wrote *The Blacks* (1958), *The Screens* (1961), *Elle* (1989) and *The Penal Colony*.[8] *The Balcony* is often regarded as a transitional play in Genet's works, since it marks a shift from inside to outside, from private to public space. This is often attributed by critics to the development in Genet's concerns from the introspective autobiographical presentation of homosexuality and criminality, or the existentialist preoccupation with the formation of identity, to an increasing engagement with politics and human rights.[9] I argue that, in addition, this opening onto wider landscapes can also be read from ecological perspectives.

While the world outside Madame Irma's brothel does not appear on stage, gunfire and shelling in the streets are constantly heard: Arthur, a pimp, is shot through the window of Irma's boudoir, and the façade of the brothel is blown apart. Genet stipulates in his prefatory comments that it should never be clear if the revolutionary insurrection is taking place outside, or inside the brothel. The rebels waging war in the streets are just as preoccupied with their image and appearance, as the bankers, clerks and gasmen who enact their sexual fantasies as archetypes of authority – bishops, judges and generals – in the bedrooms of the brothel. Therefore, whereas the mortal threat posed by the outside world in Genet's early plays is literal – the prisoners, maids and gangsters all live in constant fear of the possibility of the scaffold – in *The Balcony*, this outside world is derealized into an appearance, atomized into an image. This development is relevant to the evolution of Genet's ecological imaginary, as I explain presently.

As in *The Balcony*, Genet's representation of landscapes and environments in *Elle* and *The Penal Colony* is tentative and complex. The stage for *Elle* is framed by monumental gilt doors, which open onto 'nothing'.[10] In *The Penal Colony*, too, the outside world is theatricalized. While the play is set against the backdrop of a blistering azure sky typical of the equatorial climes where overseas detention camps were located, the décor represents an enclosed setting comprising prison walls patrolled by guards. Yet, the play differs from Genet's preceding theatre because of the way the outside elements are keenly felt by prisoners and guards, notably the relentless sun that, in the words of one prisoner, beats down like arrows from a windless sky.[11] Most remarkably in *The Penal Colony* from an ecological perspective, the Sun and Moon are included as characters that enjoy their own tableau, where they describe, in an arcane manner, their respective properties. The outside is most prominent in Genet's last plays, *The Blacks* and *The Screens*. In *The Blacks*, one group of black actors plays 'Negroes', who reconstruct the murder of a white woman, and the other plays a colonial White Court that accuses one of the Negroes of that murder. As the White Court descends into the bush to conduct the trial, the white Queen's Valet warns the Bishop, 'be careful that the train of the Queen's cloak and your (*belches*) white (*belches*) purple skirt don't get caught in the cactus. Damn it, what dust! Mouth's full of it!'.[12] The colonials construct a vision of the landscape whereby it is dangerous and hostile, and must be tamed. Finally, in Genet's most ambitious play, *The Screens*, which stages an Arab uprising against colonial power, the author stipulates that landscapes of deserts and mountains should be painted on the paper screens that constitute the play's scenography, and lend it their name.[13] The screens feature fields of palms, cactuses, mountains, and the cycle of day and night, represented by the rising sun, the moon, and star constellations. The intricate brickwork, drapes and furnishings of Genet's early theatre give way to vast geographical landscapes.

The word 'scenery', used to describe picturesque views of the countryside often admired by tourists as objects of visual consumption, originates in theatre, where it denotes a painted set. Ecocritic Lawrence Buell warns that the environment in fictive literary genres can become a mere 'setting', a 'set', which 'deprecates what it denotes, implying that the physical environment serves for artistic purposes merely as backdrop, ancillary to the main event'.[14] In Genet's theatre, landscapes are not reduced to a mere background to human activity; but they are certainly presented as a product of human activity. To demonstrate this, it is necessary briefly to evoke the literary genre that most typically represents landscapes and the 'natural' environment, the pastoral tradition. I go on to suggest how Genet's theatre coincides with pastoral conventions in paradoxical ways. While the first manifestations of pastoral literature – the poetry of Theocritus (*c.* 316–260), which described the lives of shepherds[15] – emerged long before humans were aware of their harmful impact on the environment, the pastoral became most popular during the Romantic period of the late-eighteenth and nineteenth centuries, where depictions of the countryside and rurality increased in counterpoint to the Industrial Revolution's destruction of natural spaces for the purposes of mining, road and canal construction, and the expansion of urban metropolises. The Romantics thus countered the Enlightenment humanist philosophy of the previous centuries, for which human Culture distinguished itself from Nature, all the better to dominate and exploit it.[16]

The pastoral is often accused of stylizing or 'romanticising' the countryside, creating a fantasy of pure, untouchable Nature in strict

opposition with humanity, especially urbanism. Genet does not
idealize Nature, but he constructs it with no less ideological bias
than the Romantics. Since the 'green turn' in the 1990s, ecocritics
have questioned the mythologized version of Nature as a solid,
immovable, eternal physical universe, impervious to historical
change. For one, the natural world constantly grows, evolves and
mutates. In addition, since at least the eighteenth century, human
impact has irreversibly altered the natural environment.[17] In
The Blacks, Genet alludes to the impact on the environment of
technological modernity when the Queen boasts of her 'stacks',
her 'avalanches' of emeralds, copper and mother-of-pearl, that she
has plundered from the African continent.[18] For another reason,
too, nature cannot be seen as a permanent entity. Since the 1970s,
the poststructuralist philosophies of thinkers like Derrida, Gilles
Deleuze and François Lyotard have challenged the notion of an
ahistorical, transcendent reality. The human concept of Nature is
determined by the social, political and economic factors of any
given historical period. For this reason, green cultural critic Jhan
Hochman distinguishes between *Nature* as a cultural construct,
and *nature* as the material world of plants, non-human animals
and elements, while still remaining attendant to the fact that
the barrier between the two can sometimes be 'leaky'.[19] Nature
must consequently be perceived within cultural discourse, rather
than separate from it. Without cultural paradigms with which to
describe the natural world, Nature has no meaning. To humans,
at least.

For the editors of *Readings in Ecology and Performance*, an epic,
expansive dramaturgical structure is preferable in order to testify
to the sheer temporal and spatial scale of ecological issues – 'the
stories of glaciers, rivers, and species unfold over millennia'.[20] To my
mind, the opening out of Genet's theatre onto natural landscapes
performs a different function. Genet reveals how Nature, as it is
perceived, portrayed and projected, is a human construct, not a
wilderness beyond human agency. Genet's natural world is viewed
self-consciously through human eyes. Notably, in *Elle* he provides
a parody of the pastoral tradition, when the Pope describes how he
spent his childhood, as a shepherd, in communion with nature.[21]
Since the play revolves around the idea of creating and propagating
the ideal image of the Pontiff, it becomes clear that this 'communion'
is a human fantasy.

Returning to *The Blacks*, unlike in Genet's earlier plays, the outside world is non-urban and non-human. However, this 'natural' world is no less constructed by human discourses, which in this case are white, European and colonial.[22] Crossing the jungle to conduct the trial of the black murderer, the Governor, a member of the White Court, warns, 'All is swamp, quagmires, arrows, felines. ...'[23] He continues:

Here, from the skin of their bellies the snakes lay eggs from which blinded children take wing... the ants riddle you with vinegar or arrows... the creepers fall madly in love with you, kiss your lips and eat you... here the rocks float... the water is dry... the wind is a skyscraper... all is leprosy, sorcery, danger, madness...[24]

The Judge adds, addressing the Queen, 'Our pioneers tried grafts on our garden cabbage, on the Dutch peony, on rhubarb. Our plants died, madam, murdered by those of the tropics'. The Queen responds, 'Even their botany is wicked'.[25] The African bush is snake-infested, rabid, poisonous, perilous. African Nature is evil and the indigenous Africans are portrayed as an integral part of this treacherous 'natural' world. Throughout the play, wild beasts like jackals, panthers, tigers and leopards are associated with the Africans.[26] In the words of Village, the man accused of murdering the white woman, both 'the antelope and the Negro are fair game of the colonials.[27] In addition, both terrain and native pose a threat to the colonialists' religion, military authority and civilization, and must be hunted and tamed, or killed. The Queen's Bishop cautions, 'Every thicket hides the grave of a missionary'; and the Governor grieves, 'There the north, there the east, the west, the south. On each of these shores, at the river's edge, on the plains, our soldiers have fallen'.[28] Genet even foreshadows the racist fears and prejudices with which immigrants to metropolitan centres were confronted after the colonies gained independence, as the Queen utters in disgust, 'The odor of that tree's flowers spreads all the way to my country and tries to capture and destroy me'.[29] If the African 'natural' world and the indigenous inhabitants with which it is conflated are wild, barbaric and savage, the colonialists can justify the 'civilising' occupation of their land and superior attitude to the indigenous inhabitants. Genet thus reveals the narrowness of the Nature/culture divide, demonstrating how the latter shapes perceptions of the former. This becomes all the more clear when the White Court describe their journey across the hazardous bush. It at once contains cactuses, quagmires, creepers and thickets. Is it a thorny desert? Or a mosquito-infested swamp? Or a poisonous jungle? Or an impenetrable forest? The flagrant inconsistencies in their account reveal how Nature is not so much a simple material phenomenon, but an aesthetically and ideologically inflected treatise.

Whereas the 'wickedness' in the 'vegetable kingdom' is feared and condemned by the colonials in *The Blacks*, in *The Screens* it becomes the arm of the colonized. Nettles provide the Mother of the main protagonist, Saïd, with the poison, the silent and unrelenting strength, with which she and her compatriots will 'hurt the world' and overcome the colonial occupiers:

> I belong ... to the nettle family. Near ruins, tangled with shards, their bushes were my cruelty, my hypocritical meanness that I kept, with one hand behind my back, in order to hurt the world! I tamed them and they held in their venom, drew in their needles. In their leaves I steeped my delicate hands: hemlock would not have frozen my veins. Everything wicked in the vegetable kingdom was won over to me. When the wind blew over and through the nettles, it scraped its skin, but not I.[30]

François Regnault, dramaturg for one of *The Screens*' major productions in 1984 by Patrice Chéreau, writes, 'Nettles show a total disregard for enclosures and the notion of private property. They have an authentic entitlement to the Earth, that comes from the gods'.[31] Most gardeners consider nettles to be weeds, another example of culture determining the contours of Nature. Unwanted, cast out of the well-kept garden, nettles are the representative *par excellence* of Genet's marginal protagonists: criminals in *Deathwatch*, *Splendid's* and *The Penal Colony*; servants in *The Maids*; revolutionaries in *The Balcony*; people of African origin in *The Blacks*; the colonized in *The Screens*. Concurrently, nettles have the 'god-given' right to grow wherever their herbaceous roots happen to spread, and demonstrate no respect for property or propriety. Regnault, echoing Sartre's major literary biography of Genet, *Saint Genet: Actor and Martyr* (1952), unifies in the symbol of the nettle the being who is at once excluded and blessed, outcast and saint. Brownish or greenish and small, nettle flowers, in comparison with conventionally more attractive blooms like wisteria or periwinkles, also appearing in Genet's literary flowerbeds, would be considered by a conventional gardener to be plain, undistinctive, of no value. Moreover, rather than inviting the florist to gather them into a posy, nettles sting, unless one knows how to touch them without brushing against the direction of their poison-filled trichomes, or stinging hairs. These anti-flowers are enlisted by Genet to champion forgotten members of society whose value is overlooked, and to represent their attacking defiance.

The Screens and The Blacks self-consciously highlight the artifice of the natural environments they also conjure, through the acting style recommended by Genet.[32] In The Screens, the Mother and Saïd's wife, Leïla, evoke their rural home by uttering barnyard cries – chickens, cocks, a dog and pig.[33] Genet's stage directions state that the Negroes' voices in The Blacks should make the sounds of the 'croaking of the toad, hoot of the owl, a hissing, very gentle roars, breaking of wood, moaning of the wind ... cracking of branches, cries, caterwauling, etc. ... rustling of leaves ... and other sounds that suggest the virgin forest', and that these sounds grow 'louder and louder'.[34] Genet's foregrounding of falsehood is all the more powerful and pertinent because this scene in the forest takes place just before the sheet is removed from the murdered white woman's coffin, only to reveal that there is no coffin, and consequently uncovering the grossest fabrication of all: the Negroes never raped, attacked or murdered a white woman. Nature in Genet's theatre is certainly not romantically idealized. But as with Romanticism, it becomes a highly stylized artifice.

Flowers deconstructed

Across Genet's works, the authenticity, veracity and reality of narrative or character are continually uprooted. With reference to flowers, I examine the uncertainty, instability and ambiguity that characterize Genet's theatre, before proposing that the provisionalities implicit in radical poststructuralism are not at odds with ecocriticism's concrete commitment to political change.[35]

More than any other motif, flowers, plants and shrubs feature across Genet's works. The Screens begins with the words 'Rose!

I said rose! The sky's already pink as a rose'.[36] Twenty years previously, flora appear in Genet's first works. 'The Man Condemned to Death' (1942) – a poem to Maurice Pilorge, Genet's lover executed for murder – features the head of the poet's beloved adorned with a crown of thorns; and a pimp splayed, ready and erect, across a bed of carnations and jasmines.[37] Flowers also feature in the titles of both Genet's first and second novels, *Our Lady of the Flowers* (1943) and *Miracle of the Rose* (1946). And Genet's characters are also named after flowers: in *Our Lady of the Flowers* the transvestite prostitute Divine gives her/himself names that resemble rose varieties: 'the Very Crimson, the Purplish One, Her Eminence', and fellow prostitutes are called 'Mimosa I, Mimosa II, Mimosa the half-IV'.[38] Equally in *The Screens*, the Arab prostitute visited by insurrectionary troops is called Warda, the Arabic for rose.

Flowers implicitly embody transformation. In a matter of days, or hours, they bud, bloom, fade and fall. Flourishing and wilting, youth and age, life and death, are sheathed in the petals of a single flower. In *The Thief's Journal* (1949), Genet's autofictional account of his youth spent travelling across Europe as a petty criminal and prostitute, he enlists his own surname to reveal the protean quality of the flower. *Genet* is the French word for *genisteae*, commonly known as broom, a shrub with small yellow flowers. Genet mentions two specific genera of the shrub. The first, the 'winged broom', bears pointed petals that resemble arrows.[39] Genet scholar Myriam Bendhif-Syllas notes that the plant's Latin name, *chamaespartium sagittale*, evokes Saggitarius, the archer-centaur.[40] The second, 'Spanish broom' – the nickname that poet Jean Cocteau gave to Genet – is a hermaphrodite variety of the bush. Human, horse, male, female, and shrub interpenetrate.[41] Derrida explores further the anatomical ambiguity of flowers: 'When a flower opens up, "blows", the petals part, and then there rises up what is called the *style*'.[42] Like the labia of a vagina, petals open to disclose the flower's stigma, which in fact resembles the head of a penis. Derrida's study also reveals that the flower's *style*, the supportive stalk connecting the stigma to the ovary, is phallic in shape, but is in fact the female organ of the flower, the *gynoecium*.[43] Bendhif-Syllas adds that *style* derives etymologically from the Latin term 'stylos', meaning column, emphasizing further the resemblance of the pistil (stigma, style and ovary) to a penis.[44] Flowers thus bear an ambiguous status, denoting or connoting male and female, life and death, and also other blurred categories. Derrida describes how the word 'Rose' with which *The Screens* opens is both an adjective denoting a colour – pink – and a noun – a flower. 'Rose' is also both a female noun – 'la rose' (the flower); and a male noun – 'le rose' (the colour pink).[45] From the start of the play, the first word, 'rose', presents the audience with the metamorphosing potential central to Genet's writing: flowers can be both male and female, and Arab subjects can be both colonized and empowered. Genet thus enlists flowers in his attack on stable meaning.

As with so much in Genet's theatre, flowers are far from just decorative. They do not serve simply to create scenes of pastoral beauty. They become primary vectors of meaning, although this meaning is never stable. In *Deathwatch*, Green Eyes recounts to his fellow inmates how he seduced his victim with a spray of lilac blossoms held between his teeth, thus explaining his nickname, Paulo with the Flowery Teeth.[46] Flowers in *Deathwatch* represent sex and seduction.[47] They are also associated with the victim's and with Green-Eyes' death, since he left lilacs on her body, providing the police with a clue that inevitably leads him to the scaffold.[48] Equally, flowers perform the typical Genetian function of blurring perceived opposites. The murdered girl is found with lilacs, rather than blood, in her hair and between her teeth, rather than blood.[49] Maurice also brags that when he becomes a murderer, he will 'turn into a rose and be plucked!'[50] Violence, bloodshed, death and depravity evaporate behind the pastel shades of the lilac and the fragrance of the rose in *Deathwatch*, as they do in 'The Man Condemned to Death', where a murderer is transformed by a crown of thorns into Christ on the cross, and a seedy pimp reclining on a bed of flowers appears as a virgin maid. Notions of criminality and legitimacy, outrage and attraction, all quiver like the petals of the flowers by which Genet symbolizes them.

One of the first stage directions of Genet's best known and most performed play, *The Maids*, is '*Flowers in profusion*'.[51] As in *Deathwatch*, flowers can symbolize seduction and adornment, as Madame tucks a flower in Claire's hair; and, in Solange's words, Madame fills her life with 'her flowers and perfumes and gowns and jewels and lovers'.[52] As in Genet's prison play and poem, flowers in *The Maids* also convert the base into the noble, as Solange touches her washing-up gloves as if they were a bouquet.[53] Mainly, however, flowers in *The Maids* are 'the very opposite of a celebration!' in

Madame's words, since they anticipate the death that the Maids plan for her.[54] The narrator in *The Thief's Journal* wishes to offer gladioli to the little old woman thief whom he thinks could be his mother.[55] Derrida remarks that gladioli derive from the Latin *gladiolus*, meaning 'small sword', thus creating an association between flowers and death.[56] Whether wittingly or not, Madame highlights the maids' morbid intentions as she moans, 'You're quietly killing me with flowers and kindness. One day I'll be found dead beneath the roses'.[57]

In *The Penal Colony*, the association between flowers and death continues, as Ferrand, the guard responsible for assembling the guillotine, refers to his assistants as rose bushes.[58] In *Splendid's*, 'Wreaths of flowers' exemplify the vulgar ostentation of gangster funerals.[59] Flowers are also associated with death in *The Blacks*, which opens with a catafalque centre-stage adorned with '*bouquets of flowers: irises, roses, gladiolas, arum lilies*', and a parade of Negroes who '*pluck flowers from their bodices and lapels and lay them on the catafalque*'.[60] With the flowers, the Negroes both consecrate and desecrate the coffin. One of them, Snow, chews up a flower and spits it out. Does she hyperbolize the racist stereotype of savagery imposed upon Blacks by colonial discourses? Or does her defiant act constitute a protest against the fact that the Negroes are wrongly incriminated, since no murder has actually taken place? Sex, seduction, death, flamboyance, barbarism, resistance – the signification of flowers proliferates across Genet's works.

Across *The Screens*, Genet cultivates nettles, rather than flowers. In Derrida's words, *The Screens* takes place 'in a sort of rose garden full of nettles'.[61] The colonial landowner Mr Blankensee boasts 'one of the finest rose gardens in Africa'.[62] This, and his orange grove, become emblems of the colonial occupation and exploitation of the land. For this reason, perhaps, Mr Blankensee states that the thorns on the stem of a rose are as important as the blooms: they are a reminder of the violence implicit in imperialism.[63] The 'Nettles Family', comprising Saïd – a thief and the poorest man in the region – his mother, and his wife Leïla – the ugliest woman for miles – become the unlikely, unwitting heroes of the anti-colonial insurgency. When insulted by her husband, Leïla moans, '[I'm going] to wipe my nose in the garden, to wash away my snot and tears, and to comfort myself in the nettles'.[64] Nettles, not celebrated for their obvious beauty, become emblems of abjection and simultaneously of insurrection. Like Leïla and Saïd, nettles, as configured by Genet, rebelliously resist conforming with norms of beauty or tidiness. The French word for nettle, *ortie*, derives from the Latin *urtica*, stemming etymologically from *urere*, 'to burn'. The abasement endured by nettles exists in counterpoint with their stinging attack, their burning assault on those who dictate the norms of propriety and acceptability. Like real nettles, which both inject histamine and other irritants into passers-by and serve medicinal purposes, Genet's nettles, like Derrida's *pharmakon*, are both toxic and therapeutic. They constitute both poison and cure, both attack and liberation.[65]

This by no means comprehensive account of flowers in Genet's works serves a specific purpose. It illustrates the ways in which the significations attributed by Genet to words and images multiply, propagate, flourish, cross-pollinate. Flowers can represent male, female, masculine, feminine, noun, adjective, sex, seduction, death, pomposity, ignominy, criminality, legitimation, consecration, desecration, civilization, barbarism, colonial occupation, imperial aggression, anti-colonial insurgency, marginalization, saintliness... Collapsing, conflating, confusing conventionally opposing categories becomes a dynamic that dominates Genet's entire oeuvre, as signification becomes as predictable and grounded as pollen in the wind.

Absurdism and ecocriticism

Since no meaning in Genet's works exists outside discourse, artifice and theatricality, where does reality reside? Esslin describes Genet's theatre as 'wholly absurd – it is futility mirroring itself'. Further on, he suggests, 'each apparent reality is revealed as an appearance, an illusion, which in turn is revealed as again part of a dream or an illusion, and so on, *ad infinitum*'. He concludes, 'Reality is an unattainable goal'.[66] Genet's theatre becomes 'a device to uncover the fundamental absurdity of being, its nothingness'.[67] Genet himself employs the term 'absurd' on a number of occasions. Archibald, Master of Ceremonies in *The Blacks*, describes the play-within-the-play as an 'architecture of emptiness and words', and as 'absurd'.[68] And in his essay 'What Remains of a Rembrandt Torn into Little Squares All the Same Size and Shot Down the Toilet', Genet writes,

'It's only those kinds of truths, the ones that are not demonstrable and even "false", the ones that one cannot without absurdity lead to their conclusion without coming to the negation of them and of oneself – those are the ones that must be exalted by the work of art'.[69] Here, and in other versions of the same axiom across Genet's works, the function of art is to take to an absurd extreme the relativist logic that denies stability to meaning.[70]

What kind of ecological politics might this apparent nihilism produce? Both Genet, and Derrida in *Glas*, seem to take an ecocritical stance *avant la lettre*, when emphasizing that flowers in the poet's works are not simply reduced to signifiers bearing constantly deferred signifieds. In *Miracle of the Rose*, Genet writes, 'The scents and colours of the flowers were unchanged, yet it seemed to me that they were becoming more essentially themselves. I mean that they were beginning to exist for me with their own existence, with less and less the help of a support: the flowers'.[71] Derrida appears to elucidate: 'Departed are those who thought the flower signified, symbolized, metaphorized, metonymized, that one was devising repertories of signifiers and anthic figures, classifying flowers of rhetoric, combining them, ordering them, binding them up in a sheaf or bouquet. ...'[72] Flowers are attributed such a diversity of meanings by Genet, that any definitive meaning evaporates into a haze. By refusing ever to establish the meaning of flowers, Genet also allows them to exist in their own right, independent of human agency. And Genet's ecopolitics reside precisely in the manner in which he seeks for non-human animate entities, and even the inanimate, to exist not as secondary or subsidiary to humans, but in their own right. While revealing self-consciously how Nature is a human construct, as I have demonstrated, Genet simultaneously acknowledges that it bears an autonomy beyond human comprehension or control, that humans will never grasp.

Nobody comments with more force on the political potential of deconstruction in Genet's works than postcolonial critic Edward Said. For him, the greatness of *The Screens* lies in 'its deliberate and logical dismantling not just of French identity – France as empire, as power, as history – but of the very notion of identity itself'.[73] Deconstruction is compatible with ecocriticism in that it exposes contradictions in systems of meaning, and can therefore contribute towards disassembling the humanist narcissism and sense of sovereignty that have led to the current ecological crisis. The rejection of origin, authenticity and truth provides an affirmative possibility to envisage other futures, rather than a nihilist abnegation of responsibility towards the future. It is, no doubt, for this reason that Genet's friend and commentator Lydie Dattas insists, perhaps referring to other more pessimistic absurdists like Ionesco, 'Right from the start, an abyss separates [Genet] from the corrupters of his time: not a drop of cynicism in his entire oeuvre'.[74]

'Every object possesses its own magnificence': Biospherical egalitarianism

In 'What Remains of a Rembrandt', and in a text on the artist Alberto Giacometti, Genet describes a moment when, sitting on a train opposite an ugly, repugnant old man he was obliged to acknowledge that 'any man was exactly – sorry, but I want to emphasize "exactly" – "worth" any other man. "Anyone at all", I told myself, "can be loved beyond his ugliness, his stupidity, his meanness."'[75] In his posthumously published masterwork, *Prisoner of Love*, Genet reiterates this sentiment, insisting that there is no absolute 'distinction between the highest and the humblest'.[76] Numerous critics comment on the fact that according to Genet's writing and political life, no human inherently enjoys sovereign status. As Hélène Cixous states in her recent book on Genet, he 'despises well brought-up white folk in power who claim not to know that every person is worth the same as any other'.[77] However, few critics remark that humans themselves also lose sovereignty in Genet's works, since he denies them domination over other animate or inanimate elements.

Lexically, the term 'ecocriticism' responds to the notion of *crisis*. The global ecological situation is critical, as no small number of intellectual figures cautions. Cultural critic Slavoj Žižek warns that it threatens 'the very survival of humankind', as well as 'our most unquestionable presuppositions, the very horizon of our meaning'.[78] This apocalyptic tone is reiterated in the first line of another cultural critic, Félix Guattari's *The Three Ecologies*: 'The Earth is undergoing a period of intense techno-scientific transformations. If no remedy is found, the ecological disequilibrium this has generated will ultimately threaten the continuation of life on the planet's surface'.[79] Climate change, oceanic pollution, radioactive contamination, the proliferation of toxic agents, the loss of landscapes, habitats and species, all threaten to change the planet irreversibly. The most important political, economic, social and cultural questions in the history of humanity must be posed today, and two different responses have emerged. The first, environmental politics, recommends adjustments to consumer habits: offsetting carbon emissions on low-cost flights, eating in veggie cafés, making donations to save turtles. These 'green' actions are woesomely trivial compared with the gravity of the crisis and, contrary to their good intentions, can simply fuel the problem by buying into capitalist consumerism rather than combating it. Fittingly, the term 'absurd' occurs in Guattari's text precisely to describe the environmental dead-end towards which global capitalism is heading us: 'The huge subjective void produced by the proliferating production of material and immaterial goods is becoming ever more absurd'.[80] For this reason, several eco-philosophers seek a far 'deeper', more radical solution to the ecological crisis than what politics specialist Andrew Dobson terms 'a managerial approach to environmental problems', which rests secure in the belief that the crisis 'can be solved without fundamental changes in present values or patterns of production and consumption.[81] The 'Deep Ecology movement', advocated by philosopher Arne Naess, calls for an end to human domination, and instead for 'biospherical egalitarianism'.[82] Guattari broadens the remit of this end to human exceptionalism advocated by 'deep ecology' by implicating individual, social, political and economic factors, as well as environmental ones. In particular, he proposes that capitalism's effects must be confronted not by a minority of nature-loving consumers, but in the domain of mental ecology: 'individual, domestic, material, neighbourly, creative or one's personal ethics'.[83] Žižek recommends that we rethink 'our most unquestionable presuppositions, the very horizon of our meaning'. Our dominion 'over every living thing that moves on the earth', to quote the Old Testament, must end.[84] In varied and complex ways, Genet's theatre provides an imaginative counter-discourse to the gross imbalances imposed by humanity, a critical metadiscourse to the humanist conceit that has precipitated the environmental destruction we now face.

It is true that both flora and fauna are co-opted in Genet's theatre in order to serve the self-interest of specific human groups. I have already noted instances such as the jackals or snakes that connote savagery in *The Blacks*, or the multiple symbolic significations attributed by him to flowers. However, there are numerous indications that he considers humans to bear no more or less importance than non-human forms, for instance, non-human animals. The '*opposition* between the human and the animal' is as contested as the Nature/culture divide since this distinction, too, could be perceived as a human construct.[85] Derrida's title *The Animal that Therefore I am* plays on the foundational humanist philosopher René Descartes's renowned maxim, 'I think therefore I am', a hymn to the all-knowing, all-reasoning God-like transcendental subject, the supposedly cosmic self. For Derrida, the metaphysical superiority of human- over non-human animals is determined solely by human language, human discourse. He thus coins the term *animot*. *Animot* is both a homophone of *animaux*, the French plural of 'animal', and is composed of *animal* and *mot*, the French for 'word'.[86] Derrida thus highlights how the opposition between humans and non-human animals is nothing more than linguistic. As I have demonstrated, Genet repeatedly emphasizes the linguistic discursivity of his characters' words and views, meaning that, as readily as he establishes a distinction between one human and another or one species and another, he undermines it. Immediately after declaring that 'any man [is] exactly … "worth" any other man', Genet describes Giacometti's sculpture of a solitary emaciated dog sniffing the ground. He quotes the artist saying, 'It's me. One day I saw myself in the street like that. I was the dog'. Genet goes on to remark that this dog constitutes the 'supreme magnification of solitude'.[87] Since Genet has just explained that solitude originates in the fact that no human bears sovereignty over any other, one can infer that the dog, too, is no less important than any other being. When, in *The Screens*, one of the Arab women explains that she bears children solely in order for flies to be able to eat the crust in the corners of their eyes; and the Cadi presiding over a trial declares that God can be found in 'a wasp in the sun', the superior status of humans and their world is clearly overturned.[88] Non-human animals are *animots*: linguistic constructs whose separation from human animals is theatrical, rather than actual.

Across Genet's theatre, there are instances where characters imitate non-human animals. In *Deathwatch*, Green Eyes describes how, to escape his destiny as a criminal, he 'tried to be a dog, a cat, a horse, a tiger, a table, a stone! I even tried, me too, to be a rose!'[89] In *The Balcony*, a prostitute poses in a sexual roleplay as the General's horse, complete with girth, harness, bridle and bit.[90] In *The Blacks*, as I have indicated, Negroes recreate the sounds of the jungle with their voices, and at the end of the play, the Missionary '*moos like a cow*' and '*walks about on all fours, pretends to graze, and licks the feet of the Negroes*', as the Whites finally morph into cattle, reminiscent of the chattel to which African slaves were once reduced.[91] And in *The Screens*, as I have also mentioned, the Mother and Leïla utter barnyard cries to represent their rural home, and bark like a pack of dogs when they are chased away from a funeral for being related to a thief.[92] Guattari and his collaborator, philosopher Gilles Deleuze, argue for the concept of 'becoming animal'.[93] Despite the fact that 'becoming animal' does not involve imitating non-human animals in the ways that I have just noted, it is useful for understanding the significance of Genet's bestiary. 'Becoming animal' involves abandoning the certitude of a dualist world where non-human animals are dominated by humans, the latter endowed with the reason that the former lack. Instead, human animals must envisage other modes of perception that exchange certainty and stasis, for becoming, altering, transforming. The transformatory potential of the actor is, of course, demonstrated when she or he plays a horse, dog or owl. In addition, the perpetual metamorphosis of meaning across Genet's theatre demonstrates a deconstruction of humanist ascendency that allows for the possibility to imagine other more egalitarian modes of cohabiting the planet.

Not only non-human animals, but also the inanimate world bears equal value to human animals in Genet's cosmos. Green-Eyes recounts how he tried to become not only 'a dog, a cat, a horse, a tiger', but also 'a table, a stone! … a rose!' In *The Thief's Journal*, Genet expresses his desire to mingle both with animals, and with creepers. And in *Prisoner of Love*, he writes of his sympathy towards animism, accounting for how animists 'approach everything, [themselves] included, with equal respect and without undue humility'.[94] Genet's 'animism' can be elucidated by returning to his text on Giacometti. He narrates how the artist described, when observing a towel draped over a chair, that he came to the realization that no object was more or less significant than any other.[95] For Giacometti, even the dust gathering on old bottles cluttering a table in his studio is no less 'pretty' than his canvases and sculptures.[96] As the old revolutionary, Ommou, reminds the audience in *The Screens*, 'The lords of yesterday will tell the lords of today that nothing must be protected so much as a little heap of garbage... Let no one ever throw out all her sweepings... '.[97] Writing in another text on Rembrandt, 'Rembrandt's Secret', Genet expresses a radical sense of egalitarianism which resonates with Giacometti's insistence that dust and dogs are no less significant than human animals:

> This effort brings him to rid himself of all that could lead him back to a differentiated, discontinuous, hierarchic vision of the world: a hand has the same value as a face, a face as the corner of a table, a table corner as a stick, a stick as a hand, a hand as a sleeve... and all that, which is perhaps true with other painters – but what painter, up to now, has made something lose its identity in order to exalt it more? – all that, I say, relates back to first the hand, the sleeve, then to painting, of course, but starting from that instant, endlessly from one to the other, and in a dizzying pursuit, toward nothing.[98]

The manner in which Genet notes how all elements on Rembrandt's canvas lose their identity resonates with the anti-identitarian ethics that Edward Said detects in Genet's own writing. At the same time, identity is 'exalted', specificity is maintained, as all entities safeguard their uniqueness rather than merging into one totalized whole. Human hand and face, inanimate paint and texture, illusory table, stick and sleeve, are treated by Rembrandt with an absolute disregard for hierarchy, propelling them all into a vertiginous void. Rather than a nihilist postmodern dematerialization of all elements, can this void be upheld as a celebration of all living and non-living entities? François Regnault notes the prominence of 'dirt', 'shit' and 'rubbish' in the theatres of Genet and of fellow playwright Samuel Beckett, and proposes that both playwrights reduce human subjects to garbage, indicated by the dustbins from which characters emerge in Beckett's *Endgame* (1957), and the 'muck', 'sordidness' and 'shittiness' into which Saïd and his family sink in *The Screens*.[99] Contrarily, I propose that, rather than reducing everything to dust, to an absurdist nothingness, Genet might 'exalt' everything, elevate everything to the status previously occupied solely by humans. When, with reference to Rembrandt's paintings, he declares, '*this* is nothing more than *that*, and nothing less', does he not celebrate, rather than deflate, the possibility of greater equality between human, non-human, animate and inanimate?[100] In *The Thief's Journal* he writes, "The atmosphere of the planet Uranus appears to be so heavy that the ferns there are creepers; the animals drag along, crushed by the weight of the gases. I want to mingle with these humiliated creatures which are always in their bellies.' When he wishes to mix with the universe's most humiliated beings, is it not precisely to afford them the visibility and prominence of which they have always been deprived? While it would be exaggerated to declare Genet a biocentrist or ecocentrist who consciously champions the view that all organisms and inanimate phenomena are part of an interconnected network, his systematic disassembling of the illusion of human separation from the rest of the animal and inanimate world surely goes some significant way towards engaging with the notion of ecological accountability.

How does this radical democratization of elements manifest itself in Genet's theatre? Genet diffuses the attention usually enjoyed by the canonical Aristotelian components of theatre – sequential plot, character and dialogue – in order that the spectator might enjoy a glittering array of theatrical elements: scenography, stage properties, lighting, music, acoustics, gestures, rhythms, vocal tones, costumes, make-up, hairstyles … . This is most evident in his later plays like *The Balcony*, *The Blacks*, *The Penal Colony* and, especially, *The Screens*. However, the apparent conventionality of Genet's earlier theatre is deceptive. Certain critics see *The Balcony* as a turning point from the classical unity of his earlier plays, with their single location and brief time span.[101] I would argue that none of his plays offer the reassuring resolution and conclusion often implicit in French neoclassical unity. With their self-consciously literary, image-charged dialogue, which pirouettes vertiginously from one existential crisis to another, his early plays fragment *drama*, deriving etymologically from the Greek for 'action', into sequences of isolated dramatic effects, or what in contemporary theatre studies is referred to as the 'postdramatic'.[102] Moreover, Genet disassembles characters into 'signs charged with signs', and even recommends that they be played by puppets, effacing the psychological recognizability associated with French neoclassical theatre, as well as reducing human pre-eminence further.[103] Since plot and character do not provide the foundational structure of Genet's theatre, meaning is distributed across a 'herbaceous' network of scenic elements. In Robert Wilson's

FIGURE 8 *Robert Wilson's production of Jean Genet's* Les Nègres (The Blacks) *at the théâtre de l'Odéon, Paris, October 2014.* © *Lucie Jansch.*

FIGURE 9 *Robert Wilson's production of Jean Genet's* Les Nègres (The Blacks) *at the théâtre de l'Odéon, Paris, October 2014.* © *Lucie Jansch.*

recent production of *The Blacks* (théâtre de l'Odéon, Paris, October 2014; see Figure 8 and 9) the technicolour nightclub costumes, spirals of glimmering fairy lights, neon desert palms, midnight African sky, multiple acting areas on different levels, choreographed hand gestures, stylized facial expressions, Afrobeat tunes... played no less of a central role than Genet's own text, in theatricalizing and simultaneously deconstructing any essentialist notion of a black identity.[104] As theatre theorist Odette Aslan writes, 'Objects in Genet's works are no longer simple accessories; they become primary players'.[105] I have already highlighted the central role played by flowers. Genet applies the radical egalitarianism he expresses in 'Rembrandt's Secret', where he declares that 'every object possesses its own magnificence, neither more nor less than any other', to his theatre, thereby contributing towards the evolution of the twentieth-century art of *mise en scène*, where non-textual, visual and acoustic features become key elements in theatrical expression.[106]

But does a non-hierarchical, non-differentiated approach to the inclusion and arrangement of theatrical elements necessarily take part in an ecological ethics? No. And yes. It would be naïve at best to assume that solutions to our unprecedented global ecological crisis could be purely aesthetic. For some ecocritics, notably Buell, the only truly ecological art is nature writing, where the environment is presented by literal, mimetic means. He identifies criteria that ecocritical texts must meet: 'The nonhuman environment is present not merely as a framing device but as a presence that begins to suggest that human history is implicated in natural history'. In addition, 'a spirit of commitment to environmental praxis' must be evident.[107] Human accountability to the environment is not as explicitly part of the text's ethical orientation in Genet's theatre as it might be in nature writing.[108] Moreover, since Genet's relativist philosophy is concerned with enabling humans to perceive and feel differently, it could be seen as perpetuating anthropocentrism, rather than affording agency to non-humans.[109] However, Buell does indirectly enable texts that do not present landscapes according to realist modes, or express their environmental commitment, to be considered as ecological: 'What sort of literature remains possible if we relinquish the myth of human apartness? It must be a literature that abandons, or at least questions, what would seem to be literature's most basic foci: character, persona, narrative consciousness'.[110] For him, this 'aesthetic of relinquishment' manifests itself predominantly in environmental non-fiction like nature writing rather than in lyric poetry or prose fiction, which rely on 'the most basic pleasures of homocentrism: plot, characterisation and dialogue'.[111] He does not consider theatre such as Genet's, where, surprisingly in the words of Buell rather than Lehmann, 'nonhuman agents' are accommodated 'as bona fide partners',[112] theatre where traditional anthropocentric components like characters are accorded no more importance than scenic elements such as scenography or acoustics. In the extent to which Genet's theatre critiques humans as the undisputed authors of the world and occupants of the stage; to which he values the particularity, the 'thusness' of all things; to which he displaces the self-as-ego with the self as interconnected, embedded and implicated in wider ecologies; and to which the term *ecocriticism* implicitly involves 'critique' of human hegemony, Genet's dramatic works can be considered ecocritical.

In parallel, rather than in tension, with his engagement with a radical deconstruction of meaning, Genet was a political activist. From the 1960s, he was deeply implicated in struggles for equality and justice, campaigning alongside real-life 'Nettles Families' like the black civil rights movement in the United States, immigrants in France and, most notably, the Palestinians in the Middle East.[113] Furthermore, he was not unaware of environmental political issues. As the Valet in *The Blacks* reads out the prices of rubber and gold on the stock exchange, members of the White Court '*rub their hands*'. The Queen also boasts of her 'cellars full of chests full of pearls fished up by them from their mysterious seas, diamonds, gold, pieces of eight unearthed from their deep mines'.[114] Genet's consciousness of the greedy consumption of natural resources fuelled by capitalism – the *real* absurdity of human existence – is apparent in several plays.[115] Esslin explains how Genet's theatre constitutes social protest, although he 'resolutely rejects political commitment, political argument, didacticism, or propaganda'.[116] In his most explicit, and yet characteristically opaque, manifesto on political theatre, his 'Avertissement' to *The Balcony*, Genet warns, 'A few poets, these days, go in for a very curious operation: they sing the praises of the People, of Liberty, of the Revolution, etc., which, when sung, are rocketed up into an abstract sky and then stuck there, discomfited and deflated'.[117] Politics are emptied of their vitality and potentiality when they become empty slogans chanted by artists. Genet himself insists, 'I'm not part of any party!'[118] But this does not preclude

Genet's theatre from bearing profound political significance.[119] Genet proposes a radical, 'deep' re-evaluation of the importance of humanity, which is 'neither more nor less' significant than any other animate or inanimate entity, an ethics that is reflected both in his destabilization of fixed categories, and in his inclusive theatrical aesthetics, where the sun and moon can be characters, and where paper screens can carry as much meaning as words.

Will the rampant consumption of fossil fuels exacerbating climate change, the devastating deforestation, the bleaching of coral reefs, and disappearance of over half the world's wildlife population in the past fifty years, be reversed via philosophical debates played out on theatrical stages on the subjects of the performativity of Nature as constructed by humans on anthropocentrism, or on the relativism of human sovereignty? Almost certainly not. Will herbaceous aesthetics and postdramatic paradigms save the planet? Almost certainly not. Genet states in his first-ever interview, 'It's very rare for us to make a conscious effort to go beyond this stupefied state'.[120] Genet does not provide us with a programme of ecological solutions. It is up to us, readers and spectators of his works, to stir from our stupor, and to make conscious connections between poet and planet: between mental ecology and the environment. It is up to us to 'become animal', to alter our perceptions and actions with as much dynamism as the fluid meanings that Genet attributes to his lilacs, carnations and roses. Just as no scenic element on Genet's stage steals the spotlight, humans are not the Earth's sole and autonomous occupants, existing in solipsistic isolation. In Edward Said's words, Genet dismantles identity itself. He dissolves differences between human and non-human, animate and inanimate, subject and object, self and other, dualisms that have arguably precipitated the human destruction of the environment. He celebrates nettles, dog roses, dogs and dust, according equal value to each, without, for that matter, conflating or erasing their unique specificity. Nobody is suggesting that dog roses or dust might rise up and rule the world. But a shift in human mentality is crucial to our survival. The word *culture* originates in the Latin *colere*, meaning to 'attend to, cultivate, respect'.[121] It is up to us as readers, as spectators and as inhabitants of the Earth, to employ what we learn from culture, from theatre, from Genet's anti-anthropocentric ethics and aesthetics, to care for our environment as much as we care for ourselves.

Works cited

Adorno, Theodor and Max Horkheimer, *Dialectic of Enlightenment*, trans. E. Jephcott. Stanford, CA: Stanford University Press, 2002.

Arons, Wendy and Theresa J. May (eds), *Readings in Ecology and Performance*. Basingstoke: Palgrave, 2012.

Aslan, Odette, '*Les Paravents* de Jean Genet', *Les Voies de la création théâtrale*, vol. 3 (1972), pp. 13–107.

Atterton, Peter and Matthew Calarco (eds), *Animal Philosophy: Ethics and Identity*. London: Continuum, 2004.

Bendhif-Syllas, Myriam, 'Filiation et écriture végétales de Jean Genet, une affaire de styles', in Hadrien Laroche (ed.), *Pour Genet*. Saint-Nazaire: Maison des Écrivains Étrangers et des Traducteurs, 2011, pp. 170–9.

Bharucha, Rustom, *Terror and Performance*. London and New York: Routledge, 2014.

Bolouki-Raskédian, Mahtab, '"L'Air" dans la dramaturgie de Jean Genet', *L'Infini*, vol. 97 (autumn 2006), pp. 106–14.

Bradby, David and Clare Finburgh, *Jean Genet*. London and New York: Routledge, 2011.

Buell, Lawrence, *The Environmental Imagination: Thoreau, Nature Writing, and the Formation of American Culture*. Cambridge, MA: Belknap Press, Harvard University Press, 1995.

Cixous, Hélène, *Entretien de la blessure: Sur Jean Genet*. Paris: Galilée, 2011.

Dattas, Lydie, 'Jean de Neige', in *Genet*, catalogue for 2006 exhibition at the Musée des Beaux-Arts de Tours, Farrago, 2006, pp. 55–6.

Deleuze, Gilles and Félix Guattari, *A Thousand Plateaus: Capitalism and Schizophrenia*, trans. B. Massumi. Minneapolis, MN: University of Minnesota Press, 1987 [1980].

Deleuze, Gilles and Félix Guattari, 'Becoming Animal', in Peter Atterton and Matthew Calarco (eds), *Animal Philosophy: Ethics and Identity*. London: Continuum, 2004, pp. 233–309.

Derrida, Jacques, 'Plato's Pharmacy,' in *Dissemination*, trans. B. Johnson, London: Athlone Press, 1981, pp. 61–172.

Derrida, Jacques, *Glas*, trans. J. P. Leavey and R. Rand. Lincoln, NE: University of Nebraska Press, 1986 [1974].

Derrida, Jacques, *The Animal That Therefore I am*, trans. D. Willis. New York: Fordham University Press, 2008 [2006].

Dobson, Andrew, *Green Political Thought*, 3rd edn. London and New York: Routledge, 1995.

Esslin, Martin, *The Theatre of the Absurd*, 3rd revised and enlarged edn. London: Methuen, 2001.

Finburgh, Clare, 'Unveiling the Void: Presence and Absence in the Scenography of Jean Genet's *Les Paravents*', *Theatre Journal*, vol. 56, no. 2 (May 2004), pp. 205–24.

Fredette, Natalie, *Figures baroques de Jean Genet*. Montreal, Quebec: XYZ, 2001.

Genet, Jean, *The Blacks: A Clown Show*, trans. B. Frechtman. New York: Grove Press, 1960 [1959].

Genet, Jean, *The Screens*, trans. B. Frechtman. New York: Grove Press, 1962.

Genet, Jean, *Miracle of the Rose*, trans. B. Frechtman. London: Anthony Blond, 1965 [1946].

Genet, Jean, *The Thief's Journal*, trans. B. Frechtman. Harmondsworth: Penguin, 1965 [1949].

Genet, Jean, *The Complete Poems of Jean Genet*, trans. D. Fisher et al. San Francisco, CA: ManRoot, 1981.

Genet, Jean, *The Maids and Deathwatch*, trans. B. Frechtman. London: Faber, 1989.

Genet, Jean, *Our Lady of the Flowers*, trans. B. Frechtman. London: Faber, 1990 [1943].

Genet, Jean, *The Balcony*, trans. B. Wright and T. Hands. London: Faber, 1991 [1962].

Genet, Jean, *Splendid's*, trans. N. Bartlett. London: Faber, 1995 [1993].

Genet, Jean, *Jean Genet Théâtre Complet*. Paris: Gallimard coll. Pléiade, 2002.

Genet, Jean, *Le Bagne*, in *Jean Genet Théâtre Complet*, Paris: Gallimard coll. Pléiade, 2002.

Genet, Jean, *Elle*, in *Jean Genet Théâtre Complet*.

Genet, Jean, *Fragments of the Artwork*, trans. C. Mandell. Stanford, CA: Stanford University Press, 2003.

Genet, Jean, *Prisoner of Love*, trans. B. Bray. New York: New York Review of Books, 2003 [1986].

Genet, Jean, *The Declared Enemy*, trans. J. Fort. Stanford, CA: Stanford University Press, 2004.

Gifford, Terry, *Pastoral*. London: Routledge, 1999.

Guattari, Félix, *The Three Ecologies*, trans. I. Pindar and P. Sutton. London: The Athlone Press, 2000 [1989].

Harvey, Graham, *Animism: Respecting the Living World*. New York: Columbia University Press, 2006.

Hargreaves, Martin, 'Dancing the Impossible: Kazuo Ohno, Lindsay Kemp and *Our Lady of the Flowers*', in Clare Finburgh, Carl Lavery and Maria Shevtsova (eds), *Jean Genet: Performance and Politics*. Basingstoke: Palgrave Macmillan, 2006, pp. 106–16.

Hochman, Jhan, *Green Cultural Studies: Nature in Film, Novel, and Theory*. Moscow ID: University of Idaho Press, 1998.

Kerridge, Richard and Neil Sammels (eds), *Writing the Environment: Ecocriticism and Literature*. London: Zed Books, 1998.

Kershaw, Baz, *Theatre Ecology: Environments and Performance Events*. Cambridge: Cambridge University Press, 2007.

Koltès, Bernard-Marie and François Regnault, *La Famille des orties. Esquisses et croquis autour des* Paravents *de Jean Genet*. Paris: Éditions Nanterre/Amandiers, 1983.

Laroche, Hadrien, *The Last Genet: A Writer in Revolt*, trans. D. Homel. Vancouver, BC: Arsenal Pulp Press, 2010 [1997].

Lavery, Carl, *The Politics of Jean Genet's Late Theatre: Spaces of Revolution*. Manchester: Manchester University Press, 2010.

Lehmann, Hans-Thies, *Postdramatic Theatre*, trans. K. Jürs-Munby. London: Routledge, 2006 [1999].

Naess, Arne, 'The Shallow and the Deep, Long-Range Ecology Movement: A Summary', *Inquiry*, vol. 16 (spring), pp. 95–100.

Said, Edward W., 'On Jean Genet's Late Works', in Ellen Gainor (ed.), *Imperialism and Theatre: Essays on World Theatre, drama and performance 1795-1995*. London and New York: Routledge, 1995.

Sartre, Jean-Paul, *Saint Genet Actor and Martyr*, trans. B. Frechtman. Minneapolis, MN: University of Minnesota Press, 2012 [1952].

Steffen, Will, Paul J. Clutzen and John R. McNeill, 'The Anthropocene: Are Humans Now Overwhelming the Great Forces of Nature?', *Ambio*, vol. 38 (2007), pp. 614–21.

Stewart, Harry E., 'The Case of the Lilac Murders: Jean Genet's *Haute Surveillance*', *The French Review*, vol. 48, no. 1 (October 1974), pp. 87–94.

Thody, Philip, *Jean Genet: A Study of His Novels and Plays*. London: Hamish Hamilton, 1968.

Vaïs, Michel, *L'Écrivain scénique*. Montreal: Presses de l'Université de Québec, 1978.

Westling, Louise, 'Literature, the Environment and the Question of the Posthuman', in Catrin Gersdorf and Sylvia Mayer (eds), *Nature in Literary and Cultural Studies: Transatlantic Conversations on Ecocriticism*. Amsterdam, New York: Rodopi, 2006, pp. 25–47.

Žižek, Slavoj, *Looking Awry: An Introduction to Jacques Lacan through Popular Culture*. Cambridge, MA: MIT Press, 1991.

8

The Secluded Voice: The Impossible Call Home in Early Pinter

Mark Taylor-Batty and Carl Lavery

In the original 1961 publication of Martin Esslin's *Theatre of the Absurd*, Harold Pinter was included, among a set of thirteen other playwrights, in the chapter titled 'Parallels and Proselytes', as 'one of the most promising exponents' of the proposed genre.[1] He remained tucked away there in the re-edition of 1968, and his work was only later promoted to a chapter of its own in the 1980 third edition, the earlier section now expanded to include commentary on the dramas written in the interim. As part of his argument that Pinter's writing shares generic traits with the output of Samuel Beckett, Arthur Adamov, Eugène Ionesco and Jean Genet, Esslin presents Pinter's imagery and stage spaces in terms of the workings of the unconscious mind, accommodating them predominantly within an existential perspective.

Writing of *The Room* (1957), for example, Esslin describes the bedsitting space as 'the small area of light and warmth, that our consciousness, the fact that we exist, opens up in the vast ocean of nothingness from which we gradually emerge after birth and into which we sink again when we die'[2]; and Stanley's abduction from Meg and Petey's guest-house in *The Birthday Party* (1958) is defined as an 'allegory of death – man snatched away from the home he has built for himself'.[3] Similarly, Esslin argues that 'the key to understanding [*The Homecoming* (1965)] is simple enough' and states that it can be seen as an Oedipal 'fantasy, a wish-fulfilment dream'.[4] The problem with metaphors as comfortable envelopes for interpreted signification, as Una Chaudhuri explains in *Staging Place: The Geography of Modern Drama* (1995), is that 'these supposedly "hidden" meanings are so common, so instinctive in our culture, that their ready identification in acts of interpretation is suspect, unsatisfactory'.[5] The critical risk is that to fix too quickly upon habitual metaphors for interpretative purposes can promote an easy belief that one has engaged with the meaning of a text and that such knowledge can be fixed and exists outside of an experience of that work. This potentially undermines the organic, aesthetic process of allowing the play to engage with one *in situ*, in the darkened auditorium, and it is this process, this dynamic in Pinter's early work that we might seek now to appreciate in ecologically inflected terms of displacement, recovery and attempted homecoming.[6] In this essay, Pinter's early plays are read by engaging with Jean-François Lyotard's idiosyncratic and ontological examination of the word 'ecology', which takes its prefix from the Greek word *oikos* meaning home or hearth. This understanding of ecology as homecoming will then be placed briefly in dialogue with Pierre Bourdieu's analysis of social suffering to investigate the relationship between dwelling and social ecology in Pinter. The phrase social ecology in this essay is used in the same way that Murray Bookchin and Félix Guattari use it, that is to say, as a concept that understands our relationship to the non-human *bios* as a symptom of our ability – or more accurately inability – to exist together as a human *socius*.[7] So although references to nature and the elements in Pinter's early work often function to contextualize his characters and their isolation, his investigations into the discourses, dispositions and systems that create both *habitus* and *socius* tell us much about our ecological relationship to the world in general.[8]

It is understandable why a critical approach that sought symbols and metaphors was often adopted in early readings of Pinter's work. Esslin sees Riley, the black character who rises from the dark, damp basement in Pinter's first play, *The Room* (1957), as an '[emissary] from another world'.[9] In Esslin's view, Riley's demand that the principal character Rose return with him both foregrounds the vulnerability of her tenancy and suggests a return to another (perhaps original) home that she has abandoned or even forgotten.[10] Given Riley's basement residence and behaviour, it is perhaps inevitable that he has invited a number of Freudian readings, in which he is perceived as a blind id that rises from the unconscious, inspiring both fearful and libidinous responses from Rose as well as insisting upon a return to an earlier, primal state.[11] Riley in such interpretations is figured as representative of the *unheimlich*, a concept that, in Freud's essay 'The Uncanny' (1919), is defined as a feeling or mood that is both familiar and strange, kin and unkind. The spatiality inherent in Pinter's play recalls, too, Gaston Bachelard's and Carl C. Jung's alignment of the cellar with the sinister, the unknown.[12] But given the context of this collection of essays, with its emphasis on 'greening the Absurd', how might we move beyond psychoanalysis as a critical end in itself, and shift the focus to ecology? A good place to start, perhaps, is with the later writing of the French philosopher Jean-François Lyotard. In the text '*Domus* and the Megalopolis' (1988), Lyotard offers an example of how to break with the sclerotic hold that psychoanalysis exerts on extant models of interpretation. Lyotard achieves this by reading the *unheimlich* not in terms of psychic malaise, as Freud does, but rather as an ontological condition, which he associates with a disruptive, inarticulable voice, located at the very heart of the *domus*, the home, the domestic unit:

> Even more than the city, the republic or even the flabby and permissive associations of interests and opinions called contemporary society – it is strange that, even more than with any of these states of assembling the diverse, the *domus* gives the untameable a chance to appear. As though the god-nature which cultivates it were doubling himself with an anti-god, an anti-nature, desperate to make the bucolic lie. The violence I am speaking of exceeds ordinary war and economic and social crisis.[13]

By configuring the *unheimlich* as ontology rather than symptology, Lyotard proposes a form of subjectivity that is internally divided, disrupted by the palpable presence of a 'secret' that we experience in our bodies, but whose meaning remains undecipherable. The secret, Lyotard insists, 'consists only in the timbre of a sensitive, sentimental matter [and] is inaccessible except to stupor'.[14]

In 'Domus and Megalopolis', Lyotard contends that the root of our current ecological crisis is to do with developed capitalism's inability to accept the opacity of the secret, what he also calls the 'insoluble *différend*' (a kind of constitutive difference or dispute that defies resolution).[15] Instead of letting the secret be, accepting its untameability, neo-liberal rationality attempts, Lyotard argues, to destroy it by setting it to work, making it mean something: 'It [the secret] must be exterminated because it constitutes an empty opacity for the programme of total mobilisation in view of transparency. ... The untameable has to be controlled'.[16]

In Lyotard's view, society's attempts to discipline the secret, to tame the *unheimlich*, is evidenced in spatial terms by the increasing trend to build ever bigger cities, enormous urban conglomerates, megalopoli. According to Lyotard, this desire to metabolize nature, to reduce the alterity of the world, has produced a crisis in dwelling, which he associates, like the philosopher Martin Heidegger, with the abandonment of the countryside as well as with the destruction of the life of the peasant. In Lyotard's bucolic view, the peasant lives a frugal but sustaining relationship with nature, in which what he calls '*fruges*' (the products of nature's cycles) are respected: 'The *fruges* are obtained by nature and from nature. They produce, destroy and reproduce themselves ... according to nature's care for itself, which is called frugality'.[17]

If Lyotard were to posit the *domus* as a lost origin, a pastoral paradise that we could return to, then his ecological thinking would be close to the dangerous romanticism of Heidegger, a romanticism in which the celebration of 'nature' hides a violent tendency to discriminate against others who are not native to the territory or homeland (see 'Introduction', pp 20–2). That Lyotard does not make this mistake – in the essay he openly criticizes Heidegger's support for Nazism as an example of the '*domus* mocked' – is predicated on the fact that his ontology allows no place for a return to origins.[18] In Lyotard, the *domus* is where the secret is located, an uncanny, differential space that resists ever coming into existence as an actual location. In a beautiful sentence, Lyotard describes the *domus* as something that 'never existed, except as a dream of the old child awakening and destroying it on awakening'.[19] However, in the extent to which the *domus* is key to Lyotard's notion of what constitutes a progressive ecology, then how, one might legitimately ask, are we to encounter and care for it, if it is only ever 'a mirage, an impossible dwelling'?[20] Lyotard's answer is simple: we should give up trying to ground or appropriate the *domus*, and instead relate to it as a 'future horizon, a coming which will have to be deferred'.[21]

In the essay 'Oikos' (1988), Lyotard clarifies the argument advanced in '*Domus* and the Megalopolis' by explicitly associating the home – and thus the *unheimlich* – with ecology. He does this by switching his linguistic focus from Latin to Greek. As he points out in the essay, the Greek word for *domus* is *oikos*, which forms the etymological root of the contemporary terms ecology (*oikeion*) and economics (*oikonomikos*).[22] Crucially, though, for Lyotard, to be ecological is not to engage in the scientific study of a given ecosystem (*Umwelt*), and neither is it to partake in a kind of parsimonious and careful home economics. Rather, as Lyotard explains, it is to remain open to the uncanny strangeness, the constitutive alterity, of being itself: '"*oikeion*" is an otherness that is not an *Umwelt* at all, but [an] otherness in the core of the apparatus'.[23] In Lyotard's radically singular definition, ecology (*oikeion*) is perhaps best defined in terms of an impossible *oikos* or home that resists being reduced to territorial maps and which refuses to serve a utilitarian function:

> What I mean by *oikeion* or my version of ecology ... is impossible to describe in terms of function. You can look at it as an entropy and certainly, functionally speaking, the unconscious (to use Freudian terminology) is the dysfunctional entity par excellence. It provokes only trouble, that is, paradoxes and even silences or noises, which are the same thing.[24]

Although ecology (*oikeion*) exceeds the political in the extent to which it is an ontological condition, politics, Lyotard tells us, is always trying to police and discipline it. This is because politics, in Lyotard's view, is imagined as a closed system that seeks to put everything in its place, to guard against the unproductive and excessive play of difference, conflict and chaos. Whereas politics wants to make everything public, to produce a false transparency, the *oikeion* (and the people, spaces and things that represent it) insists on remaining secluded – hence its close relationship with the tragic:

> In Greek, there is a very clear opposition between *oikeion* and *politikon*. ... *Oikeion* is everything that is not *öffenlich* [public]. ... It is the shadowy space of all that escapes the light of public speech, and it is precisely in this darkness that tragedy occurs.[25]

As Lyotard conceives it, then, ecology concerns the fight to sustain a type of experience and mode of existence that refuses to be controlled because its very meaning is to resist all order, to defy all utilitarian notions of *ratio*. From this we can deduce why the spatial tropes of domesticity, belonging and homecoming as well as the figures of the stranger and guest possess such important ecological purchase in Lyotard's work. For it is ultimately the home that, for him, embodies the *oikeion,* the site to protect on the condition that what is sustained in the *domus* is a shadowy voice that evades capture and remains untameable.

If Aristotelian modes of tragic drama have, through the centuries, constructed entertaining crises from establishing and examining the frictions between public sanction and private will, Harold Pinter's tragic manoeuvres are more directly aligned, like Lyotard's, with the shady spaces of secluded domestic environments. It is surely no coincidence that most of Pinter's early plays are located in the home. *The Room* takes place in a single space into which a bed, a stove, table and chairs are crammed; *The Caretaker* (1960) is similarly situated in a cramped room overflowing with domestic junk; the three acts of *The Birthday Party* play out in the dining/ sitting room of a seaside guest-house (and therefore both a private and public space); and those of *The Homecoming* (1965) fit into a family sitting room that has a back wall obtrusively removed to open out onto a former hall.

In all of Pinter's early plays, moreover, there is a battle, we might even call it a war, waged over the meaning and possibility of home and homecoming, a domestic battle that has important consequences for social ecology.[26] Indeed, when examined through the lens of the *oikos* or *domus,* we might usefully contemplate Pinter's early writing as a process of interrogating the threat to our social ecology that occurs when subjects are either forcibly ejected from the home or try to make themselves at home in ways that overlook the call of the *oikeion*, the domestic voice that renders any foundationalist or essentialist notion of homecoming impossible. When, in 1984, Pinter sought to recover his early dramas by insisting they were political in ambition, his argument hinged upon the moments of subversion and articulations of resistance that they contain.[27]

With Lyotard in mind, we might identify these resistances as acts that insist upon, albeit often negatively, a more progressive and inclusive notion of social ecology. For, in them, a repressed voice from the *oikos* irritates the demands of political and economic systems that would attempt to produce a homogeneous and sterile world, in which everything is parcelled out, made transparent, forced to make sense.

In *The Theatre of the Absurd*, Martin Esslin quotes from an interview that Pinter gave to Kenneth Tynan in 1960, in which he explained that the people in the enclosed rooms of his early plays 'are scared of what is outside the room. Outside the room there is a world bearing upon them which is frightening'.[28] Importantly (and this is easily overlooked), the playwright immediately qualified that statement with a link to the real social world in which the interview took place: 'I am sure it is frightening to you and me as well'.[29] In Pinter's early plays, that fear is often manifested in terms of an organic natural world that challenges the individual or group, one that breaches the binds of its domestication. In *The Room*, this is presented in straightforward terms of harsh, wintry weather and conditions. In the first scene alone, there are eight references to the cold and wind.[30] Later, in *The Homecoming*, Ruth complains of her life in America in terms of an arid landscape, 'all rock. And sand. It stretches ... so far ... everywhere you look. And there are lots of insects there'.[31] With reference to Ruth's statement, Chaudhuri highlights how the representation of America in *The Homecoming* presents a sterile 'alien land capable of providing a restricted set of pleasures' but which is 'essentially inhospitable to human life' and ultimately 'fully exposes its futility as a new paradigm of home'.[32]

In his early work, Pinter repeatedly presents the elements as symptomatic of a greater hostility that the characters must face, overcome or bypass. His characters are either pitted against these natural conditions (Bert in the final scene of *The Room* expresses his domination of the icy conditions outside in quasi-sexual terms of control of his van), or present a temperament more in tune with their environments, and therefore face greater threat from those systems that would impose structure upon the organic. Petey in *The Birthday Party*, for example, is pictured as part of an idyllic beach scene, arranging and collecting deck chairs, at one with the leisure and comfort afforded by nature. By situating his characters against a non-human environment that qualifies their behaviour, Pinter allows us to see how a relationship with the natural world serves in part as an indicator of the relationship each character has with his or her domestic and social environment. This presents a crucial link between social and natural ecologies. Petey's harmonious relationship with the environment suggests a simple vulnerability that is exposed at the end of the play when he can offer no more than an ineffectual 'don't let them tell you what to do' as Goldberg and McCann cart a tortured Stanley off to be 'adjusted', 're-orientated' and 'integrated'.[33]

Such environmental placement is more than a simple framing device or example of instructive symbolism; rather, the agency of place is a central aspect of Pinter's early work. In his novel *The Dwarfs* (written between 1952 and 1956, but unpublished until 1990), the rooms that contain his characters are frequently given as responsive environments ('The room is moving', 'The room grunted, slapped'; 'The room stopped').[34] In Chapter 3, we meet the character of Virginia who contemplates how because she stands up from the sofa the 'posture of the room changed. The sunlight jolted. The room settled'.[35] In this way, the author lends Virginia the same outlook on the agency of place as the narrative voice, and this alignment contributes to a reader's investment in her, and subsequent disapproval of her boyfriend Pete, whom she speculates might argue that to 'attribute bias or active desire to a room was merely the projection of a sick or deluded mind or the symptom of an emotional binge'.[36] In this way, Pinter's antipathies are seemingly built against those (exemplified in the character of Pete) who would have no awareness of environmental positioning and accept, instead, only positivist, transparent versions of reality. These characters seek to tame the world by avoiding the rupture in self-presence, the primordial separation, that the *oikos* produces, and which homecoming can never resist or repair.

Just as his rooms in *The Dwarfs* were given a form of agency, so Pinter extends the inferred agency of the environment to infect domestic objects in his early plays. For example, Davies in *The Caretaker* worries about the potential of a disconnected gas cooker to nonetheless poison him, and Lenny in *The Homecoming* claims to be bothered by a ticking clock (notably the remnant of an earlier sketch from which *The Homecoming* evolved). *The Dumb Waiter* (1959) takes this as a central dramatic premise, with the service apparatus of the title acting as an agent of change, command, threat and communication: the dumb waiter rattles alarmingly into action, carrying impossible requests for food down to Ben and Gus in the basement. The inside/outside opposition that Pinter postulates in his Tynan interview is therefore something more than a binary; the inside and outside are combined, part of an impossible whole that demands to be written, to be examined. These imaginative expressions of environmental agency in his work foreground the disruptive and differential agency of the *oikos* in the relationships he investigates as well as suggesting the dissidence against orthodoxy that is to emerge within the characters.

Pinter's artistic curiosity around the potential of the relationship between a character in pursuit of control or dominance in relation to inside/outside spaces (and the *domus*/social discourse they might present) is first apparent in three early texts: the two short prose pieces 'Kullus' (1949) and 'The Examination' (1955) and the poem 'The Task' (1954).[37] In the two prose pieces, for instance, the character of Kullus confounds the owner of a room by re-organizing the environment and thereby eventually taking ownership of the space – Kullus, for instance, demonstrates a preference for closed curtains during the day and open curtains at night. In the poem, the narrative voice speaks again from the position of a room (shifting from an object of control to an object with startling agency) and charts the progress of Kullus from the passive ('seen') to the active ('saw') against a natural process of a flowering plant. First 'the leaf obeyed the bud' then, inversely 'the leaf alarmed the bud' before 'the bud about to break' brings forth 'a bell'.[38] The bell-shape of the flower as it opens reinforces 'alarm' as a natural process, which declares its morphing presence in the world.[39] Again, here, in Pinter's earliest work, we can detect a dissident ambition embedded in imagery that interweaves natural and social ecologies, and this 'Kullus' imperative develops as something of a trope in his first plays, a creative itch that is repeatedly scratched. Kullus is a figure who inhabits the 'shadowy space of all that escapes the light of public speech'.[40] He is the unknown, the organic threat to domestic stability that has its root inside, not outside the home. Riley in *The*

Room, the Matchseller in *A Slight Ache* (1959) and even Ruth in *The Homecoming* are obvious extensions of the Kullus prototype. This is the source of Pinter's so-called 'comedy of menace', the consistent application of a threat to the status quo that is the engine to all his early plays. If we consider this repeated appearance of the Kullus form in Pinter's early creative writing as a symptom of the emerging author's repeated return to resolve and articulate a particular compulsion – namely, the attempt to connect social and natural ecologies through processes of domination – we might appreciate how the Kullus-drive in his pre-dramatist writing accommodates Lyotard's unpacking of the *oikeion* as a sort of troublesome guest:

> We have to imagine an apparatus inhabited by a sort of guest, not a ghost, but an ignored guest who produces some trouble, and people look to the outside in order to find out the external cause of the trouble. But probably the cause is not outside, that is my idea. So we can call it entropy, but probably the more interesting thing is to try to touch it, not approach it, because it is not an object available for a cognitive touch.[41]

The Kullus figure – the 'ignored guest who produces some trouble' – was first embodied in Pinter's drama in the character of Riley in *The Room* who comes to persuade Rose to leave her cold, confining bed-sitting space and return 'home'. Addressing her as 'Sal' (suggesting a past identity that has been abandoned or shed) and doing so as, or on behalf of, her father, he half seduces and half implores her to depart with him before Rose's husband returns to put an end to the potential (re)union. In constructing the character of Riley, then, Pinter furthers the action of displacement that the Kullus character initiated in his early writing, and adds the dimension of this call home ('come home' is repeated five times in quick succession) as a central function of the Kullus persona.[42] It is as if the voice of the *oikeion* was rising from the basement to demand a return to a place of obscure origin, which in itself is no more than an ambition, a point of mysterious otherness that is positioned as existing somewhere beyond the physical home that Rose occupies. Some critical responses to the appearance of Riley at the end of *The Room* foreground the mixed ethnic identity captured in the seeming juxtaposition between his name and skin colour.[43] This in part acts as an immediate index of social concerns around the 'othering' of certain ethnic groups in 1950s Britain.

But most critical responses to Pinter's first play tend to fold Riley's ethnicities into the play's elusive symbolic structure, regarding his perceived 'otherness' as an operation of subconscious resistance, a way of avoiding difficult psychological realities.[44] Instead, and as a means of further considering the significance of social ecology in Pinter's texts, we might address the issue of race in direct, historical terms.

Historically, Pinter's choice of character is noteworthy: there were few lead roles for black actors on the British stage before Shelagh Delaney's *A Taste of Honey* (1958), and contemporary representations of black characters on television and film in the United Kingdom fell into two broad categories: on the one hand, an essentially reactionary or conservative worldview that offered unapologetic representations of colonial attitudes and nostalgias, and, on the other, representations that sought to offer more progressive counter-narratives that centred on social conflicts or disturbances attached to issues of migration and integration.[45] Certainly, the arrival of black and Asian migrants to the United Kingdom in the mid-twentieth century foregrounded issues in domestic politics of social integration and equality.[46] And in this socio cultural context, Pinter's choice of a black lead character in a theatrical environment where there were few black actors (and no lead roles) could not be taken without an awareness that such a character would trigger a social realist reading, especially if that character, like Riley, is a victim of the insulting language of parasitism and prone to violent attacks by those who claim ownership of the environment.[47] Bert exclaims 'Lice!' as he strikes Riley, after a speech about his domination of his van, the road and the weather.[48]

If Pinter mobilizes a social realist frame to bring focus to the close of his first drama – deliberately effacing previously activated metaphorical insinuations by revealing, for example, that the man waiting in a dark cellar is blind and so needs no light – he nonetheless clearly does not do so to engage overtly with the political issues surrounding race and integration that might be attached to such a frame. The seeming shift in register, though, serves to alert an audience by establishing an expectation that a 'message' is to follow, an expectation that is subsequently unfulfilled. By making Riley, instead, the mouthpiece of a demand for re-integration, Pinter simultaneously enacts and resists the simplistic racist demand for the non-native to 'go home', by complicating and partially inverting representations of victimhood. Riley is both same and other, margin and centre, inside and outside, an intruder who simultaneously represents himself as family. He speaks with the voice of the father demanding that Rose return home. Riley belongs to the shadowy realm of the *oikeion*, the guest who inhabits and disrupts the meaning of the traditional domestic apparatus. His presence on stage and brutal fate at the hearth of the home (his head is kicked against the iron stove) suggest that we look not to the outside, not to that triggered by social realism (a deliberate misdirection), to understand the external cause of that trouble, but to what is displaced, lost, inarticulate. We are directed this way by our confusion, experienced immediately in a fast-moving moment of theatrical shock. This process of exhorted recuperation – the declaration of a need to return home arrested by the reassertion of the authority of establishment – is the first key movement in Pinter's nascent drama. A social realist aesthetic might be triggered in order to be rejected in this way, but in being invoked and left unresolved, it forms a persistent skin, as it were, around the drama that foregrounds real social context – a skin, moreover, that we are unable to shed as we leave the theatre.

Representations of race, diaspora and displacement in Pinter's other early plays reinforce the trope directly associated with constructions of 'home' and our relationship to those constructions. As signalled through Riley, one means by which Pinter sets up the relationship between difference and aggression is with the mobilization of explicit or implicit racism. Most notably, we have the crass, casual racism that the character of Davies spouts in *The Caretaker*. From almost the very first words that he speaks, Davies is presented as harbouring petty and ignorant racist views. He complains of the 'Poles, Greeks [and] Blacks' whom he castigates for his recent misfortune, and later he ludicrously blames the black family next door for his own snoring, suspecting too that they are entering the house to use the toilet facilities.[49] When he talks of the possibility of getting a job in a café, he makes an assumption about his superiority in the labour market on the basis of his skin colour, which he equates with Englishness: 'They want an Englishman to pour their tea, that's what they want, that's what they're crying out for. It's only common sense, en't?'[50] Given the racial tensions in London in the late 1950s, marked notoriously by the Notting Hill riots in September 1958, less than two years before the play's first production, it is tempting to locate Pinter's representation of such casual racism again as a clear index of social realism. But, once again, however, there is calculated misdirection in such a trigger. Davies's claim of being an Englishman performs a certain irony, deliberate on Pinter's behalf, and with both comic and dark charges. The character bears two names – Davies and Jenkins – one of which is an alias (perhaps they both are), and both of which are characteristically Welsh and Cornish, locating the character ethnically as originating from Celtic territories, on the margins of Anglo-Saxon England. Further, Davies's given peregrinations around London suggest displacement, an existence that has lost its roots, or that can no longer define itself in terms of a place of origin. References in the play to London place names imply a circuitous migration around the western suburbs of the city (Watford, The North Circular Road, Wembley, Acton, Shepherd's Bush, Goldhawk Road, The Great West Road). References to places more distant, such as Luton or Sidcup, indicate an extended, confirmed, deracination, which is also attached to Davies's very identity. His claims that the papers that would lend him an authentic identity are being kept at Sidcup (in the 1950s, the location of the Army Pay Office) suggest a recognition of the authority of the social narratives that he simultaneously resents and seeks to evade – in this context, the monastery near Luton and papers in Sidcup might even represent the poles of church and state. Davies operates on the boundary between social integration and social rejection, and might function creatively as an *oikieon* if his inclination was not so clearly parasitic within the adopted *domus*. His failure to find his way home produces his racism, allowing him to maintain an illusory sense of propriety by rejecting those who might not belong. As a homeless vagrant who fails to recognize the compromises he must adopt in being invited to settle in a new home, he represents a further failed homecoming in Pinter's early drama. In many ways, *The Caretaker* presents the possibility that the only form of progressive homecoming to which we might aspire is a kind of 'care-taking', sheltering others weaker and more dispossessed than ourselves. Indeed, in Lyotard's terms, we might go further still, and read Aston's uncompromised and unconditional ability to tender care to Davies as a function of his own ability to recognize the *différend* that exists in any *oikos*. Aston's home is the incomplete, unachievable dream of a home. He realizes that belonging is never permanent, the *oikos* not something we can own. In this respect, Aston has accepted the uncanny; he does not try to tame or possess it.

In *The Birthday Party*, the Jewish Goldberg and the Irish McCann participate in Pinter's development of displacement in relation to iterations of home. McCann presents two Irish folk songs during the play, first whistling 'The Mountains of the Morne', and later, during the party, singing a verse of 'Come Back Paddy Reilly to Ballyjamesduff'. The former song is told from the perspective of an Irish migrant, writing home to his loved one about the strangeness he perceives in the behaviour of the Londoners who now surround him. As such, it is a text of the Irish diaspora, and one that foregrounds cultural difference and a longing for return. McCann's second song 'Come Back Paddy Reilly to Ballyjamesduff' is of the same genre, but written now from the perspective of the migrant who maintains a loyal nostalgia for his place of birth. The songs, then, not only contribute to the trope of diaspora and displacement in Pinter's early writing, but also speak directly to the issue of being called back, of a return 'home', which is enforced in the case of Stanley in *The Birthday Party*, or coercive in the case of Rose in *The Room*. Goldberg, too, presents a number of instances of dislocated identity, albeit in a more subtle fashion, or at least in ways that are less obvious to contemporary ears than McCann's folk tunes. His numerous references to traditional London Jewish families and social realities tend to facilitate our desire to root him in a lineage of orthodoxy and tradition, but a few indicators disrupt or disallow this. While the references to childhood seaside holidays in Brighton, Canvey Island and Rottingdean accurately capture the habits of many London Jewish families in the mid-century (although they represent very distinct destinations for different wealth brackets), locating his Uncle Barney in Basingstoke is a notionally deliberate act of placing a wealthy Jew in a non-Jewish area. Another notable reference he makes is to the Ethical Hall in Bayswater where Goldberg claims to have given a successful lecture. This is the only point at which he locates his acknowledged esteem and authority in the real world beyond the play. And yet, it is curious that a character so embedded in and indebted to tradition, Jewish or otherwise, might be so displaced as to give a lecture in a forum of progressive liberal humanism. Such displacement suggests that even the dominant voices have no stable home, no place to return to. By eliding 'native' and 'foreign' in these ways, questions of social ecology are made overt in early Pinter. What we are ultimately left with is a crisis in dwelling, in which subjects who feel ill at ease and dislocated try to identify with a dominant system that subjects them to pressures that they either fail to recognize or else strive to repress in their desperate desire to belong.

The sociologist and philosopher Pierre Bourdieu who sought to grasp the hidden causes of individual alienation and misery offers a frame for contemplating the unease experienced by Pinter's characters. Reflecting his ethnographic training, Bourdieu does this by avoiding the limitations of existential psychology and, instead, focuses on issues pertaining to social ecology. In *In Other Words: Essays Towards a Reflexive Sociology* (1990), Bourdieu asked, 'How can behaviour be regulated without being the product of obedience to rules?' as a starting point for considering how individuals tend towards conformity even when there are no explicit governing laws demanding such conformity.[51] In this way, he attempted to express the sense in which cultural practices develop to form normative attitudes that then go on to structure conformist behaviour. Bourdieu crafted his response to the question posed above by developing the idea of the *habitus*, a concept that explains how individuals manifest a socially constituted disposition to certain modes of physical or mental behaviours which are 'beyond the grasp of consciousness, and hence [which] cannot be touched by voluntary, deliberate transformation, cannot even be made explicit'.[52] Bourdieu's quest to get to the very heart of social conformity might be usefully aligned at this point with Lyotard's ambition to give voice to the *oikeion*, which the latter describes as 'a relation with something that is inscribed at the origin in all our minds, souls or psychic apparatuses' making us 'the object of a lot of meanings' that need to be conquered, rewritten.[53] 'We try all our lives to understand what was expected of us. It is too late because these expectations are already part of our life'.[54] Although their two projects are very different, in terms of discipline and approach (Bourdieu might even be accused of reducing all cultural production to the object of sociological enquiry), their implied political positions intersect in a concern to isolate and consider the means by which power is ceaselessly and seamlessly produced and reproduced within the systems they examine. When Petey in *The Birthday Party*, for instance, tells Stanley 'don't let them tell you what to do', he is evoking a kind of Lyotardian resistance to the controlling and limiting constraints of the Bourdieusian *habitus* that is inscribed in us.[55]

We might certainly consider Pinter's characters in terms of how they express and experience discomfort from the *habitus* that defines or contains them, and how this expresses political concerns in terms of the individual within society. A more interesting angle, for our purposes, is to consider Bourdieu's later, associated conception of the 'misère de position' ('positional suffering'), which he proposed as a means of overcoming standard sociological approaches of identifying an individual's or group's 'misère de condition' ('material suffering') – the concrete economic or social conditions that limit, oppress or distress people. For, what is useful about Bordieu's 'misère de position' in this context is that it provides the means for exploring the source of suffering as something which takes place within rather than outside the apparatus, which immediately has more in common with Lyotard's approach. In the multi-authored *The Weight of the World* (1993), Bourdieu surveys the displacement from affluent society, and even citizenship, of a group of interviewees by defining their 'misère de position', a nebulous form of suffering that has its root in self-despair brought about by an indefinable sense of being alienated from the social microcosm. Importantly, this is not associated directly with social position, class or material poverty (the external factors associated with the 'misère de condition'), but rather with deeply rooted perceptions of powerlessness and inferiority that over-determines their relationship to and position within any system or group. In pursuit of a social ecological reading of Pinter, it is valuable to consider his characters as manifesting a 'misère de position' due to a 'position occupied in the social microcosm ... determined, or at least modified, by the directly experienced effects of social interaction within these social microcosms'.[56] Doing so allows us to circumvent conventional readings that would see those characters as simply manifesting symptoms of 'un misère de condition', either in straightforward social realist terms (unemployment, disability, poverty, social marginalization) or in metaphorical or existential terms (a discomfort with being). Goldberg and McCann present themselves as constituent parts of the same system that Stanley has sought to escape. Their undoubted power to overwhelm him, though, is qualified by the discomfort that the task brings them. McCann's hope that his work would be 'accomplished with no excessive aggravation' is unfulfilled, and even Goldberg suffers a breakdown in confidence when he finds himself unable to complete the sentence 'I believe that the world ...'.[57]

The Dumb Waiter, written immediately after *The Birthday Party*, might be considered as a means of further examining this positional phenomenon through the crisis of belief that the character of Gus has begun to experience in the system that employs him as a killer. Goldberg and McCann and Ben and Gus adopt positions within a system of authority that is more concerned with self-perpetuation than with the protection of those who serve to perpetuate it. Tellingly, the status it affords them begins to erode once they begin to gain consciousness of this fact. They have people 'above' them who deliver orders and those 'below' them who are the subjects of those orders, but in acting upon their instructions, Pinter has them confronting what the melancholia of the 'misère de position' conceals: namely, Lyotard's 'discourse of the secluded', 'the thing that has not become public, that has not become communicational, that has not become systematic'.[58] As proponents of the system challenged by that which is unsystemic, they experience a disturbing, momentary recognition of the artificial constructs of the establishment and its discourses of power. In ecological terms, this refers to the possibility, then, of escaping stasis, of adding complexity, and thus life, to an otherwise closed and static social system. The Bourdieusian relationality that Pinter activates goes beyond the representation of negotiated status within a simple hierarchy; it foregrounds the impossibility of ever finding comfort or safety within a power system as well as the dangers that ensues when one tries to evade that system. In his early plays, then, Pinter presents his characters not so much at the mercy of one another, but as dependent on governing principles – dominant discourses – that contaminate them all, victim and victimizer alike. The dominant discourses precede our existence, construct the environments in which subjectivity defines itself and control the languages of that self-definition.

Those who have sought a place outside a system, such as Rose, Stanley, Aston or Davies, or who threaten to become unproductive within it, such as Gus, nonetheless offer no solution, no drive, no potency. If Aston has found a protected position beyond establishment, Davies lacks the humility that would gain him a place in the same sequestered unproductiveness. Rose is comfortable in the limiting construct of housewife and the dishevelled Stanley declares that there is 'nowhere' else to go, settling for an ersatz family and artificial home rather than seeking to live with the troubling presence of the *oikos*.[59] Perhaps Stanley's declaration of there being 'nowhere' to escape to is an expression of his awareness that an authentic home is impossible, or perhaps it simply articulates the indolence that contributes to his eventual downfall. Nonetheless, this repeated lack of drive in Pinter's characters reveals how susceptible the *oikos* is in contemporary society to capture and control. It is not until we meet the character of Ruth in *The Homecoming* that Pinter composes an invader, a dangerous parasite, who not only challenges the system from within, but who also reconfigures its discourses of power to her own advantage. The homecoming of the matriarch might (temporarily) bind that group of men, but at significant risk to the integrity of their already dysfunctional system, which is finally rendered unsafe, unsettled. The ending of *The Homecoming* presents no clear sense of what might follow in that household beyond a new *différend* taking centre-stage. In this respect, Ruth deconstructs and re-assembles the patriarchy, mastering its discourse, but refusing to provide a panacea to the failed attempts of the family to belong. She remains a stranger, a troubling guest, whose behaviour cannot be predicted and who renders the *domus/oikos* uncanny. The realization that the *domus/ oikos* must remain unstable is the progressive moment in Pinter's early writing, and in turn contributed to the halting punctuation mark in his career. After an active period of eight years (including six stage plays, six teleplays and five film screenplays), he seemingly ground to a halt, writing little more than two short plays in the next four years. This might indicate that *The Homecoming* is something of a conclusion to an artistic journey begun in 1957.

By rendering authentic or essentialized homecoming impossible to achieve, Pinter interrogates the threat to our social ecology that occurs when dominant systems and processes seek to repress this impossible knowledge, and produce in its stead a fake *domus*, a proper territory. In seeking a metaphorical key to the seeming socio-political mysteries of these dramas, and by positioning Pinter's artistic writing as activating an absurdist worldview, Martin Esslin was looking behind the ecosystem of human relationships that Pinter was constructing or reflecting. However, given the social limitations of Esslin's existentialism, we might be better served mobilizing Bourdieu's notion of 'misère de position' to locate the positional stresses that determine the behaviour of Pinter's characters within distinctly recognizable social structures. These positional stresses foreground the inside/outside pressures that so many of Pinter's protagonists seek to resolve between a compromised 'home' that simultaneously reflects and produces the violence of the system that constitutes it, and the discovery of a more progressive *oikos* that might soothe and protect them, but which remains elusive. By concentrating on the disruptive, impossible presence of the *oikos* in his work, we might start to detect the recuperative, positive movements towards home in Pinter's early plays – those invitations for escape and redefinition that suggest human potential, so often betrayed. It is notable that after having resolved a creative fascination with gender and power in *The Homecoming*, this movement in relation to home is pursued no longer in terms of a battle of the sexes over domestic territories, but in relation to the stability of family structures. In plays such as *Monologue* (1973), *Betrayal* (1978), *A Kind of Alaska* (1982) and *Moonlight* (1993), the family unit is explored as a structure which might buffer against the positional suffering of social systems; and in *One for the Road* (1984), *Mountain Language* (1988) and *Party Time* (1991), it risks being assaulted and fragmented by such systems.[60]

Ultimately, though, the comforts of home are never achieved in Pinter, and the homecoming always remains an objective, a destination. In 'Oikos', Lyotard argues that 'we have to fight the heritage of meaning ... to deconstruct, to dismember, to criticize the defences that are already built into our psyche'.[61] Accordingly, then, for Lyotard, ecology is both a political and ontological process, a method for dismantling interior and exterior defences in the hope that we might be able to welcome the voices of the secluded – the *oikeion* – who refuse to identify with or become part of any system of belonging. In so far as Pinter adopts a similar strategy in his work, we might say that he encourages us to affirm an alternative mode of dwelling, one in which the *domus* or *oikos* remains unstable and thus unfit for habitation by reactionary and defensive systems that only corrupt through the very stability they seek to impose. This is the essentially positive ecological dynamic that Pinter's plays impress upon us: resist the system that would contain us, and find modes of grouping together that would affirm the home as a temporary place, always on loan. This acceptance of impossibility, this porous house, is where the significance of Pinter's ecology resides.

Works cited

Bachelard, Gaston, *The Poetics of Space*, trans. M. Jollas. Boston, MA: Beacon Press, 1994.

Bookchin, Murray, *The Philosophy of Social Ecology*. Montreal: Black Rose, 1992.

Bourdieu, Pierre, *Outline of a Theory of Practice*, trans. J. Goody and R. Nice. Cambridge: Cambridge University Press, 1977.

Bourdieu, Pierre, *In Other Words: Essays Towards a Reflexive Sociology*, trans. M. Adamson. Stanford, CA: Stanford University Press, 1990.

Bourdieu, Pierre, et al., *The Weight of the World: Social Suffering in Contemporary Society*, trans. P. Ferguson et al. Stanford, CA: Stanford University Press, 1993.

Chaudhuri, Una, *Staging Place: The Geography of Modern Drama*. Ann Arbor, MN: The University of Michigan Press, 1995.

Esslin, Martin, *The Theatre of the Absurd*. London: Eyre & Spottiswoode, 1962 [1961].

Esslin, Martin, *The Theatre of the Absurd*, 3rd revised and enlarged edn. Harmondsworth: Penguin, 1991.

Gabbard, Lucina Paquet, *The Dream Structure of Pinter's Plays: A Psychoanalytic Approach*. Cranbury, NJ: Associated University Press, 1976.

Guattari, Félix, *The Three Ecologies*, trans. I. Pindar and P. Sutton. London: Continuum, 2008.

Jung, C. J., *Analytical Psychology: Notes of the Seminar Given in 1925*, trans. C. E. Long. Princeton, NJ: Princeton University Press, 1989.

Lyotard, Jean-François, '*Domus* and the Megalopolis', in *The Inhuman: Reflections on Time*, trans. G. Bennington and R. Bowlby. London: Polity, 1991.

Lyotard, Jean-François, 'Oikos', in *Jean- François Lyotard: Political Writings*, trans. B. Readings and K. Gaiman. Minneapolis, MN: University of Minnesota Press, 1993.

Osterwalder, Hans, 'Dreamscapes: Harold Pinter's *The Room* and Franz Kafka's "Auf der Galerie"', *Zeitschrift für Anglistik und Amerikanistik*, vol. 52, no. 1 (March 2014), pp. 53–62.

Pinter, Harold, 'Interview with Kenneth Tynan', BBC Home Service, 28 October 1960.

Pinter, Harold, 'A Play and its Politics', an interview with Nick Hern, *One for the Road*, London: Methuen, 1985.

Pinter, Harold, *The Dwarfs*. London: Faber and Faber, 1990.

Pinter, Harold, *A Slight Ache*, in *Plays One*. London: Faber and Faber, 1991.

Pinter, Harold, *The Birthday Party*, in *Plays One*. London: Faber and Faber, 1991.

Pinter, Harold, *The Room*, in *Plays One*. London: Faber and Faber, 1991.

Pinter, Harold, *The Caretaker*, in *Plays Two*. London: Faber and Faber, 1996.

Pinter, Harold, *The Homecoming*, in *Plays Three*. London: Faber and Faber, 1997.

Pinter, Harold, *Various Voices: Sixty Years of Prose, Poetry, Politics 1948-2008*, 3rd edn. London: Faber and Faber, 2009.

Taylor-Batty, Mark, *The Theatre of Harold Pinter*. London: Bloomsbury, 2014.

Epilogue: 'The ruins of time (I've forgotten this before)'

David Williams

I'm on the inside of anything I can imagine.
I wanted to distribute the present, not secure the future.
What could I say that was lasting?

So. Now. What/how

As an undergraduate student of French and Drama at an English university in the late 1970s, with a furrowed brow and a cigarette-fuelled enthusiasm for Camus, Genet, Ionesco and above all Beckett, I possessed a much thumbed and annotated copy of Martin Esslin's *The Theatre of the Absurd*. Esslin's book became a point of reference and orientation for me at that time, mapping and distilling certain thematic and formal patterns of which I felt I had intuited something without being able to organize those feelings into anything resembling coherent thought. At an impressionable, receptive period it was foundational for me, offering a window into affective landscapes of theatre, as well as leading me towards a wide range of other texts and readings. Initially it also spawned a bunch of adjectives that provided a kind of shorthand for complex 'worlds' and structures of feeling, words to be tossed around in undergraduate seminars and conversations as if there was a knowing, nodding consensus as to what they actually meant: 'Beckettian', 'Kafkaesque', 'Pinteresque' etc., as well as 'absurdist'. Ultimately, and more productively, it helped seed a life-long interest in the 'unlessenable least best worse' and 'nohow on'[1] of Beckett's writings. The late Herbert Blau once located Beckett's work as 'the *locus classicus* of the problematic of the future'[2] – and, on this hundredth anniversary of the outbreak of the First World War, as conflict continues unabated in various war zones around the world, Beckett will be a shadow companion in much of what follows:

> Let us do something, while we have the chance! It is not every day that we are needed. Not indeed that we personally are needed. ... But at this place, at this moment of time, all mankind is us, whether we like it or not. Let us make the most of it, before it is too late![3]

I still have that original copy of Esslin's book, although until recently I had not opened its battered covers for many years. Almost forty years later, it is frankly disarming to revisit this text via the filter of my underlinings and scribbled notes, encountering these barely decipherable invitations to read and think as 'someone else' once read and thought. For these sub-Krapp marginalia offer the perspectives of a dimly remembered and prematurely world-weary nineteen-year-old, his (my) unconvincing performance of hip Left Bank-ish anomie concretized in an omnipresent, decaying donkey jacket stuffed with papers and books (no carrots or pebbles), and an impenetrable micro-climatic pall of ('Camusian') smoke. I was clearly seduced and somehow affirmed by what I took – in my limited understanding of existentialism as a philosophical *style*, a grey cloak of ideas to be tossed over young shoulders and worn – to be revelatory representations of impossibility and inertia, of the inadequacies of reason, language and received regimes of the self, of disenchantment and meaninglessness in the face of mortality. In retrospect, I had little sense of the gravity and matter of such thoughts in and as lived experience.

Over the next few years, increasingly and joyously immersed in the chaotic, dissident explosion of new popular music at that time, and associated leftist politics, I came to read some of these plays as proto-'punk' manifestations, affectively rhythmed and charged mechanisms to prise the lid off the blind assumptions, repressed power-plays and dead-ends of naturalized middle-class 'normality' and conformity, education, culture, science-as-progress, entrepreneurship, meaningful action, the future. (One of my notes

in the margins of Esslin's book comically reads 'Cf. Pistols?!').
In their defamiliarizing shocks to thought and conventional
aesthetic values, as much as in their pitch-black humour, these
plays seemed to have a critical status politically and socially, both
presenting lived situations as uncomfortable, uncanny image-
worlds – *how it is* – and implicitly positing the possibility of
and need to conceive of *how it might be*, otherwise, in a 'world
to come'. I began to realize that these were not exclusively
essentialist metaphysical myths of nihilism and despair, scorched
ahistorical outlines of the inevitability of the house burning down
and total collapse through proliferation or entropic diminution,
but also and at the same time abrasive, startling, excavatory calls
to question and think and reimagine what Beckett in his short text
'Enough' characterized as 'stony ground *but not entirely*'.[4] Calls
to *make* meaning where it apparently recedes and dissolves – in
paradox, contradiction, oxymoron, double-bind, the uncanny, the
im/possible, the Unnamable – or to learn how to *live with* not-
meaning.[5] Esslin suggested as much, perhaps, but somehow the
insistent privileged framing of these plays, via a very particular
conception of absurdity as anguished existential ontology, has
served to insulate and defuse their potential critical, political
charge.[6]

So. Now. What/how one might live in relation to others. What/
how one might be. What/how one might do. At this place, at this
moment in time, all mankind is us. Whether we like it or not.

The mess ('deep stuff')

To swim is true, and to sink is true. One is not more true than the
other. ... I am not a philosopher. One can only speak of what is
in front of him, and that now is simply the mess.[7]

If one were to consider the unfolding ecology of Esslin's book over
time, arguably one of the by-products of its title as received idea has
been the production of proliferative meme-like stereotypes of some
of these writers and their work, reductive clichés or line-drawing
silhouettes that travel through time and different media as popular
culture doxa. Received shorthand ideas of an alienated 'Absurdist'
landscape are characterized by, for example, an interior stifled

beneath infinitely reproducing chairs or an ever expanding corpse (Ionesco), scurrying puppet-like maids apparently manipulated by forces beyond their control (Genet), or victimized figures trapped forever in an oppressive and hermetically sealed room (Pinter). The *Waiting for Godot* meme/silhouette – the wholly meaningless (and incomprehensible) doing of waiting in some desolate no-man's land – is reiterated in parodic form in an episode of *Sesame Street,* a Muppet 'Play for Today' sequence called 'Monsterpiece Theatre' introduced by Alistair Cookie (the Cookie Monster's alter ego)[8]: 'Today we are proud to present a modern masterpiece, a play so modern and so brilliant it makes absolutely no sense to anybody, including Alistair. Maybe you can figure it out. The puzzling story of two monsters waiting for their friend. A play called *Waiting for Elmo*'. Two muppets wait by a bare tree. They rehearse the possibilities – Elmo arriving, which would make them 'so happy'; Elmo never showing up, which would make them 'so angry'. Although the sequence is less than three minutes long, it packs in a great deal of repetition, over-acting and looping game playing: 'How dare he keeps us by this tree, waiting, waiting, waiting'. 'What are we going to do? What are we going to do?' If one of them were to leave, the other would be sad on his own, 'alone in the world, waiting, waiting, waiting'. Finally – and astonishingly – the tree, apparently inert to this point, sprouts a woody face and intervenes as an enraged meta-theatrical critic, as if this were a Forced Entertainment show: 'Okay, that does it, I've been standing out here waiting for this play to make some sense. I don't get it! It's the most ridiculous thing I've ever seen! I'm outa here. Why couldn't they do *Oklahoma*? I understand *Oklahoma*!' As the tree shuffles offstage singing from *O(a)klahoma*, the two muppets charge off after him, condemned to wait for their friend by the tree, even if it moves. Back to Alistair in his stage-side box: 'Mmm, that's deep, deep stuff. But now for something that makes a lot more sense ...' and he consumes a bowl of cookies with messy abandon.

This sophisticated if throwaway distillation of a *version* of Beckett's play hilariously compacts a number of core ideas and tensions within the original play that are, indeed, 'deep stuff': the busy-ness and full-ness of waiting and of passing time as 'nothing' happens; the lived experience of ignorance and unknowability, and of push/pull entrapment within the dynamic immobility of the quintessentially Beckettian palindrome 'no'/'on'; the swim-then-sink jostle of joy and suffering in the couple's impossible *nec tecum nec sine te,* and the precarious salvation this relation paradoxically may offer; and so on. In addition, the animation and agency of the tree offers an intriguing refashioning of Beckett. The tree's interruptive talking back to the play and refusal to endure any further witnessing of an absurd (i.e. in this context, meaningless and ridiculous) mode of theatre is symptomatic of a deep-seated conservatism in terms of perceptions of legitimate models of dramaturgy and the parameters of meaning making – Rodgers and Hammerstein's *Oklahoma* as the paradigm of what is desired *ad infinitum,* escapist post-war musical theatre (about trees, it seems): 'Oh what a beautiful morning!' – the Empire of the Selfsame. The vibrant matter of the sentient tree ('nature') resists, uproots itself and moves – like Birnam Wood – in search of more 'meaningful' company and representations that it can recognize and understand. This movement to make the most of it while it still can, before it's too late, in turn provokes a miniature existential and environmental crisis for the two Muppet-shaped shadows of Vladimir and Estragon – dragged in the tree's wake, moving but not moving, forever chained to a (shonky stand-in for) 'nature' that does not recognize or value their world. The surreal inversion of this comically'monstrous' mess takes us, perhaps, into the domain of ecology....

Heart/break ('I've forgotten this before')

There is an ecology of bad ideas, just as there is an ecology of weeds, and it is characteristic of the system that basic error propagates itself.[9]

This timely collection of essays endeavours to revisit and extend Esslin's book for readers in contemporary contexts given our current concerns, predicaments and emergent structures of feeling. The editors and authors have realigned the geometry of attention away from Esslin's umbrella notion of the absurd as existentialist ontology, towards critical and political perspectives afforded by contemporary conceptions of ecology and ecophilosophy. Their aim is to reclaim and reanimate through a range of ecological lenses the generative meaning-making potentiality and momentum of the work of some of the core artists discussed in the original book – Beckett, Adamov, Ionesco, Genet, Pinter, Albee, and a number of Eastern European writers – as well as exploring the implications of more recent work by Sam Shepard, Caryl Churchill, Mirosław Bałka and Gerard Byrne.

Contemporary ecology proposes a heightened contouring of the understanding of the becoming of things in our 'Anthropocene' age through the tracking of networks in a mesh[10] of connective interrelations and turbulent flows. So, for example, in her remarkable book *Nilling* (such a Beckettian word), the Canadian poet Lisa Robertson proposes a dynamically embodied, relational and porous model of ecology for anatomizing and thinking into the domestic – the locus of so many 'absurdist' plays:

> The time of the body is generative, commingled, gestural, enacted; in a temporal interpretation of the domestic, power innovates itself as an *improvised co-embodiment*. In this sense, ecology rather than economics might provide the circulatory model of a mutually embodied and temporally vulnerable power-in-relationship, as long as one considers ecology in terms of *complex processes of disequilibrium and emergence instead of a harmonised closure.*[11]

So ecology in this context should be conceived of in much broader terms than those of an instrumental environmentalism, which is often profoundly conservative and anthropocentric in its focus on the preservation of a reified and idealized 'nature' out there, comprising designated 'natives' and 'invasive' others. The authors of the essays in this volume draw on theorists of ecology in different disciplines, such as Gregory Bateson,[12] Félix Guattari,[13] the 'ecocritique' of Timothy Morton's 'dark ecology',[14] and Jane Bennett's writings on the swarming vitalities of matter and heterogeneous agency,[15] to elaborate more complex, challenging and respect-ful conceptions of 'nature', subjectivity, human and non-human life, the sensible and the aesthetic, immanent materialism (Latour's 'parliament of things') and ethical responsibility.

Such conceptions of ecology are rooted in the inextricable intertwining of thinking and sensibility, social and political structures and material environment, and their ongoing status as relational, circulatory 'works-in-progress' (these are the 'three ecologies' of Guattari's transversal 'ecosophy': 'mental', 'social', 'environmental'). This feedback model suggests that toxic thoughts and ideas are entangled with/in pathogenic regimes and structures of behaviour that will have implications for a 'nature' in which we are always already imbricated. Shit ideas internalized and naturalized in-form poisonous working conditions, domestic situations and civic relations (and vice versa), and will pollute the rivers, the land, the sky, the flora and fauna, our bloodstreams, our affective relations, our minds and dreams and thoughts – and so it circulates in a transversally constituted ecosystem's expanded field: a turd in every pool.

Unfortunately there are an awful lot of toxic ideas that have purchase in the contemporary world, instances of an abject 'absurding the green' if you like: the belief that coercive violence and dehumanizing occupation will ever provide a resolution without repercussions; racisms, fundamentalisms, nationalist wars of all kinds; capitalism's pathological stoking of the infinite desire and drive to possess and consume yet more 'stuff' in the face of diminishing finite resources; governmental inaction internationally in the face of global warming; contemporary practices of slavery, and child labour; the continuing commitment to financing the proliferation of weapons technology research; the panicked endeavour internationally to create structures to bury nuclear waste with a half-life of over 100,000 years, an impossible period of time to begin to imagine, let alone predict (beyond the design of the sealed subterranean containers themselves, how on earth to construct hazard signs whose speed of semiotic 'decay' will be *slower* than that of the radioactive decay of the isotopes they signal to future generations?); and so on, *ad nauseam*.

> We are suicidal and genocidal. We are randomly destructive. We violate our space by the mere living of it. ... The damage we've done to the world is appalling, immeasurable. We are the ruins of time'.[16]

What is perhaps most mysterious and disappointing in all of this catastrophic ego-logical madness is our apparent inability or unwillingness at a macro-political level, and all too often at a local micro-political level, to look and listen, learn evaluatively from history and experience, and place attention and resources there where we might evolve a panoply of much better ideas. As Sven Lindqvist writes in *Exterminate All The Brutes*: 'You already know enough. So do I. It is not knowledge we lack. What is missing is the courage to understand what we know'.[17] And the courage not to deny or repress, and retreat to the default of disavowal ('bury it'). Our recurrent histories of forgetting are a bit like the uncanny temporal Möbius strip in that line by the laconic American comedian Steven Wright: 'Right now I'm having amnesia and déjà vu at the same time – I think I've forgotten this before'. Although our memories and knowledges are unquestionably partial and compromised (and isn't that the way with all knowledges?, as Beckett proposed), we remember and know enough, surely, at least to rewrite some of the absurdly toxic stories we tell ourselves.

For example, if we could only let go of our compulsion to dress transience in mourning, and instead confer value on impermanence and change, might we not be less fearful? Might we not 'inherit the Earth'? Why not lament (briefly) the very notion of permanence and move on with an understanding of the mortality of all forms? 'Truth', 'Progress', 'Fate', 'Absolute', 'Mine', 'Border', 'Inside(r)', 'Outside(r)' – it looks to me like these are all cover stories, formative human delusions. Let their heartbreak go, why not? Finding other languages and swerving shapes to accommodate the confusing mess of certainty's unravellings would be an act of kindness, of realistic optimism, and an occasion for invention. We've been pointing in the wrong direction. So in our efforts to 'mend the lesion between action and reflection',[18] and to distribute a morphing present rather than secure a future that is often a fantasy of a lost past, let's use the fact of transience – the ecological becomings of things and of *the others that are us* – for our fictions. Whether we like it or not, that's part of the way to turn a death story into a life story, as Beckett did with such unflinching attention, courage and compassion in his own writing of the disaster. Writing that perhaps, in its vision of a 'humanity in ruins' (*but not entirely*), offers 'an inkling of the terms in which our condition is to be thought again'.[19]

Nohow on …

4 August 2014
London

Works cited

Abbott, Porter H., *Beckett Writing Beckett: The Author in the Authograph*. Ithaca: Cornell University Press, 1996.

Adorno, Theodor, *Aesthetic Theory*, eds. G. Adorno and R. Tiemann, trans. R. Hullot-Kentor. Minneapolis, MN: University of Minnesota Press, 1997 [1970].

Bateson, Gregory, *Steps to an Ecology of Mind: Collected Essays in Anthropology, Psychiatry, Evolution, and Epistemology*. Chicago, IL: University of Chicago Press, 2000 [1972].

Beckett, Samuel, *Waiting for Godot*. London: Faber, 1965.

Beckett, Samuel, *Samuel Beckett: The Complete Short Prose 1929-1989*, ed. S. E. Gontarski. New York: The Grove Press, 1995.

Beckett, Samuel, 'Worstward Ho', in *Nohow On*. New York: Grove, 1996.

Bennett, Jane, *The Enchantment of Modern Life: Attachments, Crossings, and Ethics*. Princeton, NJ: Princeton University Press, 2001.

Bennett, Jane, *Vibrant Matter: A Political Ecology of Things*. Durham and London: Duke University Press, 2010.

Blau, Herbert, *Blooded Thought: Occasions of Theatre*. New York: PAJ Publications, 1982.

Blau, Herbert, *Take Up The Bodies: Theatre at the Vanishing Point*. Urbana, IL: University of Illinois Press, 1982.

Cavell, Stanley, 'Ending the Waiting Game: A Reading of Beckett's *Endgame*', in *Must We Mean What We Say?* Cambridge: Cambridge University Press, 1996 [1969], pp. 115–62.

Gontarski, S. E. (ed.), *The Edinburgh Companion to Samuel Beckett and the Arts*. Edinburgh: Edinburgh University Press, 2014.

Guattari, Félix, *The Three Ecologies*, trans. I. Pindar and P. Sutton. London: Athlone Press, 2000 [1989].

Latour, Bruno, *We Have Never Been Modern*, trans. C. Porter. Cambridge, MA: Harvard University Press, 1993 [1991].

Lindqvist, Sven, *Exterminate All The Brutes*, trans. J. Tate. London: Granta, 1997.

Morton, Timothy, *Ecology Without Nature: Rethinking Environmental Aesthetics*. Cambridge, MA and London: Harvard University Press, 2007.

Morton, Timothy, 'Poisoned Ground: Art and Philosophy in the Time of Hyperobjects', *Symploke*, vol. 21, no. 1–2 (2013), pp. 39–53.

Robertson, Lisa, *R's Boat*. Berkeley, CA: University of California Press, 2010.

Robertson, Lisa, *Nilling*. Toronto: Bookthug, 2012.

Sesame Street, *Monsterpiece Theatre: 'Waiting for Elmo'*, YouTube, 1996, http://www.youtube.com/watch?v=ksL_7WrhWOc.

NOTES

Introduction

1 Martin Esslin, *The Theatre of the Absurd*, 3rd revised and enlarged edn, Harmondsworth: Penguin, 1980, p. 28.

2 We use the word 'inevitably', since the contemporary designates the present as a time of crisis. To be contemporary is to be untimely, to fail to coincide with one's self, to be haunted by the past and future. For a more detailed discussion, see the art historian Boris Groys's discussion of the meaning of contemporary art in the essay 'Comrades of Time', *E-Flux Journal* 11, December 2009 [accessed 2 February 2015].

3 Isabelle Stengers, *Cosmopolitics I*, trans. R. Bononno, Minneapolis, MN: University of Minnesota Press, 2010, p. 35.

4 Ibid., p. 23.

5 See, for instance, Lionel Abel, *Metatheatre: A New View of Dramatic Form*, New York: Hill and Wang, 1963; Robert Brustein, *The Theatre of Revolt: Studies in Modern Drama from Ibsen to Genet*, Boston: Little and Brown, 1964; Geneviève Serreau, *Histoire du nouveau théâtre*, Paris: Gallimard, 1966; J. L. Styan, *Dark Comedy: The Development of Modern Comic Tragedy*, 2nd edn, Cambridge: Cambridge University Press, 1968; George Wellwarth, *The Theatre of Protest and Paradox: Developments in the Avant-garde Drama*, New York: New York University, 1971; Robert Mayberry, *Theatre of Discord: Dissonance in Beckett, Albee and Pinter*, Rutherford, PA: Fairleigh Dickinson University Press, 1989; Michael Y. Bennett, *Reassessing the Theatre of the Absurd, Camus, Beckett, Ionesco, Genet and Pinter*, Basingstoke: Palgrave Macmillan, 2011.

6 The painting is also known as *Fight with Cudgels*, and sometimes as the *Strangers* or *Cowherds*.

7 See Robert Hughes, *Goya*, London: Vintage, 2004; and Juan José Junquera, *The Black Paintings of Goya*, London and New York: Scala, 1999.

8 Michel Serres, *The Natural Contract*, trans. E. MacArthur and W. Paulson, Ann Arbor, MI: University of Michigan, 1995 [1990], p. 1.

 9 Ibid., p. 3.
10 Ibid., p. 4.
11 See in this context, Bonnie Marranca, *Ecologies of Theatre*,
    Baltimore, MD: Johns Hopkins Press, 1996; Stephen Bottoms and
    Matthew Goulish, *Small Acts of Repair: Performance, Ecology and
    Goat Island*, London and New York: Routledge, 2008; Carl Lavery,
    'The Ecology of the Image: The Environmental Politics of Philippe
    Quesne and Vivarium Studio', *French Cultural Studies*, vol. 24, no.
    3, (2013), pp. 264–78; Carl Lavery and Simon Whitehead, 'Bringing
    it all Back Home: Towards an Ecology of Place', *Performance
    Research*, vol. 17, no. 4 (2012), pp. 111–19.
12 The phrase 'more than human' highlights the extent to which human
    beings are part of a larger world that refuses to be defined in terms
    of normative binaries between 'nature' and 'culture'. See David
    Abrams, *The Spell of the Sensuous: Perception and Language in a
    More Than Human World*, New York: Vintage, 1996.
13 Peter Szondi, *Theory of the Modern Drama*, trans. M. Hays,
    Cambridge, MA: Polity Press, 1987 [1965], p. 7.
14 Ibid.
15 Erika Fischer-Lichte, *History of European Drama and Theatre*, trans.
    J. Riley, London and New York: Routledge, 2002 [1990], p. 2.
16 Una Chaudhuri, '"There Must be a Lot of Fish in that Lake":
    Toward an Ecological Theater', *Theater*, vol. 25, no. 1 (1994),
    pp. 23–31.
17 Peter Brook, *The Empty Space*, London: Penguin, 1990 [1968], p. 11.
18 The phrase 'more than human world' refers here to organic and
    inorganic material that exists beyond, and that affects, human
    agents. Importantly, it denotes manufactured objects as much as
    natural ones.
19 See for instance Lourdes Orozco, *Theatre and Animals*, Basingstoke:
    Palgrave Macmillan, 2013; Jennifer Parker-Starbuck, *Cyborg
    Theatre: Corporeal/Technological Intersections in Multi-Media
    Performance*, Basingstoke: Palgrave Macmillan, 2011; Minty
    Donald, 'The Urban River and Site-Specific Performance',
    Contemporary Theatre Review, vol. 22, no. 2 (2012), pp. 213–23;
    and Marlis Schweitzer and Joanne Zerdy (eds), *Performing Objects
    and Theatrical Things*, Basingstoke: Palgrave Macmillan, 2014.
20 Richard Schechner, *Performance Theory*, revised and expanded edn,
    London and New York: Routledge, 2004 [1977]; see also Richard
    Schechner, 'The End of Humanism', *Performing Arts Journal*, vol. 4,
    no. 1/2 (1979), pp. 9–22.
21 See for instance Baz Kershaw, *Theatre Ecology: Environments and
    Performance Events*, Cambridge: Cambridge University Press, 2007;
    David Williams, in Alan Read (ed.), 'The Right Horse, The Animal

Eye: Bartabas and Théâtre Zingaro', 'On Animals': *Performance Research*, vol. 5, no. 2 (2000), pp. 29–40; and Alan Read, *Theatre, Intimacy and Engagement: The Last Human Venue*, Basingstoke: Palgrave Macmillan, 2008; Jane Goodall, *Performance and Evolution in the Age of Darwin: Out of the Natural Order*, London and New York: Routledge, 2002.

22 Guattari's ideas are influenced by the thinking of the UK anthropologist and ecologist Gregory Bateson. In the epigraph to *The Three Ecologies*, Guattari references Bateson's comment from his 1972 publication *Steps to an Ecology of Mind: Collected Essays in Anthropology, Psychiatry, Evolution and Epistemology* that 'there is an ecology of bad ideas just as there is an ecology of weeds'. See Félix Guattari, *The Three Ecologies*, trans. I. Pindar and P. Sutton, London: Continuum, 2000 [1989], p. 19.

23 Downing Cless, *Ecology and Environment in European Drama*, London and New York: Routledge, 2010, and Wendy Arons and Theresa J. May (eds), *Readings in Performance and Ecology*, Basingstoke: Palgrave Macmillan, 2012.

24 Erika Munk, 'Introduction', *Theater*, vol. 25, no. 1 (1994), pp. 5–6, p. 5.

25 Ibid., p. 6.

26 Ibid., p. 5.

27 Kurt Heinlein, *Green Theatre: Promoting Ecological Preservation and Advancing the Sustainability of Human and Nature*, Saarbrücken: VDM Verlag, 2007.

28 Nelson Gray and Sheila Rabillard (eds), 'Theatre in an Age of Eco-Crisis', *Canadian Theatre Review*, vol. 144 (2010); Dee Heddon and Sally Mackey (eds), 'Environmentalism', *Research in Drama and Education: The Journal of Applied Theatre and Performance*, vol. 17, no. 2 (2012); and Stephen Bottoms, Aron Franks and Paula Kramer (eds), 'On Ecology', *Performance Research*, vol. 17, no. 4 (2012).

29 This definition echoes the classic description given by Cheryll Glotfelty in the Introduction to the *Ecocriticism Reader: Landmarks in Literary Ecology*, in which she states that 'ecocriticism shares the fundamental premise that human culture is connected to the physical world, affecting it and affected by it'. Cheryll Glotfelty, 'Introduction: Literary Studies in an Age of Environmental Crisis', in Cheryll Glotflety and Harold Fromm (eds), *The Ecocriticism Reader: Landmarks in Literary Ecology*, Athens, GA: University of Georgia Press, 1966, pp. xv–xxxvii, p. xix.

30 Una Chaudhuri, *Staging Place: The Geography of Modern Drama*, Ann Arbor, MI: University of Michigan Press, 1996; Sheila Rabillard, '*Fen* and the Production of a Feminist Ecotheater', *Theater*, vol. 25, no. 1 (1994), pp. 62–71.

31 Simon Starling, 'Never the Same River (Possible Futures, Probable Pasts)', in Amelia Groom (ed.), *Time: Documents of Contemporary Art*, Cambridge, MA and London: MIT Press, 2013, pp. 30–4, p. 30.

32 Ruby Cohn, 'Introduction: Around the Absurd', in Enoch Brater and Ruby Cohn (eds), *Around the Absurd: Essays on Modern and Postmodern Drama*, Ann Arbor, MI: University of Michigan Press, 1990, pp. 1–9, p. 2. Harold Pinter joined Esslin's 'Big Four' in the 1980 edition of the text, when he was accorded his own chapter.

33 See Guattari, *The Three Ecologies*, pp. 19–20.

34 Timothy Morton, *The Ecological Thought*, Cambridge, MA: Harvard University Press, 2010.

35 Timothy Morton, *Ecology without Nature: Rethinking Environmental Aesthetics*, Cambridge, MA: Harvard University Press, 2007, p. 181.

36 Samuel Beckett, *Endgame* in *Samuel Beckett: The Complete Dramatic Works*, London: Faber and Faber, 1986, p. 97.

37 Ibid., p. 98.

38 Greg Garrard, '*Endgame*: Beckett's Ecological Thought', in Yann Mével, Dominique Rabaté and Sjef Houppermans (eds), *Samuel Beckett Today/Aujourd' hui 23*, Amsterdam: Rodopoi, 2011, pp. 383–97.

39 Joanna Macy and Molly Young Brown, *Coming Back to Life: Practices to Reconnect Our Lives, Our World*, Gabriola Island: British Columbia, 1998.

40 See Brater and Cohn (eds), *Around the Absurd*; and Bennett, *Reassessing the Theatre of the Absurd*.

41 Theodor Adorno, 'Trying to Understand Endgame', *New German Critique*, trans. M. T. Jones, vol. 26 (1982) [1958], pp. 119–50, p. 123.

42 Ibid.

43 See Jonathan Bate, *The Song of the Earth*, Cambridge, MA: Harvard University Press, 2000; and Laurence Buell, *The Environmental Imagination: Thoreau, Nature Writing and the Formation of American Culture*, Cambridge, MA: Harvard University Press, 1995.

44 Ken Hiltner, 'Second Wave Ecocriticism', in Ken Hiltner (ed.), *Ecocriticism: The Essential Reader*, London and New York: Routledge, 2015, pp. 131–3, p. 131.

45 Timothy Morton, 'Queer Ecology', *PMLA*, vol. 125 (2010), pp. 273–82, p. 277. The Theatre of the Absurd tends to provide the type of negative ecocritique that Morton seems so interested in championing. This doubtless explains Morton's ubiquity throughout this current collection.

46 Eugène Ionesco, 'Dans les armes de la ville', *Cahiers de la Compagnie Madeleine Renaud - Jean-Louis Barrault*, 20 (October 1957), cited in Esslin, *The Theatre of the Absurd*, p. 23.

47 Albert Camus, *The Myth of Sisyphus and Other Essays*, trans.
    J. O'Brien, New York: Random House, 1955, p. 5.
48 Esslin, *Theatre of the Absurd*, p. 22.
49 Ibid., pp. 399, 408.
50 Ibid., p. 281.
51 Ibid., pp. 26–7.
52 Gertrude Stein's participation in the English-speaking Dadaist
    movement, and its influence on the Theatre of the Absurd, is
    afforded one paragraph.
53 Ibid., p. 16.
54 Marranca, *Ecologies of Theatre*, p. xvi.
55 Esslin, *Theatre of the Absurd*, p. 23.
56 Ibid., p. 406.
57 Andrew Dobson, *The Green Reader*, London: Andre Deutsch,
    1998, p. 5.
58 As Gabriel Egan explains, ecocriticism is always ecopolitical;
    its agenda is to argue for a fundamental transformation in how
    humans relate to the planet, which necessarily impacts on issues of
    economics and resource management. See Gabriel Egan, 'Ecopolitics/
    Ecocriticism', in Ken Hiltner (ed.), *Ecocriticism: The Essential
    Reader*, London: Routledge, 2015, pp. 278–300, p. 287.
59 See Caridad Svich, *The Way of Water* (2012); Steve Waters, *The
    Contingency Plan* (2009); Andrew Bovell, *When the Rain Stops
    Falling* (2009); and Richard Bean, *The Heretic* (2011). In this
    context, one could also mention Platform's on-going audio walk
    and play entitled *And While London Burns: An Operatic Tour
    Across the City*.
60 Rachel Carson, *Silent Spring*, New York: Houghton Mifflin, 2002
    [1962].
61 Both Hiltner and Garrard credit Carson with catalysing interest in
    environmental and ecological politics. See Hiltner, *Ecocriticism, The
    Essential Reader*, p. xiii; and Greg Garrard, *Ecocriticism*, 2nd edn,
    London: Routledge, 2012 [2004], p. 1.
62 Raymond Williams, *Marxism and Literature*, Oxford: Oxford
    University Press, 1977, p. 132.
63 Ibid.
64 In *Marxism and Literature*, Williams suggests that experience is a
    more accurate word than feeling. However, he refrains from using
    it because of its association with the 'past tense which is the most
    important obstacle to recognition of the area of social experience
    which is being defined'. Ibid., p. 132.
65 Theatre is, in our opinion, the perfect medium for capturing
    the emergence of this new 'structure of feeling'. For, as Williams
    explains, a structure of feeling is 'a social experience which is still

in process', that is, a collective mood whose parameters cannot be clearly delimited in some historicist desire for closure. Like a structure of feeling, theatre, too, resists historical constraint and simplistic periodization. Meaning in theatre seeps and flows; it dislodges and displaces, and remains, as Shakespeare's Hamlet realised, always 'out of joint'. But such disjuncture in the theatre is always and inherently double-edged, dialectical. For what theatre does, what it cannot help but accomplish, is to reconnect disparate temporalities, to assemble heterogeneities in an open-ended historical dialogue. Theatre is a memory machine, a historiographical methodology in and by itself, in which the past is not simply represented as a static thing, a mere object of experience, but rather something that is made palpable, quite literally conjured, in the present, the time of watching a series of dramatic images unfold together. Concatenating Williams's position with our own, we might say that theatre, *pace* Old Hamlet, allows the emergence of an ecological structure of feeling to haunt the present as a ghost that refuses to disappear, that neglects to leave the stage.

66 See Bruno Latour, *We Have Never Been Modern*, trans. C. Porter, Cambridge, MA: Harvard University Press, 1993 [1991]. According to Latour, modernity - the period when humans started to alter the Earth's crust on a molecular level - is predicated on a disavowal of our dependence on and implication in 'nature'. For Latour, such a denial is ecologically and environmentally irresponsible, as it sets us apart from the world of things.

67 Beckett, *Endgame*, p. 97.

68 This resonates with what the historian and philosopher R. G. Collingwood terms the 'idea of nature' in *The Idea of Nature* (1960). Greg Garrard makes a similar point but adopts a different perspective. For Garrard, Clov's deconstruction highlights the uncontrollable alterity of nature in a world of global warming. 'There is no more nature', in other words, because we are unable to predict its movements and pattern. See Gerrard, 'Endgame: Beckett's Ecological Thought', pp. 383–5.

69 Lynn Gardner was one of the few critics to pick up on the ecological significance of *Happy Days*. See Lynn Gardner http://www. theguardian.com/stage/theatreblog/2011/may/23/beckett-happy-days-father-ted [accessed 31 May 2013].

70 Polythene bags (plastic made from petroleum) do not decompose easily. Although estimates vary, it is commonly assumed that they take up to 1000 years to biodegrade, simply breaking down into smaller and smaller units of toxic waste.

71 Serres, *The Natural Contract*, p. 33.

72 See Arne Naess, 'The Deep Ecological Movement: Some
    Philosophical Aspects', *Philosophical Enquiry*, vol. 8, no.1 (1986),
    pp. 10–31. For 'deep green thinkers', the point is not to alleviate
    environmental degradation, but to produce a radical transformation
    in how we exist as ontological agents. The difficulty here is that
    this transformation is often predicated upon a celebration of
    phenomenological connectedness with the biosphere which tends to
    overlook social, economic and political factors. As Murray Bookchin
    and Félix Guattari point out, ecology should not be used as an alibi
    to abandon deep-rooted social problems. For a good description
    of deep ecology see Garrard, *Ecocriticism*, pp. 23–6. See also Carl
    Lavery's definition in Franc Chamberlain, Carl Lavery and Ralph
    Yarrow, 'Steps Towards an Ecology of Performance', *University of
    Bucharest Review*, vol. XIX, no. 1 (2012), pp. 1–37, pp. 12–13.
73 For Heidegger, technology constitutes the essence of humanity's
    relationship to the world. As such, the issue centres on how we use
    technology in a pragmatic way. See Martin Heidegger, *Discourse on
    Thinking*, trans. J. Anderson and E. Freund, New York: Harper and
    Row, 1966, p. 56.
74 See Murray Bookchin, *Philosophy of Social Ecology: Essays on
    Dialectical Naturalism*, 2nd revised edn, Montreal: Black Rose
    Books, 1995; and Val Plumwood, *Feminism and the Mastery of
    Nature*, London: Routledge, 1993.
75 Giorgio Agamben, *State of Exception*, trans. K. Attell, Chicago, IL:
    University of Chicago Press, 2005 [2003].
76 Our scepticism with regard to a simplistic notion of biocentrism here
    can be explained by a dangerous ethical and political position that
    tends to privilege 'nature' over culture. A more progressive definition
    of the term would see human life as being part of the *bios*. That way,
    human life would not be sacrificed to 'save' the environment.
77 Paul Davies, 'Strange Weather: Beckett from the Perspective of
    Ecocriticism', in S. E. Gontarski and Anthony Uhlmann (eds),
    Beckett After Beckett, Gainesville, FL: University of Florida Press,
    2006, pp. 66–78, p. 73.
78 Timothy Morton, *The Ecological Thought*, Cambridge, MA:
    Harvard University Press, 2010, p. 7.
79 Verena Andermatt Conley, *Ecopolitics: The Environment in
    Poststructuralist Thought*, London and New York: Routledge,
    1997, p. 10.
80 Camus, *The Myth of Sisyphus*, pp. 13–15.
81 See the essays in Edward J. Hughes (ed.), *The Cambridge
    Companion to Camus*, Cambridge: Cambridge University Press,
    2007; and Matthew H. Bowker, *Rethinking the Politics of Absurdity:*

Albert Camus, Postmodernity, and the Survival of Innocence, London: Routledge, 2013.

82 It is unfair to criticise Esslin for failing to deal with ecology, when ecology, as we use the term in this collection, had yet to become an accepted object of academic study and form of political critique.

83 Camus, *The Myth of Sisyphus*, p. 11.

84 Morton explains that, 'The strange stranger is not just "the other" – the "self" is this other. Since there is no (solid, lasting, independent, single) self, we are the strange stranger'. Morton, *The Ecological Thought*, p. 87.

85 Gabriella Giannachi and Nigel Stewart (eds), *Performing Nature: Explorations in Ecology and the Arts*, Bern: Peter Lang, 2005. The book came out of an important conference held at Lancaster University in 2002 entitled 'Between Nature: Explorations in Ecology and Performance'. See also in this context, Wallace Heim, Bron Szerzynski and Clare Waterton (eds), *Nature Performed: Environment, Culture and Performance*, Blackwell: Oxford, 2003.

86 Camus, *Myth of Sisyphus*, p. 91.

87 Ibid.

88 This hopeful ecological reading of the Absurd is close to Michael Y. Bennett's philosophical reassessment of Camus. For Bennett, the Absurd is a positive philosophy, a way of thinking that attempts to give meaning to existence. See Michael Y. Bennett, *Reassessing the Theatre of the Absurd*, pp. 14–26.

89 Beckett provides an excellent gloss on Sisyphus's embrace of immanence in the final line of the prose text *Faux Départs*: 'When it goes out no matter, start again, another place, ... never see, never find, no end, no matter'. Samuel Beckett, 'Faux Départs', in S. E. Gontarski (ed.), *Samuel Beckett: The Complete Short Prose 1929-1989*, New York: The Grove Press, 1995, pp. 271–4, p. 274.

90 See, for instance, Wendell Berry, *Home Economics: Fourteen Essays by Wendell Berry*, New York: North Point Press, 1987.

91 Jean François Lyotard, 'Oikos', in *Political Writings*, trans. B. Readings with K. Geiman, London: UCL Press, 1991, pp. 96–107, p. 102.

92 Ibid., p. 105.

93 Ibid., p. 100.

94 Ibid., p. 105.

95 Morton, *Ecology Without Nature*, p. 177.

96 Chaudhuri, *Staging Place*, p. 11, p. xii.

97 Gregory Bateson, *Steps to an Ecology of Mind: Collected Essays in Anthropology, Psychiatry, Evolution, and Epistemology*, Chicago: University of Chicago Press, 2000 [1972], p. 495.

98 Samuel Beckett, 'The Capital of the Ruins', in S. E Gontarski (ed.), *Samuel Beckett: The Complete Short Prose 1929-1989*, New York: The Grove Press, 1995, pp. 275–8, p. 278.

99 See for instance Hans-Thies Lehmann's summary of the melancholic *Weltanschauung* that dominates his account of the Theatre of the Absurd in *Postdramatic Theatre*, trans. K. Jürs-Munby, London and New York: Routledge, 2006 [1999], pp. 53–5.

100 William Cronon, 'Foreword: The Pain of a Poisoned World', in Brett L. Walker (ed.), *Toxic Archipelago: A History of Industrial Disease in Japan*, Seattle, WA: University of Washington Press, 2010, p. x.

101 Michihiko Hachiya, *Hiroshima Diary: The Journal of a Japanese Physician, August 6 – September 30, 1945*, ed. and trans. W. Ellis, Charlotte: North Carolina Press, 1955.

102 Joachim Radkau, *Nature and Power: A Global History of the Environment*, trans. T. Dunlap, Cambridge: Cambridge University Press, 2008 [2002], p. 266.

103 Michel Serres, *Times of Crisis: What the Financial Crisis Revealed and How to Reinvent Our Lives and Future*, trans. A. Feenberg-Dibbon, London: Bloomsbury, 2014 [2009], p. 14.

104 Dipesh Chakrabarty, 'The Climate of History: Four Theses', *Critical Enquiry*, vol. 35, no. 2 (2009), pp. 197–222, p. 198.

105 Chakrabarty is aware of the ethical and political tensions involved in designating human beings as a single species, but he argues that the 'crisis of climate change calls on academics to rise above their disciplinary prejudices'. Chakrabarty is calling, in other words, for a form of inclusive thinking that would bring together different disciplines and ideas – biology and history, politics and science, etc. – that have historically been separated. Ibid., p. 215.

106 Serres, *Times of Crisis*, p. 14.

107 Egan, 'Ecopolitics/Ecocriticism', p. 278.

108 Radkau, *Nature and Power*, p. 266.

109 For two excellent articles on the influence and aesthetics of *Silent Spring*, see Kenny Walker, '"Without Evidence, there is No Answer": Uncertainty and Scientific Ethos in *Silent Springs* of Rachel Carson', *Environmental Humanities*, vol. 2 (2013), pp. 101–16; and Amanda Hagood, 'Wonders with the Sea: Rachel Carson's Ecological Aesthetic and the Mid-Century Reader', *Environmental Humanities*, vol. 2 (2013), pp. 57–77.

110 Carson, *Silent Spring*, p. 188.

111 Bert O. States, *Great Reckonings in Little Rooms: On the Phenomenology of Theatre*, Berkeley, CA: University of California Press, 1985.

112   For a discussion of Tynan's criticism of Ionesco, see 'The London
      Controversy', in Eugène Ionesco, *Notes and Counter Notes: Writings
      on Theatre*, trans. Donald Watson, New York: Grove Press, 1964,
      p. 93. See also Carl Lavery's essay in this collection, pp. 165–90.

113   In this context, see Chaudhuri's reference to Pinter's *The Caretaker*
      (1960), '"There Must be a Lot of Fish in that Lake"', p. 30.

114   Playwrights such as Beckett, Ionesco and Churchill have more
      in common with the work of contemporary ecological thinkers
      like Timothy Morton and Nigel Clark than they do with
      phenomenological philosophers like Martin Heidegger, Emmanuel
      Levinas and Maurice Merleau-Ponty, who were used by ecocritics
      in the 1980s and 1990s to develop a deep green mode of reading.
      For Clark et al., the primacy that these philosophers place on the
      capacity of human beings to 'world the world' is no longer tenable
      in the face of the agency of 'nature' itself. Worlding is always an
      intentional activity; earthquakes, tsunamis and climate change
      make such intentionality redundant. See Nigel Clark, *Inhuman
      Nature: Sociable Life on a Dynamic Planet*, London: Sage, 2012,
      pp. 27–54.

115   Will Steffen, Paul J. Crutzen and John R. McNeill, 'The
      Anthropocene: Are Humans Now Overwhelming the Great Forces
      of Nature?', *Ambio*, vol. 38 (2007), pp. 614–21, p. 614.

116   Rosi Braidotti, *The Posthuman*, Cambridge, MA: Polity, 2013, p. 13.

117   Ibid., p. 15.

118   Jean Genet, *The Balcony*, trans. B. Wright and T. Hands, London:
      Faber and Faber, 1991, p. 63.

119   In ecology, negative feedback is a sign of health and stability within
      a given ecosystem. Positive feedback, by contrast, is an indicator
      of stress and disturbance, the process that sends the system out of
      balance.

120   James Knowlson, 'Tradition and Innovation in Ionesco's *La
      Cantatrice chauve*', in Enoch Brater and Ruby Cohn (eds), *Around
      the Absurd: Essays on Modern and Postmodern Drama*, Ann Arbor,
      MI: University of Michigan Press, 1990, pp. 57–72, p. 58.

121   For Derrida, deconstruction '[uses] against the edifice the
      instruments or stones available in the house'. Jacques Derrida,
      Margins of Philosophy, trans. A. Bass, Chicago, IL: University of
      Chicago Press, 1982, p. 135.

122   Elinor Fuchs, 'Another Version of Pastoral', in *The Death of
      Character: Perspectives on Theater After Modernism*, Bloomington,
      IN: Indiana University Press, 1996, pp. 92–107, p. 93.

123   This resonates with Nigel Clark's claim that if we are to come
      to terms with life on an increasingly dynamic and precarious

planet, then we will need to affirm 'a kind of primordial passivity, a susceptibility in the face of all that is not ours to make or even know'. Clark, *Inhuman Nature*, p. 52.

124 Desmastes's focus on absurdist theatre is somewhat abbreviated. Only Beckett's work is discussed in any depth. His focus is really on neo-absurdist theatre. See William Desmastes, *Theatre of Chaos: Beyond Absurdism into Orderly Disorder*, Cambridge: Cambridge University Press, 1998, pp. 56–64.

125 Ibid., p. 56.

126 Ibid., xvi.

127 Ibid., p. 169.

128 Ibid., p. 170.

129 There are other inconsistencies in his claims. In Chapter 2 of his book, Beckett is enlisted by Desmastes as a neo-absurdist playwright, despite the fact that he plays such a pivotal role in Esslin's text. Likewise, Desmastes's discussion of the 'total randomness' of absurdist theatre fails to see that 'chaos' in these works is always tightly structured and composed, otherwise there would be no theatrical experience to speak of. Ibid., p. xvi.

130 Braidotti, *The Posthuman*, p. 100.

131 See Alain Badiou, *On Beckett*, trans. N. Power and A. Toscano, London: Clinamen, 2002.

Chapter 1

1 'Dark ecology' is conceived by Timothy Morton. See *The Ecological Thought*, Cambridge, MA: Harvard University Press, 2010, p. 59.

2 Max Stafford-Clark, interview, in Mireia Aragay, Hildegard Klein, Enric Monforte and Pilar Zozaya (eds), *British Theatre of the 1990s: Interviews with Directors, Playwrights, Critics and Academics*, Basingstoke: Palgrave Macmillan, 2007, pp. 27–40, p. 28.

3 Ibid.

4 Martin Esslin, *The Theatre of the Absurd*, 3rd revised and enlarged edn, London: Methuen, 2001, pp. 23–4.

5 Ibid., p. 432.

6 Michael Y. Bennett, *Reassessing the Theatre of the Absurd: Camus, Beckett, Ionesco, Genet, and Pinter*, Basingstoke: Palgrave Macmillan, 2011, p. 4. Bennett counters Esslin's take on the Absurd by arguing against his misunderstanding of a key citation by Ionesco and a misreading of Camus as an existentialist in order to lay claim to the Absurd as not about nihilistic despair, but as a 'revolt' against meaninglessness. Ibid., p. 2.

7 Caryl Churchill, 'Not Ordinary, Not Safe: A Direction for Drama?', *The Twentieth Century* (November 1960), pp. 443–51, p. 445.

8 Ibid. Churchill moves from her reference to Beckett's *Waiting for Godot* into brief reflections on John Osborne's *Look Back in Anger*.

9 Ibid.

10 Ibid., p. 447.

11 Caryl Churchill, quoted in Judith Thurman, 'The Playwright Who Makes you Laugh about Orgasm, Racism, Class Struggle, Homophobia, Woman-Hating, the British Empire, and the Irrepressible Strangeness of the Human Heart', *Ms* (May 1982), pp. 51–7, p. 54.

12 For details regarding this shifting political landscape, see my discussion of Churchill's short play, *This is a Chair* (1997) in Elaine Aston, 'Feeling the Loss of Feminism: Sarah Kane's *Blasted* and an Experiential Genealogy of Contemporary Women's Playwriting', *Theatre Journal*, vol. 62 (2010), pp. 575–91, pp. 578–9.

13 Jacques Rancière, *Disagreement: Politics and Philosophy*, trans. J. Rose, Minneapolis. MN: University of Minnesota Press, 1999 [1995], p. 1.

14 Aristotle cited by Rancière, *Disagreement*.

15 Ibid.

16 Rancière, *Disagreement*, p. 27.

17 Ibid., p. 30.

18 Caryl Churchill, Interview, *Plays and Players* (January 1973). The interview can be found in p. 40 of the journal and p. 1 of a special insert containing the script of *Owners*. Here, p. 1.

19 Ibid.

20 Ibid.

21 Caryl Churchill, *The Ants,* in *New English Dramatists*, vol. 12, Harmondsworth: Penguin, 1969, pp. 89–103, p. 93.

22 Ibid.

23 Ibid.

24 Ibid., p. 91.

25 Luce Irigaray, 'Animal Compassion', in Peter Atterton and Matthew Calarco (eds), *Animal Philosophy: Essential Readings in Continental Thought*, London: Continuum, 2004, pp. 195–201, p. 196.

26 Ibid., p. 201.

27 Ibid., p. 200.

28 Churchill, *The Ants*, p. 103.

29 Peggy Ramsay, quoted in Philip Roberts, *About Churchill: The Playwright & The Work*, London: Faber & Faber, 2008, p. 16. Capitalization in the original.

30 Elin Diamond, 'On Churchill and Terror', in Elaine Aston and Elin Diamond (eds), *The Cambridge Companion to Caryl Churchill*,

Cambridge: Cambridge University Press, 2009, pp. 125–43, pp. 127–28. Making her observation, Diamond cites a passage from Grandfather's speech in which he verbalizes how 'out there they're all dropping bombs, bang, bang, bang' (*The Ants*, p. 100).

31 Caryl Churchill, *The Skriker*, London: Nick Hern Books, 1994, p. 1.

32 This aesthetic was promoted by the choice of image for the playbill and book cover of the script: the Man Ray photograph, *La Marquise Cassati* (1922), famed for the doubling of the eyes.

33 Spink's dance collaborations with Churchill had previously included *Lives of the Great Poisoners* (1991) which experimented with exploring a physical language for the thematic treatment of poison. Churchill acknowledges that she would 'never have written *The Skriker* that way if [she] hadn't already worked on other shows with dancers and singers'. Caryl Churchill, 'Introduction', *Caryl Churchill: Plays 3*, London: Nick Hern Books, 1998, p. viii.

34 Jacques Derrida, 'The Animal that Therefore I am (More to Follow)', *Critical Enquiry*, vol. 28, no. 2 (Winter 2002), pp. 369–418, p. 399. Somewhat in contrast to Rancière, Derrida is more thoroughly concerned with critiquing the binary divide between human and animal. To this end, he revisits philosophical thinking for the way in which it has repeatedly conceived of the ontological difference between being human and being animal, elucidating how the idea of 'the animal' in the 'singular' and 'without language' renders 'the animal ... without the right and power to "respond" and hence without many other things that would be the property of man' (p. 400).

35 Caryl Churchill, *Top Girls*, London: Methuen, 1982, p. 87.

36 For a discussion of *Fen's* socialist-feminist politics mapped with ecological concerns, see Sheila Rabillard's '*Fen* and the Production of a Feminist Ecotheater', *Theater*, vol. 25, no. 1 (1994), pp. 62–71.

37 Esslin, *Theatre of the Absurd*, p. 402.

38 For further discussion of 'deep ecology' in tension with questions of 'environmental justice' related to Churchill's theatre, see Sheila Rabillard's highly perceptive essay, 'On Caryl Churchill's Ecological Drama: Right to Poison the Wasps?', in Elaine Aston and Elin Diamond (eds), *The Cambridge Companion to Caryl Churchill*, pp. 88–104.

39 Morton, *The Ecological Thought*, p. 59.

40 Ibid., p. 17.

41 Churchill, *The Ants*, p. 97.

42 R. Darren Gobert, *The Theatre of Caryl Churchill*, London: Bloomsbury Methuen Drama, p. 23.

43 Churchill, *The Skriker*, p. 4.

44 Benedict Nightingale, *The Times*, 29 January, p. 16.

45 Caryl Churchill, Interview, *Late Theatre*, BBC2, January 1994.

46 Churchill, *The Skriker*, p. 1.

47 Ibid., pp. 4–5.

48 For an extended discussion of this point, see Candice Amich's highly insightful essay, 'Bringing the Global Home: The Commitment of Caryl Churchill's *The Skriker*', *Modern Drama*, vol. 50, no. 3 (Fall 2007), pp. 394–413, p. 398.

49 Churchill, *The Skriker*, p. 12.

50 Ibid.

51 Ibid., p. 14.

52 In the mid-1990s, at the time of the play's production, right-wing, Conservative politicians were leading a crusade against 'lone mothers' and 'home alone' children, a social context that heightened the sense of the girls' marginality. For further discussion see Elaine Aston, *Caryl Churchill*, 3rd edn, Tavistock: Northcote House, 2010, pp. 30, 98.

53 Churchill, *The Skriker*, p. 17.

54 Ibid., p. 27.

55 Ibid., p. 30.

56 Ibid., p. 31.

57 Ibid., p. 33.

58 Ibid., pp. 48–9.

59 Ibid., p. 52.

60 Ibid.

61 This resonates with Morton's idea that 'ecological thought is the Trickster, thinking of the Trickster', who commands us to figure out the tricksterish question of who counts as human and who does not, or rather to revise the inequalities of our binarized thinking of human and non-human by thinking towards our interconnectedness. Morton, *The Ecological Thought*, pp. 82–3.

62 Churchill, *The Skriker*, p. 44.

63 Ibid., p. 52.

64 Ibid., p. 43.

65 Morton, *The Ecological Thought*, p. 3.

66 Ibid., emphasis added.

67 The front cloth was painted by Alistair Brotchie; the designer was Ian McNeil, and the sound designer Paul Arditti. For further details on the staging of *Far Away*, see Aston, *Caryl Churchill*, p. 117.

68 Caryl Churchill, *Far Away*, London: Nick Hern Books, 2000, p. 12.

69 Ibid., p. 14.

70 Ibid., p. 6.

71 Ibid., pp. 14–15.

72 Irigaray, 'Animal Compassion', p. 201.

73 Churchill, *Far Away*, p. 30.

74 Ibid., p. 34.
75 Ibid., p. 33.
76 Ibid.
77 Ibid., pp. 34–5.
78 Ibid., p. 37.
79 Ibid.
80 Ibid., pp. 37–8.
81 Irigaray, 'Animal Compassion', p. 201. For Irigaray, birds have restorative powers; their 'song heals many a useless word'; and she observes that 'it is not for naught that the bird appears as the spiritual assistant, even the spiritual master, in many a tradition'. Ibid., p. 197.
82 Churchill, *Far Away*, p. 37.
83 Ibid., p. 38.
84 For details of the Royal Court's staging of the parade, see Aston, *Caryl Churchill*, p. 119.
85 Bruno Bettelheim, *The Informed Heart: Autonomy in a Mass Age*, New York: The Free Press, 1960, p. 151. I am grateful to Nina Kane, University of Huddersfield, whose PhD thesis on Sarah Kane's *Cleansed* directed me to Bettelheim's postulation of 'the walking corpses'.
86 Churchill, *Far Away*, p. 26.
87 Ibid., p. 27.
88 Todd admits that he watches the televised trials of the prisoners (p. 20); Joan's 'pity' is reserved for the hats that get destroyed, rather than the 'bodies' that 'burn' along with them (p. 25).
89 I am taking my cue from Rancière who posits politics as subject to disappearance when it is no longer possible to make visible the democratic count of those who do not count, when all that remains is 'consensus democracy', which closes the 'gap between a party to a dispute and a part of society'. Ibid., p. 102.

Chapter 2

1 Sam Shepard, *States of Shock, Far North, Silent Tongue: A Play and Two Screenplays*, New York: Vintage, 1993, p. 167.
2 The original source of Greeley's famous phrase is a matter of historical dispute.
3 Albert Camus, *The Myth of Sisyphus and Other Essays*, trans. Justin O'Brien, New York: Random House, 1955 [1942], p. 5.
4 Martin Esslin, *The Theatre of the Absurd*, 2nd revised and enlarged edn, Harmondsworth: Penguin, 1968, p. 301.

5 See Ruby Cohn, *From Desire to Godot: Pocket Theater of Postwar Paris*, London: Calder, 1998.

6 Esslin, *Theatre of the Absurd*, pp. 23–4.

7 Camus, *Myth of Sisyphus*, p. 23.

8 Ibid., p. 38.

9 Ibid., p. 11.

10 Jane Bennett, *Vibrant Matter: A Political Ecology of Things*, Durham, NC and London: Duke University Press, 2010, p. 10.

11 Leo Marx, *The Machine in the Garden: Technology and the Pastoral Ideal in America*, New York: Oxford University Press, 1964, p. 3.

12 Greg Garrard, *Ecocriticism*, London and New York: Routledge, 2004, p. 34.

13 Marx, *The Machine in the Garden*, p. 3.

14 Ibid., p. 276.

15 Camus, *Myth of Sisyphus*, p. 10.

16 Edward Albee, *The American Dream and The Zoo Story*, New York: Signet, 1961, p. 11.

17 Philip C. Kolin, 'Albee's Early One-act Plays: "A New American Playwright from whom Much is to be Expected"', in Stephen Bottoms (ed.), *The Cambridge Companion to Edward Albee*, Cambridge: Cambridge University Press, 2005, pp. 16–38, p. 21.

18 Albee, *Zoo Story*, p. 43.

19 Timothy Morton, 'Queer Ecology', *PMLA*, vol. 125, no. 2 (2010), pp. 273–82, p. 274.

20 Albee, *Zoo Story*, p. 20.

21 Ibid., p. 37.

22 Ibid., p. 28.

23 Ibid., p. 36.

24 Ibid., p. 30.

25 Ibid., p. 32.

26 Ibid., p. 35.

27 Ibid., p. 36.

28 Ibid., pp. 39–40.

29 Ibid., p. 45.

30 Latour quoted in Bennett, *Vibrant Matter*, p. 49.

31 See Albert Camus, *The Outsider*, trans. S. Smith, London: Penguin, 2013 [1942].

32 Albee, *Zoo Story*, p. 47.

33 Ibid., p. 49.

34 Esslin, *Theatre of the Absurd*, p. 23.

35 Camus, *Myth of Sisyphus*, p. 26 and p. 40.

36 Albee, *Zoo Story*, p. 49.

37 Theodor Adorno, *Negative Dialectics*, trans. E. B. Ashton, New York: Continuum, 1973, p. 375.

38 Camus, *Myth of Sisyphus*, p. 34.
39 Henry David Thoreau, *Walden; or, Life in the Woods*, Mineola, NY: Dover, 1995, p. 10.
40 Thoreau, *Walden*, p. 182.
41 Thoreau, *Walden*, pp. 2, 4.
42 Marx, *The Machine in the Garden*, p. 5.
43 Sam Shepard, *Rock Garden*, in his *Fifteen One-Act Plays*, New York: Vintage, 2002, p. 126.
44 Ibid., p. 128.
45 Ibid., p. 132.
46 Morton, 'Queer Ecology', p. 274.
47 Shepard, *Fourteen Hundred Thousand*, in his Fifteen One-Act Plays, p. 212.
48 Ibid., p. 221.
49 Ibid., p. 217.
50 Ibid., p. 211.
51 Ibid., p. 215.
52 Ibid., pp. 213, 221.
53 Ibid., p. 227.
54 Thoreau, *Walden*, p. 171.
55 Shepard, *Fourteen Hundred Thousand*, p. 220.
56 Ibid., p. 229.
57 Ibid., p. 230.
58 Thoreau, p. 1.
59 Shepard, *Fourteen Hundred Thousand*, p. 218.
60 Ibid., p. 219.
61 Ibid., p. 216.
62 Ibid., p. 228.
63 Ibid., p. 215.
64 Ibid., p. 231.
65 Ibid.
66 Ibid., p. 232.
67 Ibid.
68 Ibid., p. 233.
69 Ibid.
70 My thanks to Carl Lavery for this formulation.
71 Edward Albee, *The Goat; or, Who is Sylvia?*, London: Methuen, 2004, pp. 15, 40.
72 Ibid., p. 40.
73 Ibid., p. 24.
74 See the final chapter of Henry Nash Smith's *Virgin Land: The American West as Symbol and Myth*, Cambridge, MA: Harvard University Press, 1974.
75 Albee, *The Goat*, pp. 49–50.

76   Jacques Derrida, *The Animal That Therefore I Am*, trans. D. Wills, New York: Fordham University Press, 2008 [2006], p. 4.

77   Albee, *The Goat*, p. 35.

78   J. Ellen Gainor, 'Albee's *The Goat*: Rethinking Tragedy for the 21st Century', in Stephen Bottoms (ed.), *The Cambridge Companion to Edward Albee*, Cambridge: Cambridge University Press, 2005, pp. 199–216, p. 208.

79   Ibid.

80   The original quotation is 'Who is Silvia? What is she, That all our swains commend her?' (IV.ii).

81   Albee, *The Goat*, p. 39.

82   Ibid., p. 53.

83   Thoreau, *Walden*, p. 183.

84   Albee, *The Goat*, p. 48.

85   Ibid., pp. 46–7.

86   Ibid., p. 36.

87   Ibid., p. 51.

88   Derrida, *The Animal That Therefore I Am*, p. 12.

89   Albee, *The Goat*, p. 67.

90   Ibid., p. 54.

91   Derrida, *The Animal That Therefore I Am*, p. 12.

92   Albee, *The Goat*, p. 61.

93   Ibid., p. 70.

94   William Cronon, *Uncommon Ground: Rethinking The Human Place in Nature*, London: Norton, 1996, p. 72.

95   Thoreau, 'Walking' (1862), cited in Cronon, *Uncommon Ground*, p. 69.

96   Sam Shepard, *Kicking a Dead Horse*, London: Faber and Faber, 2007, p. 20.

97   Ibid., p. 32.

98   Ibid., p. 19.

99   Ibid., p. 24.

100 Adam Sweeting and Thomas C. Crochunis, 'Performing the Wild: Rethinking Wilderness and Theater Spaces', in K. Armbruster and K. R. Wallace (eds), *Beyond Nature Writing: Expanding the Boundaries of Ecocriticism*, Charlottesville, NC and London: University Press of Virginia, 2001, pp. 325–40, p. 326.

101 Cronon, *Uncommon Ground*, p. 80.

102 Shepard, *Kicking a Dead Horse*, p. 14.

103 Ibid., p. 12.

104 Ibid., p. 22.

105 Ibid., p. 19.

106 Ibid., p. 29.

107 Shepard, *Kicking a Dead Horse*, p. 27; and Cronon, *Uncommon Ground*, p. 49.
108 Shepard, *Kicking a Dead Horse*, p. 28.
109 Ibid., p. 10.
110 Garrard, *Ecocriticism*, p. 77.
111 Shepard, *Kicking a Dead Horse*, p. 17.
112 Ibid., p. 20.
113 Ibid., p. 42.
114 Ibid., p. 40.
115 Ibid., p. 37.
116 Ibid., p. 9.
117 Ibid., pp. 39–40.
118 Ibid., p. 46.
119 Ibid.
120 Camus, *Myth of Sisyphus*, p. 91.
121 Cronon, *Uncommon Ground*, p. 89.

Chapter 3

1 Martin Esslin, *Theatre of the Absurd*, 3rd revised and enlarged edn, Harmondsworth: Penguin, 1980, p. 23.
2 Thomas Mann, *The Magic Mountain*, trans. H. T. Lowe-Porter, London: Vintage, 1999, p. 284. The relevant passage reads: 'And life? Life itself? Was it perhaps only an infection, a sickening of matter? Was that which one might call the original procreation of matter only a disease, a growth produced by morbid stimulation of the immaterial?'
3 Isabelle Stengers, *Cosmopolitics I*, trans. R. Bonnono, Minneapolis, MN: University of Minnesota Press, 2010, p. 32.
4 Félix Guattari, *The Three Ecologies*, trans. I. Pindar and P. Sutton, London: Continuum, 2008, p. 19.
5 Stafford-Clark's rehearsal technique, derived from J. L. Austin's definition of speech-acts, asks actors to identify the intentional act relevant to each verbal form in the text. See Max Stafford-Clark, *Letters to George: The Account of a Rehearsal*, London: Nick Hern Books, 1997.
6 Timothy Morton, *Ecology Without Nature: Rethinking Environmental Aesthetics*, Cambridge, MA: Harvard University Press, 2007, p. 181ff.
7 Baz Kershaw, *Theatre Ecology: Environments and Performance Events*, Cambridge: Cambridge University Press, 2007, p. 82.
8 The time period of Esslin's text runs from roughly the late 1940s to the late 1960s.

9 Krzysztof Miklaszewski, *Encounters with Tadeusz Kantor*, London and New York: Routledge, 2002, p. 34.

10 George Hyde, 'Poland', in Ralph Yarrow (ed.), *European Theatre 1960-1990: Cross-Cultural Perspectives*, London: Routledge, 1992, pp. 182–218 (esp. pp. 204–08); and Jennifer Kumiega, *The Theatre of Grotowski*, London: Methuen, 1987.

11 Email communication to author, 2013. See also Lavery's essay in this collection, pp. 1–57.

12 George Hyde, 'Afterword', in Grazyna Bystydzieńska and Emma Harris (eds), *From Norwich to Kantor: Essays on Polish Modernism dedicated to Professor G.M. Hyde*, Warsaw: University of Warsaw Press, 1999, p. 144.

13 Bruno Schulz, in Miklaszewski *Encounters with Tadeusz Kantor*, p. 37.

14 Tadeusz Kantor, in Miklaszewski *Encounters with Tadeusz Kantor*, p. 73.

15 Stengers, *Cosmopolitics* I, p. 35.

16 Morton, *Ecology without Nature*, p. 150.

17 Samuel Beckett, *Endgame*, London: Faber and Faber, 1964, p. 16.

18 Witold Gombrowicz, *Pornografia*, trans. Alastair Hamilton, London: Penguin, 1966, p. 66.

19 George Hyde, 'The word unheard: "Form" in modern Polish drama', *Word and Image*, vol. 4, no. 3–4 (1988), pp. 719–31, p. 719.

20 Morton, *Ecology Without Nature*, p. 188.

21 Hyde, 'The word unheard', p. 729.

22 Milija Gluhovic, 'The Mnemonics of Kantor's *Wielopole, Wielopole*', *Toronto Slavic Quarterly*, no. 14 (2005), Online journal: http://www.utoronto.ca/tsq/14/gluhovic14.shtml [accessed 31 January 2014]. Ibid.

23 Miklaszewski, *Encounters with Tadeusz Kantor*, p. 74.

24 Ibid.

25 Daphne Grace cites Kathleen Hyles's observation that chaos 'can be conceived as an inexhaustible ocean of information' and notes that quantum physics registers the coexistence of coherent and non-coherent states, of uniformity and difference. Daphne Grace, *Beyond Bodies: Gender, Literature and the Enigma of Consciousness*, Amsterdam and New York: Rodopi, 2014, pp. 23, 28.

26 Morton, *Ecology Without Nature*, p. 5.

27 Gluhovic, 'The Mnemonics of Kantor's *Wielopole, Wielopole*', 2005.

28 Ibid.

29 Walker, in ibid.

30 Jean-François Lyotard, 'Oikos', in *Political Writings*, trans. B. Readings with K. Geiman, London: UCL Press, 1993, pp. 106–7, p. 100.

31 For further discussion of Lyotard's concept of ecology, see Mark Taylor-Batty's and Carl Lavery's essay in this collection, pp. 1–57.

32 Lyotard, 'Oikos', p. 105.
33 Lyotard notes: 'I want to begin by saluting the mistress of us all in matters of ecology, Sascha, Dieter Beisel's Dog. She resides wherever Dieter is. She occupies a voice, an odour, a silhouette, a set of movements: such is the oikos. She takes no one to court to safeguard her property. She doesn't need a soil, a blood, or even an apartment; all she needs is to belong'. Ibid., p. 96.
34 Stengers, *Cosmopolitics I*, p. 35.
35 Tadeusz Rózewicz, *The Card Index and Other Plays*, trans. Adam Czerniawski, London: Calder and Boyars, 1969, p. 64.
36 Ibid.
37 Ibid., p. 39.
38 Ibid., p. 41.
39 Ibid., p. 40.
40 Ibid., p. 42.
41 Ibid., p. 55.
42 Ibid., p. 62.
43 Ibid., p. 76.
44 Witold Gombrowicz, *Princess Ivona*, trans. K. Griffith-Jones and C. Robins, London: Calder and Boyars, 1969, pp. 1–2.
45 Ibid., p. 8.
46 Lyotard, 'Oikos', p. 100.
47 Gombrowicz, *Princess Ivona*, p. 56.
48 Lyotard, 'Oikos', p. 99.
49 Kantor, in Miklaszewski, *Encounters with Tadeusz Kantor*, p. 11.
50 Maurice Blanchot, *Writing the Disaster*, trans. A Smock, Lincoln, NE: University of Nebraska Press, 1986 [1980].
51 Morton, *Ecology Without Nature*, p. 142.
52 Lyotard, 'Oikos', p. 100.
53 Theatre de Complicite, *The Street of Crocodiles*, London: Methuen, 1999, p. 67.
54 Ibid., p. 5.
55 Rózewicz, *The Card Index*, p. 49.
56 Complicite, *The Street of Crocodiles*, p. 13.
57 Jane Bennett, *Vibrant Matter: A Political Ecology of Things*, Durham, NC: Duke University Press, 2010.
58 Complicite, *The Street of Crocodiles*, p. 17.
59 Bruno Schulz, in Hyde, 'The word unheard', p. 727.
60 Ibid., p. 726.
61 R. M. Rilke, *Duineser Elegien*, ed. E. L. Stahl, Oxford: Blackwell, 1965, p. 19 (my translation).
62 Bystydzieńska and Harris, *From Norwich to Kantor*, p. 11.
63 J. W. Goethe, *Gedichte, Erster Band*, Stuttgart: Verlag der J. C. Cottaschen Buchhandlung, 1868, p. 216 (my translation).

64 Ibid., p. 216.
65 Gareth White, *Audience Participation in Theatre*, London: Palgrave, 2013, p. 25.

Chapter 4

1   Samuel Beckett, *Three Novels*, trans. P. Bowles and S. Beckett, New York: Grove Press, 1965, p. 414.
2   Samuel Beckett, *Six Residua*, London: Jonathan Cape, 1999.
3   I quote from a pre-publication prospectus for the current volume.
4   Samuel Beckett, *Endgame*, London: Faber, 1968, p. 12.
5   Timothy Morton, *Ecology Without Nature: Rethinking Environmental Aesthetics*, Cambridge, MA: Harvard University Press, 2007, p. 185.
6   Ibid., p. 186.
7   See also Timothy Morton, 'Thinking Ecology: The Mesh, the Strange Stranger, and the Beautiful Soul', *Collapse*, vol. 6 (2010), pp. 195–223, p. 208.
8   Samuel Beckett, *Happy Days*, London: Faber, 1970, p. 23.
9   Ibid., p. 9.
10 See Adorno's essay on *Endgame*. 'The condition presented in the play is nothing other than that in which "there's no more nature". Indistinguishable is the phase of complete reification of the world, which leaves no remainder of what was not made by humans; it is permanent catastrophe. ...' As Adorno goes on to note, however, 'One can speak only euphemistically about what is incommensurate with all experience, just as one speaks in Germany of the murder of the Jews. It has become a total a priori, so that bombed-out consciousness no longer has any position from which it could reflect on that fact'. Theodor Adorno, 'Trying to Understand *Endgame*', *New German Critique*, vol. 26, trans. M. T. Jones (Spring-Summer 1982) [1958], pp. 119–50, pp. 5–6.
11 Beckett, *Endgame*, p. 49.
12 Ibid., p. 12.
13 All the online references to this image, for example on various art-auction sites, say 'Tribadden'. There is no such mountain. I have adjusted accordingly.
14 Byrne has some previous form in this area. Several of the artist's installations have included a reconstruction of the tree designed by Alberto Giacometti (and since lost, apart from photos) for a 1961 production of *Waiting for Godot*. An earlier photographic series, *Points of View, Waiting for Godot* (2003–4), worked around a set

dressed for a production of the play, the images loosely simulating points of view of the characters. The Giacometti tree also did service at Byrne's performance installation *In Repertory*, based on audition pieces, shown at Project Arts Centre, Dublin, 2004, and at the Performa festival, New York, 2011.

15 As Byrne says in an interview with Catherine Wood, 'My attraction to theatre is connected to its provisionality, to the notion of repetition and re-interpretation, which are rites within theatre … the pinnacle of bourgeois culture's self-imaging, and simultaneously the nemesis of Friedian modernism'. Catherine Wood, in Mark Godfrey, Catherine Wood and Lytle Shaw, *The Present Tense Through the Ages: On the Recent Work of Gerard Byrne*, London: Koenig Books, 2007, p. 73. See also Bettina Funcke, 'You See? Gerard Byrne's Reconstructions', *Afterall*, vol. 17 (Spring 2008), www.afterall.org [accessed 2 July 2014].

16 The phrase 'strange stranger' is from Timothy Morton. 'We should instead explore the paradoxes and fissures of identity within "human" and "animal." Instead of "animal," I use strange stranger. … Do we know for sure whether they are sentient or not? Do we know whether they are alive or not? Their strangeness is part of who they are. After all, they might be us. And what could be stranger than what is familiar?' See Timothy Morton, *The Ecological Thought*, Cambridge, MA: Harvard University Press, 2010, p. 41.

17 Except, perhaps, for *Breath* (1969). I say perhaps. I don't suppose the landscape of 'miscellaneous rubbish' is waiting for an inhabitant either. Nor does it get one really, although birth (and death) are ever going on, somewhere. Samuel Beckett, *Breath*, in *Collected Shorter Plays*, London: Faber, 1984, pp. 210–11.

18 'Miroslaw Balka in Conversation', http://www.tate.org.uk/context-comment/video/miroslaw-balka-conversation [accessed 2 July 2014].

19 See Beckett's 1957 letter to director Alan Schneider. 'My work is a matter of fundamental sounds (no joke intended) made as fully as possible and I accept responsibility for nothing else. If people want to have headaches among the overtones, let them. And provide their own aspirin. Hamm as stated, and Clov as stated, together stated *nec tecum nec sine te*, in such a place, and in such a world, that's all I can manage, more than I could'. Samuel Beckett, in Maurice Harmon (ed.), *No Author Better Served: The Correspondence of Samuel Beckett and Alan Schneider*, Cambridge, MA: Harvard University Press, 1998, p. 24.

20 I quote Bałka's voice on the Tate's 'How It Is App'. *The Unilever Series: Miroslaw Balka How It Is*, http://www2.tate.org.uk/miroslawbalka/website [accessed 2 July 2014].

21 A production of these three plays at the Royal Court Theatre in London during January 2014, directed by Walter Asmus and featuring Lisa Dwan in all three works, was exemplary in the quality of the darkness between the plays (only occasionally interrupted by a telephone light or two).

22 Paolo Herkenhoff, 'The Illuminating Darkness of "How It Is"', in Helen Sainsbury (ed.), *How It Is*, London: Tate Publishing, 2009, pp. 50–105.

23 Gerard Byrne, 'Life in Film', *Frieze Magazine*, no. 123 (May 2009), https://www.frieze.com/issue/article/gerard_byrne_film/ [accessed 2 July 2014].

24 See James Price's film, *Mirosław Bałka: How It Is* (2009), http://vimeo.com/11669764 [accessed 2 July 2014].

25 This is very 'Krapp-like', as Carl Lavery has remarked.

26 Alain Badiou, *On Beckett*, ed. and trans. N. Power and A. Toscano, Manchester: Clinamen Press, 2003, p. 38.

27 Ibid., p. 40.

28 For more on Badiou's concept of 'subtraction', which is key to his reading of Beckett, see Peter Hallward's *Badiou: A Subject to Truth*, Minneapolis and London: University of Minnesota Press, 2003. Subtraction involves a purifying of reality by withdrawing it from its unity for the sake of a 'miniscule difference,' the inconsistency that sustains it: 'it is in this "only barely", this rare space of "immanent exception", that everything of true value happens'. Ibid., p. 162.

29 Herkenhoff, 'The Illuminating Darkness', p. 97.

30 Isabelle Stengers, *Cosmopolitics I*, trans. R. Bononno, Minneapolis, MN: University of Minnesota Press, 2010, p. 35.

31 Ibid.

32 Alongside this idea we might place Morton's recommendation that we take responsibility 'for our attitude, for our gaze' by recognizing that our own framing of an evil situation is part of the evil we condemn. When we come upon a crime scene we implicate ourselves, as soon as we acknowledge there is a scene to play and attend to. As he says, with regard to environmental catastrophe in our own here and now: 'We are all fully responsible ... simply because we are aware of it'. See Morton, 'Thinking Ecology', p. 221.

33 But here is another. 'With ghostlike faces dimly lit by their electronic devices, visitors do what they can to avoid the experience and the related reflection of a physical condition intimating a state of annihilation. To deface the darkness of Bałka's space seems to indicate a refusal to face our current condition, not least the conditions imposed by the workings of the culture machine'. Ulrich Loock, 'Some Notes on Miroslaw Balka's Work', *Cura Magazine*, no. 4 (April–June 2010), p. 84.

34 Beckett, *Endgame*, p. 50.
35 Helen Sainsbury, 'A Bitter Happiness', in Helen Sainsbury (ed.),
    Mirosław Bałka: How It Is, London: Tate Publishing, 2009,
    pp. 106–17, pp. 106–7.
36 Zygmunt Bauman, 'Strangers Are Dangers ... Are They?', in
    Helen Sainsbury (ed.), *Mirosław Bałka: How It Is*, London: Tate
    Publishing, 2009, pp. 14–25, p. 23.
37 Jen Harvie, *Fair Play: Art, Performance and Neoliberalism*, London
    and New York: Palgrave Macmillan, 2013, p. 32.
38 Beckett, *Happy Days*, pp. 32–3.
39 An immediate example that comes to mind is film director Atom
    Egoyan's commission for Artangel, *Steenbeckett* at the Former
    Museum of Mankind, London 2002, http://www.artangel.org.uk/
    projects/2002/steenbeckett [accessed 2 July 2014].
40 Steven Connor, 'On Such and Such a Day ... In Such a World:
    Beckett's Radical Finitude', *Borderless Beckett/Beckett sans
    frontières, Samuel Beckett Today/Aujourd'hui*, vol. 19 (2008),
    pp. 35–50. I quote from an online version of the keynote talk given
    at *Borderless Beckett, An International Centenary Symposium*,
    Tokyo, 1 October 2006, http://www.stevenconnor.com/finitude/
    [accessed 2 July 2014]. It is to be noted that Connor appears to
    include his own earlier work on repetition in Beckett amongst those
    gestures of infinitizing.
41 Ibid., n.p.
42 Beckett, *Happy Days*, p. 26.
43 The phrase is Badiou's. 'What is a comedy without intrigue? In this
    line of thought it is definitely Beckett who is still exemplary. Let's say
    that in the place of comedy with intrigue or plot he substitutes comic
    sequences, which, moreover, are more theatrical installations than
    performances. Voices, bodies, becomings, irruptions, are arranged
    without any plot and yet they indicate the critical power of the
    indeterminate existent. But language remains, and what language it
    is!' Alain Badiou, 'A Theatre of Operations: A Discussion between
    Alain Badiou and Elie During', in Manuel J. Borja-Villel, Bernard
    Blistène and Yann Chateigné (eds), *A Theater Without Theater*,
    Barcelona: MACBA, 2008, pp. 22–7, p. 27.
44 Beckett, *Endgame*, p. 25.
45 Morton, *Ecology Without Nature*, p. 193.
46 Beckett, *Happy Days*, p. 31.
47 Connor, 'On Such and Such a Day ...'.
48 Morton, *Ecology Without Nature*, p. 64.
49 It is worth noting that Cartesian dualism is an important part of
    Morton's version of ecological thought. As he puts it on the last page
    of *Ecology without Nature*: 'Instead of positing a nondualistic pot of

gold at the end of the rainbow, we could hang out in what feels like dualism'. Ibid., p. 205.

50   Connor, 'On Such and Such a Day ...', np.
51   Albert Camus cited in Martin Esslin, *The Theatre of the Absurd*, 3rd revised and enlarged edn, Harmondsworth: Penguin, 1983, p. 23.
52   See Søren Kierkegaard, *Fear and Trembling and the Sickness Unto Death*, trans. Walter Lowrie, Princeton, NJ: Princeton University Press, 2013.
53   Ibid., p. 83.
54   Ibid., p. 85.
55   Esslin, *The Theatre of the Absurd*, p. 23.
56   Ibid., p. 225.
57   Ibid., p. 387.
58   Beckett, *Happy Days*, p. 25.
59   Ibid., p. 47.
60   I am grateful for comments by Boyan Manchev in response to a paper given at HZT (Hochschulübergreifendes Zentrum Tanz) in Berlin, where an early version of some of these thoughts was rehearsed.
61   'The strategy of literalisation is: you say only what your words say. That's the game, and a way of winning out'. Stanley Cavell, *Must We Mean What We Say?*, Cambridge: Cambridge University Press, 2002 [1969], pp. 115–62, p. 126.
62   See Katharine Worth, *Samuel Beckett's Theatre: Life Journeys*, Oxford: Clarendon Press, 1999, pp. 77–9.

Chapter 5

1   See, for example, the opening scene. The sounds of the *britchka*, a light, horse-drawn open carriage with a folding hood, recur throughout the first half of the play, but not the film. See Arthur Adamov, *Dead Souls & Spring 71*, trans. P. Meyer, London: Oberon Books, 2006.
2   Ibid., p. 41.
3   Ibid., pp. 15, 26, 36, 41, 46.
4   Rachel Carson, *Silent Spring*, Harmondsworth: Penguin Classics, 2000 [1962].
5   Gregory Bateson, *Steps To an Ecology of Mind: Collected Essays in Anthropology, Psychiatry, Evolution and Epistemology*, St. Albans: Granada Publishing, 1973 [1972], pp. 405–6.
6   For a consideration of the connections between the work of Bateson and Guattari, see Verena Andermatt Conley, *Ecopolitics: The Environment in Poststructuralist Thought*, London: Routledge, 1997.

7 Félix Guattari, *The Three Ecologies*, trans. I. Pindar and P. Sutton, London: Continuum, 2008 [1989], p. 19.

8 Ibid., pp. 19–20.

9 Félix Guattari, 'The Ecosophic Object', in *Chaosmosis: An Ethico-Aesthetic Paradigm*, trans. P. Bains and J. Pefanis, Bloomington, IN: Indiana University Press, 1995 [1992], pp. 119–20.

10 Martin Esslin, *The Theatre of the Absurd*, 3rd revised and enlarged edn, Harmondsworth: Penguin, 1983, p. 93.

11 Arthur Adamov, 'The Endless Humiliation', *The Evergreen Review*, vol. 2, no. 8 (1959), pp. 64–95, p. 66.

12 Ibid., pp. 66–7.

13 Ibid., p. 65.

14 Ibid., p. 67.

15 Ibid., p. 80.

16 Ibid., p. 82.

17 Ibid., p. 81.

18 Ibid., p. 84.

19 Ibid., p. 88.

20 Adamov visited Artaud at Rodez, and discussed the conditions of his release from the asylum and his return to Paris with Dr Ferdière. The 'Association des amis d'Antonin Artaud' was established by Adamov to ensure that Artaud was able to meet the stipulated criterion of 'financial independence'. Figures such as Roger Blin, André Breton, Jean-Louis Barrault and Jean Dubuffet were involved in the cause and Adamov successfully persuaded Blin to read Artaud's *Nouvelles révélations de l'être* at a benefit performance at the Théâtre Sarah Bernhardt in 1946. See Mark Taylor-Batty, *Roger Blin: Collaborations and Methodologies*, Berne: Peter Lang, 2007, pp. 59–60.

21 Adamov's translation of Jung's essay 'Die Beziehungen zwischen dem Ich und dem Unbewußten' ('The Relations between the Ego and the Unconscious') was published as 'Le Moi et l'Inconscient' in 1938 (see Esslin, *Theatre of the Absurd*, p. 94). C. G. Jung, *Two Essays on Analytical Psychology: The Collected Works of C.G.Jung*, vol. 7, trans. R. F. C. Hull, Princeton, NJ: Princeton University Press, 1966.

22 Meredith Sabini (ed.), *The Earth has a Soul: C.G. Jung on Nature, Technology, and Modern Life*, Berkeley, CA: North Atlantic Books, 2002, p. 207.

23 Esslin, *The Theatre of the Absurd*, p. 400.

24 Ibid., p. 402.

25 Ibid.

26 Arthur Adamov, *The Invasion*, in Bert Cardullo and Robert Knopf (eds), *Theater of the Avant-Garde 1890-1950: A Critical Anthology*, New Haven, CT: Yale University Press, 2001, p. 489.

27   As this is a book on the Theatre of the Absurd aimed specifically
     at an English-speaking audience, I have chosen to look at all of
     Adamov's plays that could be considered as belonging to Esslin's
     category, and that have been translated into English.
28   Esslin, *Theatre of the Absurd*, p. 401.
29   This gives the lie to Adamov's claim that *Professor Taranne* was the
     first play in which he mentioned a real place.
30   Adamov, *The Invasion*, p. 491.
31   Gary Genosko, *Félix Guattari: An Aberrant Introduction*, London:
     Continuum, 2002, p. 110.
32   Esslin, *Theatre of the Absurd*, p. 101; and Carlos Lynes, Jr., 'Adamov
     or "le sens littéral" in the Theatre', *Yale French Studies*, vol. 14
     (1954), pp. 48–56, p. 51.
33   Ibid.
34   Esslin, *The Theatre of the Absurd*, p. 102.
35   John H. Reilly, 'Deciphering the Indecipherable', in Bert Cardullo
     and Robert Knopf (eds), *Theater of the Avant-garde 1890-1950:
     A Critical Anthology*, New Haven, CT: Yale University Press, 2001,
     pp. 468–71, p. 469.
36   Ibid., p. 470.
37   Adamov, *The Invasion*, p. 474.
38   Guattari, *The Three Ecologies*, pp. 31–2.
39   Adamov, *The Invasion*, p. 491.
40   Guattari, *The Three Ecologies*, p. 42.
41   Ibid.
42   Arthur Adamov, *Two Plays: Professor Taranne and Ping Pong*, trans.
     P. Meyer and D. Prouse, London: John Calder, 1962, p. 19.
43   Esslin, *Theatre of the Absurd*, p. 109.
44   Adamov, 'The Humiliation', p. 67.
45   Ibid., p. 72.
46   See Gilles Deleuze and Félix Guattari, *A Thousand Plateaus:
     Capitalism and Schizophrenia*, trans. B. Massumi, London: The
     Athlone Press, 1988, pp. 232–309.
47   Adamov, *Professor Taranne*, p. 30.
48   Guattari, *Three Ecologies*, p. 38.
49   *Tanaka Min à La Borde* (dir. Joséphine Guattari and François Pain)
     1987, https://www.youtube.com/watch?v=IrHGwSRTjKQ [accessed
     4 May 2014].
50   Adamov, *Ping-Pong*, pp. 71 and 111.
51   Ibid., p. 48.
52   Ibid., pp. 50–1.
53   Ibid., p. 113.
54   Arthur Adamov, *Paolo Paoli: The Years of the Butterfly, A Play in
     Twelve Scenes*, trans. G. Brereton, London: John Calder, 1959, p. 44.

55 Ibid., p. 9.
56 Ibid.
57 'The Butterfly Baron: How an Indiana Jones-style adventurer
     amassed the greatest collection in history', *The Mail Online*,
     2 March 2009 [accessed 30 June 2014].
58 Jennifer Price, *Flight Maps: Adventures with Nature in Modern
     America*, New York: Basic Books, 1999, pp. 57–8.
59 Ibid., p. 84.
60 Jennifer Price, 'Hats Off to Audubon', *The Audubon Magazine*
     (December 2004), http://archive.audubonmagazine.org/features0412/
     hats.html [accessed 4 May 2014].
61 See Douglas R. Weiner, 'Community Ecology in Stalin's Russia:
     "Socialist" and "Bourgeois" Science', *Isis*, vol. 75, no. 4 (December
     1984), pp. 684–96.

Chapter 6

1 Peter Sloterdijk, *Terror from the Air*, trans. A. Patton and
    S. Corcoran, Los Angeles, CA: Semiotext(e), 2009 [2002], p. 102.
2 This attack on committed art is a constant refrain in Ionesco's work
    and is articulated also in *The Killer* (1959) and *A Stroll in the Air*
    (1962).
3 Eugène Ionesco, *Notes and Counter Notes: Writings on Theatre*,
    trans. D. Watson, New York: Grove Press, 1964, p. 93.
4 Eugène Ionesco, *The Lesson* in *Rhinoceros and Other Plays*, trans.
    D. Watson, Harmondsworth: Penguin, 1962, p. 214.
5 Ibid., p. 215.
6 I borrow the word emancipation from Jacques Rancière's ideas on
    radical, democratic pedagogy in *The Ignorant Schoolmaster: Five
    Lessons in Intellectual Emancipation*, trans. K. Ross, Stanford, CA:
    Stanford University Press, 1991 [1987].
7 Martin Esslin, *The Theatre of the Absurd*, 3rd revised and enlarged
    edn, Harmondsworth: Penguin, 1980, pp. 128–99.
8 See for instance *Notes and Counter Notes*; and Eugène Ionesco,
    Present Past Past Present: A Personal Memoir, trans. H. Lane,
    New York: Grove Press, 1971. Both Marie-Claude Hubert in her
    monograph, *Eugène Ionesco*, Paris: Seuil, 1990, and Emmanuel
    Jacquard in his exhaustive 'Introduction' to *Eugène Ionesco: Théâtre
    Complet*, Paris: Gallimard, 1991, continue to base their research on
    Ionesco's reflections on his own practice. An attempt to dissent from
    this tradition was initiated by Steve Smith in a special edition of
    Nottingham French Studies dedicated to Ionesco's work. Although

there was a discussion of some of Ionesco's more minor plays in the issue, the majority of the contributors continued to rely on Ionesco's own reading of his work. See Steve Smith, 'Introduction', *Nottingham French Studies*, vol. 35, no. 1 (1996), np.

9 Sloterdijk, *Terror from the* Air, p. 25.

10 Una Chaudhuri, 'Becoming Rhinoceros: Therio-Theatricality as Problem and Promise in Western Drama', in Garry Marvin and Susan McHugh (eds), *Routledge Handbook on Animals*, London and New York: Routledge, 2014, pp. 194–207.

11 Rosette C. Lamont, 'Air and Matter', *French Review*, vol. 38 (1965), pp. 349–61; Jacques Guicharnaud (with June Guicharnaud), *Modern French Theatre from Giraudox to Genet*, Yale, CT: Yale University Press, 1967; and Mircea Eliade, 'Lumière et transcendance dans l'oeuvre d' Eugène Ionesco', in Marie-France Ionesco and Paul Vernois (eds), *Ionesco: Situations et Perspectives*, Paris: Pierre Belfond, 1980, pp. 117–28.

12 Interestingly, the first draft of Beckett's *Happy Days* started with an explicit reference to nuclear catastrophe, in which an offstage voice stated, 'Nuclear War has been declared; London's gone, New York's gone'. See 'Interview with Simon Critchley', http://www.necronauts. org/interviews_simon.htm [accessed 31 May 2014].

13 Theodor Adorno, 'Trying to Understand *Endgame*', trans. M. T. Jones, *New German Critique*, vol. 26 (1982) [1958], pp. 119–50, p. 125.

14 Ballard's science fiction novel is increasingly viewed as a novel about climate change.

15 Eugène Ionesco, *The Chairs: A Tragic Farce*, in *Plays*, vol. I, trans. D. Watson, London: Calder and Boyars, 1958, p. 43.

16 The others are *The Killer*, *Rhinoceros* and *A Stroll in the Air*.

17 The French title of the play is cleverly metatheatrical: it reminds the audience that theatre is an art of dying, a medium where time passes.

18 Eugène Ionesco, *Exit the King*, in *Plays*, vol. 5, trans. D. Watson, London: Calder and Boyars, 1963, p. 31.

19 Ibid., pp. 19–20.

20 Eugène Ionesco, *A Stroll in the Air*, in *Plays*, vol. 6, trans. D. Watson, London: Calder and Boyars, 1965, pp. 36–7.

21 Catapulted out of heaven by a storm that is caught in his wings, Benjamin's angel is propelled backwards into the future. See Walter Benjamin, 'Theses on the Philosophy of History', in *Illuminations: Essays and Reflections*, trans. H. Zorn, New York: Harcourt Brace, 1968 [1955], pp. 245–58, p. 249.

22 Ionesco, *A Stroll in the Air*, p. 76.

23 Gaston Bachelard, *Air and Dreams: An Essay on the Imagination of Movement*, trans. E. and F. Farrell, Dallas, TX: Dallas Institute

of Humanities and Culture, 2002 [1943]; and Luce Irigaray, *The Forgetting of Air in Martin Heidegger*, trans. M. Mader, Austin: University of Texas Press, 1999 [1983].

24 Irigaray argues that Heidegger mistakenly attempts to control the feminine by associating it with 'Mother Earth', which she believes evinces a desire to ground meaning, to assign a proper place to identity. The air, by contrast, is nebulous; it cannot be controlled since it refuses to take a place; hence, Irigaray's concern to associate women with the air.

25 The reference to the *anti-monde* in the play has associations with anti-matter, which was experimented with as a way of creating nuclear fusion in the 1950s and 1960s.

26 Bennett sees the Theatre of the Absurd as offering a more positive response to existence than Esslin. See Michael Y. Bennett, *Reassessing the Theatre of The Absurd, Camus, Beckett, Ionesco, Genet and Pinter*, Basingstoke: Palgrave Macmillan, 2011.

27 Steven Connor, *The Matter of Air: Science and the Art of the Ethereal*, London: Reaktion, 2010, p. 285.

28 Oppenheimer made his famous statement in an interview recorded as part of the television documentary *The Decision to Drop the Bomb*, aired on NBC in 1965. It is taken from a line spoken by Krishna in the *Bhagavad Gita*.

29 Theodor Adorno and Max Horkheimer, *Dialectic of Enlightenment*, trans. J. Cumming, London: Verso, 1997 [1944].

30 Michel Serres, *Genesis*, trans. G. James and J. Nielson, Ann Arbor, MN: University of Michigan Press, 1997 [1982], pp. 19–21.

31 Gary Snyder, 'Four Changes', in *Turtle Island*, New York: New Directions, 1974, pp. 91–102, p. 91.

32 Rachel Carson, *Silent Spring*, Boston, MA: Houghton Miffin, 1962.

33 Eugène Ionesco, *Rhinoceros*, in *Rhinoceros and Other Plays*, trans. Derek Prouse, Harmondsworth: Penguin 1962, p. 106.

34 Ibid., pp. 68–83.

35 Ibid., p. 110.

36 Ibid., p. 124.

37 Eugène Ionesco, *Jeux de massacre*, in *Eugène Ionesco: Théâtre Complet*, Paris: Gallimard, 1991, p. 1032 (my translation).

38 Feminist critics offer a very different reading of the domestic, seeing it as a site of resistance. It remains to be seen, however, how the 'feminist domestic' might engage with notions of environmental and social toxicity.

39 Eugène Ionesco, *The Bald Prima Donna: A Pseudo-Play in One Act*, trans. Donald Watson, London: Samuel French, 1958, p. 31.

40 Ionesco, *The Bald Prima Donna*, pp. 33–4.

41 Eugène Ionesco, *Amédéé or How to Get Rid of it: A Comedy*, in *Plays*, vol. 2, London: Calder and Boyars, 1954, p. 179.

42 Elias Canetti, cited in Sloterdijk, *Terror from the Air*, p. 100.

43 Steven Connor is also sensitive to how the anxiety produced by chemicals in the atmosphere has damaging psychological consequences. See *The Matter of Air: Science and the Art of the Ethereal*, p. 257.

44 There are numerous references to the contagious quality of ideology in *Rhinoceros*. In a direct allusion to fascism in the 1930s, Dudard talks about how rhinoceritis will 'spread to other countries'. Ionesco, *Rhinoceros*, p. 104.

45 Sloterdijk, *Terror from the Air*, p. 101.

46 Eugène Ionesco, *Frenzy For Two … and the same to you*, in *Plays*, vol. 6, trans. Donald Watson, London: John Calder, 1965, p. 85.

47 Ibid., p. 104.

48 At the end of *Bubbles*, Sloterdijk suggests that in the twentieth century, the human being can no longer find 'shelter' in the spherical spaces of theological and/or metaphysical truths; rather, we are like isolated bubbles in a foam world, exposed to the play of the 'monstrous', or what he also calls 'immensity'. See *Spheres. Volume 1: Bubbles – Microspherology*, trans. W. Hoban, Los Angeles, CA: Semiotext (e), 2010 [1998], p. 630.

49 Karl Marx and Friedrich Engels, *The Communist Manifesto*, London: Verso, 2012 [1848], p. 38.

50 Eugène Ionesco, *The Killer*, in *Plays*, vol. 3, trans. D. Watson, London: John Calder, 1960, pp 22–3.

51 Strindberg's expressionist dramas such as the trilogy *The Road to Damascus* (1898–1901) and *A Dream Play* (1901) seek to stage the spiritual life or soul of a character as opposed to exploring her or his psychology or dissecting her or his passion.

52 Eugène Ionesco, *Hunger and Thirst*, in *Plays*, vol. 7, trans. D. Watson, London: John Calder, 1968, p. 10.

53 Ibid., p. 35.

54 Ibid., p. 50.

55 Ibid.

56 Ibid., p. 35.

57 In an article published in *Le Figaro* on 5 February 1990, Ionesco addressed the ecological problems besetting the present via a series of apocalyptic images. Echoing Martin Heidegger's comment in his infamous interview with *Der Spiegel* in 1966, Ionesco states, 'only God can save us' (my translation). Eugène Ionesco, *Théâtre Complet*, ed. Emmanuel Jacquart, Paris: Gallimard, 1990, p. CV.

58 See, for instance, Jacques Derrida, *Spurs: Nietzsche's Style*, trans. B. Harlow, Chicago, IL: University of Chicago Press, 1979 [1978].

59 See in particular the chapters 'Post-Anthropocentrism: Life Beyond the Species' and 'The Inhuman: Life Beyond Death', in Rosi Braidotti, *The Posthuman*, Cambridge, Polity Press, 2013, pp. 55–104 and pp. 105–42.

60 Gregory Bateson, *Steps to an Ecology of Mind: Collected Essays in Anthropology, Psychiatry, Evolution, and Epistemology*, Chicago, IL: University of Chicago Press, 1990 [1972], p. 455.

61 Ibid., p. 492.

62 Donna Haraway, *When Species Meet*, Minneapolis, MN: University of Minnesota Press, 2008, pp. 4–5.

63 Ibid., p. 31.

64 Timothy Morton, *Ecology without Nature: Rethinking Environmental Aesthetics*, Cambridge, MA: Harvard University Press, 2007, p. 205.

65 Ibid., p. 205.

66 Timothy Morton, 'Queer Ecology', *PMLA*, vol. 125, no. 2 (2010), pp. 273–82.

67 Ionesco, *Exit the King*, p. 15.

68 Ibid., p. 57.

69 Ibid., pp. 51–2.

70 Ibid., p. 68.

71 Ibid., pp. 76–7.

72 Much has been written on the existentialist function of laughter in Ionesco's work. But no one has attempted to think through its ecological implications, as I have done here. See, for instance, Jean Onimus, 'Quand le terrible éclate de rire', in Marie-France Ionesco and Paul Vernois (eds), *Ionesco: Situations et Perspectives*, Paris: Pierre Belfond, 1980, pp. 143–57.

73 Julia Kristeva, *The Powers of Horror: An Essay on Abjection*, trans. Leon S. Roudiez, New York: University of Columbia Press, 1983, p. 206.

74 Ionesco, *Exit the King*, p. 63.

75 Albert Camus, *The Myth of Sisyphus and Other Essays*, trans. J. O'Brien, New York: Alfred A. Knopf, 1955 p. 88.

Chapter 7

1 I am grateful to the intellectual ecology that has contributed invaluably to this essay and that is constituted by Christophe Brault, Mairéad Hanrahan, Elizabeth Stephens and David Williams.

2 Deleuze and Guattari write of how a central tree-like axis that governs all peripheral structures can be replaced with a system of

dispersed rhizomes, themselves giving rise to new plants, that evade the discipline of an overarching order. Gilles Deleuze and Félix Guattari, *A Thousand Plateaus: Capitalism and Schizophrenia*, trans. B. Massumi, Minneapolis, MN: University of Minnesota Press, 1987 [1980], pp. 1–26.

3 Jean Genet, *Le Bagne*, in *Jean Genet Théâtre Complet*, Paris: Gallimard coll. Pléiade, 2002, p. 802.

4 Jacques Derrida, *Glas*, trans. J. P. Leavey and R. Rand, Lincoln, NE: University of Nebraska Press, 1986, p. 18, translation modified.

5 Martin Esslin, *The Theatre of the Absurd*, 3rd revised and enlarged edn, London: Methuen, 2001, pp. 219–20.

6 Richard Kerridge and Neil Sammels (eds), *Writing the Environment: Ecocriticism and Literature*, London: Zed Books, 1998, p. 4. Lawrence Buell, too, writes, 'the environmental crisis involves a crisis of the imagination'. Lawrence Buell, *The Environmental Imagination: Thoreau, Nature Writing, and the Formation of American Culture*, Cambridge, MA: Belknap Press, Harvard University Press, 1995, p. 2.

7 Wendy Arons and Theresa J. May (eds), *Readings in Ecology and Performance*, Basingstoke: Palgrave, 2012, p. 5.

8 For detailed discussions of Genet's theatre in text and production, see David Bradby and Clare Finburgh, *Jean Genet*, London: Routledge, 2011.

9 See Philip Thody, *Jean Genet: A Study of His Novels and Plays*, London: Hamish Hamilton, 1968, p. 179, and Hadrien Laroche, *The Last Genet: A Writer in Revolt*, trans. D. Homel, Vancouver, BC: Arsenal Pulp Press, 2010, p. 66.

10 *Elle*, in *Jean Genet Théâtre Complet*, p. 447.

11 Genet, *Le Bagne*, p. 791.

12 Jean Genet, *The Blacks: A Clown Show*, trans. B. Frechtman, New York: Grove Press, 1960, p. 91.

13 Jean Genet, *The Screens*, trans. B. Frechtman, New York: Grove Press, 1962, p. 11. For a discussion of the play's scenography, see Clare Finburgh, 'Unveiling the Void: Presence and Absence in the Scenography of Jean Genet's *Les Paravents*', *Theatre Journal*, vol. 56, no. 2 (May 2004), pp. 205–24.

14 Buell, *The Environmental Imagination*, p. 85.

15 Terry Gifford, *Pastoral*, London: Routledge, 1999, p. 15.

16 Adorno and Horkheimer trace this Enlightenment 'logic of domination' to the Olympian deities, who symbolized the elements, rather than actually being identical with them, and to the Old Testament which proclaims, 'and let [man] have dominion over the fish of the sea, and over the fowl of the air, and over the cattle, and over all the earth, and over every creeping thing that creepeth on

the face of the earth' (Gen. 1.26): 'Enlightenment behaves towards things as a dictator toward men. He knows them in so far as he can manipulate them'. Theodor Adorno and Max Horkheimer, *Dialectic of Enlightenment*, trans. E. Jephcott, Stanford, CA: Stanford University Press, 2002, pp. 5–6.

17 The notion of the Anthropocene articulates the irreversible impact that humans are having on the environment. See Will Steffen, Paul J. Clutzen and John R. McNeill, 'The Anthropocene: Are Humans Now Overwhelming the Great Forces of Nature?', *Ambio*, vol. 38 (2007), pp. 614–21.

18 Genet, *The Blacks*, p. 94.

19 Jhan Hochman, *Green Cultural Studies: Nature in Film, Novel, and Theory*, Moscow, ID: University of Idaho Press, 1998, p. 2.

20 Arons and May, *Readings in Ecology and Performance*, p. 5.

21 Genet, *Elle*, p. 461.

22 Genet recalls the reaction of Black Panther David Hilliard when invited to give a lecture at Stony-Brook university, 60 kilometres outside New York City: 'There are still too many trees'. Genet explains this strange comment: 'for a Black only thirty years old, a tree still didn't mean what it did to a White – a riot of green, with birds and nests and carvings of hearts and names intertwined. Instead it meant a gibbet'. To people of African origin in the Americas, as opposed to picturesque tranquillity, the wilderness can represent lynchings or slave labour. Jean Genet, *The Declared Enemy*, trans. J. Fort, Stanford, CA: Stanford University Press, 2004, p. 55.

23 Genet, *The Blacks*, p. 94.

24 Ibid.

25 Ibid.

26 Ibid., pp. 26, 43, 64. On the other hand, snow, lilies and doves are associated with the Europeans in *The Blacks* (pp. 24, 106). Genet then subverts this oppositional imagery by calling one of the negro characters Snow. In *Deathwatch*, too, the prison's hardest criminal, a black man, is called Snowball.

27 Ibid., p. 25.

28 Ibid., p. 94.

29 Ibid., p. 103.

30 Genet, *The Screens*, pp. 112–13.

31 Bernard-Marie Koltès and François Regnault, *La Famille des orties. Esquisses et croquis autour des* Paravents *de Jean Genet*, Paris: Éditions Nanterre/Amandiers, 1983, p. 19, my translation.

32 It is important to credit many of the theatrical effects described in Genet's stage directions to Roger Blin's productions of *The Blacks* (1959) and *The Screens* (1966).

33 Genet, *The Screens*, pp. 25, 29. `

34 Genet, *The Blacks*, p. 94.

35 It would be a rash generalization to propose that deconstruction is by nature apolitical, as many of Derrida's writings, notably *The Politics of Friendship* and *Specters of Marx*, illustrate.

36 Genet, *The Screens*, p. 11.

37 Jean Genet, 'The Man Condemned to Death', in *The Complete Poems of Jean Genet*, trans. D. Fisher et al., San Francisco, CA: ManRoot, 1981, pp. 15, 19.

38 *Our Lady of the Flowers*, trans. B. Frechtman, London: Faber, 1990, pp. 52, 109. For a detailed account of flowers in this novel see Natalie Fredette, *Figures baroques de Jean Genet*, Montreal, Quebec: XYZ, 2001, pp. 49–58.

39 Genet, *The Thief's Journal*, p. 65.

40 Myriam Bendhif-Syllas, 'Filiation et écriture végétales de Jean Genet, une affaire de styles', in Hadrien Laroche (ed.), *Pour Genet*, Saint-Nazaire: Maison des Écrivains Étrangers et des Traducteurs, 2011, p. 174.

41 'Except for Rose, he could not have found a more fertile surname', writes Hélène Cixous, *Entretien de la blessure: Sur Jean Genet*, Paris: Galilée, 2011, p. 11.

42 Derrida, *Glas*, pp. 21–2. Also see p. 47.

43 Ibid., pp. 249–51.

44 Bendhif-Syllas, 'Filiation et écriture végétales', p. 171. Lindsay Kemp's dance response to *Our Lady of the Flowers* – *Flowers: A Pantomime for Jean Genet* (1968) – bears witness to the gender ambiguity represented by flowers in Genet's works. See Martin Hargreaves, 'Dancing the Impossible: Kazuo Ohno, Lindsay Kemp and *Our Lady of the Flowers*', in Clare Finburgh, Carl Lavery and Maria Shevtsova (eds), *Jean Genet: Performance and Politics*, Basingstoke: Palgrave Macmillan, 2006, pp. 106–16.

45 Derrida, *Glas*, pp. 126–7, 58.

46 Jean Genet, *The Maids and Deathwatch*, trans. B. Frechtman, London: Faber, 1989, p. 124. See Harry E Stewart, 'The Case of the Lilac Murders: Jean Genet's *Haute Surveillance*', *The French Review*, vol. 48, no. 1 (October 1974), pp. 87–94.

47 In *The Balcony*, flowers also symbolize seduction. Rather than dressing in ecclesiastical robes or pompous uniforms, one client chooses to dress as a tramp, the Little Old Man. Genet's botanical motif features in this play only in the form of a bunch of artificial flowers, which the Little Old Man offers to an ungrateful prostitute. Jean Genet, *The Balcony*, trans. B. Wright and T. Hands, London: Faber, 1991, p. 21.

48 Ibid., p. 135.
49 Ibid., p. 120.
50 Ibid., p. 127.
51 Jean Genet, *The Maids and Deathwatch*, trans. B. Frechtman, London: Faber, 1989, p. 35.
52 Ibid., pp. 74, 92.
53 Ibid., p. 36.
54 Ibid., p. 68.
55 Genet, *The Thief's Journal*, p. 15.
56 Derrida, *Glas*, p. 50.
57 Genet, *The Maids and Deathwatch*, pp. 77, 78. This association between vitality and mortality encapsulated in the flower formed the basis of Japanese *butoh* performances by Tatsumi Hijikata and Kazuo Ohno, notably *Divinariane* (1960). See Hargreaves, 'Dancing the Impossible', p. 111.
58 Genet, *Le Bagne*, p. 766.
59 Jean Genet, *Splendid's*, trans. N. Bartlett, London: Faber, 1995, p. 13.
60 Genet, *The Blacks*, p. 7.
61 Derrida, *Glas*, p. 58.
62 Genet, *The Screens*, p. 69.
63 Ibid., p. 74.
64 Ibid., p. 28.
65 Jacques Derrida, 'Plato's Pharmacy', in *Dissemination*, trans. B. Johnson, London: Athlone Press, 1981), pp. 61–172.
66 Esslin, *The Theatre of the Absurd*, pp. 210–11, 220.
67 Ibid., p. 211.
68 Genet, *The Blacks*, p. 126.
69 Jean Genet, 'What Remains of a Rembrandt Torn into Little Squares All the Same Size and Shot Down the Toilet', in *Fragments of the Artwork*, trans. C. Mandell, Stanford, CA: Stanford University Press, 2003, p. 91.
70 See Genet, *The Screens*, pp. 155, 195.
71 Jean Genet, *Miracle of the Rose*, trans. B. Frechtman, London: Anthony Blond, 1965, p. 107.
72 Derrida, *Glas*, pp. 40–1.
73 Edward W. Said, 'On Jean Genet's Late Works', in Ellen Gainor (ed.), *Imperialism and Theatre: Essays on World Theatre, Drama and Performance 1795-1995*, London and New York: Routledge, 1995, p. 236.
74 Lydie Dattas, 'Jean de Neige', in *Genet*, catalogue for 2006 exhibition at the Musée des Beaux-Arts de Tours, Farrago, 2006, p. 55.
75 Genet, 'What Remains of a Rembrandt', p. 49.

76 Jean Genet, *Prisoner of Love*, trans. B. Bray, New York: New York Review of Books, p. 68.

77 Cixous, *Entretien de la blessure*, p. 76.

78 Slavoj Žižek, *Looking Awry: An Introduction to Jacques Lacan through Popular Culture*, Cambridge, MA: MIT Press, 1991, p. 35.

79 Félix Guattari, *The Three Ecologies*, trans. I. Pindar and P. Sutton, London: The Athlone Press, 2000, p. 27.

80 Ibid., pp. 46, 53.

81 Andrew Dobson, *Green Political Thought*, 3rd edn, London and New York: Routledge, 1995, p. 2.

82 Arne Naess, 'The Shallow and the Deep, Long-Range Ecology Movement: A Summary', *Inquiry*, vol. 16 (Spring 1973), p. 95.

83 Guattari, *The Three Ecologies*, p. 49.

84 For an excellent introduction to ecocriticism, the end of humanism and the posthuman, see Louise Westling, 'Literature, the Environment and the Question of the Posthuman', in Catrin Gersdorf and Sylvia Mayer (eds), *Nature in Literary and Cultural Studies: Transatlantic Conversations on Ecocriticism*, Amsterdam, New York: Rodopi, 2006, pp. 25–47.

85 Peter Atterton and Matthew Calarco (eds), *Animal Philosophy: Ethics and Identity*, London: Continuum, 2004, p. xvi.

86 Jacques Derrida, *The Animal That Therefore I am*, trans. D. Willis, New York: Fordham University Press, 2008, p. 32.

87 Jean Genet, 'The Studio of Alberto Giacometti', in *Fragments of the Artwork*, p. 50.

88 Genet, *The Screens*, pp. 40, 50.

89 Genet, *Deathwatch*, p. 131.

90 Genet, *The Balcony*, p. 16.

91 Genet, *The Blacks*, p. 121.

92 Genet, *The Screens*, p. 45.

93 Gilles Deleuze and Félix Guattari, 'Becoming Animal', in Peter Atterton and Matthew Calarco (eds), *Animal Philosophy: Ethics and Identity*, London: Continuum, 2004, pp. 233–309.

94 Genet, *Prisoner of Love*, p. 41. For animists, the world is populated by 'persons, only some of whom are human'. These 'persons' can be non-human animals, plants, rocks, clouds or other elements of the natural surroundings. See Graham Harvey, *Animism: Respecting the Living World*, New York: Columbia University Press, 2006. Aside from its problematic anthropocentrism, whereby non-human entities are perceived as possessing human attributes such as a spirit or soul, animism considers the non-human to be of no less value than human animals.

95   Echoing this, Leïla in *The Screens* flatters a pair of Saïd's trousers
      for having more shapely thighs than its owner (Genet, *The
      Screens*, p. 25). While highlighting her husband's puniness, she
      also underscores the weighty presence that objects can command.
      For Mahtab Bolouki-Raskédian, Genet dematerializes objects and
      people, rarefying them into an ether. I argue, contrastingly, that
      Genet accords weight to them by enabling them to enjoy autonomy
      independent of human agency. Mahtab Bolouki-Raskédian, '"L'Air"
      dans la dramaturgie de Jean Genet', *L'Infini*, vol. 97 (Autumn
      2006), pp. 106–14.

96   Genet, 'The Studio of Alberto Giacometti', p. 56.

97   Genet, *The Screens*, p. 191.

98   Jean Genet, 'Rembrandt's Secret', in *Fragments of the Artwork*, p. 89.

99   Koltès and Regnault, *La Famille des orties*, pp. 38–9.

100   Genet, 'What Remains of a Rembrandt', p. 87, Genet's emphasis.

101   Michel Vaïs, *L'Écrivain scénique*, Montreal: Presses de l'Université
      de Québec, 1978, p. 171.

102   Hans-Thies Lehmann, *Postdramatic Theatre*, trans. K. Jürs-Munby,
      London and New York: Routledge, 2006.

103   Jean Genet, 'Letter to Jean-Jacques Pauvert', in *Fragments of the
      Artwork*, pp. 37–8.

104   For Genet's own explanation of this dynamic between staging and
      debunking black stereotypes, see his 'Preface to *The Blacks*', trans.
      Clare Finburgh, in Carl Lavery, *The Politics of Jean Genet's Late
      Theatre: Spaces of Revolution*, Manchester: Manchester University
      Press, 2010, pp. 227–34.

105   Odette Aslan, '*Les Paravents* de Jean Genet', *Les Voies de la création
      théâtrale*, vol. 3 (1972), pp. 13–107, p. 26, my translation.

106   Genet, 'What Remains of a Rembrandt', p. 87.

107   Buell, *The Environmental Imagination*, pp. 7, 430. Baz Kershaw's
      examination of performance and ecology focuses on more obvious
      examples than Genet of ecologically engaged performance makers,
      such as John Arden and Margaretta D'Arcy, John McGrath
      and 7:84, Ann Jellicoe and Welfare State International; and on
      more 'DiY' cultural interventions like Reclaim the Streets. Baz
      Kershaw, *Theatre Ecology: Environments and Performance Events*,
      Cambridge: Cambridge University Press, 2007.

108   Nature writing strives towards a more unified relationship between
      humans and nature by seeking to overcome oppositions between
      mind and matter, subject and object, thinker and thing.

109   I use the term 'anthropocentrism', remaining mindful of the
      contradictions inherent in the assumption that there is a clear
      distinction between the human (*anthropos*) and non-human.

110 Buell, *The Environmental Imagination*, p. 145.
111 Ibid., p. 168.
112 Ibid., p. 179.
113 See Genet's political writings in *The Declared Enemy* (2004). And for an account of the politics of his later plays, see Carl Lavery, *The Politics of Jean Genet's Late Theatre: Spaces of Revolution*, Manchester: Manchester University Press, 2010.
114 Genet, *The Blacks*, pp. 19, 25.
115 Imperial capitalist exploitation of the land is also alluded to in *The Screens*, where Arab brothel customers work in phosphate mines; Sir Harold has cleared indigenous agriculture to make way for his orange groves; and Mr Blankensee has planted cork oaks, declaring, 'It's we who made [this country], not they!' (Genet 1962, pp. 22, 73).
116 Esslin, *The Theatre of the Absurd*, p. 233.
117 Genet, *The Balcony*, p. xiv.
118 Genet, *The Declared Enemy*, p. 118, translation modified.
119 Rustom Bharucha's most recent work warns that Genet rejects all moral and political absolutes or solutions. While agreeing with this, it is my view that Genet does not, or cannot, preclude the reader/ spectator from occupying political positions based on his proposals. Rustom Bharucha, *Terror and Performance*, London and New York: Routledge, 2014, p. 42.
120 Ibid., p. 17.
121 *Oxford English Dictionary*.

Chapter 8

1 Martin Esslin, *The Theatre of the Absurd*, London: Eyre & Spottiswoode, 1962 [1961], p. 205.
2 Martin Esslin, *The Theatre of the Absurd*, 3rd revised and enlarged edn, Harmondsworth: Penguin, 1991, pp. 235–6.
3 Ibid., p. 241.
4 Ibid., p. 255.
5 Una Chaudhuri, *Staging Place: The Geography of Modern Drama*, Ann Arbor, MI: University of Michigan Press, 1995, p. 102.
6 Ibid., p. 27.
7 Félix Guattari, *The Three Ecologies*, trans. I. Pindar and P. Sutton, London: Continuum, 2008 [1989]; and Murray Bookchin, *The Philosophy of Social Ecology*, Montreal: Black Rose, 1992.
8 *Habitus* designates the complex nexus of corporeal, mental and social attitudes that define a given society's worldview or structure.
9 Esslin, *The Theatre of the Absurd*, 3rd edn, p. 240.

10   Ibid.
11   Such readings persist: Hans Osterwalder, for example, recently
     positioned Riley as 'a figure of death, the messenger of the death-
     drive rising from the Id, which Bert tries to fight off through
     violence'. Hans Osterwalder, 'Dreamscapes: Harold Pinter's The
     Room and Franz Kafka's "Auf der Galerie"', *Zeitschrift für Anglistik
     und Amerikanistik*, vol. 52, no. 1 (March 2014), pp. 53–62, p. 56.
12   Gaston Bachelard, *The Poetics of Space*, trans. M. Jollas, Boston,
     MA: Beacon Press, 1994 [1958], pp. 95–6; and C. G. Jung, *Analytical
     Psychology: Notes of the Seminar Given in 1925*, trans. C. E. Long,
     Princeton, NJ: Princeton University Press, 1989 [1926], pp. 22–3.
13   Jean François Lyotard, 'Domus and Megalopolis', in *The Inhuman:
     Reflections on Time*, trans. G. Bennington and R. Bowlby, London:
     Polity, 1991 [1988], p. 196.
14   Ibid., p. 201.
15   Ibid., p. 203.
16   Ibid., pp. 202–3.
17   Ibid., p. 192.
18   Ibid., p. 196.
19   Ibid., p. 201.
20   Ibid., p. 198.
21   Ibid., p. 201.
22   Jean François Lyotard, 'Oikos', in *Jean-François Lyotard: Political
     Writings*, trans. B. Readings and K. Gaiman, Minneapolis: University
     of Minnesota Press, 1993 [1988], pp. 96–107, p. 105.
23   Ibid., p. 103.
24   Ibid., p. 100.
25   Ibid., pp. 101–2.
26   Guattari, *The Three Ecologies*. p. 9.
27   Harold Pinter, '"A Play and its Politics", An Interview with Nick
     Hern', in Harold Pinter, *One for the Road*, London: Methuen,
     1985, p. 8.
28   Harold Pinter, 'Interview with Kenneth Tynan', BBC Home Service,
     28 October 1960, quoted in Esslin, *The Theatre of the Absurd*,
     3rd edn, p. 235.
29   Ibid.
30   Harold Pinter, *The Room*, in *Plays One*, London: Faber and Faber,
     1991, pp. 85–9.
31   Harold Pinter, *The Homecoming*, in *Plays Three*, London: Faber and
     Faber, 1997, p. 61.
32   Una Chaudhuri, *Staging Place*, p. 115.
33   Harold Pinter, *The Birthday Party*, in *Plays One*, London: Faber and
     Faber, 1991, p. 80, pp. 77–8.

34 Harold Pinter, *The Dwarfs*, London: Faber and Faber, 1990, pp. 29, 129, 170.

35 Ibid., p. 23.

36 Ibid.

37 All three texts are published in Harold Pinter, *Various Voices: Sixty Years of Prose, Poetry, Politics 1948–2008*, London: Faber and Faber, 2009.

38 Harold Pinter, 'The Task', in *Various Voices: Sixty Years of Prose, Poetry, Politics 1948–2008*, London: Faber and Faber, 2009, p. 158.

39 The Clematis 'Küllus' plant, a vine that grows to dominate where it is planted, and whose flower, indeed, reveals itself first with a bell-shaped bud, before opening out, would be a suitable origin for this most peculiar character name, if it were not for the fact that this breed was cultivated, in Estonia, in the 1980s. 'Küllus' is Estonian for 'abundance' and may still represent the etymology of the unusual character name.

40 Lyotard, 'Oikos', p. 102.

41 Ibid., p. 100.

42 Pinter, *The Room*, pp. 108–9.

43 Of course, to be black and Irish (Riley is an anglicization of Ó Raghallaigh) was not impossible in the 1950s. If the juxtaposition was noteworthy in 1957 and into the 1960s, we might speculate that this was because it could rouse reactionary assumptions about race, ethnicity and origins.

44 Lucina Paquet Gabbard interprets Riley as the suppressed unconscious and invokes Norman Holland's *The Dynamics of Literary Response* in which he argues that 'the forbidden love objects can be symbolised by any dark, unknown, obscure, banished or debased persons'. Such associations stand to be accused of unresolved, systematized racism in themselves. Lucina Paquet Gabbard, *The Dream Structure of Pinter's Plays: A Psychoanalytic Approach*, Cranbury, NJ: Associated University Press, 1976, p. 34.

45 Given that Pinter's 1957 play didn't receive its first professional performance until three years after its debut at Bristol University Drama department, we might more accurately state that Delaney's play was the first to stage a key black character on the London Stage, in 1958.

46 The key moment in British political history centred on the provision of the 1948 British Nationality Act, which conferred citizenship upon the people of the British colonies.

47 The first agency for black actors in Britain was established in 1956 by Pearl Connor-Mogotsi and her husband Edric Connor; in the same year, the West Indian Drama group was founded by Joan

Clarke. These facts in themselves indicate that the appearance of Black British characters, and actors to represent them, was only nascent in the United Kingdom in the mid-twentieth century.

48 Pinter, *The Room*, pp. 109–10.
49 Harold Pinter, *The Caretaker*, in *Plays Two*, London: Faber and Faber, 1996, p. 6.
50 Ibid., p. 25.
51 Pierre Bourdieu, *In Other Words: Essays Towards a Reflexive Sociology*, trans. M. Adamson, Stanford, CA: Stanford University Press, 1990, p. 65.
52 Pierre Bourdieu, *Outline of a Theory of Practice*, trans. J. Goody and R. Nice, Cambridge: Cambridge University Press, 1977 [1972], p. 94.
53 Lyotard, 'Oikos', p. 103.
54 Ibid., pp. 103–4.
55 Pinter, *The Birthday Party*, p. 80.
56 Pierre Bourdieu, Alain Accardo, Gabrielle Balazs, Stephane Beaud, François Bonvin, Emmanuel Bourdieu, Philippe Bougois, Sylvain Broccolichi, Patrick Champagne, Rosine Christin, Jean-Pierre Faguer, Sandrine Garcia, Remi Lenoir, Françoise Œuvrard, Michel Pialoux, Louis Pinto, Denis Podalydes, Abdelmalek Sayad, Charles Soulie and Loic Wacquant, *The Weight of the World: Social Suffering in Contemporary Society,* trans. P. Ferguson et al. Stanford, CA: Stanford University Press, 1993, p. 4.
57 Ibid., pp. 24, 72.
58 Lyotard, 'Oikos', p. 105.
59 Pinter, *The Birthday Party*, p. 20.
60 I pursue this aspect of family formation in Pinter in my chapter 'The Impossible Family' in Mark Taylor-Batty, *The Theatre of Harold Pinter*, London: Bloomsbury, 2014, pp. 128–58.
61 Lyotard 'Oikos', pp. 104–5.

Epilogue

1 Samuel Beckett, 'Worstward Ho', in *Nohow On*, New York: Grove, 1996, pp. 106, 116.
2 Herbert Blau, *Blooded Thought: Occasions of Theatre*, New York: PAJ Publications, 1982, p. 148.
3 Vladimir in Samuel Beckett, *Waiting for Godot*, London: Faber, 1965, p. 79.
4 Samuel Beckett, *The Complete Short Prose 1929-1989*, New York: Grove 1995, p. 187. Italics added.

5 It was only much later that I came across Adorno's negative
   dialectics and other critical perspectives contesting an 'absence' of
   meaning in Beckett: 'Beckett's plays are absurd not because of the
   absence of any meaning, for they would be simply irrelevant, but
   because they put meaning on trial; they unfold its history'. Theodor
   W. Adorno, *Aesthetic Theory*, eds. Gretel Adorno and Rolf Tiemann,
   trans. Robert Hullot-Kentor, Minneapolis: University of Minnesota
   Press, [1970] 1997, p. 153. See also Stanley Cavell on *Endgame* as
   'not the failure of meaning (if that means the lack of meaning) but
   its total, even totalitarian success – our inability *not* to mean what
   we are given to mean'. Stanley Cavell, 'Ending the Waiting Game:
   A Reading of Beckett's *Endgame*', in *Must We Mean What We Say?*,
   Cambridge: Cambridge University Press, 1996, p. 117.
6 See H. Porter Abbott's more explicitly political recuperation of
   Beckett's work: 'Without question Beckett wants us to feel the
   weight of political injustice, the outrage of tyranny, the stifling
   inhumanity of engineered lives, the bitter residue of a system of
   self-interest. ... From beginning to end, Beckett's art is one long
   protest. It is written out of a horror of human wretchedness and
   a yearning that this wretchedness be lessened'. H. Porter Abbott,
   Beckett Writing Beckett: The Author in the Authograph, Ithaca:
   Cornell University Press, pp. 138, 147.
7 Samuel Beckett in an interview with Tom Driver, 1961, quoted in
   S. E. Gontarski (ed.), *The Edinburgh Companion to Samuel Beckett
   and the Arts*, Edinburgh: Edinburgh University Press 2014, p. 3.
8 Sesame Street, *Monsterpiece Theatre: 'Waiting for Elmo'*, 1996.
   YouTube, http://www.youtube.com/watch?v=ksL_7WrhWOc
   [accessed 30 July 2014].
9 Quoted in Félix Guattari, *The Three Ecologies*, trans. Ian Pindar and
   Paul Sutton, London: Athlone Press, [1989] 2000, p. 71.
10 Cf. Timothy Morton in his discussion of the disappearance of
   'Nature' in 'the time of hyperobjects' (global warming, nuclear
   radiation etc.): 'What we discover instead is an open-ended mesh
   that consists of grass, iron ore, popsicles, sunlight, the galaxy
   Sagittarius, and mushroom spores. ... By *mesh*, I mean something
   disturbingly entangled, without centre or edge, so finely interwoven
   that everything is caught in it. I also mean something that appears
   to us, since *mesh* stems from the word *mask*. A mesh is a screen of
   finely interwoven links'. Timothy Morton, 'Poisoned Ground: Art
   and Philosophy in the Time of Hyperobjects', *Symploke*, vol. 21,
   nos 1–2 (2013), pp. 42–3. Italics in original. By association in this
   context, I am reminded of Pozzo's interpretative titling of Lucky's

(exhausted ghost of a) dance in *Waiting for Godot* as 'The Net'. He thinks he's entangled in a net'. *Waiting for Godot*, p. 40.

11 Lisa Robertson, *Nilling*, Toronto: Bookthug, 2012, p. 76. Italics added.

12 Gregory Bateson, *Steps to an Ecology of Mind*, Chicago: University of Chicago Press, [1972] 2000.

13 Félix Guattari, *The Three Ecologies*, trans. Ian Pindar and Paul Sutton, London: Athlone Press, [1989] 2000.

14 Timothy Morton, *Ecology Without Nature: Rethinking Environmental Aesthetics*, Cambridge, MA: Harvard University Press, 2007.

15 Jane Bennett, *The Enchantment of Modern Life: Attachments, Crossings, and Ethics*, Princeton: Princeton University Press, 2001; and *Vibrant Matter: A Political Ecology of Things*, Durham and London: Duke University Press, 2010.

16 Herbert Blau, *Take Up The Bodies: Theatre at the Vanishing Point*, Urbana: University of Illinois Press, p. 7.

17 Sven Lindqvist, *Exterminate All the Brutes*, trans. Joan Tate, London: Granta, 1997, p. 2.

18 Blau, *Blooded Thought: Occasions of Theatre*, p. 142.

19 Samuel Beckett, 'The Capital of the Ruins', in McMillan, Dougald et al. (eds), *As No Other Dare Fail*, London: John Calder, 1986, p. 76.

NOTES ON CONTRIBUTORS

Elaine Aston is Professor of Contemporary Performance at Lancaster University, UK. Her monographs include *Theatre As Sign-System* (with George Savona) (Routledge, 1991); *Caryl Churchill* (Northcote, 1997/2001/2010); *Feminism and Theatre* (Routledge, 1995); *Feminist Theatre Practice* (Routledge, 1999); *Feminist Views on the English Stage* (Cambridge University Press, 2003); *Performance Practice and Process: Contemporary [Women] Practitioners* (with Geraldine Harris) (Palgrave Macmillan, 2008); and *A Good Night Out for the Girls: Popular Feminism in Contemporary Theatre and Performance* (with Geraldine Harris) (Palgrave Macmillan, 2013). She is the co-editor of *The Cambridge Companion to Modern British Women Playwrights* (with Janelle Reinelt) (Cambridge University Press, 2000); *Feminist Futures: Theatre, Performance, Theory* (with Geraldine Harris) (Palgrave Macmillan, 2006); *Staging International Feminisms* (with Sue-Ellen Case) (Palgrave Macmillan, 2007); and *The Cambridge Companion to Caryl Churchill* (with Elin Diamond) (Cambridge University Press, 2009). Elaine has served as a senior editor of *Theatre Research International* and in 2014 received an Honorary Doctorate from the University of Stockholm, Sweden. She is currently completing the monograph, *Royal Court: International* (with Mark O'Thomas).

Stephen Bottoms is Professor of Contemporary Theatre and Performance at the University of Manchester, UK. He is delighted to have been asked, for this current volume, to merge two previously distinct areas of research interest. His books include *The Theatre of Sam Shepard* (Cambridge University Press, 1998); *Albee: Who's Afraid of Virginia Woolf?* (Cambridge University Press, 2000); and as editor, *The Cambridge Companion to Edward Albee* (Cambridge University Press, 2005). He co-edited, with Matthew Goulish, *Small Acts of Repair: Performance, Ecology, and Goat Island* (Routledge, 2007), and – with Aaron Franks and Paula Kramer – the 'On Ecology edition of the Routledge journal *Performance Research* (vol. 17, no. 4, August 2012). Steve was the principal investigator on the UK's Arts and Humanities Research Council projects 'Reflecting on Environmental Change through Site-Based Performance' (2010–11) and its follow-up, 'Multi-Story Water: Sited Performance in an Urban River Context' (2012–13). For Methuen, he is currently working on *A Critical Companion to Theatre and Environment* (working title). Among Steve's other publications are *Playing Underground: A Critical History of the 1960s Off-Off-Broadway Movement* (University of Michigan Press, 2004); and *Sex, Drag and Male Roles: Investigating Gender as Performance* (with Diane Torr) (University of Michigan Press, 2010).

Franc Chamberlain is Professor of Drama, Theatre and Performance at the University of Huddersfield, UK, and a visiting professor at University College Cork, Ireland. Franc's publications include *Michael Chekhov* (Routledge, 2004) and *Sacred Theatre* (with Ralph Yarrow, Carl Lavery et al., Intellect, 2007). He co-edited *The Decroux Sourcebook* (Routledge, 2009) with Tom Leabhart and *Jacques Lecoq in The British Theatre* (Routledge, 2002) with Ralph Yarrow. He also co-edited, with Jonathan Pitches and Andre Kirillov, a special issue of *Theatre, Dance, and Performance Training* (vol. 4, no. 2, July 2013) on Michael Chekhov. Franc was editor of *Contemporary Theatre Review* (1992–9) and of *Routledge Performance Practitioners* (2000–13) and is currently on the editorial boards of several journals including *Choreographic Practices* and *Performing Ethos*. At present he is working on a jointly authored book on Theatre and Mindfulness with Deborah Middleton.

Clare Finburgh is Senior Lecturer in the Department of Drama and Theatre at the University of Kent, UK. She specializes in modern and contemporary French and UK theatre and performance, and has translated several plays from French into English. Notably, Noëlle Renaude's *By the Way* (*Par les routes*, 2005) was performed at the Edinburgh Fringe (2008). Clare's teaching and research addresses the question of how artists might reject the devalued words and images with which people are often represented in everyday life, and engage in alternative processes of perceiving and presenting subjectivity, society and history. Clare's publications include *Jean Genet* (with David Bradby) (Routledge, 2011), *Contemporary French Theatre and Performance* (ed. with Carl Lavery) (Palgrave, 2011), and *Genet: Performance and Politics* (ed. with Carl Lavery and Maria Shevtsova) (Palgrave, 2006). Alongside her interest in French performance, Clare is completing a monograph on the notion of war as spectacle in recent UK theatre (forthcoming, Methuen 2017).

Joe Kelleher is Professor of Theatre and Performance at University of Roehampton, UK, where he is also currently head of Department for Drama. He is the author of *Theatre & Politics* (Palgrave Macmillan, 2009); co-author, with Claudia and Romeo Castellucci, Chiara Guidi and Nicholas Ridout, of *The Theatre of Societas Raffaello Sanzio* (Routledge, 2007) and co-author, with Ridout, of *Contemporary Theatres in Europe* (Routledge, 2006). His writings have appeared in a range of journals including *Contemporary Theatre Review*, *Frakcija*, *Maska*, *PAJ* and *Theater* (Yale). In addition to the current volume, his recent essays have appeared in collections such as Jenny Edkins and Adrian Kear, eds. *International Politics and Performance* (Routledge, 2013) and Maria Chatzichristodoulou and Rachel Zerihan, eds. *Intimacy Across Visceral and Digital Performance* (Palgrave Macmillan, 2012). Joe's new book *The Illuminated Theatre: Studies on the Suffering of Images* is going to be published by Routledge in 2015.

Carl Lavery is Professor of Theatre and Performance at the University of Glasgow, UK. He has published widely in the fields of theatre and performance with a specific emphasis in recent years on issues pertaining to ecology and environment. He has also been involved in a number of the UK's Arts and Humanities Research Council (AHRC) projects looking at sustainability and toxicity. His recent publications include *The Politics of Jean Genet's Late Theatre: Spaces of Revolution* (Manchester University Press, 2010); *'Good Luck Everybody: Lone Twin: Journeys, Performances, Conversations'* (with David Williams) (Performance Research Books, 2011); *Contemporary French Theatre and Performance* (with Clare Finburgh) (Palgrave Macmillan, 2011); and 'On Foot', *Performance Research* (with Nicolas Whybrow) (vol. 17, no. 2, April 2012). He is currently working with the artist Lee Hassall on a series of performances called 'Return to Battleship Island'.

Mark Taylor-Batty is Senior Lecturer in Theatre Studies at the University of Leeds, UK. He has enjoyed the challenge of positioning his knowledge of Pinter's work and artistic ambitions within an eco-critical framework and is grateful for the joint venture with Carl Lavery. He has published widely on Pinter, most notably *The Theatre of Harold Pinter* (Bloomsbury, 2014) and *About Pinter: The Playwright and his* Work (Faber and Faber, 2005). Other publications include *Roger Blin: Collaborations and Methodologies* (Peter Lang, 2007). With his wife, Juliette Taylor-Batty, he has co-authored three children and one book, Samuel Beckett's *Waiting for Godot* (Continuum, 2009). He is associate editor of the *Performing Ethos* journal and co-editor of the Methuen Drama Engage series of books.

David Williams is Professor of Performance Practices at Royal Holloway, University of London, UK. Over the past thirty years, he has taught and made performance in England, Europe and Australia. His research – on performance, contemporary directors, animals, weather, waste and Sicily – has been published internationally. He has edited collections on the work of Peter Brook's CICT, Ariane Mnouchkine's Théâtre du Soleil and Lone Twin, and was co-author, with David Bradby, of *Director's Theatre*. He has been a contributing editor with *Performance Research* since its inception. He is currently dramaturg with the British performance duo Lone Twin, and with choreographers Jane Mason (UK) and Malgven Gerbes/David Brandstaetter (Berlin).

Ralph Yarrow is Emeritus Professor of Drama and Comparative Literature at the University of East Anglia, UK. He has directed over fifty theatre productions in English and French in UK, India and South Africa (e.g. Beckett, Ionesco, Sartre, Genet, Pirandello, Strindberg, Rózewicz, Kokoschka, Dickens, Orton, Pinter, Caryl Churchill, Shakespeare, Tanvir). His teaching and research links aesthetic experience, performance practice and consciousness with reference to drama and literature in India, South Africa and Europe, including absurd theatre, feminist theatre, theatre and development/social change. His publications include *Improvisation in Drama* (with A. Frost) (Macmillan, 1990; second edition

Palgrave, 2007; third edition in preparation); *European Theatre 1960-90* (Routledge, 1992); *Consciousness, Literature and Theatre: Theory and Beyond* (with P. Malekin) (Macmillan, 1997); *Indian Theatre: Theatre of Origin, Theatre of Freedom* (Curzon, 2000); *Lecoq in Britain* (ed. with F. Chamberlain) (Routledge, 2001); and *Sacred Theatre* (with F. Chamberlain, W. S. Haney II, C. Lavery, P. Malekin) (Intellect, 2007).

INDEX

Page numbers in bold refer to figures.